JOSEPH NAVEH   SHAUL SHAKED

MAGIC SPELLS AND FORMULAE

MAGIC SPELLS AND FORMULAE

Aramaic Incantations of Late Antiquity

by

JOSEPH NAVEH SHAUL SHAKED

THE MAGNES PRESS, THE HEBREW UNIVERSITY, JERUSALEM

Published with the generous help of
The Louis and Minna Epstein Fund of
The American Academy for Jewish Research
The Ada G. and Leon H. Miller Memorial Endowment Fund
The Research Comittee
of The Faculty of Humanities
The Hebrew University of Jerusalem

Distributed by
The Magnes Press, P.O. Box 7695, Jerusalem 91076, Israel

ISBN 965-223-841-6
Printed in Israel
at Kesset Press, Jerusalem

CONTENTS

List of Illustrations 9
Preface 11

Introduction

1. Hekhalot literature and the Jewish magic tradition in Palestine and Babylonia 17
   a. Jewish magic and Hekhalot literature 17
   b. The Jewish magic tradition in Palestine and Babylonia 20
2. Magic and Jewish liturgy: Biblical verses in magic practice 22
3. Magic and medicine 31

Texts and Commentary

I. Amulets from Palestine and Syria

For Amulets 1-15 see *AMB*.

Amulet 16. Ḥorvat Marish (ancient Meroth?). Bronze. Yose son of Zenobia seeks power over the townspeople. Israel Antiquities Authority, 84-317 43

Amulet 17. Tiberias. Silver. Healing Ina daughter of Zeʿirti from fever and other sickness. Institute of Archaeology, Hebrew University, Jerusalem, No. 2028 50

Amulet 18. Provenance unknown. Gold. Removing an evil spirit from Klara daughter of Kyrana. Bernard Gimbel Collection, Saddle River, N.J. 57

Amulet 19. Ḥorvat Kannah. Bronze. Removing various kinds of fever from Simon son of Kattia. Private collection 60

Amulet 20. Provenance unknown. Silver. Removing (evil) dreams from... and from Maximion. Bernard Gimbel Collection, Saddle River, N.J. 67

Amulet 21. Provenance unknown. Silver. Healing for Melekh son of Guzu. Geoffrey Cope Collection, Herzlia 68

Amulet 22. Provenance unknown. Silver. Amulet for Theodosius son of Theodora. Bible Lands Museum, Jerusalem 73
Amulet 23. Provenance unknown. Bronze. Healing for Teo daughter of Matrona from excrescence. Leonard A. Wolfe Collection, Jerusalem 77
Amulet 24. Provenance unknown. Silver. Healing for Qaduma son of Cyrill. Geoffrey Cope Collection, Herzlia 80
Amulet 25. Provenance unknown. Bronze. Removing the evil spirit from Nonn[a] daughter of Megale. Geoffrey Cope Collection, Herzlia 85
Amulet 26. Provenance unknown. Copper. For Ḥabibi son of Ḥerta against evil encounters. Skirball Museum, Hebrew Union College, Los Angeles, California 87
Amulet 27. Irbid. Silver. For the protection of Marian daughter of Sarah and her foetus. New York Public Library 91
Amulet 28. Irbid. Silver. For the protection of Marian daughter of Sarah and her foetus. New York Public Library 95
Amulet 29. Irbid. Bronze. For the protection of Georgius son of Megautes from the evil eye. New York Public Library 99
Amulet 30. Irbid (?). Bronze. For Surah daughter of Sarah, against premature delivery. The Metropolitan Museum of Art, New York 101
Amulet 31. Provenance unknown. Silver. Healing for Cassianus son of Domitia. Leonard A. Wolfe Collection, Jerusalem 105
Amulet 32. Provenance unknown. Christian Palestinian Aramaic. Bronze. Healing for Makaria and Timop... Geoffrey Cope Collection, Herzlia 107

II. Incantation Bowls from Mesopotamia

For Bowls 1-13 see *AMB*. No precise provenance is known for any of the following bowls.
Bowl 14. Protection for the house of Dabara son of Shelam with seven seals. Fiorella Cottier-Angeli Collection, Geneva 113
Bowl 15. Removing spirits from Goray son of Burzandukh and his family. Bible Lands Museum, Jerusalem 115
Bowl 16. Syriac. Expelling demons from the house of Yoyiʿa son of Rašnendukh. Leonard A. Wolfe Collection, Jerusalem 118

Bowl 17. Syriac. Confounding the evil eye that smote Yoyiʿa son of Rašnendukh. Bible Lands Museum, Jerusalem 120
Bowl 18. Removing the Tormentor from Panahurmizd son of Rašndukh and his household. Leonard A. Wolfe Collection, Jerusalem 122
Bowl 19. Healing and protection for Mihroy son of Ghušnay and others. Einhorn Collection, Tel Aviv 124
Bowl 20. Healing for Karkay son of Abaroy. Einhorn Collection, Tel Aviv 126
Bowl 21. Protection for Duday d. of Immi and others, using the story of an egg that runs after humans. Einhorn Collection, Tel Aviv 127
Bowl 22. Incantation for Marutha d. of Duda, to be protected by four angels on all sides. Einhorn Collection, Tel Aviv 130
Bowl 23. Amulet to protect Sergius son of Barandukh. Alexander L. Wolfe Collection, Jerusalem 132
Bowl 24. Wine-charm for Burz-Bahrām son of Dutay. Geoffrey Cope Collection, Herzlia 133
Bowl 25. Healing for Mahoy son of Imma, named Barshuti. Smithsonian Institution, Washington D.C. 137
Bowl 26. Syriac. Protection for Khusro son of Qaqay and Shelta daughter of Qayumta. Smithsonian Institution, Washington D.C. 139
Bowl 27. Protection for Berikhishi (?) son of Ahata. Leonard A. Wolfe Collection, Jerusalem 142

III. Amulets and Fragments of Magic Books from the Cairo Geniza

For Geniza 1-8 see *AMB*
Geniza 9. T-S K 1.15. Four pages from a book of magic recipes: for easy birth, hatred, and for other purposes 147
Geniza 10. T-S K 1.18 + T-S K 1.30. Amulet on paper for a pregnant woman, Ḥabiba daughter of Zahra 152
Geniza 11. T.-S. K 1.19. Four pages from a book of magic recipes: for a barren woman, for opening locks, and for other purposes 158
Geniza 12. T-S K 1.42. Amulet against ʿAlī b. Nūḥ the Ishmaelite 164
Geniza 13. T-S K 1.57. Fragment from a book of magic recipes: For entering the presence of a sultan and for a safe journey 166

LIST OF ILLUSTRATIONS

Figures

(All drawings by Dr. Ada Yardeni, unless otherwise noted)

Plates

(Photos on Pls. 4, 5, 9-11, 18, 20, 22, 24-29, 32 by Z. Radovan)

Plate 8. Amulet 21. Courtesy of Dr. Geoffrey Cope, Herzlia
Plate 9. Amulet 22. Courtesy of the Bible Lands Museum Jerusalem
Plate 10. Amulet 24. Courtesy of Dr. Geoffrey Cope, Herzlia
Plate 11. Amulet 25. Courtesy of Dr. Geoffrey Cope, Herzlia
Plate 12. Amulet 26. Courtesy of the Hebrew Union College Skirball Museum, Los Angeles. Photo Erich J. Hockley
Plate 13. Amulet 27. Courtesy of the New York Public Library
Plate 14. Amulet 28. Courtesy of the New York Public Library
Plate 15. Amulet 29. Courtesy of the New York Public Library
Plate 16. Amulet 30. Courtesy of The Metroppolitan Museum of Art, New York
Plate 17. Amulet 31. Courtesy of Mr. Leonard A. Wolfe, Jerusalem. Photo kindly supplied by Moriah Artcraft, Inc., New York
Plate 18. Amulet 32. Courtesy of Dr. Geoffrey Cope, Herzlia
Plate 19. Bowl 14. Courtesy of Mrs. Fiorella Cottier-Angeli, Geneva
Plate 20. Bowl 15. Courtesy of the Bible Lands Museum Jerusalem
Plate 21. Bowl 16. Courtesy of Mr. Leonard A. Wolfe, Jerusalem
Plate 22. Bowl 17. Courtesy of the Bible Lands Museum Jerusalem
Plate 23. Bowl 18. Courtesy of Mr. Leonard A. Wolfe, Jerusalem
Plate 24. Bowl 19. Courtesy of Mr. Yizhak Einhorn, Tel Aviv
Plate 25. Bowl 20. Courtesy of Mr. Yizhak Einhorn, Tel Aviv
Plate 26. Bowl 21. Courtesy of Mr. Yizhak Einhorn, Tel Aviv
Plate 27. Bowl 22. Courtesy of Mr. Yizhak Einhorn, Tel Aviv
Plate 28. Bowl 23. Courtesy of Mr. Leonard A. Wolfe, Jerusalem
Plate 29. Bowl 24. Courtesy of Dr. Geoffrey Cope, Herzlia
Plate 30. Bowl 25. Courtesy of the Smithsonian Institution, Washington, D.C.
Plate 31. Bowl 26. Courtesy of the Smithsonian Institution, Washington, D.C.
Plate 32. Bowl 27. Courtesy of Mr. Leonard A. Wolfe, Jerusalem
Pls. 33-34. Geniza 9. Courtesy of the Cambridge University Library (= CUL)
Pls. 35-36. Geniza 10. CUL
Pls. 37-38. Geniza 11. CUL
Plate 39. Geniza 12. CUL
Pls. 40-41. Geniza 13. CUL
Pls. 42-43. Geniza 14. CUL
Pls. 44-45. Geniza 15. CUL
Pls. 46-48. Geniza 16. CUL
Pls. 49-52. Geniza 17. CUL
Pls. 53-62. Geniza 18. CUL
Plate 63. Geniza 19. CUL
Plate 64. Geniza 20. CUL
Plate 65. Geniza 21. CUL
Pls. 66-67. Geniza 22. CUL
Pls. 68-69. Geniza 23. CUL
Pls. 70-71. Geniza 24. CUL
Pls. 72-73. Geniza 25. CUL
Pls. 74-75. Geniza 26. CUL
Plate 76. Geniza 27. CUL
Pls. 77-78. Geniza 28. CUL
Pls. 79-80. Geniza 29. CUL

PREFACE

In 1985, when the Magnes Press and E.J. Brill published our *Amulets and Magic Bowls: Aramaic Incantations of Late Antiquity* (= *AMB*), we believed that we had used all extant Palestinian Aramaic amulets. In the years that have elapsed, however, many additional texts have come into our hands, and it was felt that the time had come to assemble a new collection of metal amulets, accompanied by Babylonian incantations on earthenware bowls and magic texts from the Cairo Geniza. This was partly due to the increased interest of collectors, who were kind enough to place their items at the disposal of the authors and to colleagues who drew our attention to the existence of further pieces in different collections.

In *AMB*, 15 Palestinian amulets, 13 Babylonian incantation bowls and 8 Geniza texts were published. The present volume contains additional texts in all three categories: 17 new amulets (A 16-32), 14 bowls (B 14-27) and 21 Geniza texts (G 9-29). Among the 52 new texts, the Palestinian amulets, incised on gold, silver or bronze plates, are of special importance. Until 1985 our knowledge of this field was very limited. Six previously known amulets were republished with new readings in *AMB* (A4, A5, A6, A7, A8 and A9). Three amulets from Irbid, published in 1911 by Montgomery (kept in the New York Public Library), were not incorporated in that book, as it was not possible to arrive at reliable readings on the basis of the photographs then available. Thanks to Dr. Roy Kotansky, who specializes in Greek amulets, and who provided us with better photographs, we were able to improve on Montgomery's readings. These are given in the present volume (A 27, A 28 and A 29). The other amulets that Dr. Kotansky brought to our attention are A 26, A 30 and A 31 (A 26 is in the Skirball Museum, in Los Angeles and A 30 in the Metropolitan Museum of New York). A relatively large number of amulets were in the possession of Mr. L. Alexander (Lenny) Wolfe; some are owned by Dr. Geoffrey Cope of Herzlia. The publication of A 16 and 19 was made possible by the permission of the late Dr. Zvi Ilan. A 17 is in the Collection of the Institute of Archaeology at the Hebrew University. A 22 is now in the possession of the Bible Lands Museum, Jerusalem.

Some further items which have recently come to light have not been included in the present volume: two Aramaic amulets from the Paul Getty Museum were published by Kotansky 1991, and a bilingual one in Aramaic and Greek, from the Ashmolean Museum of Oxford (see Kotansky, Naveh and Shaked 1992). Some additional Aramaic and Syriac amulets are now being studied by the authors for future publication.

The majority of the magic bowls included in this volume are in private collections (Wolfe, Jerusalem; Einhorn, Tel Aviv; Cope, Herzlia; and Cottier-Angeli, Geneva) and in the Bible Lands Museum Jerusalem. B 25 and B 26 are in the possession of the National Museum of Natural History, the Smithsonian Institution, Washington D.C.

In recent years several other bowl texts have been published. Mention may be made here particularly of the articles by Smelik 1978, Franco 1978/9, Gordon 1984, Geller 1986, and Gawlikowski 1988. A Mandaic amulet was published by Greenfield and Naveh 1985. In *AMB*, reference to Stübe 1895 was omitted by an oversight from the bibliography, and this is rectified in the present volume.

The magic texts from the Cairo Geniza manuscripts were neglected for close to a whole century. Our attention to this material was drawn by Professor Yaakov Sussmann about ten years ago. Thus, after the edition of a number of such texts in Gottheil and Worrell 1927, Mann 1931/1935, pp. 90-94, and Margalioth 1966, the first systematic treatment of texts from the Cairo Geniza was done in Schäfer 1984 (from the point of view of the Hekhalot literature) and in *AMB*. Schäfer in collaboration with S. Shaked have now undertaken to publish an exhaustive collection of texts from the Cairo Geniza in the series Texte und Studien zum Antiken Judentum, and Schiffman and Swartz have also prepared a volume of Geniza texts.

The amulets and magic books in the Geniza were written in the Middle Ages, mostly between the tenth and the fourteenth centuries, but they follow the tradition of Palestinian Jewish magical texts of Late Antiquity. The Geniza texts reflect the language (Palestinian Jewish Aramaic) and formulae of Palestinian Jewish magic. They contain elements of Hebrew, as do also the Palestinian amulets, and they are influenced by Jewish Arabic, and possibly also by Babylonian literature. In the selection of the Geniza material we have been guided primarily by the desire to find parallel texts to those of the Palestinian amulets included in this volume. Such parallels sometimes make it possible to reconstruct the texts of the amulets which are often damaged or incoherent, and make their reading and understanding in general much easier. Thus, the Geniza material, which essentially belongs to the Palestinian idiom of magic, is important for the decipherment of Palestinian magic in Late Antiquity. The selection of these texts was done partly from microfilms at the Jewish National and University Library in Jerusalem, and partly by working directly on the Geniza collection in Cambridge. Their study was based largely on photographs obtained from the Genizah Research Unit at the Cambridge University Library. The photographs included in this volume are reproduced with their kind permission.

All the texts are published here, as in *AMB*, with transliteration, translation and commentary. They are accompanied by the best available photographs (many of them done by Zeev Radovan); the metal amulets are also illustrated by facsimile drawings done by Ada Yardeni.

The Introduction examines some specific problems of Jewish magic in Late Antiquity, such as the relationship between magic and medicine on the one hand, and magic and other types of Jewish religious expression on the other, in particular the magic formulae occurring in standard Jewish prayers, especially the biblical verses used in magical texts.

A number of important surveys and studies of the magic material have been published in recent years. Particular mention may be made of the collection of Greek magical papyri in English translation prepared under the general editorship of Betz (1986). Alexander 1986 provides a comprehensive view of the whole field. One special focus of attention has been the relationship between the Merkava and Hekhalot literature, the Qumran writings, and Jewish liturgy and magic. In this general field, which is partly touched upon in our introduction, several studies have been published. We should like to mention in particular Halperin 1988; Schiffman 1982, 1987; Schäfer 1988b; Weinfeld 1976, 1979, 1982, 1990; Nitzan 1986; and Bar-Ilan 1985, 1987. This list is far from exhausting a subject which currently draws a great deal of scholarly attention.

We should like once again to express our gratitude to Dr. Ada Yardeni, who prepared the drawings included in the volume, and as usual her drawings reflect an independent view of the text, which contributed to our reading and understanding. The reader should be warned that the drawings are not always in perfect harmony with our readings.

It is a pleasant duty to thank Mr. Yuval Harary, who worked on the glossary. Prof. H.D. Betz made observations on some of the texts. Prof. Y. Sussmann helped to solve talmudic problems. Mr. Dan Benovici, Director of the Magnes Press, and his staff, especially Mr. Ram Goldberg, took every effort to bring the book out in the most satisfactory manner. The various collectors and directors of institutions who allowed us free access to documents in their possession deserve particular thanks.

The Research Committee of the Faculty of Humanities at the Hebrew University and the American Academy for Jewish Research have generously contributed towards the costs of the printing.

Jerusalem, October 1992 — *J.N., S.S*

Signs used in the transliteration of texts

( ) uncertain readings
[ ] restoration of lost writing
< > omitted by the scribe by mistake
{ } superfluous writing in the text (e.g. in the case of dittography)
(( )) gloss (written above or outside the line)
{{ }} an erasure in the original

Signs used in the translation

( ) supplemented for better comprehension
[ ] restored
« » Arabic language (either in Hebrew or in Arabic characters)

INTRODUCTION

1. *Hekhalot* Literature and the Jewish Magic Tradition in Palestine and Babylonia

a. Jewish magic and Hekhalot literature

There can be little doubt that there were certain connections between the practice of magic in Palestine in the period of Late Antiquity and the literature of the *Hekhalot*, although the details of these connections have not yet been precisely determined. Some of the relationships are visible even from the small corpus of Palestinian amulets at our disposal. It may be stated at the outset that not all magical texts show an awareness of this literary tradition, and it may be assumed that there were practitioners of magic who followed a tradition independent of the *Hekhalot* school. In the absence of further detailed information, one may have recourse to the analogy of late mediaeval and modern magic and its relationship with the Kabbalah. With the spread of the kabbalistic schools in the sixteenth century and afterwards, many writers of amulets were deeply influenced by the knowledge they derived from the Spanish Kabbalah and referred in their texts to some ideas that were typical of the Kabbalah writings. But on the whole, the practice of writing amulets continued without taking too much cognizance of the newly discovered kabbalistic doctrines, even though magic acquired the label of "pragmatic Kabbalah" (קבלה מעשית). The amulets of the Renaissance and of the modern period thus show formulae that are partly a continuation of ancient traditions, with no awareness of the Zohar or the writings of Isaac Luria, while other amulets do show dependence upon such learning. The case, it may be assumed, was somewhat similar with the *Hekhalot* conception of the divine world. The *Hekhalo*t literature constituted a new trend which may have exercised influence over some writers of amulets, while traditional formulae went on being used without showing any influence of the *Hekhalot* school.

How are we to describe the *Hekhalot* literature? We can hardly do better than quote the concise presentation given to it by P. S. Alexander:

> The so-called *hekhalot* literature, produced by the Merkabah mystics of the Talmudic and early Gaonic periods, abounds in magic of a theurgic nature. The adepts were interested in acquiring secret knowledge about various subjects — the heavenly world, the mysteries of nature, the esoteric meanings of Torah, the future course of human history — and they used theurgic techniques to obtain this knowledge. Sometimes by means of ritual and incantation, they ascended to heaven, at others they conjured a powerful angel down to earth and compelled him to impart the desired information. Some of their incantations take the form of hymns or prayers which they believed to be part of the angelic liturgy ... They [the adepts] also used magic names of great power by means of which the angels could be controlled and forced to do their will. The *Hekhalot* tracts are full of *nomina barbara* and other unintelligible magic formulae. ... The names, as well as the rituals they practised in their conventicles, are very similar to those found on Jewish amulets and incantation bowls, in *Sefer ha-Razim* and in the Greek magical papyri (Alexander 1986, p. 361).

The Jewish magic texts found in Palestinian amulets on metal contain several elements which are usually associated with the *Hekhalot* literature. Among such elements (which are not necessarily exclusive to the magical and *Hekhalot* literature, but are also found, for example, in liturgical texts) one may mention the custom of using various names and epithets of God, sometimes side by side. The names are, for example, "the God of Israel" (אלהי ישראל, A1:23; A7:14. This is a typical usage of the *Hekhalot* texts; cf. Bar-Ilan 1987, p. 12); the use of the word מלך (A1:24; A3:1,3; A15:24; A16:4; A24:9. Cf. Bar-Ilan 1987, p. 11) is another instance of this style, and so are epithets like קדוש, מפואר, מהדר in Hebrew (A17:22f., 28f., 34ff.) or Aramaic (A7:16), and phrases describing the actions of God (A9:5ff.). Similarly we find in the amulets references to the angels standing before the throne (A7:4-5, 15-16).

Typical of this is the hymnic style (A3:1-3; A24:6-10), which is also most often a prayer. Such prayers also found their way into the Jewish prayer book, for example האל הגדול הגבור והנורא (Deut. 10:17.

Cf. A1:8; A7:15), ברוך (A3:18; A16:3-4; A24:10). Bar-Ilan's study (1987) tries to show that several poetic compositions were borrowed into the standard Jewish prayer-book from the *Hekhalot* literature.

Particularly striking are two amulets, A21 and A22, parts of whose texts are actually identical with passages in the *Hekhalot* literature. The right column of A21 contains a list of *nomina barbara* and of angel names arranged in alphabetical order. The middle column consists largely of figurative representations which seem to depict the celestial world, within which are scattered various letters in the Hebrew, Greek and ancient Hebrew (or Samaritan) scripts. One particular symbol which catches the eye in this medley of forms is a ladder, and next to it the Hebrew word מכונם is written: that means "their abode", and refers presumably to the place of residence of the angels.

The text of A 22 contains a list of angels who are said to "rule" over various areas, such as the heavens, the *she᾿ol*, the sun, the moon and the ocean. These angels are accompanied by other beings who are said to be their servants. The two amulets A 21 and A 22, made for the personal use of Melekh son of Guzu and of Theodos(i)us son of Theodora respectively, thus contain fragments of texts that form part of the *Hekhalot* literature. In these instances we see the mutual dependence and interpenetration of the two types of writings, that of amulets for practical purposes and that of the theoreticians and mystics of the Hekhalot compositions. The *Hekhalot* books use the magical style of incantations and amulets, while the magic texts of Late Antiquity, for their part, were deeply impregnated by the *Hekhalot* tradition. At the same time, since magic is an ancient and conservative craft, much of its practice went on using older moulds, without explicit reference to the theoretical developments made by the authors of the *Hekhalot* texts.

The *Hekhalot* literature uses the techniques of magic in order to acquire secret knowledge concerning the heavenly world, whereas magic, as the practical counterpart of the mystical preoccupation, endeavours to harness the powers of the supernatural world to its purposes: to gain certain pragmatic aims for a particular person.

This literary tradition has its roots in Palestine. Some of its early manifestations are present in the Dead Sea Scrolls. The fragments 4Q 510-511 (first published by Baillet 1982) contain hymns, written in two different hands, to ward off evil spirits. As pointed out by Nitzan 1986, these texts show marked affinity with the magical literature (although on pp. 41ff. she argues against attributing magical character to these texts). These hymns contain lists of demons and evil spirits which the authors wish to banish and whose influence they wish to annul. Other commentators (cf. Ta-Shma, listed under Nitzan 1986) have pointed out that this is a genre that continues a tradition begun in the Book of Psalms and that they display the custom of applying the Book of Psalms for magical purposes, a custom that has been in current use until modern times.

b. The Jewish magical tradition in Palestine and Babylonia

In his important book on magic in the Talmudic period, Ludwig Blau, almost a century ago, expressed an opinion that is still widely held nowadays. "The Babylonians", he says, "were infected by the belief in magic more than the Palestinians". (Blau 1898, p. 23). He based his statement on the observation that there is much less magic material in the body of literature that stems from Palestine than in that of Babylonia. He may have had in mind also the consideration, not expressed in this connection, that magic, which he certainly considered to be on a lower level than religion (as can be seen from the choice of the verb "infected", in German *angesteckt*), was a product largely of foreign influences on Judaism. Although he is well aware of the magical elements which exist in the Old Testament, he seems to hold the view that Judaism in its pure state was not capable of harbouring magic, and he may have been pleased by the thought that in Palestine, the home of the Jewish faith, the religion existed in a state as close to perfection as possible, and as a result had little or no magic in it.

We cannot share such preconceived ideas either concerning Judaism or regarding the relationship between religion and magic. The latter is in the eyes of Blau, as in those of other nineteenth-century scholars, sheer superstition, in contrast to religion, which is based on elevated ideas. Our present concern is however with the factual statement that magic was less prominently present in Palestine than in Babylonia, which proves to be wrong. It may be well to quote the words of a great Talmudic scholar, the late Saul Lieberman:

> The civilized world believed in charms; observation proved that they sometimes helped and cured; the ancients did not yet discriminate between real medicine and the magic of the "medicine-man", between charms and experimental science (Lieberman 1942, p. 100).

It is fundamentally an error to generalize and say that in Palestinian

> Talmudo-Midrashic literature fewer "superstitions" are found than in the Babylonian. To adhere to this view would mean to maintain that the Palestinian Jews were less civilized than the Babylonian, that they were not men of their time and place. Palestine, situated between Egypt on the one hand and Babylonia on the other, could not escape the influence of the wisdom of that time.... True, the Babylonian Talmud records many incantation-formulas, whereas the Palestinian Talmud mentions only a few, yet this fact does not prove that the Palestinian Jews resorted to incantations less frequently than the Babylonian (Lieberman 1942, p. 110).

The amulets from Palestine and its environment which we have collected in the two volumes, *AMB* as well as the present volume, clearly bear out Lieberman's contention. They contain magical material which is as much part of a living tradition as the magical texts from Babylonia. One may go even further and say that a comparison of the metal amulets from Palestine and surrounding countries to the magic bowls from Mesopotamia shows in several cases clear Palestinian influences and only rarely if ever can one detect influences in the other direction. Palestine and Mesopotamia had two separate traditions, each with its own style and set of formulae. When however formulae from the two geographical areas converge, it may be invariably established that the origin of the theme is Palestinian, rather than Babylonian.

This is obvious in the case of the story of the *Semamit* (A15 and B12a, B12b). The Greek words *pelagos*, *sideros*, which occur, uncharacteristically, in the Mesopotamian bowl carrying this story, and the Palestinian Aramaic words, like ארתק (cf. Kutscher 1971, col. 274), which occur in all the versions of the text, but which the writers of the Babylonian bowls B12a and B12b did not understand — all these details demonstrate that the origin of the text is quite definitely Palestinian.

A similar case is the formula ... שיר תשבחות למלך עלמיה which occurs in A3 as well as in certain bowls (Isbell 1975, Nos. 67 and 69). That this formula is of Palestinian origin can be shown from the fact that it is written with a Palestinian orthography in the bowls. The few linguistic features which the Palestinian texts share with the Mesopotamian bowls (for which see *AMB*, pp. 34f.) can all be explained as having travelled from Palestine to Mesopotamia, rather than the other way round. The *alef* occurring in the ending of certain words in the Palestinian texts is no proof to the contrary. In the Palestinian texts we do not encounter the typical Babylonian and Persian magical terms which are so common in the Mesopotamian bowls. The only such term that occurs in the metal amulets is the Persian *dēw*, and that is a term attested only in Syriac (A6), not in Jewish Palestinian Aramaic texts.

It may be useful to try and present a short list of magical terms which seem to be typical of the one tradition in contrast to the other. Since the linguistic corpus of the amulets is still quite limited, the list should be regarded as tentative; the discovery of new texts may show that terms that seem at the moment to be only typical of one tradition turn up in the other. Jewish Babylonian magical terms unknown so far in Jewish Palestinian magic texts are the following: זידניתא, חברא, חומרא, חרשא, לוט (to curse) and לוטתא, מחי (to smite), מעבדא and ע(ו)בדא, סכר, סרודתא, בעגלה. Names and terms for angels and spirits unique (so far) to Jewish Babylonian texts are: איסתרא, בגדנא, בלתי, דיוא, דנחיש, לטבא, ליליתא, מבכלתא, מלויתא, פתכרא. This state of affairs may strengthen the feeling that Palestinian formulae were generally adopted in Babylonia, but not the other way round.

2. **Magic and Jewish Liturgy: Biblical Verses in Magic Practice**

Jewish incantation texts very often make use of biblical verses. This phenomenon is clearly visible in all varieties of Jewish magic, in the Mesopotamian bowls, the Palestinian amulets, as well as the magic material from the Cairo Geniza, and is also widely attested in late mediaeval and modern Jewish magic practice. Biblical verses are also commonly quoted in Jewish liturgy, and this is one of the factors which sometimes make it hard to distinguish between prayers and spells. As we shall see below, there are also non-biblical formulae which are commonly used in the Jewish prayer book and which turn up in magic texts. There are even rare cases of rabbinic quotations, of the kind that may be used in prayers, that are dragged into the magical context, even though their immediate relevance to the incantation is not always apparent. A curious example for this is in Geniza 18, p. 11:1 ff., where Mishna Shabbat 2:7 is quoted, apparently, like the rest of the context, for magic purposes.

The use of biblical verses in magic contexts is of course often derived from their liturgical prominence. In some cases it may be shown however that certain verses came to be specifically used for magic aims. The evidence for this is rather early. Already in the Mishna there are warnings not to use certain verses which commonly serve the needs of sorcerers. A telling passage of this type is the following: כל ישראל יש להם חלק לעולם הבא ... ואלו שאין להם חלק לעולם הבא ... והלוחש על המכה ואומר כל המחלה אשר שמתי במצרים לא אשים עליך כי אני ה׳ רפאך (Mishna Sanhedrin 10:1). "All Israelites have a share in the world to come ... And these are those who have no share in the world to come: (...), and he that utters a spell over a wound, saying, 'I will put none of the diseases upon thee which I have put upon the Egyptians, for I am the Lord that healeth thee' (Ex 15:26)" (following Danby's translation; see also Bavli Sanhedrin 90a, and Tosefta Sanhedrin 12).

Ex 15:26 occurs rather frequently in incantation texts. It is used in Amulet 13:12-22, which, as will be recalled, was discovered in the synagogue of Maʿon. This verse is very close in contents to Dt 7:15: והסיר יהוה ממך כל חלי וכל מדוי מצרים הרעים אשר ידעת ולא ישימם בך ונתנם בכל שנאיך. "And the Lord will take away from you all sickness and will put upon you none of the evil diseases of Egypt which you know, but will put them upon all those who hate you". The words "all sickness" in Dt 7:15 are given the following comment in Bavli Bava Meṣiʿa 107b: והסיר ה׳ ממך כל חולי אמר רב זו עין "'And the Lord will take away from you all sickness' — Rav said, this is the (evil) eye". In Geniza 8:21-27, Ex 15:26 is quoted after the first five words of Dt 7:15.

Quoting just the first or last few words of a verse, and making them stand for the entire text, or alluding to a verse by some other form of abbreviation, is quite common. This is the method often used in the Samaritan amulets engraved on metal pendants or rings. According to this method, Ex 15:26 is sometimes represented by the last four words: כי אני יהוה רפאך (Zertal 1977; Reich 1985), or by the last two: יהוה רפאך (Kaplan 1967).

Dt 7:15 is quoted in full in T-S K 1.158, and also in *Havdala de-Rabbi ʿAqiva* XII:9-10 (Scholem 1980/1, p. 280), and on a door-post found at Palmyra (see below). Ex 15:26 occurs in its entirety in *Qeriʾat Shemaʿ ʿal ha-miṭṭa*, as given in Ashkenazi prayer-books. The earliest reference to the essential part of this prayer (המפיל חבלי שינה) is found in Bavli Berakhot 60b; prayer books use a formula similar to that found in the Talmud, but this is amplified by a whole series of verses, as follows (based on Baer 1868, pp. 573ff.):

1. Dt 6:4-9 (beginning שמע ישראל). The words ברוך שם כבוד מלכותו לעולם ועד are inserted between verses 4 and 5.
2. Ps 90:17 (beg. ויהי נועם).
3. Ps 91 in its entirety (beg. יושב בסתר עליון).
4. Ps 3:2-9 (beg. יי מה רבו צרי).
5. Gen 48:16 (beg. המלאך הגואל אותי).
6. Ex 15:26 (beg. ויאמר אם שמוע תשמעו).
7. Zach 3:2 (beg. ויאמר יהוה אל השטן).
8. Cant 3:7-8 (beg. הנה מטתו של שלמה).
9. Num 6:24-26 (beg. יברכך יהוה וישמרך).
10. Ps 12:4 (beg. הנה לא ינום ולא יישן).
11. Gen 49:18 (לישועתך קויתי יהוה). These three words are recited, in addition to the normal order of words, in the five other possibilities of word-order, and are said altogether in six different ways.
12. Ps 4:5 (beg. רגזו ואל תחטאו).
13. Ps 128 in its entirety (beg. שיר המעלות אשרי כל ירא יהוה).

There are insertions of non-biblical material between items 4 and 5. Certain items are repeated three times each. The following text is recited three times after item 11: בשם יי אלהי ישראל מימיני מיכאל ומשמאלי גבריאל ומלפני אוריאל ומאחורי רפאל ומעל ראשי שכינת אל (a text familiar also from certain amulets; cf. *AMB*, p. 42).

The Sephardi and Oriental prayer-books contain certain variations on the selection of texts and the order of the Prayer before Sleep. One feature of the currently most common form of the "Oriental" prayer book is that it incorporates the rhymed composition אנא בכוח גדולת ימינך תתיר צרורה, attributed popularly to R. Neḥunia ben ha-Qana (cf. Tal 1984, p. 194). The acrostic of this *piyyuṭ* is said to constitute the 42-letter divine name, which is very frequently used in late magic formulae (cf. Trachtenberg 1939, p. 95 and note 41). Otherwise the *piyyuṭ* אנא בכוח figures in most prayer books among the morning prayers (cf. Baer 1868, pp. 14, 49).

The elaborate order of the Prayer before Sleep described above is a relatively late development. It does not yet occur in the prayer-book of Rav Saadia Gaon (tenth c. CE), where only the bare blessing is given (*Siddur Rav Seʿadya Gaon*, p. 87). The prayer-book of Amram Gaon, which represents in the form in which it reached us a later redaction, contains a wide range of texts which make up this prayer (cf. *Seder R. Amram Gaon*, p. 54 f.).

Some of the items which make up this prayer in its more elaborate versions are frequently used also in Jewish incantation texts. Thus, Dt 6:4 (שמע ישראל) occurs in two bowls (Isbell 1975, No. 35:1; Isbell 1976, p. 18). The combination of that verse with Ps 91:1 (יושב בסתר עליון), done by quoting successively a word from each one of the two verses, occurs a number of time (cf. Bowl 11:6-7 and the references given in *AMB*, p. 187). In *Havdala de-Rabbi ʿAqiva* IX (Scholem 1980/1, p. 272), the words of ... שמע ישראל are interwoven with Ps 90:17 (ויהי נועם יי אלהינו). There follow Ps 91 (יושב בסתר עליון) and Ps 121 (אשא עיני אל ההרים) which are also interwoven with שמע ישראל. An interweaving of the first words of שמע ישראל with יושב בסתר עליון occurs also in a bowl published by Gordon 1978, p. 233. Ps 90:17 is quoted in *Havdala* I:16-17 as well as Ps 91, with the names of God and magic names interspersed after every few words.

Dt 6:4-9 is engraved on a lintel found at Palmyra together with the door-post on which Dt 7:15 is written (see further below). Dt 6:4 is frequently represented on Samaritan amulets by the last two words of the verse, either in the Hebrew original (יהוה אחד) or in the Greek version (ΕΙΣ ΘΕΟΣ). The Greek formula is also common in Christian amulets and dedicatory inscriptions (Peterson 1926a). It is even attested at least once in a Jewish dedicatory inscription from Dmer in Syria (Lifshitz 1967, p. 48; Peterson 1926a, pp. 27-28). An early Islamic oil lamp carries the word שמוע in the Christian Palestinian Aramic script, presumably alluding to the Syro-Palestinian version of the verse: שמוע איסראיל מרא אלהך מרא חד הו (see Naveh 1988, pp. 39-40).

Ps 91 (beginnning יושב בסתר עליון) is called in Bavli Shevuʿot 15b either by the epithet "a song of afflictions" (שיר של פגעים) or "a song of plagues" (שיר של נגעים), based on verses 7 and 10. Both these verses occur in Isbell 1975, No. 52:9.

Zach. 3:2 is perhaps the most commonly used verse in the magic texts. Isbell 1975, p. 195, lists it in five bowls, and it occurs also in Bowl 11:5-6 above, and in a Palestinian amulet (Amulet 1:56).

Cant. 3:7-8 occurs in Bowl 12B, as well as in Isbell 1975, No. 66:3-4, where it is follwed by the Blessing of the Priests, just as in *Qeriʾat Shemaʿ ʿal hammiṭṭa*.

"The Blessing of the Priests", Num. 6:24-26, is much used in magic formulae. Its history can now be traced through two and a half millennia, thanks to a recent discovery. On two silver amulets found in a burial cave in Ketef Hinnom in Jerusalem (to be dated to the 6th century

BCE), Ada Yardeni managed to decipher the fragmentary texts that are almost identical with Num. 6:24-26 (see Barkay 1986, pp. 29-30; Yardeni 1991). The text of these verses, יברכך יהוה וישמרך follows in both these amulets some other, so far unidentified, texts. Palaeographically, the date favoured for these amulets is the sixth century B.C.E., most probably from the exilic period, and the archaeological data do not contradict such a dating. In view of such an early dating, the relationship between the text on the amulets and the biblical text is not clear. It seems likely, at any rate, that the Blessing was not necessarily confined to priests only, so that it need not be assumed that the burial cave was that of a priestly family. That it was quoted and used outside the priestly context already at a very early period may be shown by Ps 67:2 אלהים יחננו ויברכנו יאר פניו אתנו, where the "Blessing of the Priests" is used without immediate connection to a milieu of priests. The amulets in Ketef Hinnom show deviations from the "Blessing of the Priests". In the one place where the whole text can be reconstructed, it may be seen that the words ויחנך ישא יהוה פניו אליך are missing. This omission may be due to an error by ***homoioteleuton***, but it may also alternatively be the result of a textual variant.

We have evidence in the Talmud that the Priestly Blessing was used for magic purposes. In Bavli Berakhot 55b it is said that a person who wishes to have his dream interpreted in a good sense, should recite a formula to that effect while the priests stretch out their hands and say their blessing. A similar attestation for a fairly early magic use of the Priestly Blessing occurs in the *Hekhalot* literature (Schäfer 1981, pp. 298-299, 981-985).

That the "Blessing of the Priests" was indeed said by the priests is of course evident from its original setting in Num. 6:22ff. This is strengthened by various other references, e.g. 1QSerekh 2:1-4 (see also the references in Elbogen 1972, pp. 54-57). Apart from ברכת כוהנים, "The Blessing of the Priests", it is also called by the name "the Raising of Hands" (נשיאת כפים) as well as "the Triple Blessing" (הברכה המשולשת). The latter appellation is commonly used in the *ʿAmida* prayer, where it is recited by the priests, prompted by the *šeliaḥ ṣibbur*. It occurs not only in the various versions of the Prayer before Sleep, even as early as in the prayer book of Rav Amram Gaon (cf. *Seder R. Amram Gaon*, p. 55), but also in the Prayer for the Safety of a Journey (תפילת הדרך) (cf. e.g. Baer 1868, p. 580), obviously recommended for recitation in both cases by laymen as well as by priests. Indeed, it is so common as a potent magic formula, that its use in amulets can be documented from the early amulets in Ketef Hinnom through the Babylonian material (Isbell 1975, No. 66) and the Geniza texts (Geniza 7 above; *Havdala de-Rabbi ʿAqiva* X:13-16) to modern amulets (Shachar 1971, Nos. 5, 775, 785, 810, 839, 884 etc.). In these latter the formula is frequently represented by the initial letters only: ייוייפאוייפאולש (see Shachar 1971, No. 924).

Often the verses of the "Blessing of the Priests" are combined with the mysterious formula אנקתם פסתם פספסים דיונסים, consisting of twenty-two letters. One of the earliest attestations of this combination is provided by Geniza 7:33-37 above. Elbogen 1972, p. 56, claims that the association of these words with the "Blessing of the Priests" is late and was made under the influence of the Kabbala. The meaning of these four words has been the subject of several attempts at explanation, none of which seems entirely convincing (Heller 1908; Krauss 1908; Sperber 1977, p. 43).

The verse Gen. 49:18 לישועתך קויתי יהוה is very common in magic texts. It is quoted both forward and backward in *Havdala de-Rabbi ʿAqiva* X:13, coming before Num 6:24-26, discussed above. It is recited in three different word-orders in the Prayer for the Safety of a Journey (תפילת הדרך) (cf. Baer 1868, p. 580), and in six different word-orders in the Prayer before Sleep (Baer 1868, p. 576). The practice of inverting the order of the words of verses is quite widespread in magic texts too, and Gen. 49:18 is quoted in three different word-orders also in T-S K 1.168, at the beginning of an amulet, just after the opening formula בשם יי נעשה ונצליח. G 13, p. 2:4 ff. quotes Ex 15:16 forwards and backwards, and the same procedure is attested in the Blessing of the Moon (ברכת הלבנה), cf. Baer 1868, p. 338. Dt 29:22 is quoted forwards and backwards in a magic bowl (Schwab 1890, pp. 327-328). Ps 55:9 is quoted similarly in Geniza 7:23-25.

Gen. 49:18 לישועתך קויתי יי is most often quoted in three different word-orders in modern amulets by the initial letters לקי קיל ילק; see Shachar 1971, No. 775. Quite often the initial letters representing this verse are accompanied by the initial letters of its Targum version, לפורקנך סברית יי, i.e. לסי; this is the case in the amulets given in Shachar 1971, Nos. 782, 784, 789, 804, 833. A formula which combines the abbreviation of both the Hebrew and the Targum in all three modes occurs in Shachar, No. 834: לקי קיל ילק לסי סיל ילס

In *Qeriʾat Shemaʿ ʿal ha-miṭṭa*, Gen. 49:18 is followed by the formula: בשם יי אלהי ישראל מימיני מיכאל ומשמאלי גבריאל ומלפני אוריאל ומאחורי

רפאל ועל ראשי שכינת אל. This is a characteristic magic text. It occurs, with some variants, in Amulet 1:1-3; 14:8; Bowl 22:2-3; Geniza 5, p. 2:9-10, and is also used in modern amulets; cf. Shachar 1971, No. 791. A similar text is known in Syriac: גבריאל מן ימינה ומיכאל מן סמלה אשרה אל שדי אדוני לעל מן רשה וכרובא̈ מן קדמוהי וסרפא̈ מן בסתרה (Gollancz 1898, p. 88). *Havdala de-Rabbi ʿAqiva* 3:26-28 has the following variation on this theme: גבר גבור יה מן ימינינו וברוך מן שמאלנו אלהים מלפנינו אדיר מאחורינו ושכינת אל על ראשינו. The Prayer for the Safety of a Journey as given in *Seder R. Amram Gaon*, p. 184, has a similar formula: כשיוצא אדם בלילה בלוא שעה אומר: מימיני אל ומשמאלי עוזיאל ומלפני נמואל ומאחורי שעשיאל שכינת אל על ראשי הצילני ה׳ מפגע רע ומשטן רע. This is reminiscent of the fragmentary text preserved in Amulet 14. Further parallels are found in Kropp 1931, III, p. 71 n. 1; Polotsky 1937, pp. 241f.

The boundary between prayers and magic incantations is not always very clear. Thus, the Prayer for the Safety of a Journey occurs in the Geniza magical fragment G 13, p. 1:5-10, and one of the verses used in that prayer, Gen. 32:3, occurs in Geniza 5, p. 2:2-4. In a recent study, Bar-Ilan 1985 has shown that the benediction *Yoṣer ha-adam* is used in the following contexts: (1) the marriage service; (2) after relieving oneself; (3) in the *Hekhalot* literature; (4) in the benediction after meals for mourners; (5) in the preliminary morning service; and (6) in a magic bowl (Isbell 1975, No 42:12), which only alludes to it. The whole of this benediction, one may add, occurs in a fragment of a magic book found in the Geniza; cf. G 9, p. 1:1-4.

Samaritan inscriptions on buildings usually contain verses from the Pentateuch, which were also employed in the Samaritan liturgy. This has led scholars to assume that these were inscriptions engraved on the walls of Samaritan synagogues, although no similar inscriptions have been found in any of the three ancient Samaritan synagogues so far uncovered in Palestine (in Shaʿalabim, Tell Qasile and Bet-Shean), and the archaeological context of the Samaritan inscriptions is uncertain (see Reeg 1977, p. 537). It seems quite likely that there was no essential difference between the Samaritan synagogues and the contemporary Jewish ones. The inscriptions found in Jewish synagogues, whether done in mosaic or stone, and in the three Samaritan ones so far known (in all cases inlaid in mosaic pavements), are generally dedicatory in nature. The Samaritan inscriptions we are discussing, however, contain only verses from the Pentateuch, and abbreviations of most of these texts are found engraved in Samaritan amulets. The decalogue, which is very common in the Samaritan inscriptions, never occurs either in the Jewish liturgy or in Jewish incantation texts, but other texts employed in the Samaritan inscriptions are quite well known from Jewish magic. The Samaritan version of Ex 15:3 יהוה גיבור במלחמה יהוה שמו (for which the short version in Samaritan amulets is יהוה גיבור), appears in our Amulet 1:8 רבא גיברא ודחילא and in Amulet 7:15: אלה רבה תקיפה ודחילה. This corresponds to the Hebrew formula האל הגדול הגבור והנורא of the *ʿAmida* prayer.

As for the decalogue, it is, as mentioned above, frequently used in Samaritan, but never in Jewish, liturgy and magic. There is, however, evidence for an early Jewish use of it in the Nash Papyrus, a 25-line long manuscript from the second century B.C. (Cook 1903; Albright 1937). In that papyrus, which may have been used as an amulet, both the decalogue and Dt 6:4-5 are written. The *tefillin* from Qumran also show the close dependence between the decalogue (Dt 5:6-21) and the *Shemaʿ* (Dt 6:4-9); cf. Yadin 1969. From some date later on we have an explicit rabbinic decision to exclude the decalogue from the liturgy. This is expressed in Yerushalmi Berakhot I:8, 3c, where it is intimated that although the decalogue should ideally be recited every day, it is not actually recited. The reason given is: "מפני טינת המינים" (this is the version in a Geniza fragment; cf. Urbach 1985, pp. 168f.) "because of the spite of the *minim*", and this is explained: "In order to prevent them from saying that only they [i.e. the Ten Commandments], and nothing else, was given to Moses on Mount Sinai". A parallel, though less explicit, tradition is found in Bavli Berakhot 12a. The identity of the *minim* mentioned in this text is not clear (cf. full discussion in Urbach 1985, pp. 131ff.). Although it is not easy to determine who were the "minim", the fact that the decalogue is used quite frequently in Samaritan liturgy and magic may serve as an illustration for one kind of people who might fit the allusion of the Talmud.

The idea of God's oneness, expressed in Dt 33:26 by the words אין כאל ישורון appears in a Samaritan inscription on a lamp, and is very common in Samaritan amulets. The idea is also expressed in a magic bowl by a quotation from Hannah's prayer in ISam 2:2: "There is none holy as the Lord" (Gordon 1984, p. 238).

Another element which occurs in the Samaritan inscriptions is the reference to the divine *fiat*. The same idea is expressed also in Hebrew in a number of magic texts: בשם ... שאמר והיה העולם (Geniza 4:5-6; see also Isbell 1975, No 66:2-3). The benediction ברוך שאמר והיה העולם, which makes use of the same motif, is included in the Sabbath prayer.

The benediction ברוך אומר ועושה, also found in the Sabbath prayer, has its equivalent in Geniza 3:1, which begins with the words בשם אומר ועושה.

Num. 10:35 is quoted in a Samaritan inscription from Beyt al-Māʾ, near Shechem: קומה יהוה ויפוצו איביך וינסו משנאיך מפניך. Similarly in T-S K 1.140. Bowl 3:5 starts with the same verse, from the beginning: ויהי בנסוע הארון. This verse and the following one, Num 10:36, are given in a shortened form in T-S AS 142.40. Samaritan amulets use the short formula קומה יהוה, and on an oil lamp one finds the single word קומה in the Samaritan script, which undoubtedly stands for the whole verse (cf. Naveh 1988). According to *Sefer gemaṭriyot*, Num. 10:35-36 is assigned for the safety of a journey (v. Trachtenberg 1961, p. 110).

The conclusion to be drawn from this is that the Samaritans wrote on doorposts and on house entrances various prophylactic texts derived from the Pentateuch with the aim of protecting the house and its inhabitants from harm and affliction. An explicit verse written in an ancient Samaritan inscription at Emmaus is Ex 12:23 ופסח יהוה על הפתח ולא יתן המשחית לבא. By doing so they were continuing the practice enjoined in Dt 6:9 וכתבתם על מזוזות ביתך ובשעריך. This verse was found in a late Samaritan inscription (perhaps medieval) written on a door lintel in Gaza (cf. Ben-Zvi 1976, pl. 13), where the whole of Dt 6:4-9 was engraved. Dt 6:4 by itself is represented on Samaritan amulets, as already stated above, by the words יהוה אחד or ΕΙΣ ΘΕΟΣ.

Dt 6:4-9 occurs also on a lintel from Palmyra, where, on the left doorpost, the verse והסיר יהוה ממך כל חולי וכל מדוי מצרים (Dt 7:15) was engraved in the square Hebrew script. Most scholars have believed that these inscriptions were written on a synagogue structure. There is, however, no good reason to reject the idea, already expressed by Mittwoch 1902, p. 206, that they were derived from a residential house, where it was used for magical protection. The inscriptions from Palmyra are so far the only known Jewish equivalents to the Samaritan epigraphy discussed above. They are clearly distinct from ancient synagogue inscriptions elsewhere, and have the appearance of a protective writing on a house entrance. In a sense they probably continue the ancient form of *mezuza*, which was given another shape and form in the Jewish halakha. As Mittwoch points out, Muslims are still in the habit of writing passages from the Qurʾān on house entrances.

Oil lamps are another type of material on which texts with religious contents, including biblical verses, were commonly engraved. Thus we find on Samaritan oil lamps phrases such as אין כאל ישורון, or individual words like קומה, which alludes to the whole verse, or, in Palestinian Syriac, שמוע (cf. on these above). We also find the phrase נר תמד "perpetual lamp" (cf. Ex 27:20; Lev 24:2), as well as הרם הו לא תזרה לא תצמח, based on a combination of Dt 7:26 and 29:22. The whole verse of Dt 29:22 occurs in two word-orders, forwards and backwards, on a Babylonian bowl published by Schwab 1890, pp. 327-328. On another lamp the Samaritan abecedary occurs from *alef* to *nun*, and on yet another lamp the Greek alphabet, from *alpha* to *nu*, is given. The use of the alphabet also belongs, of course, to the sphere of magic.

Magical formulae of this type are, as we have seen, fairly widespread on oil lamps from the Byzantine and early Islamic periods in the Samaritan script as well as in Greek and Palestinian Syriac, the latter two languages reflecting Christian usage; they also occur in Arabic (on Muslim objects). It is however remarkable that no Jewish inscriptions of this nature have so far been found written on lamps. It is a matter for speculation to decide whether the absence of such Jewish lamps is due to mere accident or to a reason which we are as yet unable to define.

3. **Magic and Medicine**

The most conspicuous objective for which the amulets in our collection have been prepared is to address health problems. A large proportion of the amulets we have published, and many of the amulets of Late Antiquity in general, relate to problems of health and disease. They declare themselves to be efficacious in preventing disease and in curing it, sometimes mentioning a specific illness, at other times, perhaps in the majority of cases, abolishing all diseases, or curing any unspecified illness that may be caused the client for whom an amulet has been prepared.

It may be assumed, though it cannot be proven from this material, that the magical practice employed here was usually not the only method used. We know that there was medical practice of more than one kind in wide use in Late Antiquity. There was, first, the scientific practice which had been developed by the great physicians of the Greek-speaking world, such as Galen and Hippocrates, and which must have been familiar at least to the more learned of the inhabitants of Syria-Palestine and possibly also of Babylonia. In addition, there was medical knowledge based partly on local traditions formulated in handbooks in Hebrew and Aramaic in the period with which we are dealing. We have evidence for this in the Book of Asaph the Physician in Hebrew (although this may be a mediaeval work; for an early dating see Venetianer 1915/1917; Muntner 1957. For a late dating see Steinschneider 1872; 1879; Lieber 1991), as well as in a small number of Geniza fragments in Aramaic, hitherto unpublished (see below). In addition, as a third kind of medical practice, we have some information about popular medicine, as expressed chiefly in the Talmud (see a discussion of this medicine in Preuss 1923). This must have been perhaps the most common form of medical treatment in the period under question, and it was based, one may take it, on the use of herbs and practical physical treatment which perpetuated traditional lore, but which was rarely codified in books.

All of these forms of medical practice were kept more or less strictly separate from the magical method of treatment. It seems however reasonable to assume that patients or their kinspeople had recourse to different methods of treatment at the same time, especially when the danger seemed grave. In practice, we rarely find magical handbooks that give medical instruction. The medical books proper may sometimes contain instructions that seem to us naive or "magical"; such recipes however were considered, as far as we can tell, to be physically efficacious, and were not aimed at achieving magical ends, which may be characterized as being concerned with controlling the spirits and subduing the malevolent powers that cause disease. Despite a certain measure of overlapping, in practice we experience little difficulty in distinguishing between magical and medical writings.

The Cairo Geniza has preserved a number of fragments in Aramaic and Hebrew which contain semi-scientific medicine, somewhat akin to the type of treatise found in the book of Asaph the Physician. These fragments, which seem to go back to a fairly old tradition, are still unedited, and need careful study before they can be made available, as they contain a large number of problems and uncertainties. There are also some fragments of such semi-scientific treatises of a late date, which have the appearance of an anthology of recipes culled from various sources. An example of such a recipe:

שמירת בריאות העין מופלא. יקח רימונים מתוקים וחמוצים: ויעטוף אותם וישים
כל א׳ מהם לבדו לְשֶׁמֶש תוך כלי זכוכית: וִיצַלְצֵל אותם בכל חֹדש וישליך השמרים:
ואח״כ יְקַבֵּץ אותם יחד חלק שוה: ואח״כ יקח לכף וימרח מהם צַבָּר: פלפל:

> דאר פלפל: נשאדאר: מא׳ דכ׳: וישחק אותם הכל היטיב הרך: וישליך אותם במיץ הַנִזְכַר: ויכחול בו העין: וכל מה שיהיה ישן הוא יותר טוב: ומופלא:
> (T-S K 14.32; the vowel signs are in the original manuscript).
> For the preservation of the health of the eye. Remarkable. Let him take sweet and sour pomegranates. Let him wrap them and place each one separately in the sun in a glass vessel. Let him filter them once (?) a month, and throw away the dregs. Afterwards let him put them together in equal parts. Then let him place that in a ladle (?) and smear from them: a cactus fruit; a pepper; a long-pepper; sal ammoniac; ... (?); let him pound them together thoroughly, and pour this into the above-mentioned juice, and anoint the eye with it. The older it is the better. It is remarkable.

This text presents a straightforward medical recipe, despite the fact that some of the terminology in use is not quite clear. Such treatises (or whatever fragments we have of them) are marked, as a rule, by the fact that they make no use of magical practices such as incantations, even though their version of medical practice is not always in keeping with that enjoined by the more scientific forms of medicine current in that period (e.g. Galen).

From our knowledge of medieval and modern practice in Judaism, Christianity and Islam we know that recourse to the practice of magic tends to complement other, more conventional means, such as the medical practice of a physician, or general religious ritual. We may thus assume that any knowledge we try to deduct from the magic documents at our disposal will only be partial, for the magic literature which we are studying was but one way among several in which a crisis in health matters found expression. When we try to see what notions the practitioners of magic had about disease we should keep in mind the fact that this is in all likelihood only a very partial view, and that other ideas may well have co-existed at the same time. Apart from the fact that the magic literature is fragmentary, it never talks of its objects in any systematic way, because the magic text in an amulet is not designed as a theoretical presentation of a subject, but as part of a healing action, part of a pragmatic ritual which should bring about health and protection to a specific person. Any generalizations made on the basis of this kind of material are of course tentative and incomplete, and may be, in a sense, inaccurate. Nevertheless the interest of this material is in completing our very fragmentary knowledge of popular religion and of the popular notions of medical problems in the world of Late Antiquity, and particularly among speakers of Aramaic in the two areas from which our amulets are derived.

Conventional religion was no doubt also a method of dealing with health problems, and the rituals prescribed by religion were probably used at the same time if not before the magic practices. When alluding to "conventional religion" in this context we are of course treading on sensitive and unstable grounds, for the boundaries between the two fields are difficult to draw, and there is a great deal of overlapping between them. The magic texts themselves contain an enormous amount of material which is also used in conventional religion, and the normal order of service in the synagogue (and in the church as well, for that matter) is full of formulae that are also used in magic contexts (see chapter 2 of this introduction).

The texts which seek to heal the client most often use the term אסותא to indicate "healing". This comes typically in the heading of such texts, or in their beginning (see Glossaries of *AMB* and the present book). It could be accompanied by the synonym דרמנא, a word of Persian origin, which means "medicine" or "healing" (B26:12), and it seems likely that in G5, p. 1:8, where we have אסותא דרחמנא, this is a corruption from אסותא ודרמנא. *Darmana* "remedy" is attested, it is true, only in Mandaic and Syriac, not in Jewish Babylonian Aramaic.

It is typical of the magical treatment of illness that the source of the disorder is deemed to lie in the intervention of evil spirits, whether as a general phenomenon, or as a specific evil agent responsible for particular problems. Thus, in A1, it appears that "the spirit of the bones, that walks within the tendons and bones" (A1:21-22) is held to be the main source of the client's ill-health.

Very often the amulets are confined to banishing evil spirits of various kinds. We may take it that in most cases these evil spirits are supposed to be connected to physical ailments of the patients, but this is not always explicitly stated in the text of the amulet. Thus we have a general formula such as: "May there be extinguished the evil spirit and the shadow-spirit, and the demon, whether male or female, from ..." (A7:5-7), which does not specify what these spirits are supposed to have caused (or are feared of causing in the future). One amulet wishes "to save" the client "from evil tormentors, from evil eye, from spirit, from demon, from shadow-spirit, from [all] evil tormentors, from evil eye, ... from impure spirit..." (A13:5-11). Another instance of such a general banishment of an evil spirit, which is presumably connected with protection from disease is Amulet 18, where we have the invocation "Adjured are you, spirit..." (line 1), "May she be (kept) sealed from you and also from all evil" (line 6). When we translated ביש as "evil", we should bear in mind that practically the same word (usually spelled בוש, but the distinction between *waw* and *yod* in most texts is not clear) means "illness". Amulet 21 seeks to gain healing for its client "from a spirit and from a demon" (Left column, lines 4-5). It is clear that Amulet 22 is also concerned with curing a client, but its reading is uncertain in large parts and its wording is too obscure to allow a clear understanding of its contents. It does contain apparently the Greek term θεραπεία (line 3), if תרפיה is not a form of the Aramaic word for "to heal". The "evil spirit" is sought to be exorcised from the client of Amulet 25. The amulet also uses the peculiar formula of offering "a song of praise to ... the supreme God" against "all harm and all blemish" (A25:7-8).

It is not always easy to distinguish between the spirits or agents that cause disease or a particular ailment, i.e. spirits whose presence in the body "explains" the presence of disease, and factors that embody the evil motive of other people to harm the client. When we read, for example, that the amulet is intended to protect the client "from the eye of cataract (?), from the eye of a spell, [from the eye of] a talk (?), from the eye of the house, from the eye of the open space (?) ..." (A1:16-17), we cannot be sure that these "eyes" (if our translation is correct) are supposed to be sources of specific ailments, in a fashion similar to the modern explanation that ascribes certain ailments, say, to microbes. The spirits mentioned could alternatively by conceived of as evil agents that trigger off distinct mechanical causes of disease.

Some of the texts mention "sickness" without further specification. Amulet 29 seeks to protect the body of the client "from all evil and from evil eye", with several further specific eyes enumerated. "Pain and suffering and spirit and demon" are also mentioned further on as things the client should be protected from (A29:7). In a Syriac magic bowl which deals with the guarding of "the house, dwelling and body", and which seeks to cause "the tormentors, evil dreams, curses, vows, spells, magic practices, devils, demons, liliths, encroachments and terrors" to go out from the client, a clause is added to the effect: "His sickness shall be pressed down" (B1:11), as if this is but a secondary issue among others, where an all-round protection is sought. It is difficult to tell from Amulet 31 what particular illness the client has, but it is clear that the amulet seeks to cure him and preserve his life. A formula specifically said to be "for every illness" is in G18, p. 18:4.

Among health problems the most conspicuous illness seems to be fever. Fever is recognized to be not a single complaint; it consists of different symptoms, for which a variety of terms are used. "Fever and shiver and hectic fever" (אשתא ועריתא ודקיקתא) are a group of terms coming often together (A2:12; cf. also A2:2, 8). The meaning of the terms, especially the meaning of the third term, was apparently lost by the early Islamic period, as we find them undergoing bizarre corruptions. We have, for example, לאישתא רקיקתא ולעירירותא (G5, p. 1:1-2), as if the term רקיקתא, a corruption of דקיקתא, was an adjective accompanying אשתא. The series אשתא ועריתא וזעקא occurs too (G6, p. 3:12). Here we may assume that דקיקתא was transformed into זעקא (cf. also *ibid.*, p. 4:2, with further corruption). These three terms are used in a fairly accurate sense as descriptions of the complaint from which the client suffers. For good measure, "the evil eye" or "the female demons and the spirits" are added (A2:2-3, 8-9), presumably because they are considered to be the ultimate agents responsible for the trouble.

Amulet 17 seeks to remove from the body of the client "all fever, hectic fever, illness and sickness" (כל אשא דקיקה ובוש ומרע, lines 1f., 17f., 31f.), where it seems preferable to take דקיקה as an independent noun, rather than as an adjective of אשא. No particular evil spirit seems to be mentioned in connection with these ailments.

"Fever and shivering" is also the target from which the client of A3:22 is to be protected. Here the agent that causes the ailment is named as "every bad and evil-doing spirit" (A3:4). The agent causing the "fever and shiver" in another amulet is "the shadow-spirit and the male and female spirit" (A4:15). "Fever and shiver" are associated with "shadow-spirit" (A2:11-12), as well as with "evil spirit, demon, and shadow-spirit" (A24:20).

"Fever and shivering" are directly called "a spirit", which presumably affects the body of the client and causes the symptoms thus described to occur in his (in this case her) body (cf. A9:1). "Fever [and shivering]" occur after "satan and evil eye" and before "[every] spirit that shakes" (A14:2-3), indicating that these symptoms could belong to a list of spirits that cause ailments. In a Babylonian bowl text these symptoms seem to be called "a flame" and "a heat" (שלהפתא and שחמתא, respectively; B11:1). The terms אישתה ועריתה occur in Babylonian bowls; cf. Gordon 1941, p. 341; *AMB*, p. 47) and in B 27:2 spelled אישתא and ערויתא.

Amulet 19 gives us the most complete enumeration of terms relating to fever. It is "proper to expel the great fever and the tertian (fever) and the chronic (?) fever and the semi-tertian (fever)" (lines 1-3), to which are added also, presumably as agents that cause illnesses, "any spirit and any misfortune and any (evil) eye and (evil) gaze" (lines 3-4). The Aramaic term used in this amulet for "fever", apart from the usual אשתא, is חמימתה (line 32), literally "heat", or "the hot one".

A group of spirits are enumerated which seem to be the cause of a headache, designated by the Greek term ***kephalargia***, and it (or possibly one of the spirits) "goes into the bones of the chest" of the female client (A11:5). Apart from proper names, we have also generic terms such as "blast-demons, tormentors and shadow-spirits" that penetrate the bones of the chest and the head and cause complaints (A11:10). Headache is also treated by a formula given in G5, p. 3:7, which carries the title: למן דחשש ראשיה, although the text of the incantation may refer to a problem with toothache rather than with headache. A formula against headache (Arabic *ṣudāʿ*) is given in G16, p. 6:1ff. The use of certain Psalms against headache is prescribed in G21:1ff., 12ff. An amulet for various illnesses, but apparently dedicated more specifically against headache, is G29, cf. p. 2:14f.

Evil visions, perhaps connected with the act of dreaming, are the object of the cure in Amulet 20. "Evil encounters", and especially an evil spirit that is capable of taking up different forms and appearing in these forms in front of people, and that is associated with an evil glance, are the objects to be removed from the client in Amulet 26.

In Amulet 23 we have an attempt to rid the client of an excrescence (תטלטולה) of some kind. It also alludes to evil spirits and to an evil glance, as well as to some act of sorcery which is designated by a term hitherto unknown (בודינה), which may possibly designate "vision".

A health hazard which may afflict "the eyes, the nostril, the head, the tendons and the eyelids" of the client is mentioned in A5:5-6. We are not told whether this is something concrete that has befallen the client, or a general fear which the amulet is expected to allay.

A major set of problems of health dealt with by our amulets are those connected with childbirth and the good health of a new-born baby. This is the concern of A12, as well as of A15 and the parallel texts B12a and B12b. The typical cause of child mortality, according to the text of these incantations, seems to be choking, for the evil agents are accused of "strangling" the children. This expression occurs only in the Babylonian versions (B12a and B12b: V, VIIIb). In Amulet 27 we have a formula for removing "[the evil] spirit and the evil assailant and every evil des[troyer] from the body" of the client and of the foetus that is in her belly. Amulet 28 is another amulet for the same client and her foetus. The chief aim of Amulet 30 is to prevent the client from delivering her child prematurely. The verse Ps. 116:6 is quoted with a curious error שומר פתהים יייי, which makes it possible, somewhat comically, to understand it as meaning, "The Lord preserves the orifices", with an appropriate sense for this context, rather than in its original sense, "The Lord preserves the simple". Amulets for pregnant women, one to prevent abortion and another to facilitate delivery, are given in G11, p. 3:13ff. A formula against abortion is also in G18, p. 18:11ff. To prevent that a foetus should die in the mother's belly (or to enable her to deliver the dead foetus) there is an amulet formula in G16, p. 2:1ff. In Geniza 9, p. 1:6ff., we have a formula for the delivery of a child; another formula is in G25, p. 3:6. Amulets for the cure of barrenness are not rare. Our collection has one in Geniza 11, p. 1:6ff.; p. 3:5ff. For the delivery of the after-birth, an amulet is given in G16, p. 2:12ff. To stop menstrual flow, a recipe is given in G23, p. 2:5ff.

One recipe which serves for diagnosis, to see whether a woman is pregnant or not, is given in G17, p. 7:1ff.

For the unbinding of a person suffering perhaps from sexual incapacity ("a bound person") there is a formula in G16, p. 3:1ff.; for a lame woman (?) a recipe is given in G25, p. 1:12ff. Specific amulets to enable the client to sleep are also found; cf. G16, p. 1:9ff. A recipe for a leper is in G25, p. 4:3ff. Against a scorpion bite, a formula is given in G16, p. 5:12ff.

A list of sicknesses is found in a curious bowl text which is dedicated to wishing ill against a certain person (B9). The illnesses that can be identified are as follows: various limbs of the enemy, named Yehuda son of Nanay, should be dried: the tongue in his mouth, the spittle in his throat, and his legs. There should burn in him sulphur and fire (i.e., fever), and he should be scalded by them. Mental derangement should apparently occur in him (ויסתכר ויתנכיר ויעכר לעיני כל חזוהי). Shivering (here called זיעא) is wished on him. "The throat of" the client "shall not swallow and his gullet shall not eat, choking shall fall on his palate, and paralysis shall fall [on his mouth and tongue]", "with an inflammation, a purulence, an itch, a vermin, a blackening, a shiver, a vermin ...". It is of course better not to place too much emphasis on the biblical quotations which abound in this text; these are traditional, and cannot be taken at face value. Geniza 10, p. 2:13, gives a short list of illnesses from which it seeks to protect the female client: "vomiting, diarrhea, pain, unease and weakness".

Although these texts do not give us a full comprehension of the notions of illness as viewed by their authors, they enrich our knowledge of the medical terminology and are helpful in explaining some of the mechanism of disease.

TEXTS AND COMMENTARY

I. Amulets from Palestine and Syria

Amulet 16

Provenance: Ḥorvat Marish (ancient Meroth?)
Bronze
Yose son of Zenobia seeks power over the townspeople
Israel Antiquities Authority, 84-317
Plates 2-3; Figure 1

1 על חסדך ועל אמיתך
2 בשם יהוה נעשה ונצליח
3 אל חזק וגיבור ברוך שמך
4 וברוכה מלכותך היך דכבשת
5 ימה בסוסיך ורקעת ארעה
6 במסנך והיך מה דאת מכבש
7 אילנייה ביום סיתבה ועסבה
8 דארעה ביום קייטה כדין ית[כבשון]
9 [ ]תה
10 קודם יוסי ברה דזינביה יהווי
11 מימרי ומשמעי עליהון הך מה
12 דשמיה כבישין קודם אלהא
13 וארעה כבישה קודם בני
14 אנשה ובני אנשה {כבישין}
15 כבישין קודם מותה
16 ומותה כביש קודם
17 אלהא כדין יהוון עמה
18 דהדה קרתה כבישין
19 ותנ[ב]ירין ונפילין
20 קודם יוסי ברה דזינביה
21 בשם חטועע מלאכה
22 דאשתלח קודם ישראל
23 אנה עבד סימן צלח
24 צלח אמן
25 אמן סלה
26 הללויה

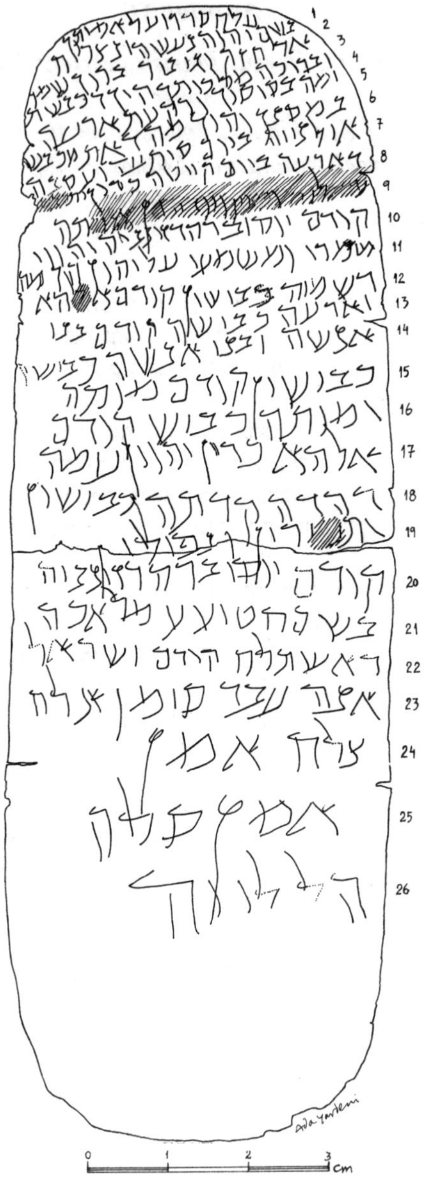

Fig. 1. Amulet 16

Translation

1 "For your mercy and for your truth" (Ps. 115:1; 138:2).
2 In the name of YHWH we shall do and succeed.
3 Strong and mighty God! May your name be blessed
4 and may your kingdom be blessed. As you have suppressed
5 the sea by your horses and stamped the earth
6 with your shoe, and as you suppress
7 trees in winter days and the herb
8 of the earth in summer days, so may [there be suppressed]
9 [...]
10 before Yose son of Zenobia. May
11 my word and my obedience be imposed on them. Just as
12 the sky is suppressed before God,
13 and the earth is suppressed before
14 people, and people are
15 suppressed before death,
16 and death is suppressed before
17 God, so may the inhabitants
18 of this town be suppressed
19 and broken and fallen
20 before Yose son of Zenobia.
21 In the name of **ḥṭw**‘‘ the angel
22 who was sent before Israel
23 I make a (magic) sign. Success,
24 Success, Amen
25 Amen, Selah,
26 Hallelujah.

Commentary

The amulet published here was found in the ruins of an ancient synagogue. It was unearthed in excavations conducted by Zvi Ilan and Immanuel Damati in Ḥorvat Marish (map reference 1998/2707), some 3.5 km. north-west of Tel Hazor in Upper Galilee. The amulet was found, folded and rolled, among the stones of the northern wall which was built in the third stage of the construction of the synagogue; this corresponds to the end of the Byzantine or the beginning of the Islamic period. The following are the main points from the excavators' description of the circumstances of the find:

The synagogue building underwent three stages in its existence. It was apparently first built in the second third of the fifth century CE. Some time after the initial building was erected, a coloured mosaic floor was placed over the original plaster floor. This mosaic includes, among other elements, the figure of a warrior and the short inscription **ywdn br šmʿwn mny**. In the second stage (later in the fifth or early in the sixth century) the synagogue floor was redone by placing stone slabs over the mosaic. In the third stage, which the excavators place in the first half of the seventh century, the whole structure was changed, and a new wall was built on the northern side over a bench which was placed originally against the northern wall. The amulet under discussion was found while a section of the northern wall built in the third stage of construction was being dismantled. It thus seems likely that the amulet is contemporary with the third stage of the building. The site has been identified by Ilan 1983 with Meroth mentioned by Josephus Flavius (*Bell.* 2,20,6; 3,3,1). See the full description in Ilan and Damati 1987:43ff.

The amulet, a bronze plate measuring 4.8 × 13.8 cm., with 26 lines of writing incised into the surface of the tablet, was unrolled and cleaned in the laboratories of the Israel Museum. The photography of the amulet was carefully made by Mr. Nahum Slepak of the Israel Museum. The drawing was made by Dr. Ada Yardeni. The first edition of this amulet appeared in Naveh 1985a.

The amulet has rounded corners, similar to those of the Greek amulet of the Monastery of the Flagellation in Jerusalem (published in Manns 1979) and to our Amulet 18. It was written on a fairly thick plaque of bronze, which did not allow the shallow incisions to come through on the reverse side of the object. Having the negative of the writing visible on the back of the plaque is sometimes helpful in deciphering thin foils of metal; the absence of this makes the reading of the shallow marks on the front side of the amulet extremely arduous. The photograph published here presents little that is decipherable. We have benefitted much from the contribution of Dr. Yardeni, who, when preparing the drawing of the script, suggested various improvements to the reading.

The text of the amulet is reminiscent of the form of ancient epistles (for a fuller discussion see Naveh 1985a). It consists of three parts:

(a) A short opening formula (lines 1-2), followed by the address

("strong and mighty God", line 3) and a greeting formula ("may your name and your kingdom be blessed", lines 3-4).
(b) The main part of the epistle, which in this case is a magical message, consists of two series of invocations (lines 4b-11a; 11b-23), each one based on a similar cycle of sayings: Just as God suppressed X, so may the people of the town be suppressed by the owner of the amulet. The second series begins with the sentence "the sky is suppressed before God". This may have followed something like: "the earth is suppressed by the sky" (cf. Geniza 9, p. 2:20-p. 3:1; Geniza 18, p. 16:1ff. has a different sequence). The following text is: "the earth is suppressed by people, people are suppressed by death, and death is suppressed by God". At the end of each series, after the name of the client, there is a statement in the first person (10b-11a; 21-23a).
(c) Greetings and blessings (23b-26).

1 Ps. 138:2; 115:1. Such a phrase occurs also in Geniza 4:2; Geniza 7:4, as well as Geniza 18, p. 16:13. Similarly also in Kotansky 1991, Amulet A:10-11, B:11.

2 The same formula occurs in Gottheil and Worrell 1927, p. 76. Geniza 6, p. 2:8-9; T-S K1.168; Mann 1931/1935, II, p. 93.

3 The phrase "a strong and mighty God" occurs in Isbell 1975, No. 67:3, and in a distorted version in A 3:6. The phrase *ha᾿el haggadol haggibbor we-hannora*, used in the *ʿAmida* prayer, is more commonly used in its Aramaic version. Cf. *AMB*, p. 43.

4-5 For the phrase "As you have suppressed the sea with your horses" cf. Habakkuk 3:15. The authority of God over the sea is also referred to in Geniza 18, p. 16:4-8.

The verb כבש, which is of great importance in magical practice, means "to suppress, to subdue", mostly with reference to human enemies and demons, as well as diseases and afflictions (which are deemed to be the work of demons). The noun is *kibša* (e.g. Montgomery 1913, No. 6; Geller 1980, p. 51), or, in Hebrew, *kibbuš* (Geniza 9, p. 2:17, and Geniza 18, p. 14:12). This noun serves in the sense of an incantation or amulet, the function of which is to suppress the demons. With regard to the sea, the verb כבש occurs in the early liturgical poem which opens with the words *azal moše* (cf. Yahalom 1978).

The formula "Just as... so..." is quite frequent in the magic texts; cf. *Sword of Moses*, in Gaster 1896, p. XXVI. Faraone 1988 discusses the use of this formula.

5-6 The verb רקע in the sense of "to tread, to trample with the feet" is actually in Hebrew, but it occurs in the Peshitta to Is. 44:24. The combination of this verb with a word for "shoe" is unusual. Comparable material in Greek is *PGM* X:36-50; IX:1-14; VII:925-968, in which the client desires to subdue and place under his feet certain people. Geniza 9 contains a recipe for subduing (p. 2:17ff.). It prescribes that the amulet on which the text is written should be placed under the foot of the practitioner while speaking the text (p. 2:18).

6-8 The intention apparently is that God causes the trees to bend under the impact of the winds of winter, and the grass to wither and dry in the heat of the summer. In the Syriac incantation bowl published by Montgomery 1913, No. 34:4-5, we read: "Just as Moses bade the Red Sea and the water stood like a wall on both sides... by that very word by which He suppressed the land and the trees..." (cf. also Epstein 1922, p. 49). The order of elements here and in the bowl of Montgomery is identical: the sea, the land and the trees.

7 סיתבה — The spelling with *bet* for *waw*, if our reading is correct, is quite common in Galilean Aramaic; cf. Kutscher 1976, 16-17; Sokoloff 1982, p. 129.

8-9 The text in line 9 is too faint for reading. The last word could be **[...qr]th**, resembling the text in lines 17-19; or **[...kl dʾmryn byš]th**, as in Geniza 9, p. 3:1-2,7.

10 The name Yose is very common. Its spelling is usually **ywsh**, both in the Synagogue inscriptions (cf. Naveh 1978, p. 152) and in the most reliable manuscripts of talmudic literature (cf. Epstein 1964, pp. 1267 f.). The name Zenobia is known chiefly as that of the Queen of Palmyra (266-273 CE). Her name in the Palmyrene inscriptions is spelled **btzby**, and only in Greek is it Zenobia. In the Pal. Talmud (Terumot 46b) the form **znbyʾ** occurs. The names Zenobia and Zenobius were in use before the time of the Queen of Palmyra (cf. Schwabe 1947, p. 150) as well as in later times (see the inscriptions in Greek from Bet Sheʿarim, Schwabe and Lifshitz 1967, Nos. 24, 183; Ashkelon, Schwabe 1947, pp. 149ff.; Kurnub, Negev 1981, No. 84; Elusa, op.cit., No. 92; Nessana,

Kraemer 1958, Nos. 79:18, 90:45,80,82, 136:5; and various sites east of the Jordan river, Canova 1954, Nos. 17, 86, 87, 211, 231, 282).

10-11 "May my word and my obedience (i.e. obedience to me) be imposed upon them": This is evidently said in the name of the client for whom the amulet is written. It is not clear who the people implied by "them" are, as the text of line 9 is not preserved. A similar wish is uttered in the Geniza texts, Geniza 18, p. 13:5-7, 12-14, and in *Havdala de-Rabbi ʿAqiva*, p. 8:21-22, where the desire is expressed in general that all that the client says be accomplished. In *Sefer ha-Razim*, p. 74, I:138ff. a similar wish is expressed.

11-17 A similar formula occurs in Geniza 18, p. 16. The structure is reminiscent of the poem *Ḥad Gadya* which forms part of the Passover Haggada, usually taken to be a late addition to the Haggada, composed in mediaeval Europe. A similar circular saying, which gives a series of objects or agents each dependent on the preceding item, and ultimately all dependent on God, occurs in *Bereshit Rabba*, p. 363, Parasha 38. BT Bava Batra 10a contains a similar text (cf. Goldschmidt 1969, pp. 98-99; Kasher 1967, pp. 190-191).

19 תבירין קודם occurs in Targum Deut. 28:7 and Judges 20:32 (for the Hebrew *niggafim lifne...*) The passive form **npylyn** translates Heb. *nofelim* in Ps. 145:14.

21-22 The name חטועע is not known from other sources. It is said here to be an angel "sent before the (Children of) Israel", an expression which may echo Ex. 23:20-21: "Now I send an angel before you... for my name is in him". In Bavli Sanhedrin 38b this angel is identified with Metatron. Among Metatron's names we have **ʿʿh** and **ḥṭṭyh** in Enoch III, chapter 48 D. In the Midrash *Otiyyot de-rabbi ʿAqiva* (Wertheimer 1980 II, p. 353) we have among Metatron's names טטנדיאל and אטטיה. Similarly, in the *Sword of Moses*, Ch. II, para. 105, various letters indicating guttural sounds occur after the names of the angels.

23 סימן is a magic term, like *naḥaš* (cf. Bavli Ḥullin 95b; Pal. Shabbat 8c). The formula **bnḥšʾ ṭbʾ wbsymnʾ mʿlyʾ** occurs in the opening of T-S K1.155 and similar formulae come at the beginning of marriage contracts of recent date, e.g. from North Africa (cf. Attal 1984, plates 2, 3). The term *siman* seems to correspond to the Greek δοκιμή, which is also used as a magic term in the Hebrew text of *Sefer ha-razim* (cf. II:86;

III:47), where it indicates a proof for the effectiveness of magic deeds (cf. Margaliot 1966, p. 4). Etymologically *siman* is no doubt related to Greek σημεῖον, which is itself used in magical contexts (e.g. in John 2:11, where it indicates the miracles of Jesus), as Roy Kotansky has pointed out to us.

23-24 צלח occurs, repeated three times, in Geniza 18, p. 16:12-13.

Amulet 17

Provenance: Tiberias
Silver
Healing Ina daughter of Zeʿirti from fever and other sickness
Institute of Archaeology, Hebrew University, Jerusalem, No. 2028
Plate 1; Figure 2

0 [ ]
1 [ברתה דז]עירתי מכל אשא דקיק[ה]
2 [ובו]ש ומרע בשם הוא יזות יה יה
3 [י]ה דהוה על ציצה כתיב דהוא
4 [גלי]ל על כלילה דאהרן כהנה רבה
5 [דה]וא הוה משמש בה ונחת למלא[ה]
6 [ ]נה הוא שמה דסבל עלאי
7 [ו]ארעאי (ר)עדין מנה הדה הוא
8 י̅ר̅פ̅א̅ ש̅ו̅מ̅ר̅א̅ך̅
9 מ̅ר̅כ̅ב̅י̅א̅ת̅ ז̅ז̅ז̅ז̅ א̅ל̅ה̅י̅ם̅ ח̅י̅י̅ם̅
10 עליזא ש̅מ̅א̅ר̅י̅ה̅
11-16 יה (*written seventy times*)
17 עקור מן גופה דאינה ברתה דזעירתי כ[ל]
18 [א]שא דקיקה ובוש ומרע בשם יׄהׄוׄהׄ
19 [י]ושב הכרובים אמן אמן סלה ברוך ה[וא]
20 [י]הוה צבאות עמנו משגב לנו אלהי יעקב
21 [ס]לה
22 קדוש קדוש קדוש
23 שמא המפואר אבלת
24 אשמאזה אזא מזה

Fig. 2. Amulet 17

25 סנבאותתייך יה שמא מה
26 קדדך הא אסמכה אסא
27 מסא פיתיה רביבאות
28 הסא זא זא שרם השם
29 קדושים מהודר מהדר
30 עקור מן גופה דאינה ברתה
31 דזעירתי כל אשא דקיקה ובוש
32 ומרע מן יומדן ועד לעלם אמן אמן
33 סלה

In the margins around lines 22-33:

left margin: 34 קדוש קדוש קדוש קדוש
below, inverted: 35 קדוש קדוש קדוש קדוש
right margin: 36 מפואר מפואר מהדר

Translation

0 [An amulet proper for saving and healing Ina]
1 [daughter of Ze]ʿirti from all hectic fever
2 [and ill]ness and sickness. In the name of **hwʾ yzwt yh yh**
3 **[y]h**, that was written on his front plate which was
4 [unrol]led on the wreath of Aaron the High Priest
5 who was serving with it, and he descended in order to fu[lfil]
6 [...] his name, who carries those on high
7 [and] those below, <and all> tremble before him [?]. This is it.
8 **yrpʾ šwmrʾk**
9 **mrkbyʾt zzzz** the living god
10 **ʿlyzʾ šmʾryh**
11-16 (*70 times* **yh**)
17 Eradicate from the body of Ina daughter of Zeʿirti a[ll]
18 hectic fever and illness and sickness in the name of **yhwh**
19 who is enthroned among the cherubim, Amen Amen Selah. Blessed be He.
20 "The Lord of Hosts is with us, the God of Jacob our refuge
21 Selah" (Ps. 46:8,12).
22 Holy (× *4*)
23 The glorious name **ʾblt**
24-28 (*magic names*)
29 holy, splendid, splendid.
30 Eradicate from the body of Ina the daughter

31 of Ze‘irti all hectic fever and illness
32 and sickness from this day to eternity. Amen Amen
33 Selah.
34-36 (*Around the margins:*) Holy (× *12*), magnificent (× *2*), splendid.

Commentary

This amulet was bought, apparently in 1938, by the Museum of Jewish Antiquities of the Hebrew University in Jerusalem (today the collection of the Institute of Archaeology of the Hebrew University) from Baruch Toledano of Tiberias, a man of considerable erudition. The amulet recently came to our notice among the collections of the Institute of Archaeology, where it is kept, accompanied by a detailed and learned note written by Toledano, which describes its contents and gives an attempt at decipherment. The main points of this note (written in Hebrew) are worth reproducing here in English:

> This is an amulet incised on a thin plate of beaten silver, rolled like thick paper, and measuring 11x4 cm. It was discovered in a tomb more than four metres deep, close to Tiberias, where tombs of Jewish sages of the Talmudic period are known to exist. The silver tablet was found rolled in a small copper container which was in such a bad state of corrosion that it split open at a mere touch. The letters are incised into the silver, and, being as bright as the silver itself, are not easily visible. The fact that the container had corroded at both sides caused the silver plate to be broken and eaten away at the top and at both sides, so that there are no margins left. Only at the bottom was the silver preserved completely.

Toledano's note contains also some quotations from rabbinical literature concerning magic, as well as a somewhat imperfect reading of the text.

0 There probably is just one line missing at the top. The text may have read as follows (according to the opening text of Amulet 2): [קמיע טב משיזבה ומאסיה אינה]. It may be noted that, like our amulet, Amulet 2 too is an incantation against various kinds of fever.

1 **זעירתי** is a feminine proper name which means "small". The ***mater lectionis*** after the ‘*ayin* could conceivably be read as *waw*, but comparison with the spelling of this name in lines 17, 31 decides the reading unequivocally in favour of *yod*. Kutscher 1976, pp. 23ff., tried at first to argue that **זעור** is a western Aramaic form, as against **זעיר**, which is eastern Aramaic. However, his own evidence led him to the conclusion that the distinction between **זעיר** and **זעור** cannot be attributed to the dialect differences, and that there are forms like **זעיר** in West Aramaic, while forms like **זעור** turn up in East Aramaic. Another problem is the existence of the final *yod* in the name **zʿyrty**. Epstein 1960, p. 119, noted that this was a regular form of the feminine adjectives in the Babylonian Talmud, and is thus a typical eastern form (it is so far unattested in Palestinian Aramaic texts). Please note that in *AMB*, p. 210, where a reference to Epstein 1960, p. 119, occurs, an error should be corrected. In the references to fem. pl. forms "pl." should be omitted. The forms discussed there are all singular, and so is the sense of Epstein's note.

We have **zʿyrty** here in a Galilean amulet, and this fact seemingly provides evidence that this feminine ending may also be used in a Palestinian text. One cannot however draw a definite conclusion from this occurrence alone, as we are dealing here with a proper name, where the *—i* ending may well reflect the pronominal possessive suffix of the first person singular, perhaps used as an affectionate form of the name, as in the name **ʾymy** (which also occurs, incidentally, only in Babylonian texts; cf. Isbell 1975, p. 97, No. 40:2; p. 127, No. 56:12).

3 The front plate of the high priest Aaron figures in one of the amulets from Irbid (A 27). As the front plate is here related to **klyl** "wreath", it is possible that the verb at the beginning of line 4 should be **[gly]l**. For the text which relates to *ṣiṣ* here cf. the tannaitic text quoted in Bavli Shabbat 63b and Sukka 5a:

> התניא ציץ כמין טס של זהב ורוחב שתי אצבעות ומוקף מאוזן לאוזן וכתוב עליו בב׳ שיטין יו״ד ה״א למעלה וקודש למ״ד למטה. ואמר ר׳ אלעזר בר׳ יוסי אני ראיתיו בעיר רומי וכתוב קדש לה׳ בשיטה אחת
>
> It was taught: *Ṣiṣ* is like a gold plate. Its width is two fingers. It extends from one ear to the other, and there is inscribed on it in two lines YH above and "*qodeš l—*" below. R. Eleazar b. Yose said: I saw it in the city of Rome, and it was written "*qodeš* to God", in one line.

Here too we have the idea that the *ṣiṣ* had something written on it. Writing on a *ṣiṣ* occurs also in Midrash Tanḥuma, *Vayeṣe* 12.

4 For the reading **glyl** cf. the text of Targum Cant. 5:14 concerning the words ידיו גלילי זהב:

> תרי עסר שבטין דיעקב עבדיה גלילן על ציץ כלילא דדהבא דקודשא גליפן על תרי עסר מרגליתא
>
> The twelve tribes of His servant Jacob are unfolded over the plate of the holy golden wreath, engraved on the twelve jewels.

5 It is not clear who is the subject of **NḤT** "to descend", and in fact what the precise meaning of the verb is in this context. As a result it is not clear how one should supplement the missing end of line 5 and the beginning of line 6. The word beginning **lml'[ ]** may be the verbal noun of **ML'**, which among its uses in Hebrew also counts the sense of "to serve (in the temple)", as is evidenced by the usage of the Targum Ex. 29:29,33,36, where the Hebrew phrase *lemalle yadam* is rendered by **lqrb' qwrbnhwn**. The difficulty about this is that it would be strange to have here the Hebrew expression transformed into Aramaic **lml'h** with the Aramaic **[qrb]nh** which we would have to supplement at the beginning of line 6. **lml'h**, or (as in Hebrew) **lml'**, may be an independent elliptical expression, which alludes to the biblical phrase *lemalle yadam*. In that case the beginning of line 6 constitutes a new phrase.

ml'.. could also be the beginning of the word **ml'kh** (although there is hardly enough room for more than one letter after the *alef*). Angels are in fact said to "descend from heaven" (**ml'kh dnḥyt mn šmy'**, e.g. in Montgomery 1913, No. 12:5), but in that case the syntax is not clear.

6 For the beginning of this line see the comments on the preceding line. If we have here an independent phrase, the first word could read something like **[rḥm]nh**, which would go well with what follows: "His name is Raḥmana". If the first word does not belong here we are left with too little to go by with **hw' šmh**, unless we take **hw'** to be a divine name (cf. line 2 and comment on line 3).

For the phrase **dsbl ‘l'y [w]'r‘'y** cf. the midrash *Genesis Rabba* s. 22 (on Gen. 4:13): לעליונים ולתחתונים אתה סובל ולפשעי לא תסבול "You bear the upper and the lower ones; would you then not bear my sin?" The sense of the verb **SBL** in this quotation constitutes a play on the double meaning "to carry, to bear" and "to bear with, to have forbearance".

For the sense "to carry" one may refer to *Sefer ha-Razim*, p. 109 (VIII:30): תולה עולם כאשכול סובל הכל "He who hangs the world like a cluster of grapes, and who bears all". The *Siddur Rabba di-Bereshit* (in Wertheimer 1980 I, p. 368) suggests another meaning to this phrase:

> דבר אחר צור עולמים שהוא דומה לצור שסובל את כל עמודי הבית אף כך הקב״ה סובל אותן קצ״ו אלפים עולמים והעולם הזה והעולם הבא תחת זרועו הגדולה ודומה כמין קמיע שהוא תלוי בזרוע גיבור
>
> Another (explanation): He is called *ṣur ʿolamim* (Is. 26:4) because He is like a rock which carries all the pillars of the house. So does God also carry the 196,000 worlds, while this world and the world to come are under His large arm, in the manner of an amulet hanging from the arm of a hero.

Such phrases are fairly common in Jewish literature. Cf. for example the expression מלך תולה עולם בזרוע in T-S K 21.95 C 1a:14 f., (see Schäfer 1984, p. 100).

The reading of the verb, whether **rʿdyn** or **dʿdyn**, partly depends on our understanding of the cosmological situation described here. If we read it with an initial *dalet*, the word is to be construed as consisting of **d—** + **ʿdyn**. The possibilities of interpretation are as follows: (1) God carries both the upper and the lower worlds, and <all> tremble before Him; (2) God carries the upper worlds, and the lower worlds tremble before Him; (3) God carries the upper worlds, and the lower worlds are like ornaments hanging (**ʿDH** [?]) from Him. Linguistically the third possibility seems less satisfactory.

A fourth possibility, which represents a different understanding of the text, is as follows. God bears (i.e. forgives) the upper and the lower (beings) that deviate from Him (**ʿdyn mnh**), i.e. that trespass against Him. This goes well with Ex. 28:38 *we-naśa aharon et ʿawon haqqodašim* "and Aaron may bear the iniquity of the holy things". The text of Ex. 28 seems to play an important part in the phrasing of our amulet, if we recall the *ṣiṣ* and the writing on it, as well as possibly the phrase *lemalle yadam* (Ex. 28:41). This explanation fits in well with *Genesis Rabba* s. 22, quoted above. The verb **ʿDH** renders Hebrew **SWR** (Targum Onk. to Gen. 49:10, Deut. 4:9), but the phrase **ʿdh mn** is not attested in the sense of "to deviate from (the way of God), i.e. to trespass against (Him)", which would be required here.

6-7 עלאי [ו]ארעאי: The forms of the emphatic masculine plural in Palestinian Aramaic are usually **—yʾ**, but here we have to do with forms which behave like gentilic adjectives, such as **yhwd'y, mṣr'y, šmr'y**, etc., for which cf. Beyer 1984, p. 454.

It may be noted that the Qumran text 4Q'Amram 2:6' (cf. Milik 1972, p. 79) contains the phrase **'ly' 'd 'r'y'** (the reading of the first word is in doubt, for the first letter has the appearance of a *ṣade*; see Plate I in Milik 1972). Several different interpretations have been offered for this phrase. Milik 1972 takes the first adjective to be singular, and the second plural; Beyer 1984, p. 212 takes them both to be plural. See also Fitzmyer and Harrington 1978, pp. 94-95.

Amulet 18

Provenance: Unknown
Gold
Removing an evil spirit from Klara daughter of Kyrana
Bernard Gimbel Collection, Saddle River, N.J.
Plate 4; Figure 3

1 משבעת רוחה בשמה דאהיה אשר אהיה ובשם מ
2 לאכוי קדישיה דתזוע ותגער ותרחק מן קלארא ברתה
3 דקיראנה ולא תהי לך עוד מכען רשו בה אסיר את ומרחק
4 מנה בשמה דאפרכאל אחיאל רפאל מפריאל אופפיאל
5 כפויאל עמיאל טוריאל ובשמה דמיכאל בסמאל נדבאל
6 חתימה מנך ועוד מן כל ביש בשמה דמימר קדיש עלמה דד ננג
7 נג חס E*E חקק (*magic characters*) עקצסכרד אפססE פגע סעצכקסס
8 (*magic characters and Hebrew letters*) גם אתי רוחה עברי מ
9 חוש קלארא θ חנפ BB AMANACHΛ AN*ANA AθA
10 יה יה יה (*magic characters and Hebrew letters*)
11 כתראת זתבדי בא במון קתר מנין דימר ליפ
12 אנברויה מיקונכוס גור תמב גסת יללוס זובה

Translation

1 Adjured are you, spirit, in the name of I-am-who-I-am and in the name of
2 His holy angels, that you may move away and be expelled and keep far from Klara daughter of
3 Kyrana, and that you may have no longer from now on power over her. May you (i.e. the spirit) be bound and kept away

4 from her, in the name of Afarkha᾿el, Aḥi᾿el, Raphael, Mafri᾿el, Ofafi᾿el,
5 Kefuya᾿el, ῾Ami᾿el, Ṭuri᾿el, and in the name of Michael, Besam᾿el, Nedav᾿el.
6 (May) she (i.e. Klara) (be) sealed (away) from you and also from all evil. In the name of the word of the Holy One of the World, **dd nnn**
7-8 **nn** (*magic characters and incomprehensible Hebrew letters*)
9 Quick, Klara. (*magic characters*)
10-12 (*magic characters and Hebrew letter combinations*).

Commentary

We are indebted to Mr. L. Alexander Wolfe for his help and cooperation in studying this amulet before it was acquired by its present owner. We are also grateful to Mr. Gimbel for his generous permission to make scholarly use of this text. The object was purchased in Europe, but its provenance was given as the area of Syria or Lebanon.

The amulet, measuring 11.0 × 4.3 cm., is written on a thin foil of gold. As in Amulets 9 and 11, the lines are not incised from top to bottom along the narrow side of the sheet, but are written in long lines along the wide side of the gold foil.

1 משבעת: This is evidently a passive participle in *aph῾el,* followed by the second person sg. of the pronoun (= **mšb῾ ᾿t**), the pronoun referring to the spirit. The spirit ("*rūḥā*") is here used consistently as a masculine noun.

2 ותגער: This verb is in the *itpe῾el,* as in Amulet 9:2.

Klara is a proper name so far unattested in these texts. It does exist however in Greek; cf. Preisigke 1922, p. 174.

3 קירא‍נה: For this name cf. Kyranan in Preisigke 1922, p. 188. The name may be possibly explained as a combination of Kyra ("lady") and Anna.

4-5 Most of the names in this list of angels, which consists of 8 + 3 = 11 names, are not widely attested in other sources. Raphael is of course well known (see the index to *AMB*), and so is Michael (see there too); but of the other names, Aḥi᾿el is mentioned in *Sefer ha-Razim* I:212; Mafri᾿el may be akin to Peru᾿el in *Sefer ha-Razim* II:40; Ofafi᾿el is attested in Amulet 3:10, **᾿pp᾿l**, as well as in Odeberg 1928, Heb. section 71, in 3Enoch 48D No. 5, **᾿ppy᾿l**.

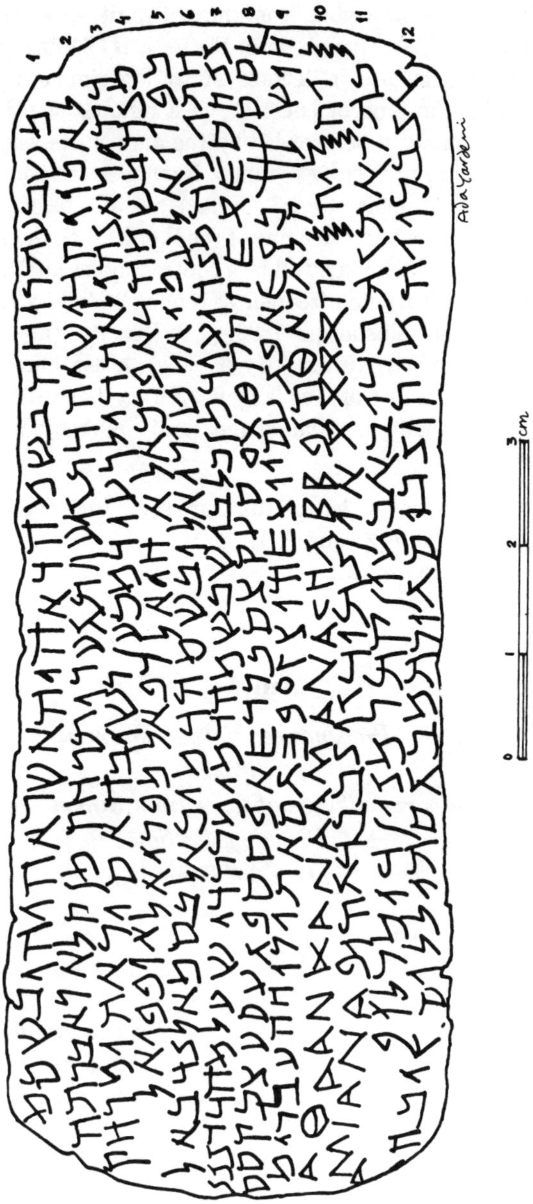

Fig. 3. Amulet 18

6 חתימה מנך: The subject of the passive participle seems to be Klara, who is to be 'sealed', i.e. protected, from the evil spirit, spoken of in the second person in lines 2-3. Although often the verb **ḤTM** has as its object the demons, in which case it denotes an action similar to that of **ʾSR**, **KBŠ**, etc., i.e. "to bind or enclose", in a number of places it takes as its object the client to be guarded by the amulet; its sense in that case is presumably "to protect by sealing". Examples are: Montgomery 1913, No. 7:2 (Jewish Aramaic); 31:1,8 (Syriac). See also below, B 15:1-4.

For the invocation "in the name of the Word..." cf. the phrase **bmʾmr qdyš** in A 3:23, which may well be a contraction of **bmʾmr qdyš ʿlmh**. The Palestinian Targums frequently render "God" by the phrase "the word of God"; cf. Ginsburger 1899, p. 3, Gen. 1:3 (**mymryh dẖ̇**), and similarly in Neophyti (**mmrʾ dyy**). The phrase here thus probably signifies "in the name of God". In B 22:3 we have the phrase **mymr qdyšʾl** (if the reading is reliable) apparently as the name of an angel, if not of God.

7-12 Among the magic letters there are some from the Greek alphabet. Compare also A 20, A 21 and A 32.

Amulet 19

Provenance: Ḥorvat Kannah
Bronze
Removing various kinds of fever from Simon son of Kattia
Private collection
Plate 6-7; Figure 4

1 קמיע טב למגעור אשתה
2 רבתה וטרטיה ואשת עדניה
3 וחמיטריטין וכל רוח וכל
4 משפט וכל עיין וכל מסקור
5 מן גופה דסימון הדן ברה
6 דקטטיה ומן כל אברוי
7 ולמסיה יתה ולמנטרה יתה
8 בשם כל אלין שמהתה
9 ואתיה קדישיה דכתיבין

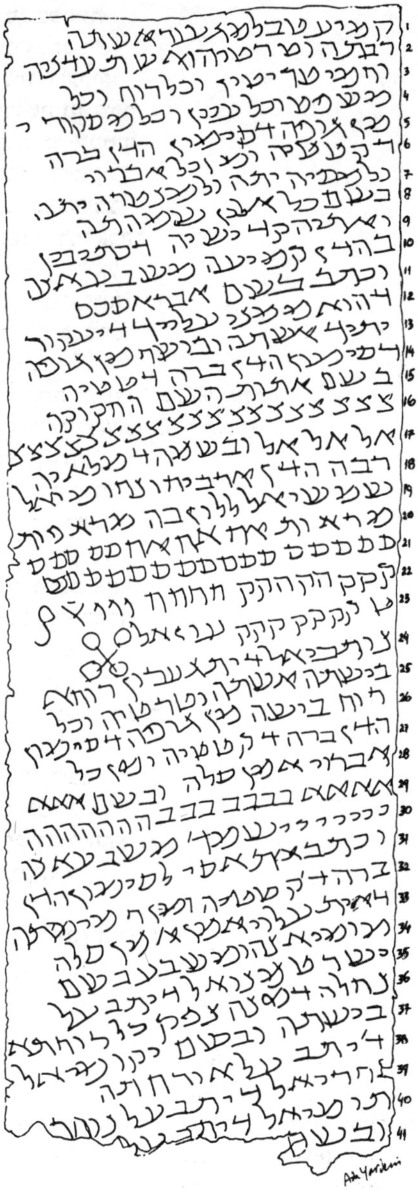

Fig. 4. Amulet 19

10 בהדן קמיעה משבע אנה
11 וכתב בשם אבראסכס
12 דהוא ממני עלייך דיעקור
13 יתיך אשתה ובושה מן גופה
14 דסימון הדן ברה <ד>קטטיה
15 בשם אתות השם החקוקה
16 צצצצצצצצצצצצצצצצ
17 אל אל אל ובשמה דמלאכה
18 רבה הדן ארביחו נחומיאל
19 שמשיאל ללוזבה מראפו(ת)
20 מראות אח אח אח ססססס
21 סססססססססססססס
22 קקק הקהק ק חחחח ווו (*magic characters*)
23 (ט) קקקקקקק עוזאל (*magic character*)
24 נותביאל דיתגערון רוחא
25 בישתה אשתה וטרטיה וכל
26 רוח בישה מן גופה דסימון
27 הדן ברה דקטטיה ומן כל
28 אברוי אמן סלה ובשם אאא
29 אאאא בבבבבבב ההההההה
30 ייייייי שמך משבע אנה
31 וכתב את אסי לסימון הדן
32 ברה דקטטיה {ח} מן חמימתה
33 דאית עלוי אמן אמן סלה
34 מומי אנה ומשבע בשם
35 ישר טמנואל דיתב על
36 נחלה דמנה נפק כל רוחתא
37 בישתה ובשם יקומיאל
38 דיתב על אורחתה
39 [נ]הריאל דיתב על (נו)[ה]ר[א]
40 תומיאל דיתב [על ...]
41 ובש[ם ...]

Translation

1 An amulet proper to expel the great
2 fever and the tertian (fever) and the chronic (?) fever
3 and the semi-tertian (fever) and any spirit and any
4 misfortune and any (evil) eye and any (evil) gaze
5 from the body of Simon, son of

6 Kattia, and from all his limbs,
7 to heal him and to guard him.
8 In the name of all these holy names
9 and letters which are written
10 in this amulet, I adjure
11 and write in the name of Abrasax
12 who is appointed over you (i.e. the fever), that he may uproot
13 you, fever and sickness, from the body
14 of Simon, the son of Kattia.
15 In the name of the engraved letters of the Name.
16 **ṣ** (*19 times*)
17 El El El, and in the name of this great
18 angel, **ʾrbyḥw nḥwmyʾl**
19 Shamshiʾel, **llwzbh mrʾpwt**
20 **mrʾwt ʾḥ ʾḥ ʾḥ sssss**
21 **s** (*16 times*)
22 **q** (*3 times*), **hq** (*2 times*), **q**, **ḥ** (*4 times*), **w** (*3 times*)
23 **ṭ**, **q** (*7 times*), ʿUzzaʾel
24 Noteviʾel. May there be driven away the evil
25 spirit, the fever, the tertian (fever), and all
26 evil spirit from the body of
27 Simon, son of Kattia, and from all
28 his limbs. Amen Selah. And in the name of
29 **ʾbhy** (*each letter repeated seven times*),
30 your name, I adjure
31 and write: You, heal Simon
32 son of Kattia, from the fever
33 which is in him. Amen Amen Selah.
34 I make an oath and adjure in the name of
35 **yšr ṭmnwʾl** who sits on
36 the river whence all evil
37 spirits emerge; and in the name of Yequmi'el,
38 who sits on the roads;
39 [Na]hariel, who sits over the [light,]
40 Tomi'el, who sits [on ...]
41 and in the na[me of ...]

Commentary

This amulet, brought to our attention by the late Dr. Zvi Ilan, was discovered in Ḥorvat Kannah, north of Biqʿat Bet Netofa in the Galilee (map reference 178.247). The amulet is incised on a thin bronze sheet, measuring 14.3 × 5.0 cm., with its bottom part damaged.

This amulet is specifically concerned with the healing of a client from various kinds of fever, and it contains valuable additions to Aramaic medical terminology. This was largely borrowed, as will be seen, from Greek; in part it was formed by way of imitation of the equivalent Greek terms.

1 אשתא רבתה seems to constitute a fixed medical term. Its Greek equivalent may be μέγας πυρετός (Liddell and Scott, col. 1088b), or μάκρος πυρετός, cf. Hippocrates, *Aphor.* IV:44; ed. Jones, p. 146. The sense may be "long, protracted fever".

2 טרטיה: We have here the Greek term τριταῖος (i.e. πυρετός) "tertian fever", a Greek loan-word in Aramaic. For this term and what follows, where we obviously have a series of borrowings from Greek, see the Introduction.

אשת עדניה means literally "the fever of the times". We assume it to denote "chronic fever".

3 חמיטריטין: The Greek medical term ἡμιτριταῖος "semi-tertian (fever)" is so well attested that there seems to be no doubt that it occurs here, even though the spelling with a *ḥet* seems unusual. For an occurrence of this term in a Greek magical context see Betz 1986, p. 301. The first part of the word looks like a derivative of the Aramaic term for fever, but one must resist the temptation to render חמי טריטין as an Aramaic-Greek expression meaning: "fevers of the tertian (type)". This, besides creating a somewhat unlikely Aramaic phrase, would be a mere repetition of טרטיה in the preceding line.

4 משפט could be associated to שופטי, שובטי occurring in magic texts. Palestinian Syriac seems to have **mšpṭ**ʾ, attested once in the version of Luke 1:4, where the ordinary Syriac version has ʿ**ny**ʾ; cf. Schulthess 1903, p. 212b. (We thank M. Sokoloff for this observation.)

The two words עיין and מסקור are similar in sense. They both denote the organ or action of seeing or looking. In this respect they are seemingly of neutral connotation. In such a magical context however they are used with an implicit pejorative sense: the *evil* eye, the *wicked* or envious gaze. The word for 'eye' has the well-known secondary sense of "evil eye"; the verb **SQR** is attested in Syriac in the sense of "to look askance, to hate", where it is used to translate the Hebrew verb שטם, e.g. in Genesis 27:41; cf. Payne-Smith 1890, II, col. 2721. The expression **msqwryt**ʾ occurs, besides ʿ**yn**ʾ **dbryyt**ʾ, in G 29, p. 1:10. In A 23:3 we have the expression **kl rwḥ byšh dsqrh bh**.

5 סימון הדן: The demonstrative pronoun is often used as a kind of article with proper names.

6 The spelling קטטיה may be a way of writing the Greek feminine name Kattia, Kittia (for the former see Frey 1936, No. 537; for the latter see Pape 1863/1870, s.v. The name Katia is also attested; cf. Pape 1863/1870, s.v.). The gemination of consonants is occasionally marked in Palestinian Aramaic by writing the letter twice; cf. Epstein 1964, II, p. 1258f. and Kutscher 1976, p. 31 n. 71.

15 The expression אתות השם החקוקה is curious, ungrammatical Hebrew. It may denote magic characters, probably referring to the letters which follow. The bizarre Hebrew is reminiscent of phrases such as בפיה תיחל מן זולתו in A 4:19, an amulet which abounds in unusual Hebrew phrases.

16 The letter *ṣade* is not rare in the magic texts, and seems to refer to the divine power. It occurs for example in A 2:4-5; B 2:9.

17 אל אל אל: Cf. A 2:4. Compare also **ʾlʾl** in *Sefer ha-Razim* I:25; **ʾlyʾl** in *Sefer ha-Razim* I:42, and elsewhere. As a magic expression it corresponds to **yh yh** etc. (e.g. A 2:3, 6).

18 ארביהו may be a variant of the angel's name **ʾrbyʾl**, attested in *Sefer ha-Razim* I:194. In that case the spelling given here should be regarded as standing for **ʾrbyhw**.

נחומיאל has its counterpart in **nḥmyʾl**, *Sefer ha-Razim* II:27.

19 שמשיאל is attested in *Sefer ha-Razim* I:212.

ללוזבה may be compared to לליזפת in the magic bowl Istanbul Museum 5363:7; cf. Jeruzalmi 1963, p. 128; also לוזפת in A 1:9.

19-20 מראפו(ת) / מראות is a sequence of names which may be associated to the well-known **mrmrʾwt** (e.g. *Sefer ha-Razim* IV:13; *AMB*, p. 61, note to A 4:25). The first name has a certain resemblance to **mrhptys** in A 1:9.

אח: Cf. אחאל in *Sefer ha-Razim* I:111. An alternative connection may be made to A 11:3, where the name אה occurs.

22-23 The letters here may be derived from the word החקוקה.

23 **עוזאל**: The forms attested so far in the amulets are עוזיאל (A 1:1; cf. also *Sefer ha-Razim* I:195) and עזאל (A 7:3).

28-30 The letters, each written 7 times, add up to make the word אבהי, which seems close in form to **ʾbhw** in Montgomery 1913, No. 7:9, and the commonly attested Greek magic name Abao, Abaot.

32 The scribe appears to have intended first to write חמימתה after קטטיה, then realized that he had to write מן first, and abandoned the *ḥet* half done.

On the term חמימתה, which seems to be synonymous with אשתא, cf. in the Introduction.

35 **ישר טמנואל**: This sequence is evidently intended to constitute a single name; cf. T-S K 21.95.P in Schäfer 1984, p. 144, where the sequence in line 10 is טמוניאל ישריאל טמניאל כראל. The same sequence occurs also in T-S NS 322.21 1b:11 (cf. Schäfer 1984, p. 153). The arrangement is evidently alphabetical, with *ṭeth* represented by Ṭemuniʾel, *yod* by Yaśriʾel-Ṭamaniʾel, and *kaf* by Karʾel. The two names Yaśriʾel-Ṭamaniʾel thus form a single epithet, perhaps by enlargement (or corruption) from a text like ours, where Yašar-Ṭemanuʾel serves as the name of the angel. A somewhat similar sequence occurs in an amulet published by Kotansky 1991, p. 270, line 2.

35-36 **דיתב על נחלה**: For the idea cf. A 6:3-5, where there are three spirits "standing in the great ford of the ocean". A 28:23-24 has דיתב על כ[ר]סיה. In Hebrew we have the expression היושב על in A 27:11. G 5, p. 4:8-9 has the expression דיתב על in the same usage as here, designating the functions of various angels. Cf. also G 9, p. 3:5-6, אילין שמהתא דיתבין על רוחתא וכבשין יתהון. The sense of this expression may be identical to the phrases where a certain angel is said to be "appointed over" something (e.g. above, line 12; A 12:2).

36 **נפק**: Singular form for a plural subject.

Amulet 20

Provenance: Unknown
Silver
Removing (evil) dreams from ... and from Maximion
Bernard Gimbel Collection, Saddle River, N.J.
Plate 5a; Figure 5

(*magic letters*) [	]	1
רנאל רדביאל נותיאל בהנאל[	]	2
אל גניאל עותיאל גער חזויא[	]	3
ו](מ)ן מכסימיון ברה מכי י(מ)	]	4

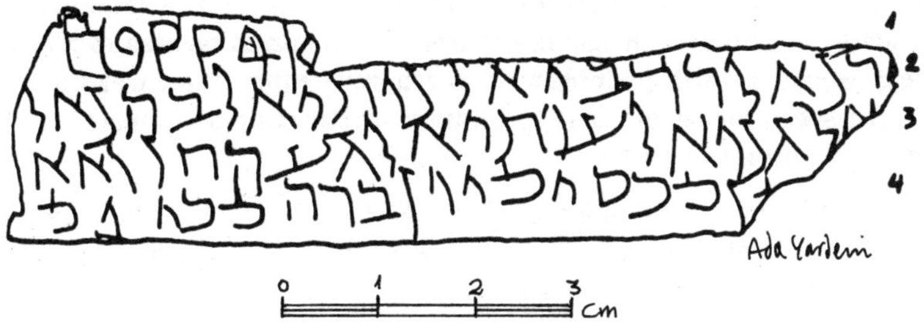

Fig. 5. Amulet 20

Translation

1 [ ] (*magic letters*)
2 [ ]**rn'l**, Radbiel, Nutiel, Bahnael
3 [ ]el, Ganiel, ʿUtiel. Drive out the visions
4 [and] from Maximion, his son. **mky y(m)**...

Commentary

This amulet is incised on a strip of silver. The extant fragment measures 9.0 × 2.3 cm.

For help with the publication of this amulet, as with No. 18, we are indebted to Mr. Leonard Wolfe and to Mr. Bernard Gimbel.

1 The characters are reminiscent of the Samaritan, or ancient Hebrew, script. The last four characters may perhaps be read as inverted *bet*, *resh*, *waw* (?) and *kaf*; one wonders whether the writer intended to express the word ברוך, "Blessed be he".

2-3 The names of the angels are not otherwise attested so far.

3 גער occurs in the singular, although a plural form would be expected here. The long vertical line of the *mem* in line 4 may perhaps be explained as part of a *waw* that was added in order to correct גער to גערו. This is far from certain, because the shape of the *waw* is of course not that of a straight vertical stroke.

חזויא: "Visions" occur very often in the Aramaic incantation texts in lists of afflictions or demons that are meant to be driven away. Some examples are: B 10:4; Geller 1980, p. 49, line 6; Isbell 1975, Nos. 38:5; 39:3,5,8; Harviainen 1981, p. 5, line 7; Greenfield and Naveh 1985, p. 99, line B24; Yamauchi 1967, No. 24:10. The form חזונא is often used in the Aramaic magic bowls from Babylonia as well as in Syriac (e.g. Gollancz 1898, p. 86 והלין חזוׄנא דהוין בלליא ובאימממא). Our amulet appears to provide the first attestation in Palestinian Aramaic of the definite plural form חזויא.

4 For the name Maximion cf. Pape 1863/1870, p. 856f. The name of the main client appears to have been written earlier, in a section of the amulet which has not survived.

ברה could also be "her son".

Amulet 21

Provenance unknown
Silver
Healing for Melekh son of Guzu
Geoffrey Cope Collection, Herzlia
Plate 8; Figure 6

Right column:

1]]כ[ ]איין ר]בה[[
2]](ח)רן[ ]א[י]אל רבה[ ]ל אאא הא[א]ל רבה אברה
3]]הא[ ](ד) יאל רבה (ח)נאל אח אא יאל רבה א(ז) מרתי
4]]מ[ ]חחח אי אי אי א אי יאל רבה חניאל חח אי אא יאל רבה

Fig. 6. Amulet 21

5 [ ](ברא)[ ]ooooo יאל רבה טביאל אה א(ה) א(ל) רבה אריאל
6 [(ר)צון]יאל הי הי הי הי הי הי יאל רבה יואל יאל רבה זהיאל
7 [ ]פיא[ל א]י אי אי[ן]אי אי אי יאל רבה יויאל ואל רבה מ(רי)ה
8 [ר]בה[א]ל רבה כרביאל ואל רבה אלשד(י)ת
9 [ ]ון[ ]הוא ה[ואל]רבה לוליאל ואל רבה אל אברה
10 [ ]ה יאל רבה מ(א)מ(יא)ל ואל רבה אל המון
11 [א]ל רבה אלוה(י)[ ]
12 [ ]רבה [ ]

Middle column:

מכונם

Left column:

1 [ ]
2 [ ] אלה רב (ד)הוא
3 יתן אסותה למלך
4 ברה דגוזו מן רוח
5 ומן שד ומן [ ]
6 ומן [ ]
7 אמן א אמן

Translation

Right column:

1 [ ] great [ ]
2 [ ] the great Ya'el [ ] ''' **h**'[ ] great '**brh**
3 [ ] the great Ya'el Ḥana'el '**ḥ** '' the great Ya'el '**z** Marti
4 [ ] **ḥḥḥ** '**y** '**y** '**y** ' '**y** the great Ya'el, Ḥaniel, **ḥḥ** '**y** '' the great Ya'el
5 [ ] OOOOO the great Ya'el Ṭabiel '**h** '**h** the great El, Ariel,
6 [ ]iel **hy hy hy hy hy hy hy** the great Ya'el Yo'el the great Ya'el Zahi'el
7 [ ]fi'e[l ']**y** '**y** '**y** **[ ]** '**y** '**y** '**y** '**y** the great Ya'el Yoyi'el the great Wa'el the great
8 [Ma]ster [ ] the great, Karbi'el, the great Wa'el, El Shaddai **t** (?)
9 [ ] the great [Wa'el,] Luli'el, the great Wa'el, El, Abra,
10 [ ] the great Ya'el, Ma'mi'el, the great Wa'el, El, Hamon,
11 [ ] the great [Wa]'el, Elohi[m]
12 [ ] the great [ ]

Middle Column:

Their abode.

Left Column:

2 ... Great God, who
3 will give healing to Melekh
4 son of Guzu from a spirit
5 and from a devil and from [ ]
6 and from [ ]
7 Amen, A<men >, Amen.

Commentary

Right Column:

The text consists exclusively of "names" and *nomina barbara*, but certain general observations may be made. It is obviously constructed according to the alphabetical principle, with the principal names being arranged according to this order. The main names which fall under this category are: Ḥanaʾel (R3) and Ḥaniʾel (R4); Ṭaviʾel (R5); Yoʾel (R6) and perhaps also Yoyiʾel (R7); Karbiʾel (or perhaps rather Keruviel) (R8); Loliʾel (R9); Ma(ʾ)miʾel (R10). In this our text has a number of parallels with the Geniza fragments which belong to the Hekhalot type of texts: T-S K 21.95 P, p. 2a (edited in Schäfer 1984, p. 143), where, in lines 4-7, we have a very similar sequence to the one preserved here: Abriel, Barkiel, Geliliel, Dalkiel, Hodiel, Vaʿdiel, Ziqiel, Ḥanuel, Ṭobiel, Yehoel, Kerubiel, Lahaṭiel, Maʾminiel, (Naṭ)liel, Sodiel (or Soriel), ʿAzriel, Penuel, Ṣefahʾel, Qantotiel, Ragšiel, Šafriel, T(ušm)aʾel. A different list occurs in the same fragment, K 21.95 P, on p. 2b, lines 9-11 (Schäfer 1984, p. 144). An inverse alphabetical series of names occurs in T-S K 21.95 T, p. 1a:9-11 (Schäfer 1984, p. 147). This requires reading in line 9 Rahbiel and not Dahbiel, and in line 10 Keluliel and not Beluliel (this was apparently already an error committed by the copyist). Similarly T-S NS 322.21 p. 1a:1-3 (Schäfer 1984, p. 153), where the beginning of the list is missing, and on p. 1b:9-13 (ibid.). Also in Bodl. Heb. a.3.25a:21-26 (Schäfer 1984, p. 156).

Another feature of this text is the repetition of certain fixed sequences: **ʾy** or **hy** repeated several times followed by **yʾl rbh** (sometimes written **wʾl rbh**) is a sequence that recurs in lines R4, 6, 7, and in a mutilated form also in line 5 (**ʾh ʾh ʾl rbh**), and at the end of line 4 (**ḥḥ ʾy ʾʾ yʾl**

rbh). Up to the middle of line 7 the spelling of the name is **y'l**, and **from** that point onwards there is preference for the spelling **w'l**.

A somewhat similar structure is seen in Amulet 22, where we have certain entities "that rule over (the sun, the moon, the ocean, etc.)" and their servants.

Middle Column:

At the top of the column one can distinguish the word מכונם, "their (= the angels') *makhon* (abode)", underneath which there are various Greek letters as well as letters resembling the ancient Hebrew (or Samaritan) alphabet. One item in the drawings around the Hebrew word looks like a ladder.

The single word **mkwnm** in the middle column is certainly related to the term *makhon* that designates, like *ma'on*, one of the seven firmaments (see Bavli Ḥagiga 12b). The word is used fairly frequently in the Dead Sea Scrolls, especially in the Thanksgiving Scroll. It also occurs quite often in the Hekhalot writings (cf. the enumeration in Schäfer 1988, p. 408), where it seems to be based quite explicitly in many cases on the Talmudic discussion. Some of the references to *makhon* in the Hekhalot texts mention a ladder; cf. for example: וסולם גדול נצב במעון וראשו מגיע למכון (Schäfer 1981, §773), וסולם נצב במכון וראשו מגיע לערבות (Schäfer 1981, §772-774).

Left Column:

This section of the sheet contains the operative formula, designed to heal a certain person: Melekh son of Guzu. Both names are quite unusual in the period under consideration, and are not easy to place. While the first name is attested in some places, cf. Zadok 1989, p. 260, the second seems so far unattested.

Amulet 22

Provenance unknown
Silver
Amulet for Theodos(i)us son of Theodora
Bible Lands Museum, Jerusalem
Plate 9; Figure 7

1 ... צבואות צור הע(ל)מים אמר ... רפאל מר ו(מ)ריה

2 ... וחצרות גודיה צבא המשרת את כבודו (א)חד ומיוחד ... אסו

3 ... ותרפיה ומרמ(וי) וטלני דכל ליליה ... או עוף מעוף חצץ המשל אסיאל קדוש

4 ... ויחפרו וירדפו ויגערו מן תידוסוס ברה דיתידורא בשם שלום אל אלוה ס אתא בארץ ...

4a ומשרתו וכל אלהה

5 ... השם המו<ש>ל בשמים אה באה יה ביה ומשרתו ... כל אחד א הכוב(ר) ערבות ...

6 ... צביאל בביאל בחור בוחר ה רבתה וגתבינן השני (*drawing*) המשל בשאול חח

7 ... משרתו ויקר(ס)נא ותפנט ספיני ספנייאל שמשא חונא חוסא אל את אות אחח למן מן

8 פנייס פנרוס בן בן רבא שלוש אות מי שמושל בבשמש יא אאא בבב ומשרתו את אנת תיאון הגדול

9 אמונא נא ... אבראות אבלא אברסס ... שמושל יה שמו לוס ממר ממר מארתו ארנות יאסיה

10 אביאות אאות רב ... מלל המושל בירח ... משרתו אלם ... גנניאל

11 עאות ... ()אות ... סנג(י)ן אגגן בר פרגגוס ... מרותה שמושנאות

12 ...

13 ... (ומ)שרתו ... המושל באוקינוס חחחחחחח ...

14 ... מכיאל מלאיתגה ... נגג ואות טרסוס חחף ... שבעואות ... אמן אמן רבה אמן

Translation

1 Sabaoth, the Eternal Rock, said ... Raphael ...
2 ... the troops (?), army, that serve His glory, one and only ... heal
3 and healing (?) and ... and shadow-spirits of every night ... or bird ... Asiel, holy.

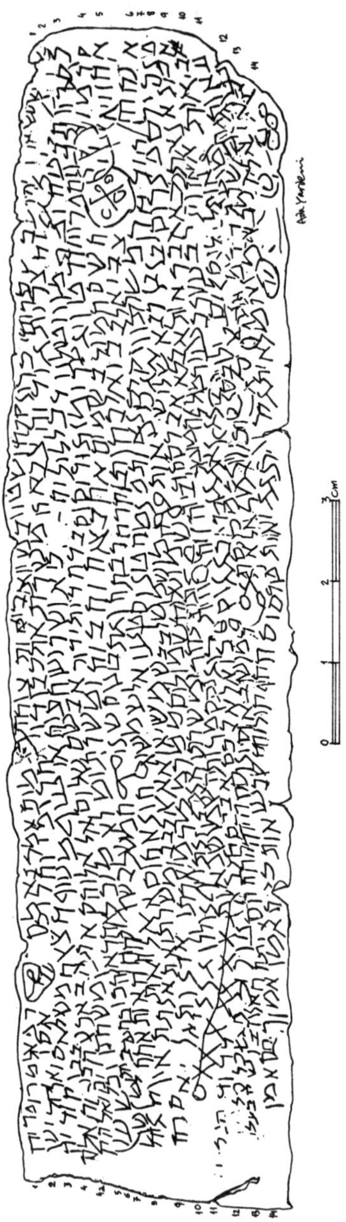

Fig. 7. Amulet 22

4 and may they be ashamed, and chased away, and driven out of Theodosus son of Theodora, by the name of Shalom El Eloah ... in the land

4a and his servant and every deity

5 the name that ru<l >es in the heaven, Ah-in-Ah, Yah-in-Yah, and his servant ... each one, A, he who rides the clouds.

6 ... Ṣeviʾel, Babiʾel, ... He who rules over Sheʾol. **ḥḥ**

7 ... his servant ...

8 ... he who rules over the sun, **y**ʾ ʾʾʾ **bbb**, and his servant you, you, Theon the Great.

9 Amuna Na ... Abraoth, Abla Abrasas, ... who rules, Yah, his name ...

10 ... Malal (?), who rules over the moon ... his servant Alam (?) ... Gananiel

11 ... Sa<sa >ngen Angen bar Faranges ...

13 ... and his servant ... who rules over the ocean **ḥḥḥḥḥḥ ...**

14 ... Amen, Amen, Great, Amen.

Commentary

The text, measuring 14.0 × 4.8 cm., is extremely difficult to read. It is very densely written, apparently by a writer who did not care much about being legible, either because he was careless, or because he sought consciously to conceal the wording of the formulae he used. The language is apparently Hebrew, although one cannot make much sense of the sequences that can be deciphered. The lines are not very clearly distinguished. Only the sequences of words and letters that could be made out with relative confidence have been transcribed here. There would be no point in copying in this edition highly doubtful sequences of letters that seem to make little or no sense. It is also impossible to offer a continuous translation of the text, apart from a number of lines where a few words form what looks like a coherent sentence. These will be given in the following notes. We would however like to urge the reader not to attach too much weight to our tentative transcription of the text. It may be pointed out that Ada Yardeni's drawing was made at an early stage of our work, and does not reflect in all deatils our later conception of the text.

It may be noted that we have here an enumeration, imperfectly preserved, of certain deities or angels that are, respectively, "ruler of the heaven" (line 5), "ruler over Sheʾol" (line 6), "ruler over the sun" (line 8), "ruler over the moon" (line 10), "ruler over the ocean" (line 13). Each one of them seems to be accompanied by a certain servant, called *mešareto* (lines 4a, 5, 7, 8, 10). This is slightly reminiscent of the text in Schäfer 1984 (Antonin 186) where we have a reference to "the holy troops that serve YHWH the God of Israel" (line 12).

3 ותרפיה may be either the Aramaic: "and may you heal him / her", or the Greek noun θεραπεία "cure" etc.

4 ויחפרו: The reading is doubtful; if it is accepted, it would represent the Hebrew verb ḤPR, which means "to be ashamed" (e.g., Is. 24:23; Jer. 50:12; Ps. 40:15, etc.). In Prov. 13:5 the Targum uses also the same root, which is otherwise rarely (if at all) attested in Aramaic.

For the names Theodosus (presumably for Theodosius) and Theodora, both of which are attested among Jews, see Frey 1936, Nos. 31, 709, 722, 723. For Theodosia, see Schwabe and Lifshitz 1967, No. 199. See also Naveh 1992, p. 116.

5 הכוב(ר) ערבות seems to be a corruption of הרוכב בערבות, Ps. 68:5.

8 The writing בבשמש contains a superfluous *beth*.

For Theon the Great cf. the deity called Bar-Theon in A 6.

9 After אברסס (= Abrasax?) a *dalet* may be written. The division of words here is particularly uncertain.

מארתו could be a corruption of משרתו "his servant".

11 We have traces of the frequent name-formula Sasangen bar Faranges here. On this name cf. A 7:10. Note the spelling of *—ng—* with **gg**, by influence of Greek orthography.

Amulet 23

Provenance unknown

Bronze

Healing for Teo daughter of Matrona from excrescence

Leonard A. Wolfe Collection, Jerusalem

Plate 5b; Figure 8

1 קמיע טב לטיו ברת מטרונ(ה)

2 דתתאסי מן טתלתולה דאחד ל[ה ומן]

3 כל רוח בישה דסקרה בה וכל דד(ח)[לתה]

4 (ד)בודינה על לבה לא קרבה בה

5 [ל](ב)ישה

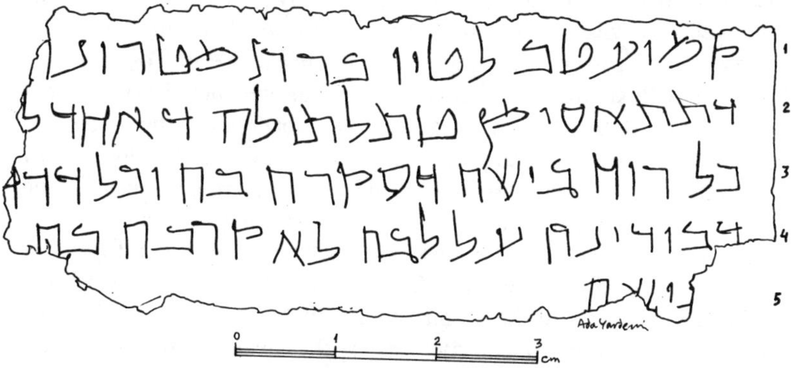

Fig. 8. Amulet 23

Translation

1 An amulet proper for Teo daughter of Matrona,

2 that she may be healed from the excrescence that has seized her [and from]

3 every evil spirit that has cast an (evil) glance at her, and every (spirit) [that has terror]

4 [of] sorcery (?) on its heart shall not approach her

5 [for] evil.

Commentary

A bronze tablet, measuring 7.7 × 3.0 cm.

1 טיו: This name could be a short form of Theodora (for which see above, A 22, line 4; Frey 1936, No. 709), Theodosia (Schwabe and Lifshitz 1967, No. 199), or a similar name, although the Aramaic *ṭeth* is not normally used for Greek *theta*. The alternative explanation for this name would be to connect it to the feminine name **ʾṭyw**, **ʾṭywn**, which occurs in Inscription No. 15 in Beth Sheʿarim III (see Avigad 1976, pp. 241-242), and which has been explained as reflecting the Latin name Attius (see Lifshitz 1962, p. 71).

מטרונה: Cf. the name Matrōna in Frey 1936, No. 46, and in a Judaeo-Greek amulet from Syria (Schwabe and Reifenberg 1945/6).

2 טתלתולה: This name of a disease is evidently a masculine noun in the determined state, to judge from the verb **dʾḥd**. Its interpretation is not entirely unequivocal. One may try to explain it by connecting it to the word **tltwl**, **tylwl**, so far attested only in Hebrew, but which may well have also existed in Aramaic, and which means "wart" or some other excrescence. Examples for this usage are in Tos. Negaʿim II:12; Bavli Bekhorot 40b. If this is accepted, one should assume that the scribe hesitated, first writing *ṭeth*, then abandoning this letter and writing the word with an initial *taw*. One may object, however, by questioning whether a wart was considered a severe enough affliction to warrant an amulet to fight it. The only alternative seems to be to take this as a form of the Greek perf. participle neuter τεθηλός or feminine τεθηλυῖα "a swelling (e.g. of the spleen, of the liver)" (cf. Liddell and Scott s.v. θάλλω), but the spelling of the Aramaic does not seem to favour such a connection. Since the meanings of the Hebrew **tltwl** and of the Greek are fairly close to each other, the possibility of a conflation of the two forms, the Semitic **tltwl** (which is probably connected with the Hebrew word **tl**, Aramaic **tlʾ** "mound, hill"; according to Even-Shoshan, *Hammillon he-ḥadaš*, it is a by-form of *dildul*) and the Greek τεθηλός (from θάλλω "to bloom") cannot be ruled out, resulting presumably in a hybrid form, *ṭeθetūlā*, which may refer to any kind of swelling, excrescence or carbuncle.

דאחד לה: Cf. the expression דאחד ליה רוחא Bavli Pesaḥim 111b "a spirit seizes him".

3 דסקרה: Cf. A19:4 וכל מסקור, which corresponds in the same text to וכל עין, and see the commentary there. מסקוריתה occurs also in A 26:15 and in Geniza 29:10.

3-4 דד(ח)[לתה] (ד)בודינה: The reconstruction of the first word is difficult. One possibility is to regard the first *dalet* as superfluous, and to read **wkl {d }dḥlh dbydynh <d >ʿl lbh** "and any fear of a court (of law) which is in her heart". For lawsuits mentioned in magic tablets see Youtie and Bonner 1937, p. 47. It may however be pointed out, against the possibility of reading בידינה, that the letter following *bet* in the first word of line 4 looks more like a *waw* than like a *yod*.

A court of law occurs in a relevant text as a place for imprisoning the demons. This is a passage from the *Book of Asaph*: וישלח מלאך אחד מן הקדושים שרי הפנים ושמו רפאל לכלה את רוחות הממזרים מתחת השמים לבלתי השחית עוד בבני האדם, ויעש המלאך כן ויכלאם בבית המשפט, אך אחד מעשרה הניח להתהלך בארץ לפני שר המשטמה לרדת בם במרשיעים לנגע ולענות בהם בכל מיני מדוה ותחלואים... (quoted from Muntner 1957, pp. 148f.; a slightly different version is given op.cit., p. 93 n.) "and he (i.e. God) sent one of the holy angels of the Presence, Raphael by name, to abolish the wicked spirits from under the sky, so that they might cause no more damage among people. The angel acted in this manner and imprisoned them in the house of judgment. But he allowed one tenth of them to function on the earth in the presence of the Prince of Mastema, to persecute the evil ones, to cause them harm and torment them by all kinds of ailment and sickness..."

Another way of solving this problem is by reading דד(ח)[יא] בבודינה (or דד(ח)[קא] בבודינה) "(a spirit) that pushes (or oppresses) her heart with deceit".

The form בודינא, בודינה is not attested elsewhere in Aramaic, but the structure of the word may be assumed to be *budyān* (*quṭlān*), like *pulḥān*, *purqān*, etc. If this is the structure of the word, בודינה may be an abstract noun meaning "falsehood, fiction", obviously derived from the root BDH / BDY "to invent (a fiction, a story)"; compare the Syriac *bedyā*. While this may indeed be the structure of our word, it is difficult to regard it as completely separate from a similar-looking word, spelled **bdyn**, **bydyn** (vowelled *biddin*), that occurs in some Targumic passages as an Aramaic equivalent of Hebrew *baddim* (Is. 44:25) or *ōv*, *ōvōt* (Lev. 19:31; 20:6, 27; Dt. 18:11; Is. 19:3). The word may thus have a magic association, meaning perhaps something like "spirit"or "sorcery".

The word בדני occurs several times in the Qumran manuscripts, twice in the War Scroll (once written אבדני) and some 18 times in the Song of the Sabbath Sacrifice (see discussion with references in Newsom 1985, pp. 235, 283-285). Its meaning is uncertain, but it has been suggested that it means "form, pattern, shape". Should בודינה, בדין and בדני be related, they may have a sense such as "image, vision".

Amulet 24

Provenance unknown
Silver
Healing for Qaduma son of Cyrill
Geoffrey Cope Collection, Herzlia
Plate 10; Figure 9

1 [ק]מיע טב ובדיק ומ[..]ה (ע)ל כל [ ]
2 [ ] וטלנין דאיה לאשכן חת(מה)
3 [ ]ה גלי וכסה מן גבריאל מלאכה
4 עירא וקדישה דייהון מאסין בה [ ]
5 י(ש)ראל לבטירות להטט אברכסיס
6 צפירים יייי יא יה מוליך רם ישב [כסא]
7 הכבוד בגוה רבה ונורא על כל סביביו
8 (ב)יה עלם דין כל המעסים אדון כל הנשמה אד[ון]
9 כל הבריה המכה ומלך רופה אל חנון ומל[ך]
10 רחום בריך רופה רופה הו(א) לכן רפה את
11 [קדומ]ה בן קירל מן אשה ומן ערוי ומן
12 [ ]ה וטלני בנדכר בן נקבה בשם אכבה
13 בסלר סנר בשם שמעלל הסר הגדול [ ]
14 [ ] המתיצב על מפ[ ] מסבל חכ[ ]
15 א אה קרי [ ]לכך מסס מסוס יא יהא [ ]
16 בא(פ)יה ביה ואאאא וההההה ייי[י]
17 א(ת)בן כסא שם הנכב<ד> הושיע ועסא רן[ ]
18 קדומה בר קירל כל ה[ ]
19 vacat הוא יתין רפואתו על קדומה
20 [ב]רה דקירל מן רוח רעה ושיד וטלנ[ית]
21 vacat סרגינוס וטסיריס (... ...)
22 דכר ונקבה ויקהרי נגע ולגלל ומראה
23 דלל רושי עלי(ך) ינה סין יה דרהי וחבה
24 (א)בכוה vacat

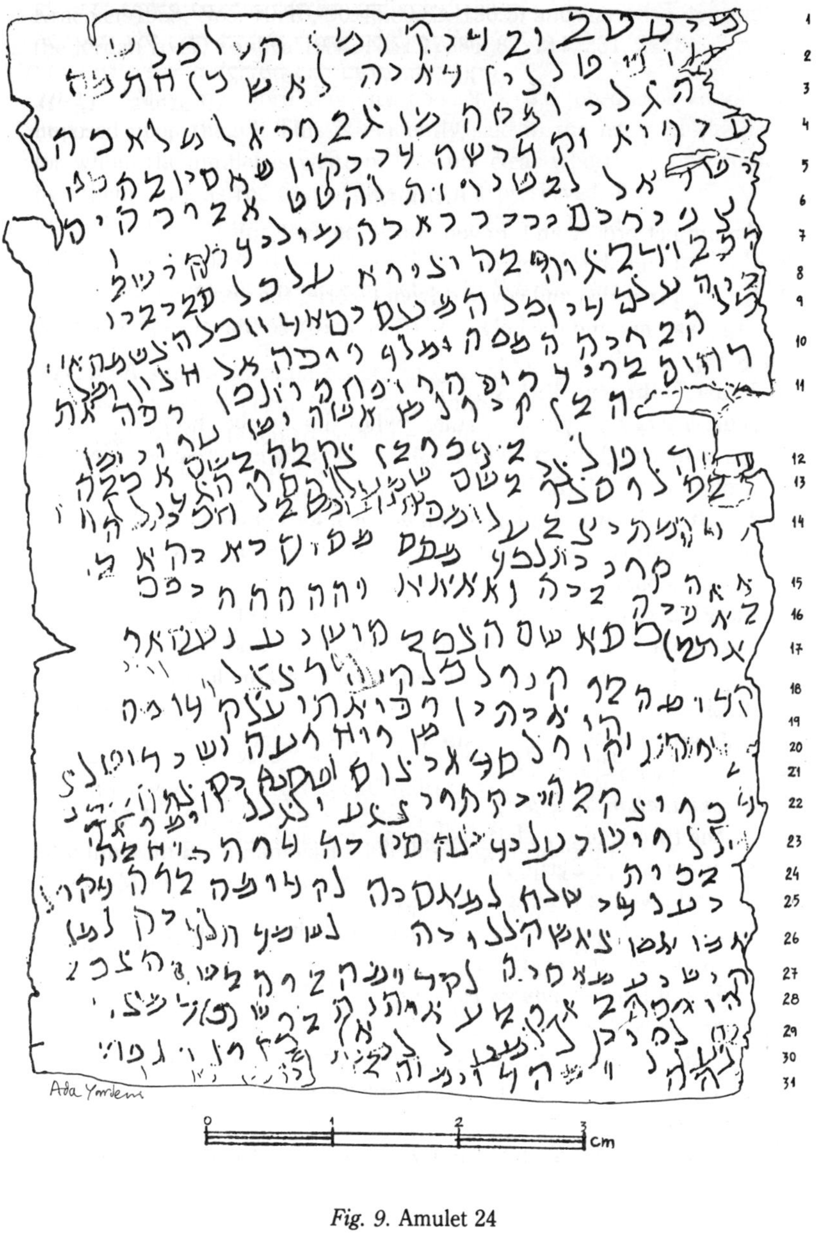

Fig. 9. Amulet 24

25 יעל דישלח למאסיה לקדומה ברה דק(רל)
26 אמן אמן נאמן הללויה לשמך הל(ל)ויה למן
27 הושיע מאסיה לקדומה ברה בש[ם] הנכ(ב)[ד]
28 (...) בארבע (... ...)
31-29 (... ...)

Translation

1 An amulet proper and proven and ... against any ...
2 [ ] and shadow-spirit ...
3 [ ] revealed and covered from Gabriel the angel
4 "the watcher and the holy one" (Dan. 4:10), so that they should heal by it [ ]
5 Israel (?) **lbṭyrwt lhṭṭ** Abraxis
6 *ṣefirim* **yyyy y' yh**, lofty ruler, (who) sits [on the throne of]
7 glory in haughtiness (which is) "great, and is awesome above all around him" (Ps. 89:8).
8 By **yh** of the world, judge of all actions, lord of all souls, l[ord]
9 of all creatures, who smites and is a healing king, merciful God and compassionate
10 ki[ng]. Blessed is the healer, a healer is He. Therefore heal
11 [Qadum]a son of Cyrill from fever and shiver and from
12 [ ] and shadow-spirit, whether male or female. In the name of **'kbh**
13 **bslr snr**. By the name of **šm'll** the great prince [ ]
14 [ ] who stands on ...
15-16 (*combinations of letters*)
17 ... the throne of the glorious name. Save and act ...
18 Qaduma son of Cyrill. All ...
19 He will give his healing to Qaduma
20 son of Cyrill from evil spirit, demon and shadow-spirit.
21 ... **srgynws** and **ṭsyrys** ...
22 male and female. *nomina barbara*
23-24 *nomina barbara*
25 and that he may send healing for Qaduma son of Cyrill
26 Amen, amen, faithful, hallelujah, for your name, hallelujah, therefore (?)
27 save, healing, for Qaduma son of <Cyrill> by the glorious name
28-31 ...

Commentary

This is a silver plaque measuring c. 8.0 × 6.0 cm. and containing 31 lines of densely written inscription, incised on the surface of the plate rather carelessly in uneven lines. The margins are damaged. Since the incisions are relatively shallow and not clearly visible, and the text is quite corrupt, the reading of the amulet has proved to be a difficult and somewhat uncertain task.

Lines 1-4 are written in Aramaic, but lines 6-10 are in Hebrew, in a style that suggests formulae that were also used in the Jewish liturgy. Lines 11f. are again in Aramaic. A similar alternation of the two languages goes on in the following lines. Lines 28ff. are impossible to make out.

1 The fourth word may be read ומ[נס]ה "and tested", for which cf. e.g. the corresponding Hebrew phrase בדוק ומנוסה, a very common expression, cf. e.g. Gaster 1900, p. 105 (20). This word could alternatively be read ומ[גנ]ה "and protecting"; cf. Targum Is. 4:5 מגנה על "to cover, protect", and Targum Jonathan to Dt. 28:15. The preposition על probably does not depend in this case on the verb מגנה, but goes back to קמיע. The translation would be: "A good, tested and protecting amulet, against [spirits, demons] and shadow-spirits". At the end of the line and the beginning of line 2 one should probably read [רוחין ושידין]; see A 13:7-8.

2 דאיה לאשכן: The words are not clear. אשכון occurs as an angel name in G 18, p. 18:6, but it may be doubted whether this is relevant in the present context. Somewhat more promising is the text in Schäfer 1984, p. 173 (T-S K 21.95A), 1a, lines 4-6, where Is. 57:15 is quoted. It should be read as follows: וגלויות ונסתרות [...] קדושים וטהורים שעמהם שכן כבוד יהוה שנאמר כי כה [אמר רם ונשא שכן עד וק]דוש שמו מרום וקדוש אשכן את דכא ושפל רוח להחיות (רוח) שפ(ל)ים. If there is a connection, our amulet may refer to spirits among whom the glory of God does not reside. Two other points of possible contact between our amulet and T-S K 21.95A (Schäfer 1984, p. 173) are as follows. (a) In our amulet, line 3, we have [...]ה גלי וכסה, and this may correspond to וגלויות ונסתרות (Schäfer 1984, p. 173, line 4). (b) Both our text, line 7, and Schäfer 1984, p. 173:10, make prominent use of Ps. 89:8, which is obviously regarded as possessing special magical power.

4 עירא וקדישה: This expression is based on Dan. 4:10. It is fairly common in the Hekhalot literature and later; cf. e.g. Schäfer 1981, p. 142:5.

דייהון מאסין בה: The verb should be דיהוון. The phrase goes back to קמיע, and the preceding words are something like one (or more) dependent clause(s).

5 י(ש)ראל: If the reading is correct, this is part of the object to the verb "to heal". The second letter could however be a *ṭeth*, and then this would be the first item in a list of *nomina barbara*.

7 גוה is a defective spelling for גאוה. רבה in Ps. 89:8 is perhaps an adverb. Here it is used as an attribute to "haughtiness", which does not occur in the biblical verse.

8 דין כל המעסים "the judge of all actions" is somewhat strange and unusual, and may be a corruption of אדון כל המעשים "the lord of all actions", which is attested in Schäfer 1981, p. 143 (T-S K 21.95.P), lines 9-10; op.cit., p. 153 (T-S NS 3.22:21), p. 1a:9-10: אל אלים חיים ומלך עולם אדון כל הבירויות אדון כל המעשים. The standard Jewish prayer book has the phrase אל ההודאות אדון הנפלאות בורא כל הנשמות רבון כל המעשים, said among the morning blessings.

אדון כל הנשמה: Cf. Scholem 1965, p. 114; *Sefer ha-Razim*, p. 109 (VII:39): ברוך שמו בפי כל נשמה ומבורך בפי כל בריה.

11 קדומה: For this name cf. Nabataean **qdmw** (*CIS*, II, 467. Cf. also Cantineau 1930/1932, II, p. 141); Καδαμος, cf. Pape 1863/1870.

קירל is apparently a form of Cyrilla, cf. Frey 1936, No. 310 (p. 244): Κυρυλλα.

אשה and ערוי are both indefinite Aramaic forms of the nouns. See the discussion on A 2:2.

12 בנדכר: written as one word, for בין דכר.

17 ועסא רן [ ]: Perhaps to be completed: ועסא רפואה ל/קדומה "and do healing to Qaduma".

21 The line may have been intended as an addition above the line to the names in line 22.

26f. למן / הושיע מאסיה: We have assumed that the first word is a corruption of לכן. It can also be taken to be a defective writing for למען. The following two words may then be infinitives, in Hebrew and Aramaic respectively.

Amulet 25

Provenance unknown
Bronze
Removing the evil spirit from Nonn[a] daughter of Megale
Geoffrey Cope Collection, Herzlia
Plate 11; Figure 10

1 [ ] בשם טרחיאל
2 [ ](א)ל (ס)תריאל ס(ננ)תיאל יה יה י[ה י]ה יה יה יהו
3 [י]הו [יהו] יהו ברוריאל ברוריאל ברכיא[ל] ברכיאל
4 פנחתיאל פנחתיאל קרבתיאל קרבתיאל סננתיאל סננתיאל
5 (*magic characters*) געורו רוחה בישתה מן נונ[ה]
6 ברתה דמגלי vacat בשם תה ובה יה יה (*magic symbols*)
7 שיר תשבחות לאלהא לאלהא עליא על כל פגע ועל
8 כל מ(ום) דאות מלאכה סנג ופרנגיס מלאכו[י קד]ישוי דינ[ ]
9 [ ]ין נחיר[ין] בישין יטרון ל[נונה ב]רתה

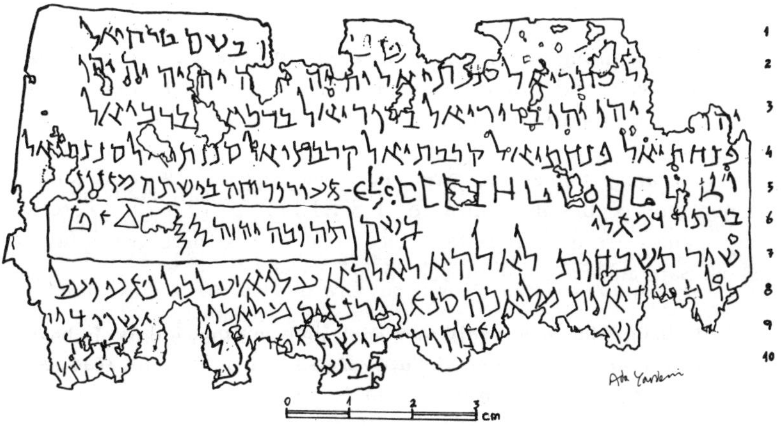

Fig. 10. Amulet 25

Translation

1 [ ] in the name of Ṭarḥiel (?)
2 [ ]el Satrial Sanantiel, **yh yh yh yh yh yh yhw**
3 **yhw [yhw] yhw yhw** Beruriel Beruriel, Barkiel Barkiel
4 Panaḥtiel Panaḥtiel Qarbatiel Qarbatiel Sanantiel Sanantiel
5 (*magic characters*) Exorcise the evil spirit from Nonn[a]

6 daughter of Megale. In the name of **th wbh yh yh** (*magic symbols*)
7 A song of praise to God, to the supreme God, against all harm and against
8 all blemish. Da'ot the angel, Sang and Faranges his holy angels ...
9 ... evil breathing (?). May they guard [Nonna] daughter
10 [of Megale ...]

Commentary

This is a bronze amulet, measuring 11.5 × 5.5 cm, which was found with its case (c. 7 cm. long), and recently bought by Dr. Geoffrey Cope of Herzlia. The inscription consists of ten lines of elegantly incised script. Because of the wear of the metal, the reading from the recto side is extremely difficult, and it is best done from the reverse. The photograph reproduced in Plate 11 shows the reverse of the bronze plaque, printed from the back side (to show the writing in the correct direction). Lines 9-10 are heavily damaged, so that very little can be retrieved from what was written in these lines.

1-2 The beginning of the text is illegible. In lines 1-2 a list of angel names is given, and this is followed by a sevenfold repetition of Yah, and a fivefold repetition of Yahu.

3-4 Five angel names are given, each one repeated twice. A similar phenomenon occurs in Geniza 18 (T-S K1.143), p. 19:6-10, where six angel names are each repeated twice. The names there are different: Eškon, Sargon, Michael, Raphael, ʿAniel, Uriel.

5 The client's name has only the first three letters, but there seems to be hardly any other way of supplementing it except by reading it Nonna. The name occurs in Frey 1936, No. 645, as that of a Jewish lady in Milan. Greek has νέννος and νόννος for "uncle", and a feminine form from this would be quite easily conceivable. Latin has nonnus, m., and nonna, f., for "monk" and "nun"; cf. also *PGM*, P6d.4 Νοννοῦς.

6 The client's mother is Megale, the Greek adjective "big". See Megas, Megalos in Naveh 1985b, p. 108, as well as Schwabe and Lifshitz 1967, Nos. 78, 145.

תה ובה may be an abbreviated reference to תהו ובהו (Gen. 1:2) or to its Aramaic equivalent תהיה ובהיה. Syriac has **twh wbwh**.

7 שיר תשבחות: See A 3:1. There and in two bowl texts (quoted in the commentary to A 3) the formula is שיר תשבחות למלך עלמיא.

8 The reading **mwm** is not certain, but this seems a possible reconstruction of the signs visible.

סנג ופרנגיס is a further variation on the very common angel name Sesengen bar Ferenges (cf. A 7:10).

מלאכו[י קדי]שוי: The endings here are somewhat unusual, with the possessive pronoun in the 3rd person singular attached to both the noun and its adjective.

9 נחירן[ין] בישין: The noun may be either connected to the verb NHR "to breathe hard", and indicate a symptom of illness, cf. Syriac *nḥārā* "heavy or stertorous breathing as in illness" (Payne-Smith); or to the Aramaic noun *nuḥrā* which means "wrath, anger", cf. Berešit Rabba p. 767 (paraša 67): עוברתיה נוחרתיה

Amulet 26

Provenance unknown
Copper
For Ḥabibi son of Ḥerta against evil encounters
Skirball Museum, Hebrew Union College, Los Angeles, California
Plate 12; Figure 11

1 משביע אני על כל אוערות ו[ ]
2 רעות רעות עם זכר עם נקבה עם אי(ש)
3 עם אשה עם גוי עם ישראל {המתג}
4 המתגרשים לבוא על חביבי ברה
5 דחרתה בשם דרקון דוקון דוקון
6 אסטקטון סלדאקליף סקופק
7 ש(נ)קק בשם אדמיאל מלאכה {ובש}
8 ובשם כוכביאל מלאכה בשם
9 מלאכיה אלין אשבעית עלכי
10 רוחא בישתה דפרחא ודשכנה
11 דילה תקרובין (ב)חביבי ברה

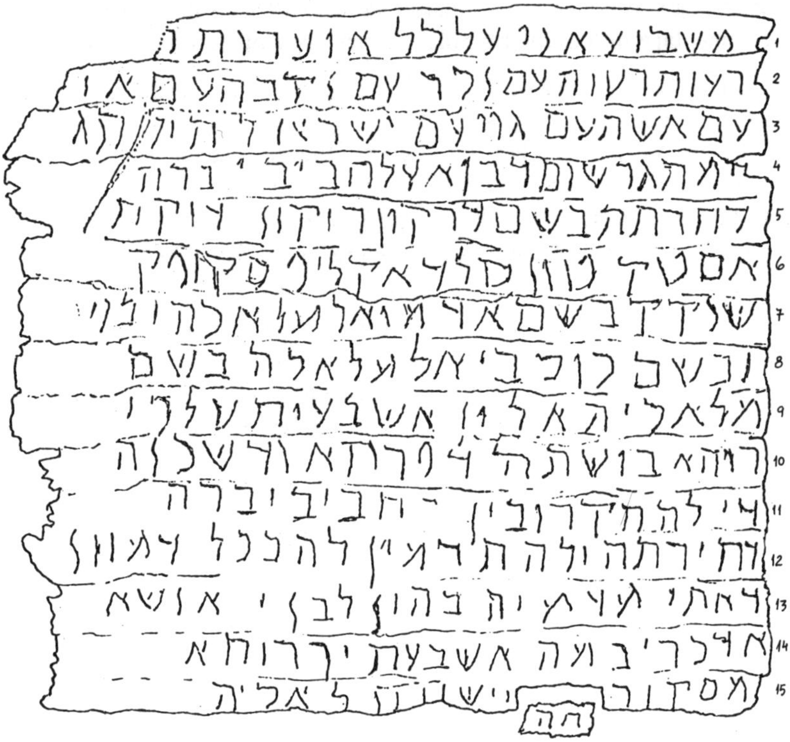

Fig. 11. Amulet 26

12 דחירתה ולה תדמין לה בכל דמוון
13 דאתי מדמיה בהון לבני אנשא
14 אדכרי במה אשבעתיך רוחא
15 מסקור[י]תה (בשם מלאכיה)
16 (...)

Translation

1 I adjure all evil occurrences (?) and [en-]
2 counters, (whether) with a male or a female, (whether) with a man
3 or a woman, (whether) with a Gentile or with an Israelite,
4 that come up rushing against Ḥabibi son of
5 Ḥerta. In the name of **drqwn, dwqwn, dwqwn**,
6 **ʾstqṭwn, sldʾqlyp, sqwpq**

7 **šnqq**. In the name of the angel Admiel
8 and in the name of the angel Kokhbiel. In the name
9 of these angels I adjure you (fem. sg.)
10 evil spirit, whether flying or resting,
11 that you should not touch Ḥabibi son of
12 Ḥerta, and that you should not appear to him by any likeness
13 by which you appear to people.
14 Remember what I have adjured you, (evil-)gazed
15 spirit. In the name of the angels ...

Commentary

The copper plate measures 3.18 × 3.18 cm.

We should like to thank Dr. Roy Kotansky for having brought this amulet to our attention. He brought us a photograph with an excellent hand-drawing of the inscription which he had done, as well as his tentative reading, and generously agreed that the first edition of the inscription should be published in this volume. The edition offered here thus owes a great deal to the collaboration of Dr. Kotansky.

The inscription starts off in Hebrew, but from line 9 on the language is Aramaic.

1 אוערות is unattested. It may be a corruption, either through metathesis or scribal error, of *אורעות, and this may possibly be a by-form of מאורעות, from the verb ארע. Cf. Syriac ארועותא "meeting, encounter, disputation, controversy", אורעא "meeting, encounter, attack". Hebrew has מאורע with a similar sense. Cases of metathesis in magic texts are not rare; cf. Epstein 1921, p. 48 on Montgomery No. 16:11. A similar case occurs in line 4, המתגרשים. On the other hand, the Aramaic Targum to Ps. 34:20 has in a manuscript quoted by Levy 1867/8, I, p. 52, סגיאין אערען לצדיקא, which corresponds to רבות רעות צדיק. In the printed editions this phrase is rendered סגיאין בישן מערען לצדיקא; the printed version may look suspiciously like a modification of the manuscript translation. If אערען is a genuine Aramaic form, a putative Hebrew plural corresponding to it might be *אערעות.

The word אוערות is followed by another plural noun ending in the next line with [ ]/רעות, which could plausibly be reconstructed as the well-known Hebrew [מאו]/רעות. This sequence makes it less likely that אוערות could be just a corruption of *אורעות, followed by the correct spelling. If that were the case, the following word would not start with a *waw*.

1-2 The reconstruction expected here is [או]רעות or [מאו]רעות.

2 עם זכר עם נקבה: We have here the preposition that goes with the noun meaning "(bad) encounters". The usual style for expressing "either ... or" is בן ... בן (e.g. A 24:12).

4 המתגרשים: This seems to be a misspelling for המתרגשים, which is the verb normally employed in the idiom מתרגשים / מתרגשות לבוא for troubles that come upon someone. For the metathesis, see above note to אוערות. התגרש itself has, among its other senses, also the meaning: "to be stirred up".

4-5 חביבי ברה דחרתה: The name of the client and that of his mother are common in Palmyrene; see Stark 1971, pp. 20, 23, 87, 90. In line 12 the spelling of the mother's name is חירתה, which is apparently the feminine equivalent of Palmyrene חירא "good, excellent" (Arabic *ḫair*); see Stark 1971, p. 88.

5 דוקון דוקון: See A 11:2.

10 דפרחא ודשכנה: In Syriac a similar expression is used for the Holy Spirit: בדמות יונא פרחת נחתת ועל רישה שכנת (J. Payne Smith 1903, p. 577; cf. also R. Payne Smith 1879/1901, p. 4152) "like a dove it flew down and settled on His head".

12 That an evil spirit is capable of appearing in various likenesses is a theme that occurs often in the bowl texts; e.g. Montgomery 1913, No. 1:12-13, and above, B 13:11-13.

דמוון is the absolute plural of דמו "likeness".

14 אדכרי is fem. imperative in *itpe*ʿ*el*. In Palestinian Aramaic (Jewish, Christian and Samaritan) DKR does not occur in *pe*ʿ*al* (except for דכיר in passive participle), but *itp.* served in the sense of "remember"; cf. Bar-Asher 1977, pp. 236-237; Sokoloff 1990, pp. 149-150. The phrase אדכר מרא אלהא "Remember the Lord God" occur in a Christian Palestinian Aramaic votive inscription: see Naveh, *apud* Kloner 1990, p. 139.

15 מסקור[י]תה: See A 19:4 מסקור, and G 29, p. 1:10 מסקוריתה

Amulet 27

Irbid
Silver
For the protection of Marian daughter of Sarah and her foetus
New York Public Library
Plate 13; Figure 12

1 ובחטרה דמשה ובציצה דאהרן
2 כהנה רבה ובעזקתה דשלמה ו[ ]
3 [ ] דדויד ובקרנתה דמדבחא ובשמ[ה]
4 [ד]אלהא חיה וקימה דיתגערון [רוחא]
5 [ב]ישתה וס(ע)יא בישה וכל מ[זיק]
6 ביש מן גופה דמרין ברתה ד[שרה]
7 ועולה דבמעיה מן יומ[ה דין]
8 ועד לעלם אמן אמן סלה [ ]
9 [ ]ענמון פיאנה[ ]א
(*magic characters*)
10 [ב]אל נתנאל ביה אברהם אגו
11 [ ] היושב על ל[ ]
12 געור מן מרין ומן עולה כל רוח
13 [ ]רתה וסתמ[ה]
14 ית מבלעיה אשבעת יתיך
15 רוחא דיתגערין מן מרין ומן
16 עולה בשם הגוער בים ויה
17 מו גליו ייי צבאות שמו [ה]ו
18 יגעור מן מרין ברתה דשרה
19 ומן עולה רוחא בישתה הדה
20 בשמה דאלהא רבה
21 מן אלפי אל כדאיא [נ]
22 ט[ר]ו למרין ברתה דשרה
23 ולעולה דלגו מעיה בשם
24 [ ]
25 מדות מלאכיה דממנ
26 ין על מ[ ]
27 יה פרוקו למרין ברת<ה>

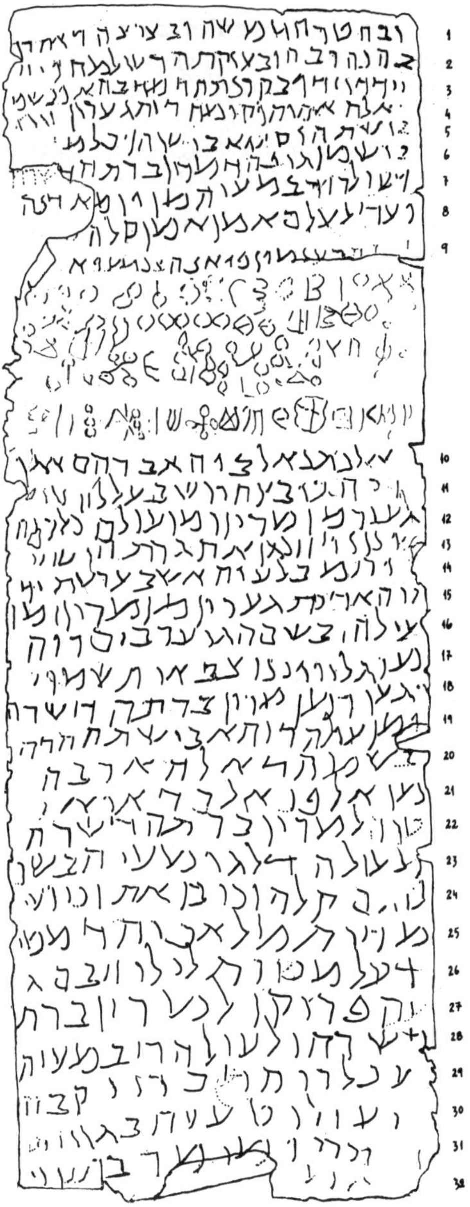

Fig. 12. Amulet 27

דשרה ולעולה דבמעיה 28
מכל רוח דכר ונקבה 29
[ ] 30
[ ] 31
[ ] 32

Translation

1 And by the rod of Moses and by the front-plate of Aaron
2 the High Priest and by the signet-ring of Solomon and [ ]
3 [ ] of David and by the horns of the altar and by the nam[e]
4 [of] the living and existent God: that you should be expelled, (you,) [the evil]
5 [s]pirit and the evil assailant and every evil
6 des[troyer] from the body of Marian daughter of [Sarah]
7 and her foetus that is in her belly from th[is day]
8 to eternity, Amen, Amen, Selah [ ]
9 [ ]ʿ**nmwn py**ʾ**nh**[ ]ʾ
(*magic characters*)
10 Baʾel Netanʾel Beyah Abraham ʾ**gw**
11 [ ] who resides over [ ]
12 expel from Marian and from her foetus all spirit
13 [ ] ... and blocks
14 her gullet. I adjure you,
15 spirit, that you should be expelled from Marian and from
16 her foetus that is in her belly. By the name of He who rebukes the sea "and its
17 waves roared YYYY Sabaoth is His name" (Is. 51:15; Jer. 31:35), may He
18 rebuke (= expel) from Marian daughter of Sarah
19 and from her foetus this evil spirit.
20 By the name of the Great God
21 **mn** ʾ**lpy** ʾ**l kd**ʾ**y**ʾ
22 [g]uard Marian daughter of Sarah
23 and her foetus that is inside her belly. By the name of
24 [ ]
25 Middot, the angels that are appoin-
26 ted over the ...
27 ... redeem Marian daughter

28 of Sarah and her foetus that is in her belly
29 from all male and female spirit
30-32 [...]

Commentary

This amulet was first published by Montgomery 1911 as Amulet A. It measures 9.5 × 3.5 cm. A first attempt at presenting a partial improved reading of the amulet was made in *AMB*, p. 22 n. 23, where the first four lines were given. Better photocopies of this group of amulets were supplied us by Dr. Roy Kotansky, as a result of which a fresh attempt was made to read the whole text.

1 The front-plate of Aaron figures also in A 17 above.

2 The signet-ring of Solomon is invoked in a magic bowl, Montgomery 1913, No. 34:8.

4 דיתגערון: 2nd person plural imperfect *ithpeʿel, di + tiggaʿarūn*. The translation is based on the structure of the sentence in line 15, where the 2nd person address in דיתגערין is unequivocal. The form דיתגערון by itself could also be 2nd person plural of *peʿal*, in an active sense, or 3rd person plural *ithpeʿel*, in a passive sense.

5 If the reading וסעיא is correct, this would be a participle of the verb סעא, attested so far only in Syriac (although the Hebrew verb, known from Ps. 55:9 מרוח סעה מסער, may have played a role here too). An alternative reading could be וסניא "enemy".

14 מבלעיה: Cf. מבלעתא "the uppermost part of the gullet" (Jastrow, p. 725). For the spirit that apparently blocks the gullet cf. A 1:21-22, where a spirit that moves in the veins and bones of a person is mentioned.

15 דיתגערין: This is apparently an *ithpeʿel* imperfect, giving a passive sense.

16-17 בשם הגוער בים ויהמו גליו יייי צבאות שמו: We have here a conflation of two biblical verses: (1) Na. 1:4 גוער בים ויבשהו; (2) Is. 51:15 (also Jer. 31:35) רגע הים ויהמו גליו יהוה צבאות שמו. This was made possible by the confusion between גער and רגע, two different verbs sharing the same consonants. The verb גער had changed its sense by the time of this amulet from the original biblical meaning "to rebuke" into the technical magical usage of "to exorcise, expel".

25 מדות: Cf. G 27:13, where מידות figures, possibly as an angel.

Amulet 28

Irbid
Silver
For the protection of Marian daughter of Sarah and her foetus
New York Public Library
Plate 14; Figure 13

1 [ ]
2 (צ)יה ומאסיה ומן[ ] גופה דמ[רין]
3 [ב]רתה דשרה ודעולה דבמעיה
4 [ ] פגעין וסטני[ן]
5 [ ] אמפנוס
6 [ר]שו לא במרין ולא
7 [ב]עולה קדוש קדוש קדוש קדוש
8-9 (*illegible*)
10 אל אלוהי הו יחיה לכל בשר
11 מלך מלכי המלכים [ ]
12-14 (*illegible*)
15 [ ] ייי צבאו(ת)
16 שמו קדוש נורא קורא קרוב יה
17 יחוש אחוש הסונה הסונה יה יה
18 חזק אחוש יחוש שווי שוי שוי
19 אהיה אשר אהיה אלוהים אלהים
20 אלוהים יה יה יה יה יה יה יה
21 יה יה יה את בש גר דק הצ ופ זע חס
22 טנ ים כל יה הויה שדי גיבור דיאס
23 [ ] ירושלים אל אות דיתב על כ[ר]
24 סיה ביפני תרי כרוביה א ייי אות ת
25 אנתאל כנפיאל יה יה כנאו שם האל

Amulet 28

Fig. 13. Amulet 28

26 הקדוש הנגלה למשה מתוך הסנה
27 יהוה יהו שמו מבורך אהיה אשר
28 אהיה יהוה צבאות יהוה אלהים יהו[ה]
29 [אח]ד [ ] השם אאאאאא
31-30 (*illegible*)
32 ה ברוך הוא עושה שחר ועי[פה]
33 דורך על במותי ארץ יייי צבאו[ת]
34 שמו בשם פנואל ותהריאל אסר[ה]
35 אסרנה ליך [ ]
37-36 (*illegible*)
38 לה למרין ברתה דשרה ולא לעולה דבמ
39 עיה [ ]
40 [ ]

Translation

1 [ ]
2 ... and to heal and to ... the body of Ma[rian]
3 daughter of Sarah and of her foetus that is in her belly
4 [ ] afflictions and enemies
5 [ ] **ʾmpnws**
6 [that they may have po]wer neither over Marian nor
7 [over] her foetus. Holy, holy, holy, holy
8-9 [ ]
10 El, my God, He shall keep every living being alive
11 King of the kings of kings [ ]
12-14 [ ]
15 [ ] YYYY Sabaoth
16 is His name. Holy, awesome, calling, near, Yah
17 **yḥwš ʾḥwš hswnh hswnh yh yh yh**
18 **ḥzq ʾḥwš yḥwš šwwy šwy šwy**
19 I-am-who-I-am Elohim Elohim
20 Elohim Yah Yah Yah Yah Yah Yah Yah Yah Yah Yah
21 Yah Yah Yah **ʾt bš gr dq hṣ wp zʿ ḥs**
22 **ṭn ym kl**. Yah, **hwyh** Šaddai Mighty **dyʾs**
23 [ ] Jerusalem El Oth, who sits on His throne
24 in front of His two cherubim **ʾ** YYYY Oth **t**
25 Antʾel Kanfiel Yah Yah Yah gave as name of the Holy
26 God who was revealed to Moses from the burning bush

27 YHWH YHW is His blessed name I-am-who-
28 I-am YHWH Sabaoth YHWH Elohim YHWH
29 [is o]ne. [ ] the name ’’’’’
30-31 [ ]
32 ... Blessed is He, "who makes the morning and dark[ness]
33 (who) treads upon the high places of the earth, YYYY Sabaoth
34 is His name" (Am. 4:13). In the name of Penuʾel and Tahriʾel...
35 I bind you [ ]
36-37 [ ]
38 neither Marian daughter of Sarah nor her foetus that is in her
39 belly [ ]
40 [ ]

Commentary

This amulet was first published in Montgomery 1911, as Amulet B. It measures 8.2 × 3.5 cm. Much of it is still illegible in the photographs available. The amulet was written for the same client as A 27, and by the same hand. It shares a number of further features with it: it also makes somewhat inaccurate use of biblical verses, and, despite the fact that it is written in Aramaic, it contains a number of hebraisms. Both have several words that begin in one line and end in the other. One may further note that they are both made of silver and have the same breadth, i.e. 3.5 cm, which may indicate that they were cut from the same silver sheet.

17-18 יחוש אחוש: This is a "name" developed from an appeal to a speedy and immediate execution of the charm (see our A 3:2; 12:25, and *AMB* p. 52). שוי also means "quickly", cf. *AMB*, p. 72.

21-22 את בש ... ים כל: We have here the whole "At Bash" sequence, the alphabetical code based on pairing the first and last letters of the alphabet, advancing towards the middle of the alphabetical order.

26 הנגלה למשה מתוך הסנה: Cf. Isbell 1975, No. 53:17, for a corresponding phrase in Aramaic; also the Ashmolean amulet, see Kotansky et al. 1992, p. 9 line 18.

Amulet 29

Irbid

Bronze

For the protection of Georgius son of Megautes from the evil eye

New York Public Library

Plate 15; Figure 14

1 [ ] צצצצצצצ [

2 [ ] [פפפפפפפ ססססססס ללללללל ייייייי חחחחחחח /פפפפ[פפפ]

3 [טרו]ן גופה דגיורגיס ברה דמגאותיס מן כל ביש ומן עין [ב׳](ש)[ה]

4 [ומ]ן עין דאימם ומן עין דנשין ומן עין דגברין ומן עין דבתול(אתא) /[ומן] עין [ ]

5 [יהוה] צבאות עימנו מיסגב לנו אלוהי יעקוב סלה אמן אמן סלה אמן/אמן [ ]

6 [ ]אפאות אמיה שאל תרדו סלי(ח)ות שמא(ות) יה יהו טור (גיאו)/רגיס [מן]

7 [ ]ומחוש וצער ורוח ושיד אמן אמן סלה אמן אפס אמיד יהוה /

8 [ ]י אל ותרדו סליחות שמרות יה יהו ט(ור גיאו)/(ר)ג[יס]

9 אמן אמן סלה אמן

Translation

1 [ ] ṣṣṣṣṣṣṣ

2 [ ] **ppppppp sssssss lllllll yyyyyyy ḥḥḥḥḥḥḥ pppppp**

3 [guar]d the body of Georgius son of Megautes from all evil and from [e]v[il] eye

4 [and fr]om the eye of the *mother and from the eye of women and from the eye of men and from the eye of virgins [and from] the eye of [ ].

5 "[The Lord] Sabaoth is with us, the God of Jacob is our fortress Selah" (Ps. 46:8, 12). Amen Amen Selah Amen Amen.

6 [ ]**ʾpʾwt ʾmyh šʾl trdw slyḥwt šmʾwt yh yhw** guard Georgius [from]

7 [ ] and pain and suffering and spirit and demon. Amen Amen Selah Amen **ʾps ʾmyd** YHWH

8 [ ]**y ʾl wtrdw slyḥwt šmrwt** Yah YHW guard Georgius

9 Amen Amen Selah Amen.

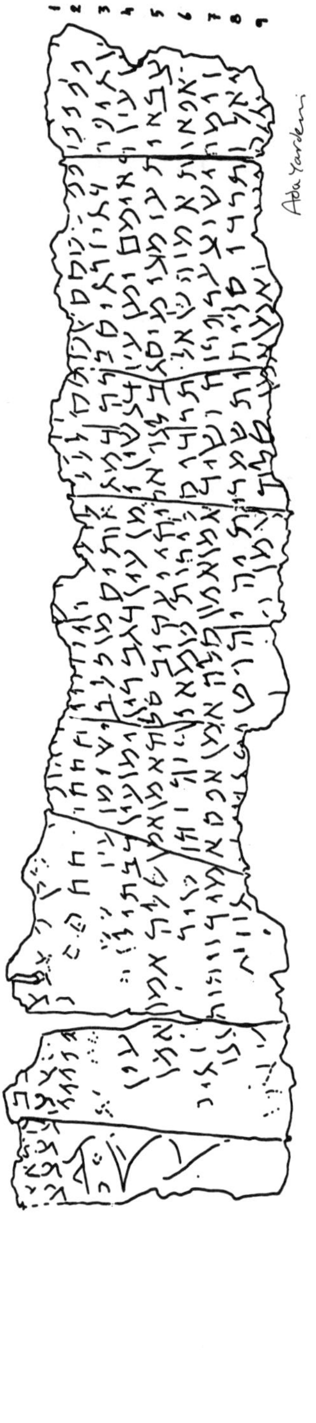

Fig. 14. Amulet 29

Commentary

This amulet was first published by Montgomery 1911, as Amulet C. Its size has not been communicated to us. The left-hand section of the amulet was apparently detached at some point, and was incorrectly joined in the photographs available to us. It has to be reversed in order to give a correct reading, as was apparently done in the photograph printed in Montgomery 1911 (which is too faint for any safe reading). Ada Yardeni's drawing gives a reconstruction of the correct position of this section. In this edition, a slash (/) indicates the limit between the main part of the amulet and the detached section.

4 דאימם: This is probably an error for דאימה. For the sequence עינא דאימא ... עינא דגברין ... עינא דנשין cf. the Warsaw amulet of 1867 reproduced in *AMB*, p. 133.

Amulet 30

Irbid (?)

Bronze

For Surah daughter of Sarah, against premature delivery

The Metropolitan Museum of Art, New York

Plate 16; Figure 15

1 [ע]ולה דסורה ברת סרה בשמה ד[...]אל ו[ ]

2 [ ]... עולה דסורה ברת סרה דלא יפוק אלא בע(דנה) [ ]

3 [ ]יתבר מני בריאל אנהואול יתבר מני סוס(גר) ארבעתי מלאכיה קדי[שיה]

4 [ע]ולה דסורה ברת סרה במעיה שומר פתהים יייי אנה את(ג)ל[ית]

5 [ ]ם אנה אתגלית ומללת עם מן דיהב במעי עולה דלותי לא [תילד]

6 [ס]ורה ברת סרה עד ימטי זמנה (*magic characters*)

7 [קרי]נה לכון מלאכיה קדישה ושמהתה טביא ותלא למל[ ]

8 [ ] הדין קמיעה אחות באדות פנותה

9 [ו]לדה דסורה ברת סרה ולדהין דכל בנת חוה דלשדלב(ס)[ ]

10 [ ] מני נפק שמשיאל מני נפק (מ)וריאל מני נפק גבריאל אנקיאל [ ]

11 [מני נ]פק פרחאל ענאל מני מני נפק אזיה ואזיזיה ובדיה ובדי[ ]

12 [ ]אל ובדרך ונדבך זוזעיה [ ]

To the left of the magic characters in line 6:

6a בט[ ] 6b ד(ס)[ורה] 6c ברת סר[ה]

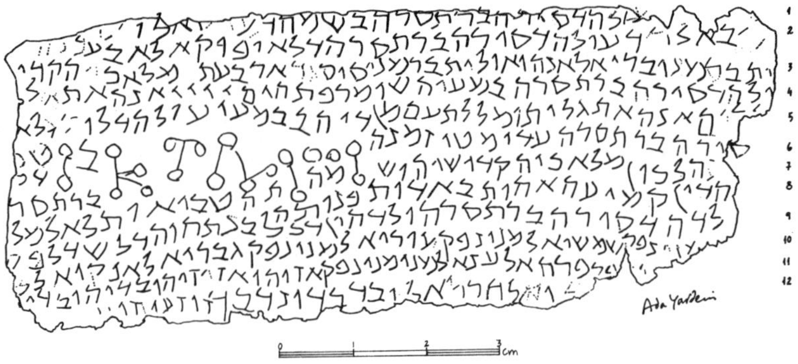

Fig. 15. Amulet 30

Translation

1 … the foetus of Surah daughter of Sarah. In the name of …

2 … the foetus of Surah daughter of Sarah, that it should not emerge except in its proper time.

3 … the four ho[ly] angels

4 the foetus of Surah daughter of Sarah in her belly. "The Lord preserves the simple" (Ps. 116:6). I have been revealed

5 … I have been revealed and have spoken with him who placed the foetus in my belly. "I was brought low" (Ps. 116:6). [She should] not [give birth,]

6 Surah daughter of Sarah, until her time comes. (*magic characters*)

7 I invoke you, holy angels and good names, and suspend …

8 … this amulet **ʾ̣hwt bʾdwt pnwth**

9 the (newborn) child of Surah daughter of Sarah, the (newborn) children of all the daughters of Eve **dlšdlbs**

10 … emerges from me, Shamshiel emerges from me, Moriel emerges from me, Gabriel (and) Anqiel emerge from me …

11 … Paraḥel (and) ʿAnael emerge from me, Azia and Azizia and Badia and … emerge from me

12 [ ]ʾl and **ddrk** and **ndbk** and **zyzʿyh** [ ]

6a **b…** /

6b of Surah /

6c daughter of Sarah.

Commentary

This bronze amulet was acquired by the Metropolitan Museum of Art in 1918. It measures 12.1 cm in breadth and 4.2 cm in height and was originally rolled to fit into a small bronze cylindrical case, 6.6 cm long. In 1919, Prof. C.C. Torrey of Yale University sent the Museum a translation of the text of the amulet. This translation has been communicated by Dr. Dietrich von Bothmer, Chairman of the Department of Greek and Roman Art at the Metropolitan Museum of Art, where the amulet is kept, in a letter to Dr. Roy Kotansky. We are reproducing it in the following:

1 (This charm) is written by Sura, daughter of Sara. In the name of Immanuel ...
2 for the protection (?) of the unborn child of Sura, daughter of Sara ...
3 There is beside me no Creator, no Immortal; beside me no Rick... and the 4 holy angels ...
4 (The child) of Sura, daughter of Sara, in her bowels. Name of the Lord of the Abyss ... Thou didst reveal thyself ...
5 ... Thou didst reveal thyself, and didst speak with the righteous ...
6 ... Sura, daughter of Sara, until her time shall come.
7 ... sing praises the Holy Angels, and the Good Names ...
8 This amulet ...
9 ... child (?) of Sura, daughter of Sara, and the children of all her children ...
10 By the number of the Angel Shamshiel, number of the Angel Muriel, number of the Angel Gabriel, Uriel,
11 Barkiel, Aniel, number of the Angel Azyahu, (A)zizyahu...
12 ... (Imma)nuel (?) ...

A short notice about this amulet was published by G.M.A. R[ichter] in the *Bulletin of the Metropolitan Museum of Art* 14 (1919), p. 94, where phrases from this translation are quoted. On p. 95 of the same issue of the *Bulletin* a photograph of the amulet is given.

We owe our knowledge of this amulet to Dr. Roy Kotansky, who handed over to us his drawing of the inscription and a transcription, as well as his correspondence with Dr. von Bothmer. All this has been a great help in our effort at establishing the reading, although several problems still remain. The main problem besetting the interpretation of the text is the fact that an undetermined portion of the amulet was lost on both right and left sides. The remaining text is in many cases too fragmentary for continuous translation. Another problem is created by the obscure language of the text, which recalls, in its use of many seemingly meaningless words, the text of A 4.

3 The first part of the line is obscure. The division of words is unclear, and more than one interpretation of them is possible. One division of words is offered in the present edition, but this is by no means preferable to several other possibilities. Instead of יתבר מני, one could think of reading [ל]יתבר מני, which occurs twice (the second time with *lamed* which may be attached to the verb); but this could also be read לית בר מני or just בר מני, and what precedes it could be regarded as a proper name of an angel. Instead of סוסגר the reading סוסיך seems also possible.

The division of words adopted in the text assumes that the invocation of the angels, repeated twice, is for something to be "broken away from" the client. It is perhaps somewhat less likely that the root TBR is here used in the sense (so far unattested) of "to give birth" or possibly "to be born"; this sense is only extant in Aramaic under the (Hebrew?) form שבר, perhaps with the specialized sense "to give birth with difficulty". This verb is attested on an ossuary from Giv'at ha-Mivtar in North Jerusalem (cf. Naveh 1970, p. 37). The noun מתברא, which corresponds to the Hebrew משבר, may indicate that the proper form of the Aramaic verb might have been TBR (see on these problems Naveh, op. cit.). If this second interpretation is considered as being at all possible, the phrase מני נפק, repeated five times in lines 10-11, may have a similar meaning, i.e. "may it (= the foetus) emerge from me".

The main consideration in the interpretation of this line may be its possible correspondence to lines 10-11, where we have a sequence of angel names with the recurring formula מני נפק "from me there goes out (or emerges)". This formula would be nicely paralleled by בר מני "out of me", i.e. "away from me", as in the common Aramaic expression (used also in Hebrew) בר מינן "(may this be) far removed from us", an expression which is used to avert an evil notion alluded to in conversation, and more particularly death. Similarly מני נפק, although not so far attested in this sense, may conceivably mean "may it go away from me", serving a similar function. If this interpretation is followed, we would have in line 3 an expression that may be reconstructed as follows: [ ]ית בר מני בריאל

[שיה]קדי אנה ואולית בר מני סוס(גר) ארבעתי מלאכיה קדי[שיה] "**[ ]yt**, away from me, Bariel, Ana and Ulit, away from me, Susgar, the four holy angels". The names of the "holy angels" occur, one may surmise, as forms of address to benevolent and helping angels. One only invokes them for help in getting rid of some menacing evil being that is responsible for the client's dangerous condition. Lines 10-11 similarly call for some evil to go away, and intersperse these calls with the names of holy angels.

4 **שומר פתהים ייי**: The whole verse **שומר פתאים יהוה דלותי ולי יהושיע** occurs in the Geniza magic book T-S K1.143 (G 18), p. 17:3-8; 18:11-19:3, in a recipe against abortion. The weakening of the gutturals caused **פתחים** ("openings, apertures") to be pronounced **פתהים**, which made it identical in sound to **פתאים**. The identity of pronunciation made it possible to use this verse in a spell for preserving the embryo.

5 It is hard to understand who is speaking in the first person and saying "I have manifested myself", for this is followed by "he who placed the foetus in *my* belly", where it is clear that the mother is speaking.

10 **נפק** can be either perfect or active participle. Somewhat less likely is the possibility that it is an imperative (which is normally **פוק**).

Amulet 31

Provenance unknown
Silver
Healing for Cassianus son of Domitia
Leonard A. Wolfe Collection, Jerusalem
Plate 17; Figure 16

1 [ ]רכן דיונתן תרמ(ון) (ס)רמ(ון) ר ס ס
2 כדרקר פניאל בשם פאלרצות מלאכה דית[ ]
3 נפשתה דחברון מעיני קבורתה דאברהם ר[פאל]
4 רב אסותה אסי ית קאסיאנוס בר דמטיא (*magic characters*)
5 בשם מיכאל רפאל גבריאל עזריאל שמשיאל
6 פלאות מלאכה בשם המלך יהוה אוגירת מר[ ]
7 לאלא זיבה נטר ית קסהיאנוס ובשם זיבה וב[שם]
8 אברן בוניון ארספה הב חיין לקאסיא[נוס]

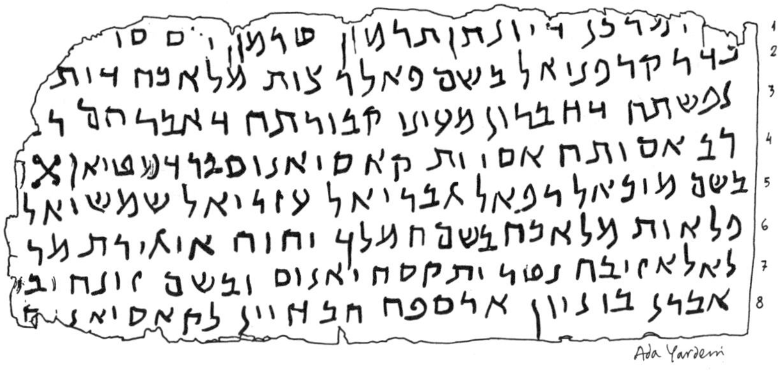

Fig. 16. Amulet 31

Translation

1 [ ]**rkn** of Jonathan **trmwn srmwn r s s**[ ]
2 **kdrqr** Peniʾel. In the name of **pʾlrṣwt** the angel who s[its over (?)]
3 tombs of Hebron from the eyes of (?) the burial of Abraham. R[aphael,]
4 the Prince of Healings, heal Cassianus son of Domitia. (*magic characters*)
5 In the name of Michael, Raphael, Gabriel, Azriel, Shamshiel,
6 Pelaʾot the angel. In the name of the King YHWH, Ogirat Mar[ ]
7 **lʾlʾ zybh**. Protect Cassianus. And in the name of **zybh**, and in [the name of]
8 **ʾbrn bwnywn ʾrsph**, give life to Cassia[nus.]

Commentary

The amulet measures 3.4 × 7.9 cm. We thank Mr. Michael Ehrenthal of Moriah Artcraft Inc. for obliging us by sending photographs of the object.

2 כדרקר: Hardly כד רקד “when he danced”.

3 נפשתה דחברון has its counterpart in the Aramaic targum to the ʿAmida, published by Gaster 1928, III, p. 51, where ומקים שבועתו עם ישני עפר is rendered: ומקים הימנותא ושבועתא דקים עם דמיכי חברון דהוו מאיכין בעיני גרמיהון כעפרא.

The expression מעיני is not otherwise attested, to our knowledge. It may be similar in usage to בעיני, לעיני “within sight of, in the presence of". In Hebrew מעין is normally used in the sense of "similar to", which would hardly fit in here. Reference may be made in this connection to the expression מעין הברכות, which occurs in the prayer מגן אברהם (known also as "מעין שבע"). Baer 1868, p. 191, explains the expression as meaning "like, similar, to the blessings", referring to Bavli Berakhot 40a: כל יום ויום תן לו מעין ברכותיו.

4 רב אסותא: Cf. the expression מרי אסואתא, Montgomery 1913, No. 8:1; מרי אסואתה, Montgomery 1913, No. 27:1, where the plural is evident.

דמטיא: For this feminine name cf. Frey 1936, No. 212, where the name is spelled Domitia. In No. 106 the feminine name in Greek characters Δομιτια is reconstructed by the editor.

6 אוגירת מרן [: Cf. A 8:5-7, where we find a sequence of words which bears a striking resemblance to the text here. In the light of our present text read in A 8 as follows: בשם / אגירת מרתי פ / ללא זיבה. Worthy of note is also the text in A 4:24f., ובשם אוגרית מר / מרמאות.

7 Note the spelling of the name with *he* to mark the vowel.

Amulet 32

Provenance unknown
Christian Palestinian Aramaic
Bronze
Healing for Makaria and Timop...
Geoffrey Cope Collection, Herzliah
Plate 18; Figure 17

1 + פלקטון למקריא ו(ל)טמופ[ ]
2 קותא כתוב יפוק צערא ד[ ]
3 בט̈ופא ור̈קותא סבר [ ]
4 (*magic letters*) דיפוג [ ]
5-6 (*magic letters*)
7 (*magic characters*)

Translation

1 A phylactery for Makaria and for Timop[ ]
2 ... write: May the torment of ... go out [ ]

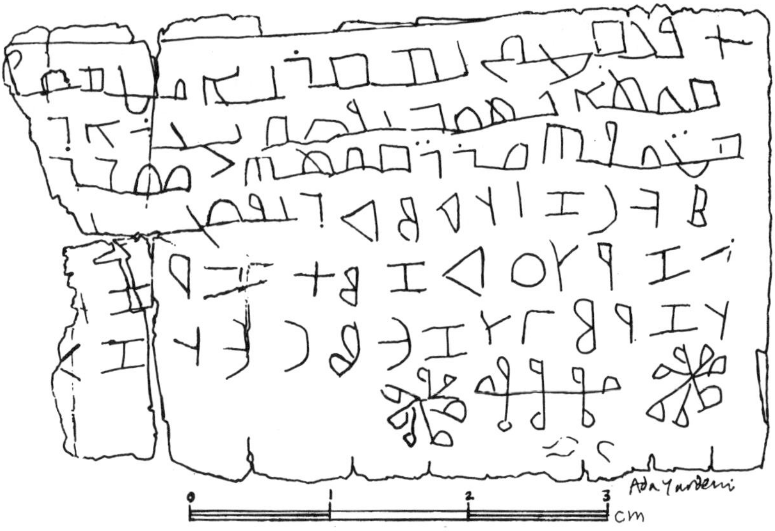

Fig. 17. Amulet 32

3 in the sailings (?) and the ... [ ]
4 (*magic letters*) that should cool [ ]
5-7 (*magic letters and characters*)

Commentary

This is the first amulet on metal so far published in Christian Palestinian Aramaic. Its Christian affiliation is indicated not only by the language and script, but also by the presence of a cross at the beginning of the inscription. In language, style, and the difficulty of interpretation, this amulet is reminiscent of the magical book published by Baillet 1963, also composed in Christian Palestinian Aramaic. Here, as there, a large portion of the vocabulary seems unintelligible. In this case the trouble may partly be attributed to the fact that we have very little text to help us in filling in the meaning of the inscription, especially when we have words that are potentially capable of bearing more than one sense.

1 פלקטון probably represents Greek φυλακτήριον "amulet".
מקריא seems to be the Greek name Μακάρια. The *—a* ending should

not, however, be taken necessarily to indicate a feminine name. It can be the Aramaic form of the masculine Μακάριος. For this one may compare, e.g., the names occurring in synagogue inscriptions of the same period: יוסטה, i.e. Iustus (Naveh 1978, No. 58); לולינא, i.e. Iulianus (Naveh 1978, No. 13); סיסיפה, i.e. Sisyphos (Naveh 1978, No. 33). This is a well-known phenomenon for Greek and Latin names in Palmyra, see Stark 1971, pp. 131f.

טמופ[ ]: This seems to be the beginning of another Greek name.

2-3 Most of the words occur elsewhere in Aramaic, but some are capable of more than one interpretation, and no combination of word-meanings makes a coherent translation possible.

קותא does not exist in the dictionaries. It could conceivably be a noun derived from the root קוא "to stay, remain" (although this is not the expected form).

כתוב: If the interpretation adopted here is correct, the scribe of this amulet apparently copied from a manual of magic, in which there was a heading: "An amulet for ..." (where he supplied the names of his clients); this may have been followed by an instruction which said: "Write [the following text on the amulet]:".

3 בטֿופא, marked here with a *siyāmē* for the plural, is defined in the dictionary as meaning "sailing, voyage".

ורקותֿא, marked similarly, could be derived from the root רק(ק) "to spit, vomit" and be a by-form of רקקותא; or it could be a by-form of רקיקותא "thinness, shallowness" or even, by a different reading of the two *resh*s, דקיקותא, דקדקותא "smallness, fineness".

4-7 These lines contain a series of magic signs; those in lines 4-6 resemble letters of the Greek alphabet, while those in line 7 belong to no known alphabet, and are characterized by small circles at the end of the lines (the type known as "Brillenbuchstaben"). To distinguish between magic signs derived from a recognized alphabet and signs that seem to be arbitrary inventions of the magical practitioners we propose to use the term "magic letters" for the former, and "magic characters" for the latter. Magic letters imitating forms of the Greek alphabet occur in A 14, 18, 20 and 21.

II. Incantation Bowls from Mesopotamia

Bowl 14

Protection for the house of Dabara son of Shelam with seven seals
Fiorella Cottier-Angeli Collection, Geneva
Plate 19

(1) אסורי אסירין וחתומי חתימין וקטורי קיטרין ולחושי לח[ישי]ן בשום ת[א]סרון
ותיחתמון (2) ותירחקון מן ביתיה ודירתיה ((ד---)) דדבארה בר שלם ודאמא [בת ---]
ומן שרשיי בת אמא ומן (3) איכומא בר אמא ומן ביתיהון כוליה ומן כולה דירתהון
כל ליליתא בישתא וכל שידי ודיוי <ו>אסרי ופתכרי [ונידרי] (4) ולוטתא וקריתא
ושיקופתא ואשלמתא וחרשין בישין ועובדין תקיפין וכל מידיעם סניא אסיריתון
בשבעה אסרין וחתימיתון בשב[עה (5) חתמין] בשמיה דאל דביר אביטני מרי (ביזא)
וקלל אמן אמן סלה חתים בשבעה חתמין ומחתם בתלתא שורין רב(רבין) ק(ד)מאה
דברי ותינינא (6) ד(גוי) וחמישְאה דזבדין בראזי ואשתיתאה חתימין שביעא(ה)
דא(פור)מין בחמא בעזקתא (דס)יהרא ובצורתא (7) דארעה ובראזה רבה דרקיעה אמן
אמן סלה

Translation

(1) Thoroughly bound, sealed, tied and charmed (may you be) by the Name. May you be bound and sealed (2) and removed from the house and residence of Dabara son of Shelam and of Ima [daughter of ---] and of Sharshay daughter of Ima and of (3) Ikuma son of Ima and of all their house and all their residence, all (you) evil liliths and all demons, dēws, bindings, idols, [oaths,] (4) curses, misfortunes, mishaps, spells, evil sorceries, mighty deeds and all hateful things. May you be bound by seven knots and may you be sealed by se[ven (5) seals]. In the name of El Devir Abitani the lord of **byz**ʾ and **qll**. Amen Amen Selah. Sealed by seven seals and firmly sealed by three large walls, the first (of which) is of the outside, the second (of which) is (6) of the inside, the fifth is of those who are equipped (?) with the secrets, the sixth (of those who) are sealed, the seventh of Afurmin (?). By the heat (?), by the ring of the moon, by the form (7) of the earth, by the great mystery of the firmament. Amen, Amen, Selah.

Commentary

The text of the first part of this bowl corresponds very closely to that of Montgomery 1913, No. 5.

1 For the readings אסורי, חתומי, etc. cf. Epstein 1921, p. 33. Epstein assumed that קיטרין in Montgomery 1913, No. 5 was a scribal error for קטירין, but our bowl has the same spelling.

בשום: If there is no ellipsis here of a divine name, the phrase alludes to "Name" in an absolute usage, referring to God. The same construction occurs also in Montgomery 1913, No. 5.

2 דבארה: The reading and the structure of this proper name are not certain.

שרשיי: Again the name is not entirely clear, unless it represents Iranian Srōšay, a proper-name formation derived from the divine name Srōš. The spelling with a *shin* however does not favour this interpretation.

3 אסרי "bindings", hence "spells, invocations", occurs frequently; cf. e.g. Geniza 9, p. 7:12; *Havdala de-Rabbi Akiva* 4:13, 6:13-14.

5 אביטני, אל דביר: The same readings seem possible also in Montgomery 1913, No. 5.

חתים בשבעה חתמין ומחתם בתלתא שורין etc.: This section, which has no correspondence in Montgomery 1913, No. 5, is somewhat incomplete. It talks of seven seals and three walls, and then goes on to enumerate the seven seals (?), but skips from the second to the fifth. The list is not easy to make out because the first two items are "of the outside" and "of the inside" respectively, but the rest seem to be described by certain actions, which are not quite clear.

6 דזבדין: From the root ZBD, although the *dalet* looks like *resh*.

בחמה: One may expect here a phrase such as: "by the heat <of the sun >", to correspond to "by the ring of the moon", "by the form of the earth", "by the great mystery of the sky" which follow. Another omission occurred here apparently.

Bowl 15

Removing spirits from Goray son of Burzandukh and his family
Bible Lands Museum, Jerusalem
Plate 20

(1) [ב]שמך אני עושה חתימין (2) וימחתמין גוריי בר בר(ז)אנדוך (3) וגושני בת איפראהורמיז וגוריי בר פרדדוך אינון (4) ויבניהון ויבנתהון ובתיהון וימדירתהון וכל רוחין בישן ושידין ושיבטין (5) ודיוין ופגעין וסטנין ומשמתתא ומבכלתא ועקרתא ותכלתא וחרשי ונידרי (6) ולוטתא ואשלמתא ויפתכרין וחומרין זידנין וטעין וטולנין ולילין וימרובין וכל מזיקין בישין (7) דיזיחון ויפקון מינהון ומן בניהון ומן בנתהון ומן בתיהון ומן מדירתהון ומן שבע איסקופתהון (8) בשודשידא וברז דעיזקתא וביתרי עשר ראזי כ(ס)י̣ וחתימי וי(נ)טירי איליי(ה)ן אתיתא נטתא תקשפרה נדא ציצלי (...) אמן אמן סלה

Translation

(1) By your name I act. May (the following) be sealed (2) and countersealed: Gōray son of Burzāndukh, (3) and Gushnay daughter of Ifra-Hurmiz and Gōray son of Frāda-dukh, they, (4) their sons, their daughters, their houses, their dwellings; and all evil spirits, demons, plagues, (5) devils, afflictions, satans, bans, tormentors, spirits of barrenness, spirits of abortion, sorcerers, vows, (6) curses, magic rites, idols, wicked pebble spirits, errant spirits, shadow spirits, liliths, educators (?), and all evil doers of harm. (7) May they move away and go out of them, of their sons, of their daughters, of their houses, of their dwellings, of their seven thresholds, (8) by the chain, by the mystery of (?) the seal-rings, by the twelve hidden, sealed and guarded mysteries. These are the letters (?): **nṭt' tqšprh nd' ṣyṣly** ... Amen, Amen.

Commentary

1 The expression "sealed and countersealed" usually applies to demons and agents of wickedness. Here it is used with regard to a group of people, who are mentioned in the place usually reserved for the clients who seek the protection of the amulet (for examples of this usage cf. A 18:6, and the not to the place). They are, however, immediately followed by a long list of demons and afflictions. If this is all part of the same phrase, it uses the root חתם in two contradictory senses: (1) to guard, protect; (2) to enclose, imprison.

It is possible, however, to understand the text differently. According to this alternative interpretation of the text, one may regard the forms derived from חתם as applying only to the clients, while the list of demons and afflictions is governed by the verbs which follow: דיזיחון ויפקון מינהון.

3 Gushnay: A well-attested Iranian name; cf. e.g. Montgomery 1913, pp. 276, 277 (s.v. **iazadpnh**); also in compounds, e.g. *Gushnasp, B 10:11. The basic word signifies a male beast.

Ifra-Hurmiz: For this name cf. Goodblatt 1976.

גוריי: A similar name, written Goroy, is in Montgomery 1913, No. 25:1, cf. op. cit., p. 28. Justi 1895, pp. 356f., identifies Guroy in Firdawsi, *Shāhnāma*, as a late development of a presumed form Warōya, which in Arabic was written **brw**ʾ. It seems simpler to assume that the late names we are dealing with in the Sasanian period are derived from the noun designating the wild boar, in Persian Gōr. A name **gwry** is attested in Palmyrene (quoted Zadok 1989, p. 292). A Semitic name with a similar appearance is quoted in Zadok 1989, 278.

Frāda-dukh: This name is presumably the same as Frata-dukh, for which see B 4:6 (*AMB*, p. 156).

4 מדירתהון: This word, which is not attested in Babylonian Aramaic, is evidently derived from the root **DWR**. It must, like the Syriac **mdyr**ʾ, also signify "a dwelling", and should be distinguished from the similar-looking word (spelled **mdwr**ʾ) which signifies a fire, a pyre.

6 טעין: This seems to be the first attestation of such a designation for a class of evil spirits; the meaning is derived from the root **Ṭ**ʿʾ, to err, to wander. In Syriac the root also means specifically to be a heretic.

מרובין: Cf. Bowl 1:9 **mrwby**ʾ, which in other versions of that text corresponds to **mr(w)byn**ʾ; see commentary there. It seems strange that this term occurs here as a designation for a class of evil beings. But cf. *Havdala de-Rabbi Akiva* IV:18 (Scholem 1980/1, p. 260 n. 40), where the term occurs for a class of demons; and the text published by Geller 1980, p. 49, lines 18-19: ומן מריבין ומן שופטי בישי (for מריבין it would be preferable to read מרובין).

7 דיזיחון: Although the spelling seems to be as transcribed, one should have expected perhaps an intransitive form, viz. **dyzwḥwn**. However, a similar spelling, with a seemingly transitive form, occurs in Gordon 1941, p. 125 (No. 6:6; Isbell 1975, No. 43).

8 שורשידא: This clear spelling of the word is an obvious error for **šwršyr**ʾ. Cf. Gordon E and F, compared to Hyvernat's bowl, in Gordon 1934b, p. 331 (= Isbell 50), where the object is called **šwšyr**ʾ. Cf. also Smelik 1978, p. 177, line 1, where it is called **šwšr**ʾ. The writer of our bowl did not understand the word and may have interpreted it as a mixed Hebrew-Aramaic expression **bšwd šyd**ʾ, i.e. "by the robbery of the demon" (?).

ובדז ד- looks like another error committed by the writer of this bowl. On the analogy of other texts, e.g. Gordon 1934b, p. 331, and Smelik 1978, p. 177, quoted above, one should have expected here the enigmatic word **zwzmry**, which seems to denote something akin to a chain or a bond. In the bowl published by Smelik 1978 the word is written apparently **bzwz wmr**ʾ; the writer of that bowl must have thought that these were two separate words. A different kind of error occurs in the bowl published by Hyvernat 1885. The writer, to whom the word was unfamiliar, replaced it by the expression ʾ**bny zymr**ʾ, where the second word, if it is genuine, could be connected to the rarely attested Mandaic word **zimara**, which denotes "bridle" or perhaps "the ring in the nose of the camel" (cf. Drower and Macuch 1963, p. 166), and which may be related to the Arabic and Persian word *zammāra* "a dog's collar". The origin of the word **zwzmry** may be sought perhaps in a corruption of Greek ζωστήρ "belt, girdle" or the like. If, as seems likely, the writer of our bowl had this word in front of him in the original from which he copied, but did not understand it, he may have misread ***zwzmr** as ***rzmr** which he "corrected" to **rz d** — "the secret of", which looks like good Aramaic, although it makes no sense in the context.

אילי(ה)ן: This looks like a badly written, or a dialect form, of the pronoun ʾ**ynhy**, perhaps in contamination with forms like ʾ**yly**, ʾ**ly**, ʾ**ylh** to which is added **hn**. Cf. for the forms Epstein 1960, p. 20; Rossell 1953, p. 29.

Bowl 16

Syriac

Expelling demons from the house of Yoyiʿa son of Rašnendukh

Leonard A. Wolfe Collection, Jerusalem

Plate 21

(1) זה דיוא ולטבא עירא ושיכבא וכול אלהותא בישתא מן (2) הנא ביתא דיויעא
בר רשדינדוך ומן דיארא̈ דבגוה שרי̈ן אסיר בישא (3) ולטבא וחומרתא דיכרא
וניקבתא ולליתא דיכרא וניקבתא דאתת ושרת בהדין (4) ביתא אסיר באסורה דאריא
וחתים בחתמה דתנינא אסיר באסורא דאיבול וחתים בחתמא (5) דאבורית אסיר
באסור זעקא̈ וחתים בחתמא דבגדנא̈ אסיר וחתים במובלא רבא דזעקא̈ דכול
שידא̈ בישא̈ (6) ולטבא̈ וחומרא̈ פתכרא̈ ואיסתרתא̈ ולליתא̈ וכול אניש אניש בשמה
וכול שידא̈ בישא̈ לותה דהנא ביתא (7) דהנא ראזא קביר בגוה לא ניקרבון לה
אסירא הדא רוחא בישתא דשריא ושידא דיוא ולליתא וכול דבהנא ביתא (8)
שרא אסיר וחתים (...) נחתין בגדנא̈ אמין

Translation

(1) Go away, demon and no-good creature, either awake or asleep, and every evil deity, from (2) this house of Yoyi'a son of *Rashnendukh and from the inhabitants who dwell in it. Bound is the evil (demon) (3) and the no-good creature and the pebble-spirit, whether male or female, and the lilith, whether male or female, who came and dwelt in this (4) house. Bound is (he) by the bond of the lion and sealed by the seal of the dragon. Bound is he by the bond of Ibol and sealed by the seal (5) of Iborit. Bound is he by the bond of the blast-demons and sealed by the seal of the Bagdanas. Bound and sealed is he by the great load of the blast-demons so that all the evil (6) demons and no-good creatures and pebble-spirits, idol-spirits and goddesses and liliths, and each individual by his name, and all evil demons who are at this house (7) in which this "mystery" is buried, should not come near it. Bound is this evil spirit who dwells (in this house), and the demon, the dēw, the lilith, and every (spirit) that dewlls in this (8) house. Bound and sealed is ... the Bagdanas descend. Amen.

Commentary

This bowl, written in the pre-Manichaean script, was written for the same client as Bowl 17, Yoyiʿa son of Rashnēn-dukh. Both bowls were formerly in the Aaron Gallery in London, where they were seen and studied by Dr. M. Geller, who prepared hand copies of both of them. Dr. Geller very kindly let us use his notes, including his finely executed hand copies. His reading and interpretation of this bowl have since been published (Geller 1986, pp. 111 f.), and it may be seen that on some points we have a different conception.

1 זה: For an explanation of this form it has been suggested that it is an imperative of זחת (Montgomery 1912, p. 436). A similar form, תיזה, which occurs in Bowl 1:11, was explained by us as deriving from אזה, related to אזל (cf. the Glossary to *AMB*, s.v. אזל). For a discussion of this imperative form cf. also Epstein 1913, p. 279, who refers to Bavli Pesaḥim 112b, where it is said: ניזהה דאריא זה זה "the spell for lions (i.e. to avert damage which may be caused by lions) is **zh zh**". This last quotation seems to support a new derivation for this form, viz. the verb נזה, נזח.

For עירא ושיכבא cf. Bavli Sanhedrin 29b: עירי ושכבי ליהוו עליך סהדי "May both those who are awake and those who sleep be witnesses against you".

2 יויעא is a name not attested so far, although we now have it in two texts belonging to the same person, our bowl and Bowl 17. How the name should be vocalized and explained is not clear. Geller read יויתא, but the reading given here is quite certain.

רשדינדוך is almost certainly an error for רשנינדוך, which is the name of the client's mother in Bowl 17, where it occurs four times. While **ršdyndwk** is not easily explained in terms of an Iranian etymology, Rašnēn-dux is a good Iranian name, derived from the name of the deity Rašn, the god of justice. The name occurs already in a Mandaic bowl of Paris, published by Lidzbarski 1902, p. 100, where, in note 6, there is an explanation of the name by Andreas.

3 חומרתא: As can be seen here too, the singular **ḥwmrtʾ** has as a plural **ḥwmr̈ʾ** (line 6).

4 אסיר באסורא דאריא וחתים בחתמא דתנינא: A similar phrase, אסירין באריא וחתמין בתנינא occurs in Montgomery 1913, No. 19:15. Montgomery made a mistake in his reading of this sequence of words, but the reading was corrected, on the basis of Montgomery's own hand-copy, already by Epstein 1921:50. Isbell 1975, No. 21, unfortunately disregarded Epstein's article, thus perpetuating Montgomery's mistake. Montgomery 1913, No.

19, contains several parallels to our present text. As already remarked by Epstein, the two beasts, lion and dragon, are also mentioned side by side in a Syriac spell in the text edited by Gollancz 1912, p. 5, where the officiant says: אריא רכיבנא וברתנינא "I mount the lion and the young dragon" (translation in Gollancz 1912, p. xxviii).

אסיר באסורא דאיבול etc.: A parallel formula (somewhat curtailed) is in Montgomery 1913, No. 19:16f.

5 אסיר וחתים במובלא רבא דזעקָא: This parallels, and helps emend the reading of, Montgomery 1913, No. 19:17. Instead of וחתימין במכילא רבא דזעוזא one should obviously read (and this is confirmed by the hand-copy provided in Montgomery): וחתימין במבולא רבא דזעקא. Milik 1976, p. 337 has come close to this reading, but his interpretation is denied by our new bowl.

6 איניש is unusual is Syriac, where the common form is אנש (with the *alef* unpronounced). A very common form in Jewish Babylonian Aramaic is איניש, and in Mandaic a commonly used spelling is עניש (cf. Glossary to Yamauchi 1967, s.v.).

7 ראזא "mystery" is of course a reference to the amulet. Cf. below, commentary to B 19:1.

Bowl 17

Syriac

Confounding the evil eye that smote Yoyiʿa son of Rašnendukh

Bible Lands Museum, Jerusalem

Plate 22

(1) תיתור ותיתמחא עינא בישתא דהי מחתה (2) ליויעא בר רשנינדוך על מא כיס ומכיס עלי כסי ליויעא (3) בר רשנינדוך על מא חמרת עלי אמר אקים דרכיבין על מא סכורא כיס (4) סכרן ליויעא בר רשנינדוך השעתא דין חמרת עלי *אמר מית אקימית וזכי ליויעא בר רשנינדוך (5) וכול מנו דנקום לאנפה הכנא נתמחא ונתבטל רוגזה כול דיליד אנתתא הו ולקיבלה קאים (6) נקום ונעור חילה דמשיחא +

Translation

(1) May the evil eye that has smitten Yoyiʿa son of Rashnendukh (2) be confounded and smitten. "Why has my fate struck and beat me, (that is,) Yoyiʿa (3) son of Rashnendukh, why have you become hot (in anger) against me?" He said: "I shall cause those that ride to stand". "Why does he that shuts beat (4) (and) shut us, [viz.] Yoyiʿa son of Rashnendukh? Now then you have become hot (in anger) against me". He said: "I have raised a dead (man) and he caused Yoyiʿa son of Rashnendukh to win. (5) Every one who stands against him shall in this manner be smitten, and the anger of every one who is born of a woman and who stands against him shall be annulled". (6) May the power of Christ rise and become awake. +

Commentary

This bowl was first in the Aaron Gallery, London, where it was studied and copied by Dr. M. Geller (see Commentary to Bowl 16). We have gratefully used his hand-copy of it.

The curious text in Bowl 17 was written for the same client as the one for whom Bowl 16 was prepared, and it makes use of the same type of Syriac script. It is remarkable for the fact that it belongs to the limited number of magic bowls in Syriac which clearly bear a Christian symbol and formula. It is also remarkable for the style which it uses, which seems to be based on a dialogue between the client for whom the bowl was written and a divine agent, probably God, and it seems to contain, in line 4, an allusion to the raising of Jesus from the dead, although this is not quite certain. The style and wording of this bowl are so unusual that our translation and interpretation can only be offered with considerable reserve.

1 תיתור belongs to the verb תור "to confound, surprise".

2 The expression כיס ומכיס is reminiscent of אכיס ומכיס in the Mandaic lead amulet published in Greenfield and Naveh 1985, e.g. B 5; D 3 עכיס ומאכאס; cf. the comments of the authors, op. cit., p. 103. The forms of the words are difficult to interpret. אכיס in Mandaic has been explained as a passive participle *peʿal*, an explanation that is not sufficient for the form we have here, but if its origin is Mandaic, it may have been copied mechanically. מכיס is not explained in the Mandaic context, but seems to be explainable as a participle of the *afʿel*.

כסי is most likely to be a reflection of the Peshitta translation of Heb. *kōs* "fate, lot". Thus, מנת חלקי וכוסי (Ps. 16:5) is rendered into Syriac by מנתא ... דכסי; מנת כוסם (Ps. 11:6) is in the Peshitta מנתא דכסהון.

3 חמרת, which is repeated in line 4, seems to refer to the anger of the divine entity with whom the dialogue is conducted. The verb חמר is not attested in Syriac, to our knowledge, in the sense required here, but only in the sense of "becoming hot" or "ferment".

אקים דרכיבין is quite obscure. For the use of אקים in the sense of "to stop" cf. Gollancz 1898, p. 79 ואקים לסהרא, but it is not certain that we have the same usage here.

4 אמר: The bowl has here אחר, but in view of the fact that *ḥet* and *mem* are only distinguished from one another by a horizontal upper stroke, which the scribe may have forgotten to put in the bowl, and since this is in close parallel to the structure of line 3, the emendation to אמר seems quite convincing.

מית אקימית may be a reference to the rising of Jesus, who, it is here promised, will cause the client to win.

5 כול דיליד אנתתא הו: we should have expected דכול דיליד אנתתא הו.

Bowl 18

Removing the Tormentor from Panahurmiz son of Rašn-dukh and his household

Leonard A. Wolfe Collection, Jerusalem

Plate 23

Around the central figure:

(1) הנה צילמה דמבכלתא דמיתחזיא בחילמי ובדמואתה (2) מיתדמיה דין איסורה מן יומא דין ולעולם אמן אמן סלה גבריאל נוריאל

In the triangles surrounding the central circle:

(3) יהוה יהו יהוה יהו יהוה יהו יהוה יהו יהוה יהו יהוה יהו יהוה יהו יהוה יהו יהוה יהו יהוה יהו יהוה יהו יהוה יהו יה

In spirals around the rim:

(4) הדין חתמא שרירא ונטרתא וחתמתא דישלמא לפנאחורמיז בר [ר]ש[נד]וך ולכוסתי
בת גיות ולבפתוי בת כוסתי ולרשנדוך בת (5) כוסתי ולכל אינשי בתיהון ולקיניניהון
ולמזוניהון ולבתיהון כוליה דתיהוי להון אסותא טבתא מן שמיא בשם אל שדי ובשום
(6) סמך ואסגר אברישך סמך אמן אמן ס(לה) אמ(ן)

Translation

(1) This is the figure of the Tormentor that appears in dreams and takes on (2) (various) forms. This is the bond from today and for ever. Amen Amen Selah. Gabriel, Nuriel. (3) **yhwh, yhw** (13 times). **yhw yh**. (4) This is the firm seal and protection and sealing of Solomon (?), for Panah-Hurmiz son of Rashndukh and for Khwasti daughter of Ga(w)yot, and for Baftoy daughter of Khwasti and for Rashndukh daughter of Khwasti, and for all the people of their houses, for their possessions, for their sustenance and for their whole houses. May there be for them good healing from heaven in the name of El Shadday and in the name of (6) Samakh, Asgar, Abrishakh, Samakh. Amen Amen Selah, Amen.

Commentary

This bowl has as its central drawing a representation of a figure, presumably female (although the sexual parts are not very clear, it seems to possess at least a well-pronounced breast), which should be in the likeness of a *mevakkalta*. There is a string that ties the two hands of the figure to each other, and which deserves the term *issura*. Lines 1-2 serve as a legend to the drawing. The text of the bowl has already been published by Geller 1986, pp. 106 f., and is here published again from photographs kindly put at our disposal by Dr. Geller.

1 הנה could be Hebrew *hinne* "behold, here", but it seems somewhat more likely that we have the Syriac form of the demonstrative pronoun, although in the following we have the forms of the demonstrative pronoun in Jewish Aramaic, **dyn**, **hdyn**.

4 דישלמא could mean, as translated here, "of Solomon" (spelled somewhat unusually with a final *alef*); but it could alternatively mean also "of wholeness, of peace".

Panāh-Hurmiz is an Iranian proper name meaning "Ohrmazd is the defence".

Rašn-dukh is another Iranian name, in which the first element refers to the deity of Justice, Old Iranian Rašnu.

Khwāsti, an Iranian name, presumably from Khwāstīg, means "She who is desirable".

גיות may be a way of writing the Iranian Gao-yaoti "pasture land" (cf. Bartholomae 1904, col. 484), although this is unknown as a personal name.

Baftoy is presumably an Aramaic derivation from Baba, the Iranian designation for "Father", with the feminine form Bavta. The *-oy* ending is again historically derived from Iranian, but it seems to have become a very common ending for Aramaic proper names as well. On this ending see Nöldeke 1888, pp. 388ff.

5 ולמזוניהון: A reference to "sustenance" occurs in Isbell 1975, No. 7 (Gordon 1941, text 11:6) in a similar context.

כוליה for כולהון.

Bowl 19

Healing and protection for Mihroy son of Gušnay and others
Einhorn Collection, Tel Aviv

Plate 24

(1) דין רזא לאסותא למיהרוי בר גושנאי ולפדרדוך בת דדי אינתתיה (2) ולברשבתי ולאימא ולמלבונאי ולגושנאי בני פדרדוך ויתסון ברחמי שמיא ויתחתמון (3) מן כל מזיקין בישין מן שידי ומן שיבטי ומן דיוי ומן פגעי ומן קירין ומן סטנין (4) ומן לילית(א) בישתא דיכרין ונוקבתא ומן כל חרשין [בי]שין ועובדין בישין ומן לוטתא ונידרא ומן קריתא (5) ואשלמתא ומן שיקופתא ומן כל מזיקין בישין (ות)[קיפ]ין אמן אמן סלה הללויה תוב מומינא ומשבענא וגזרנא (6) ומשמיתנא ומבטילנא ית כל רזי חרשין (ו)מיני חרשין וזיפין וקטרין וכיסין ומללתא ונידרי וענקתא וקריתא ולוטתא וכל (ס)טני (ורוח)י (7) בישתא ורוחי זידניתא וכל מעבדי וכל מזיקי מבטילנא יתהון במרי שמיא ובמרי ארעה ובאין ולא קדמאה דהוה בינגא (8) ובין אבהתנא ולא תיעלון לביתיה ולאיסקופתיה ולדירתיה דמיהרוי בר גושנאי ודפדרדוך בת דדי אינתתיה ולא תנזקון יתהון ולא (9) תיתחמון להון מן יומא דין ולעלם אמן אמן סלה הללויה חתים ביתיה דמיהרוי בר גושנאי הדין בחתמא ובצורתיה דאל חתים בחתמא דשדי אלהא דלא (ת)יק((ר))בון ביה כל חרשין וכל מעבדין וכל כיסי וכל (10) מללתא וכל נידרי וענקתא וקריתא בישתא וכל זיקין ומזיקין בישין

וכל סטנין תקיפין וכל מידעם [ ] (11) [ ][ד(ד)יתתסי בשמיה דאפססמט רבה אמן אמן סלה

Translation

(1) This mystery is designated for healing Mihrōy son of Gushnay; Pidardukh daughter of Daday, his wife; Bar-Shabbetay; (2) Imma; and Malbonay and Gushnay, the children of Pidardukh. May they be healed by the mercy of heaven, and may they be sealed (3) from all evil destroyers, from demons, from plague spirits, from dēws, from afflictions, from misfortunes (?), from satans, (4) from evil liliths, both male and female, from all evil sorceries and evil magic acts, from curses and vows and accidents (5) and spells and afflictions and from all evil and mighty destroyers, Amen Amen Selah Hallelujah.

Further. I adjure, invoke, decree, (6) ban and annul all mysteries of sorcerers and kinds of sorceries, falsities, knots, blows, spells, vows, necklace-charms, accidents, curses, all satans, evil (7) spirits, malicious spirits, all magical acts and all destroyers. I annul them by the Lord of Heaven and the Lord of the earth and by the primordial "Yes-and-No" (?) that was between us and (8) our ancestors — and (as a result) you shall not enter the house, the threshold and the living quarters of Mihroy son of Gushnay and of Pidardukh daughter of Daday, his wife, and you shall not cause them harm, and you shall not (9) make yourselves visible to them from this day and to eternity, Amen Amen Selah Hallelujah.

Sealed is the house of this Mihroy son of Gushnay by the seal and the figure of El. It is sealed with the seal of Shaddai the God, that you shall not approach it, (you) all sorceries and all magic acts and all blows and all (10) spells and all vows and necklace-charms and evil accidents and all blast demons and evil destroyers and all mighty satans and every thing … (11) that he may be healed by the name of **ʾpssmṭ** the great. Amen Amen Selah.

Commentary

1 רזא designates a mystery in the concrete sense of "a spell, an amulet". Cf. also B 6:1-2; B 16:7. In the following, line 6, the sorceries of evil agents, against which our amulet wishes to act, are also referred to as *raze*. Another term for the same idea is מילתא "word", as in B 7:1.

2 בני: The term is used here for both male and female children.

4 ונידרא: Apparently a singular form for the plural.

6 וזיפין: Cf. Montgomery 1913, 7:13, where a list very similar to our own occurs. Montgomery translates "hair-spirits", but the root **ZYP** allows also an association with falsehood.

וכיסין: A similar word occurs in B 17:2 (see commentary), 3. It seems however that since it occurs here independently of the verb, and in company with other harmful elements in the sorcerer's trade, it ought to have a sense which denotes something concrete that has the effect of piercing, biting or smiting. כיסי occurs also in Montgomery 1913, 7:13.

9 תיתחמון: For a similar idea cf. A 12:13, 33.

בחתמא ובצורתיה דאל ... בחתמא דשדי: The break up of the compound El-Shaddai is already attested in the Bible (Num. 24:4, 6; Job 27:13). It is discussed by Melamed 1945:182; 1961:120.

Bowl 20

Healing for Karkay son of Abaroy
Einhorn Collection, Tel Aviv
Plate 25

(1) (ב)מריהון דאסותא אסותא לקרקי (2) בר אברוי ה[ד]ין אסרה הדין חתמ[ה] [הע]ומדין (3) וקימין לעולם לאזחא ולאפ((ו))קא כל שידא דיכרא (4) ונוקבתא וכל דיוא דיכרא ונוקבתא וכל סטנא דיכרא ונוקבתא וכל (5) ליליתא דיכרא ונוקבתא וכל מבכלתא ורוחא וחו(מ)ר(ת)א דיכרא ונוקבתא (6) וניתאסרון וניתמסרון כולהון וניתחתמון וניתכבשון ונית[בטל]ון מיניה מן מהאדרגושנצף (7) בר דאטי ומן ביתיה כוליה ומן בית [ ] (ת)הוי ליה אסותא חתמא ונטרתא (8) דישלמה למהאדרגושנצף בר דאטי מן כל שידא ודיוא ורוחא ו(ח)ומרתא (9) ופתכרא ולילִיתא ומבכלתא ורוח דנחיש ושידא זניא וחתים ומחתם מהאדרגושנצף בר דאטי וביתיה כוליה (10) בשמה דרוחא דקודשה ובחתמה דמריהון דאסותה יה ביה יהוה אלהים צבאות אל שדי רבה אמן אמן סלה

Translation

(1) By the lord of healings. Healing to Qarqay (2) son of Abaroy. This is the binding, this is the sealing that exist and (3) subsist forever,

for removing and driving out every male and female (4) demon, every male and female dēw, every male and female satan, every (5) male and female lilith, every tormentor and spirit and male and female charm. (6) May they all be tied, surrendered, sealed, pressed down, [annulled] from Māh-Ādur-Gušnasp (7) son of Dātay and from his whole, whole house and from the house ... May there be healing for him. The seal and the protection (8) of Solomon for Māh-Ādur-Gušnasp son of Dātay from every demon, dēw, spirit, charm, (9) idol, lilith, tormentor, the spirit of Danaḥiš, and the fornicating demon. May Māh-Ādur-Gušnasp son of Dātay be sealed and doubly sealed and his whole house. (10) By the name of the holy spirit and by the seal of the lord of healings. Yah be-Yah, YHWH, Elohim, Sabaoth, the great El-Shadday. Amen, Amen, Selah.

Commentary

6 **וניתאסרון וניתמסרון**: The tendency to play on the similarity of sound of these two words makes them almost synonymous. Cf. Gordon 1934b, p. 326:1, where Isbell 1975, No. 52:1 correctly reads אסי(רין) ומסירין. The root MSR occurs also in the bowl published by Geller 1980, p. 49, line 11: ומימסר כל רוחי בישאתה, line 14: ומימסר כל שידי ודיוי, where it probably has a similar meaning of subduing the demons.

Bowl 21

Protection for Duday d. of Immi and others,
using the story of an egg that runs after humans
Einhorn Collection, Tel Aviv
Plate 26

(1) (מזמ)ן הדין רזא לכיבשא (2) דדודי בת אימי ורדיני בר ארו ודאברהם בר
(תוס) וסוס(יה) (3) (בת) אימי ודפריברד בר (גש) בעתה בת תרנגול(תה) אלמא
פומך פתחת (4) (עלי) (א)למא עינך מרמזת עלי אלמא (בדעתך) (מחש)[בת] [עלי]
(5) אלמא ב[רג]ליך [רה](ט)ת בתרי (מן) לילא (ההוה) בעתה ואמרה (לי) מנא [לי]
(6) פומא דפתח[נא] עלך (מ)נא לי עינ[י דרמזנא עלך ...] עלך מנא לי רגל(י דרהטת
בתרך)[(7)]בעתה שפיפ(ת ולא) [... פו]מא (לית) לך דפתחת עלי (ועיני לית) לך
ד(רמזת) עלי [ולי]בא לית לך דמחשבת עלי וריגלי לית לך דרהטת (8) (בתרי) (הכדין)

מכבשין כל סנייהו ומסיקייהו דסוניונא בר קיטין הדין דודי בת אימי וסוסיא בת אימי בהיכדין (9) דמיתכבשה מתות(א) בה (מסי)קי תחות אדלהון ונהרה תחות אדלהון מיא כן]אל כ(שיא)ל חרפיאל חרפיאל [.......]ראל ורזאל (10) ברז שמיה ברז מרי רזיה ועבד מיא וברז [...] קבליה אסר תגא למלכו ועבד שולטנא ברקיעה וכבשה לגולית ביד דויד ולפרעה ביד משה (11) ומצרים ביד יוסיף ושורא דיריחו ביד יהושע בר נון הוא יאסר תגיה דהדרא ( )תא דמלכותא על אנפוהי דסוניונא בר קיטין בשום חרסיאל וסרדיאל (12) וסריפון (בשום) דכנישין שוחין דשוחין סחפין עלהון אגני דדמא דדמא מתדנאן (עליהון) מסר דמרדותה מאמר אמרין ומודין (דימין) על (ב)פגיאנגאה דנתי סוניונא (13) בר קיטין ביגריא נובס (...) חרם חרם ניפש הדא אמר בתרהון אנה (קירחה) ואנא מנכון כול חכמיא מנכון מיד עוקבי בארעה נקיש לי וראשי (ברקיעה) ענני ברקיעה אמן אמן (14) סגי ושיתקא (כל) ( ) שוקוי ניחות מן שמיה (...) מלאכה עלך רחיצנא בת גודא בטנא מוכנתא שותא שותקאניה סכרא פומא לכל בני אדם וחוה הגיז ואמגת קלקלא כלה (15) לכל בני אדם וחוה מן סוניונא בר קיטין ביש[מיה ...]

Translation

(1) This mystery is designated for subduing (2) (in favour) of Duday daughter of Immi, Radeni son of Aru, Abraham son of [ ], Susya (3) daughter of Immi, and Friyabard son of Gaš (?).

Egg, daughter of a hen: Why do you open your mouth (4) against me? Why does your eye wink at me? Why do you consider me with your mind? (5) Why do you run after me with your foot at night? The egg spoke (?) and said: Where have I got (6) the mouth that I open at you? Where have I got the eye [that I wink at you? …] at you? Where have I got the foot that runs after you? [(7)] the egg bowed and not … You have no mouth to open against me, you have no eyes to wink at me, you have no heart to think against me, you have no feet to run (8) after me.

Thus may all the enemies and oppressors of this Sunyona son of Oitin and Duday daughter of Immi and Susya daughter of Immi be subdued, just as (9) death (?) is subdued by it (?), the oppressors underneath their ʾ**dl**ʾ and a river underneath their ʾ**dl**ʾ. K[ ]el, Kashiʾel, Ḥarpi'el, Ḥarpiʾel, … Raza'el, (10) by the mystery of heaven, by the mystery of the lord of mysteries and the slave of water (?), and by the mystery of …

He who places a crown for the kingship, and makes dominion in the sky, and who has subdued Goliath by the hand of David and Pharaoh by the hand of Moses, (11) and Egypt by the hand of Joseph, and the wall of Jericho by the hand of Joshua bar Nun, may he place the crown of glory (?) ... of kingship upon the countenance of Sunyona son of Qitin.

By the name of Ḥarsiel and Sardiel (12) and Serifon. (By the name of) ... pour over them buckets of blood (?), they judge against them the denunciation of rebellion (?), they speak and admit ... Sunyona son (13) of Qitin ... *ḥerem, ḥerem,* ... This he said after them: I am ... and I am one of you. All the wise people are of you. Thereupon at once (?) my heel knocked on the earth and my head (knocked) on the sky, on the clouds in the sky. Amen Amen. (14) ... angel, in you I trust. Bat-guda, pregnant, ..., shuts the mouth of all sons of Adam and Eve, ... destruction (15) to all the sons of Adam and Eve from Sunyona son of Qitin, in the n[ame of...]

Commentary

Much of the text is obscure, partly because the reading is doubtful, but partly also because the text is badly transmitted and may have been imperfectly understood by the scribe. Some quite doubtful readings are given in the hope that other scholars may improve on them.

At the beginning of the text there is a curious dialogue with an egg, which seems to constitute a menace to the clients of the incantation (lines 3-8). The magician asks the egg (in the feminine, according to its grammatical gender) why she opens her mouth against the client, why she winks at him, why she thinks thoughts against him, and why she runs after him. The egg denies doing these things, claiming that she does not possess a mouth, eyes, a heart, and feet which might perform the actions attributed to her. The magician asserts that the egg indeed does not have those limbs, and that she is therefore incapable of doing harm to the client. The following section, where the connection to the rest of the text is not entirely clear, contains an incantation. This is followed by an invocation to God, based on a string of biblical allusions (lines 10-11).

1f. לכיבשא ד...: This verbal noun normally comes in order to designate the action done to evil spirits. It may be assumed that its occurrence here, followed by the names of the clients, signifies subduing done on their behalf.

2 ארו, רדיני, דודי are proper names which are not easy to place ethnically. The second name could be regarded as Iranian: Rādēn may be an adjectival form from *rād* "generous", but the final vowel is not clear. The other two names are so far unattested and do not fit in with the pattern of either Semitic or Iranian proper names.

Susya seems to be the Aramaic designation "horse" (fem., in the indefinite form).

Friyaburd (?) (or Friyakard?) appears to be Iranian, and may signify: "carried tenderly", with the second element from the verb *burdan*; or "made dear", or even, if the reading is Parīburd, Parīkard, the meaning would be "carried, made, by the *paris*". If the final letter is *kaf*, the reading of the name could be Friya-bārak.

5 מן לילא is uncertain in its reading and interpretation. The sequence מן לילא ההוה בעתה may be a corruption of מללת ההיא בעתה "The egg spoke (and said)..."

8 הכדין ... בהיכדין "Thus ... just as".

For מסיקייהו cf. Bavli Bava Qama 116b, where an equation of meaning is established between מסיקין and מציקין.

Sunyona (or Sinyona), as well as the name of his mother, Qitin, belong to those names which are not transparent, and which are at present incapable of being identified ethnically.

9 אדל (אדלא): The context is obscure.

14 בטנא may be the active participle meaning "pregnant", but it may alternatively be one of the terms occurring in Bavli Ḥullin 63a (**bṭnʾy**, **bṭny**) for a kind of bird, or, as in Bava Meṣiʿa 86b **bṭnytʾ**, **by bṭnytʾ**, which is a term for a hen.

Bowl 22

Incantation for Marutha d. of Duda, to be protected by four angels on all sides

Einhorn Collection, Tel Aviv

Plate 27

(1) הדין קמיעה דחתמ[נא...] (2) מן ימינה חרביאל ומשמאלה (מ)יכאל ומלפנה סוסיאל [ומע]ליה (3) שכינת אל ומאחורה מ(ימר קד)ישאל (...אל) (4) [ ] (אלהים)

מכל שטן ומכל פגע (...) [...] (5) [...] (6) עדה עדה (עלילאל אמן אמן סלה)
(7) (דאשחת היכליה) וחן[...] וככיבי ומזלי וזיקי (וא...) ופיקדי ולטבי (8) ופתכרי
דיכרי ואיסתרתא ניקבתא [ ] מרותא בת דודא [...] (9) [...] (10) [...] ... על פי יהוה יחנו
ועל פי יהוה יסעו א]ת משמרת יהוה שמרו על (פי) [יהוה ביד משה] (11) (עלמי)
עד) ותהי עוונותם על עצמותם כי חת]ית גבורים בארץ חיים] ...

Translation

(1) This amulet that I seal [...] (2) On her right hand is Ḥarbi᾿el, on her left hand is Michael, in front of her is Susi᾿el, and [abo]ve her is the Shekhina of God and behind her is the word of Qaddish᾿el ... (4) God (?) from every satan and every trouble (5) ... (6) ... Amen, Amen, Selah ... (7) ... and stars and zodiac signs and blast-demons ... and (bad) commandments and no-good spirits (8) and male idols and female goddesses. [ ] Marutha daughter of Duda [ ] (9) ... (10) ["At the command of the Lord they encamped and at the command of the Lord they journeyed. They] kept the charge of the Lord, at the command of the [Lord by the hand of Moses]" (Num 9:23); [ ] (11) "their iniquities shall be upon their bones though they were the ter[ror of the mighty in the land of the living]" (Ez 32:27).

Commentary

The text is for the most part faded and barely legible. Only the sections that seem to give a coherent reading have been transcribed.

2-3 We have here another version of the well-known formula which invokes different angels and heavenly powers for the different directions around the body of the person. A similar formula has been encountered in A1:1-3, and parallel passages quoted in the commentary and in the "Additions and Corrections" to the Second Edition of *AMB* (p. 295). It may be noted that the "name" Ḥarbi᾿el has as its counterpart in A1:1 הרבה מאד; as the latter expression does not seem to make good sense in this context, it may be assumed to be a corruption from חרביאל. See Kotansky et al. 1992, הרביאל.

3 מימר קדישאל seems a more likely reading than מימר[א] קדישא ל[...]. For the phrase see above, A 18:6, בשמה דמימר קדיש עלמה.

7 פיקדי has not yet been attested as a name for a group of maleficent spirits.

8 Marutha daughter of Duda, a Semitic name, seems to be the client (or one of the clients) of this incantation.

11 עולמי עד: If the reading is correct, this is the end of Is. 45:17.

Bowl 23

Amulet to protect Sergius son of Barandukh
Alexander L. Wolfe Collection, Jerusalem
Plate 28

(1) אסירין ניקיטין צמידין כב(יש)ין דישין (עש)יפין כל פתיכרי (2) דיכרי ואיסתרתא ניקבתא דוריגי ונידרי ולוטתא ושיקופיתא וזיגוריתא (3) וקבלאתא ורוחי בישתא וחומרי זידניתא וכל ע(וש)פא וכל לוטתא (4) עישפא צמידא ונידרא וקיריתא ולוטתא ושיקופי(תא) (דאיכא ב)גיתא ומללתא קיריא (5) וקיבלא צעקתא ד(אית) לי (הוה) דילי אנה סרגיס בר ברנדוך בשום יזיד מחדט מלאכה (6) בשום אטון ארזין וניטר(וא)ל ופקיד(אל) דאינון קימין עים בורכתא ולוטתא וקיריתא דבני אינשה (7) בשום (גג)ראים לל... דאינון שרין עים מדינ איסרין נידרי ולוטתא וקיריתא מיניה (8) דסרגיס בר ברנדוך הדין ... ין לוטתא וקיריתא ושיקופיתא ואלהי ואיסתרתא וניחידרון על (9) אחתימא בת סרא עלה ועל ירתי בתה ועל משדריניהון אסיר וחתים שמיה וגדיה דסרגיס {בר} בר ברנדוך מן כל שידין ושיפטין (10) ורוחי בישתא וחומרי זידניתא אסירין וחתימין מן סרגיס בר ברנדוך בשום יזיד מחדט מלאכה ובישמיה דגבריאל מלאכה (11) דאיניש קיטריה לא שרי וחתמיה לא תבר אמן אמן סלהתר

Translation

(1) Bound, seized, attached, pressed down, thrashed, exorcised are all the male (2) idols and the female goddesses. Ladders (?) and vows and curses and afflictions and ... (3) and charms and evil spirits and impious charms and all exorcisms and all curses, (4) exorcism, binding, vow, calamity, curse, affliction that is (?) in the world, (magical) words, invocation, (5) charm, and cry that is with me [and that] was with me, I Sergius son of Barandukh. In the name of the angel Yazēd Māhdāt, (6) in the name of Aṭun-Arazin, Niṭru᾿el, Peqid᾿el, who stand with the blessing and the curses and calamities of the sons of man. (7) In the name of ... who exist with strife (?). Bound are the vows, curses, calamities from the same (8) Sergius son of Barandukh ... curses and calamities and afflictions and gods and goddesses. And may they go back to (9) Aḥat-

Ima daughter of Sara, to her and to those who inherit her household (?) and to those who send them. May the name and the fortune of Sergius son of Barandukh be bound and sealed from all the demons and the plagues (10) and the evil spirits and impious pebble-charms. May they be bound and sealed from Sergius son of Barandukh. In the name of the angel Yazēd Māh-dāt and in the name of the angel Gabriel (11) whose knot no man can untie and whose seal no one can break. Amen, Amen, Selah, immediately.

Commentary

1 עשיפין: This is from עשף "to exorcise"; for *ʿayin* instead of *alef* cf. Mandaic. A similar usage is in Bowl 26:2.

2 דוריגי: This is apparently the Babylonian Aramaic דרגא "step, ladder"; cf. Syriac דורגא "progress, attainment".
וזיגוריתא: or וזיבוריתא "wasps"?

4 גיתא could be the Middle Persian word *gētīg*, New Persian *gītī* "the material world, the world", with an Aramaic ending.

5 יזיד מהדט: Iranian Yazad-Māh-dāt- "created by the deity Moon".

6 אטון ארזין: This is unclear.

7 מדינ may be the Hebrew word מדין, מדון.
איסרין נידרי: Could be badly written איסרי ונידרי, but one should probably prefer emending to אסירין נידרי.

11 סלהתר: A contraction, evidently, of סלה על אתר.

Bowl 24

Wine-charm for Burz-Bahrām son of Dutay
Geoffrey Cope Collection, Herzlia
Plate 29

(1) מזמן הדין קמיעה לחמריה לביסומיה ולמנטרנותיה דחמריה דבורזבהרם בר דותאתי דותאי מן מן (2) רוסתקא דקרביל דבדיזא מאתה בישמיה דיה יה יה אות אות אות קדוש קדוש יה שמיה רבא מבורך לעלמא (3) ולעלמי עלמיא

וקסיה ססח דפריש ומפריש ליה לחמריה דבורזבהרם בר דותאי {בשום} בשום
--- יה יה יה מן בורזבהרם (4) בר דותאי חרשא טנפא ומגנא ומגזא ומפרשא
ומפרשין ומפרשא ומפ(רשה) באבנא בישמיה אה אה אה אהוי אהוי אהוי ארנו
(5) ארץ נוד לחמריה דבורזבהרם בר דותאי ניהא {בש} בסים חמריה דבורזבהרם
בר דותאי דלא ניזריק ולא ניסתפף ולא ניחת בשום איל איל אל (6) אל
אל שדא(י) אדא א(ות) קדוש חי לבורזבהרם בר דותאי בשמיה דיה יה יה
יה קדוש קדוש בשמיה דיהו יה יה אמן אמן סלה הללויה הללויה אבגדהוזח
(7) טיכך למם נן סעפף סעפצץ קרשת

Translation

(1) This amulet is designated for fermenting, sweetening and keeping the wine of Burz-Bahrām son of Dutay of (2) the village Qarbil, which is at the town Diza. In the name of Yah Yah Yah Yah, Ot Ot Ot, Holy Holy Holy. "May His great name be blessed for ever (3) and ever". **wqsyh ssḥ**. That he may distinguish and cause to be distinguished the wine of Burz-Bahrām son of Dutay. In the name of Yah Yah Yah. [May he separate] from Burz-Bahrām (4) son of Dutay the filthy sorcery, and the magic craft, and the removed (sorcerer), and the separated (sorcerer), and the separated (sorcerers), and the separated (sorcerer) and the separated (sorcerer). By the stone (?), by the heaven (?). Ah Ah Ah, Ahwi Ahwi Ahwi, Arno. (5) The Land of Nod to the wine of Burz-Bahrām son Dutay. May the wine of Burz-Bahrām son of Dutay be sweet. May it not be spilled (?), nor burn, nor go down. By the name of Il Il Il, El (6) El El, Shaddai Ada Ot, Holy Living, for Burz-Bahrām son of Dutay. In the name of Yah Yah Yah, Holy Holy. By the name of Yahu Yah Yah. Amen, Amen, Selah, Hallelujah, Hallelujah. (*There follow the letters in alphabetic sequence.*)

Commentary

This seems to be the first occurrence in Jewish magical literature of a charm seemingly dedicated to the preservation and good quality of wine (or, for that matter, of any specific commercial enterprise). In Syriac, we have some analogies in the *Book of Protection*; see Gollancz 1912, p. 19, §29: בורכתא דכ̈רמא וע̈ללתא; also p. 26 §44, an incantation for milk. The occurrence of the name of the client's place of residence, or of his origin, is another unique feature of this bowl.

1 לחמריה: This seems to be the *nomen actionis* of the verb ḤMR "to ferment". The occurrence of several terms associated with wine seems to exclude taking the word here in the widely attested sense of "charm, pebble-charm".

ביסומיה: This is a term used frequently with wine. See e.g. in Gollancz 1912, p. 19.

2 רוסתקא: This is probably the Middle Persian term *rōstag* "district, province". It is attested also in Syriac (cf. e.g. Mar Abba Qaθōlīqā in Bedjan 1895, p. 240 line 1), where it also designates "village", which seems appropriate here. The form ריסקא, which may be a corruption of this word, occurs once in II Targum Esther 6:10; cf. Geiger in: Krauss 1937, p. 385f. It is not easy to separate *rōstag* from ריסתקא (< **rāstag*?), that occurs in the Talmud in the sense of "outskirts, market", a different word, discussed by Geiger in: Krauss 1937, p. 386. The word occurring here could be either one of the above, the difference in Aramaic being only between *yod* and *waw*, which are hardly distinguishable in the script.

קרביל: The name is not attested in the available sources. It recalls however the area of Nehar Bil near Baghdad, for which cf. Oppenheimer 1983, p. 273 ff., where, on p. 275 n. 14, Arabic sources are quoted (calling the place variously Nahr Bīl or Nahr Bīn). The name Qarbil may be explained as derived from Kār Bīl "the people" or "army" of Bil, but no other toponyms are known to contain Kār as first element. It seems unlikely that קרביל should preserve an early form of the place known in Islamic times as Karbalāʾ.

דבדיזא: Diza is a name attested in different locations, though none seems to go together with either of the two associations made above for Qarbil. See Yāqūt s.vv. "Dizaq", "Dīzak". The underlying Persian word means "fortress".

2-3 יה שמיה רבא מבורך לעלמא ולעלמי עלמיא: This is a phrase from the Qaddiš, which has been established by scholars as a very early liturgical composition (cf. de Sola Pool 1909, esp. pp. 8ff., where occurrences of the formula יהא שמיה רבא מברך are quoted from Talmudic and Midrashic sources; Heinemann 1966, p. 163). The formula used here occurs also in the Hekhalot literature, cf. Schäfer 1981, p. 60 (§122) as a clear reference to an established prayer: וכיון שישראל נכנסין לבתי כניסיות ולבתי מדרשות והם עונין יהא שמיה רבא מברך אין אנו מניחין לצאת מחדרי חדרים "When Israel go into the synagogues and the places of learning and respond ʿMay His great name be blessed', we do not let (them) come out of the innermost rooms" (compare Schäfer 1987, p. 53). The corresponding Hebrew formula ברוך ומבורך שמו לעולם ולעלמי עולמים occurs in Schäfer 1981, p. 150 (§356);

ברוך שמו הגדול ... שהוא קיים לעולם ולעלמי עולמים occurs in Schäfer 1981, p. 253f. (§692).

3 דפריש ומפריש: The root **PRŠ** possesses, among its other meanings, the sense of "to distinguish, make wonderful". If this translation is correct, one has to assume that the forms derived from the same root in line 4, repeated several times, have by contrast a pejorative meaning.

4 ומגנא seems to be the same as the word מנגנא, which is attested also without the first *nun*. The word, clearly of Greek origin, seems to be predominantly attested in Palestinian texts.

ומגזא: This is apparently a participle form of the root **GZY**. The passive participle of this root (attested in Syriac) means "deprived, removed, barren".

ומפרשא ומפרשין: Pejorative forms derived from the root **PRŠ**?

באבנה בישמיה is obscure. The second word could also be "in the name of", but one would expect it to be followed by -ד.

5 ארץ נוד occurs in Gen. 4:16 as the place of dwelling of Cain after he killed Abel. Its occurrence here is difficult to explain, unless we assume a certain play on words: נוד means also "wine skin", and the expression ארץ נוד may have been jocularly used for the room where wine jars and skins were kept.

ניזריק: *Ithpe*ʾ*el* of **ZRQ** (for *nizdereq*), which means properly "to throw, sprinkle".

ניסתפף: Derived from the root **SPP**, attested in Syriac and Mandaic.

6 שדא(י): If the reading is correct, this is an unusual spelling of the divine name.

6-7 It is interesting to note that the sequence of the alphabet is used as a magical device here. Final letters are treated as independent letters. By mistake the letters *samekh, ʿayin, pe* are given twice in this list.

Bowl 25

Healing for Mahoy son of Imma, named Barshuti
Smithsonian Institution, Washington D.C.
Plate 30

(1) אסותא מן שמיה למחוי בר אימא דמתקרי ברשותי וכל שום דאית (2) ליה מן ילדותיה ויתסי מן ברקתא דיכרא וניקבתא ומן רוחא בישתא דמיתדמ(י)ה (3) ב(ד)ימינין ומן רוח נידא ומן דיוא ונידרא ומן שידא ומן טולין ומן [..]שיא ומן פגעא בישא (4) ומן זיקא ומזיקא ומן כל מידעם בישא דלא יתון עלהי דמחוי בר אימא מן יומא דנין ולעלם אמן אמן סלה /> שיר (5) ותשב(ח)ות וע(שיות ו)גברו(ת) למלך מלכי המלכים ברוך הוא

בשמיה רבא אומית ואשבעית עליכו ב(ר)ק(ת)א דיכרא וניקבתא ושידי (6) ודיוי ורוחא ד[ב]יש ונידרא בחר(ש)י ושאר כל רוחין כלהון וישאר כל מזיקי כלהון דברא אלהה דישראל בעלמא דלא תיעזקון ליה למחוי (7) בר אימא מן יומא דנין ולעלם אמן אמן סלה /> אומיתי ואשבעית עליכו ברקתא דיכרא וניקבתא דלא תיתון עלוהי דמחוי בר אימא ולא ת(כ)פתוהי (8) ולא תשלילוהי ולא תעלון במעלוניה ולא תיפקון במפקוניה ולא תי(מ)ירון בתמרורתיה ולא תיהי ליה לא תברא בימאמה ולא <ת>(ב)רא בליליה ולא תיכבשון (9) יתיה אנתי ברקת(י) דיכרא וניקבתא למחוי בר אימא לא מן ימיניה ולא מן שמאלה ולא (תיתבון) על (בית) (...) דמידמין ליה בדימינין בישין (10) ובהרהרין בישין ובב(עו)תין ולא תידמון ליה בכל צ(ב)ו ודמו דאתון מיתדמין לבני אינשא ודילא תין[.........ברקתא דיכרא] וניקבתא מיניה (11) דמחוי בר אימא מן מעלוניה ומפקוניה ודירתיה ומן ארבעא זוית ביתיה דברשותי בר אימא ותיזלון לאתר [........]תא בשום (12) [......] אמן סלה </

Translation

(1) Healing from heaven to Mahoy son of Imma, who is named Barshuti, and any other name he (2) (may) have from childhood. May he be healed from the cataract, male and female, and from the evil spirit that appears (3) in appearances and from the spirit of uncleanness (?) and from the demon and the vow and the devil and the shadow-spirit(s) and from […] and from evil occurrence (4) and from blast (demons) and harmful (spirits) and from evil things, so that they should not come upon him, Mahoy son of Imma, from this day for ever. Amen Amen Selah.

A song (5) and praise and … and might for the king of the kings of kings, may He be blessed.

By His great name, I adjure and invoke against you, the male and female cataract, demons, (6) dēws, evil spirit, vow with witchcraft, and all other spirits and all other harmful (spirits) that the God of Israel created in the world. May you not bind Mahoy (7) son of Imma from this day for ever, Amen Amen Selah.

I adjure and invoke against you, male and female cataract, that you should not come against Mahoy son of Imma, and that you should not tie him up (8) or chain him. That you should not come in through the way he comes or go out the way he goes out, and that you should not change (?) at the place where he changes (?), and that he should not have a misfortune either by day or by night, and that you should not subdue (9) him, you, the male and female cataract, (him,) Mahoy son of Imma, either from his right side or from his left side, and that you should not sit upon the house ... that they appear to him with evil appearances (10) with evil thoughts and with scary things (?). And that you should not appear to him by any thing or appearance as you appear to people. And that you should not ... [male and] female [cataract] from (11) Mahoy son of Imma, from the way he enters and the way he goes out, and his residence and from the four corners of his house, of Barshuti son of Imma, and that you should go to [another?] place ... By the name of (12) .... Amen Selah.

Commentary

We should like to thank Dr. Gus W. Van Beek, of the Smithsonian Institution in Washington, D.C., for putting a photograph of this and the following bowl (Nos. 25 and 26) at our disposal.

3 טולין, which occurs in a list seemingly consisting of singular nouns, may also be a singular *ṭulyān*, rather than the plural of טולא "shadow" (which is not attested for a shadow-spirit). A singular טולין, presumably related to the plural form טלני, is so far unattested.

5 עליכו: This could also be read עליכי, and the same ambiguity exists throughout the text.

7 אומיתי: This is a very widespread form of the 1st person singular, cf. Gordon 1941, No. 2:6 (Isbell 1975, No. 39:6). Rossell 1953, p. 47f.

10 צ(ב)ו: The reading is uncertain. Another possibility which presents itself is צפר, for which we may compare B 10:9 בת דמו כציפרא.

11 ארבעא should of course have been ארבע.

Bowl 26

Syriac

Protection for Khusro son of Qaqay and Shelta daughter of Qayumta

Smithsonian Institution, Washington, D.C.

Plate 31

(1) ל(קי)טין אסירין זריזין חליצין קמיטין וחתימין חרשא̈ ושא̈(ד)ין [...] (2) דיתבין
(דו)כ(י)א ורטנן ריטנא ועשפן עשפא ליליא וימאמא ודכול דנסיב ש(וחד)א ו(מ)קביל
(קו)רבנא (3) ודכול דשאתא (מיא) מן [...] (ו)עדילתא וב(ע)קא דנדרין לה לכוסרו בר
קאקי ולשלתא בת קיומתא ולפרוכ[דעד ולבירו] (4) ולגושני בנה ובנתה [דש]לתא
ליתקטר̈ון וליתאסר̈ון באסרא דביש ותקיף וקמיט כתיב̈ין חתימין דלא נעבר̈ון פור̈היא
דלא [...] (5) דלא לפחון ולא לרמ̈ון אלא ליתהפכ̈ון לות משדרני̈הון וקר̈יביהון
בשום פקר̈ון זיוא רבא דשימשא ואלפישרא רבא דמיא [... לכ]וסרו בר קאקי (6)
ולשלתא בת קיומתא ולפרוכדעד ולבירו ולגושני בנה̈ ובנתה̈ ד[ש]לתא מן כול דלעלא
אמין אמין איך דהנא קניא דמן גו ב(ית)א אתא ותוב לאגמא לא אזל ותוב (7) חיא
לא הוין לה̈ון הכנא לא תהוא בה̈ון חיותא בחרשא̈ דבניאנשא̈ דעבדין לה לכוסרו בר
קאקי ולשלתא בת קיומתא ולפרוכדעד ולברו וגושני בנה̈ ובנתה̈ דשלתא אין (8) ואמין
אמין סלחה וה̈ללוהי אבגד הוז חטי כלמנן סעפצ קרשתת אמין אמין סלח /
אבגד הוז חטי כלמנן סעפצ קרשתת אמין אמין סלחה (9) (*magic characters*) אף
אנתון (ר)וחא וחומרא ולליתא פתכר̈א דכר̈א ואיסתר̈תא ניקבתא (10) אסיר וחתים
ביתא ואנשיה אילין בבה וסליקין איגרה (א)ב(א)ה חקלה ובירה וקנינה אסיר וחתים
בעיזקתא דחתימא בה שמיא וארעא ובחתמא דחתמה נוח לכיולה ובעיזקתה דשלימון
(11) דחתימין בה שאדא ודי̈וא ובחתמא רבה חתימין מזרזין ומבדר̈ין קמע̈יא
הל̈ין דאתכתב̈ו לאסיותה ולנטרתה דכוסרו בר קאקי ושלתא בת קיומתא ופרוכדעד
ובירו וגושני בנה̈ ובנתה̈ דשלתא על(א) (12) אסר גוס אסר אסיר̈ין וקטר קטר̈ין אמין
אמין אמין סלח הללוהי לשמך אלהא חיא אלהא דבטיל כול שאדין וכל דיואין
אסיותא וחולמנא ודרמנא וחתמתא וק(ימ)תא ונטרתא דחיא (13) מן שמיא אנא
כתבתי אלהא נאסא (א)מן הש ולעלם אין ואמין אמין סלח

Translation

(1) Gathered, bound, girded, tied, clasped and sealed are the sorcerers and the demons ... (2) who sit in purity (?) and who mumble a mumbling and exorcise an exorcism by day and by night. Any one who takes a gift and who accepts a present, (3) and any one who drinks water (?) from ... and the accusation and convulsion that they pour down on Khusrau son of Qaqay and Shelta daughter of Qayumta and Farrokhdad and Biru (4) and Gushnay the sons and daughters of Shelta, may they be tied

and bound by an evil, strong and clasping binding. May they be written and sealed so that they should not transgress against the *warnings and not ... (5) and that they should not blow or cast, but that they should return to those who sent them and to those who are near them.

By the name of Paqrun, the great splendour of the sun, and Alpishara, the lord of water ... [save ... Kh]usrau son of Qaqay (6) and Shelta daughter of Qayumta and Farrokhdad and Biru and Gushnay the sons and daughters of Shelta from everything that is (written) above. Amen Amen.

As this reed, which comes from the inside of the house and does not go back to the marsh, and which has (7) no more life, so may there be no vitality in the sorceries of the people, which they perform against Khusrau son of Qaqay and Shelta daughter of Qayumta and Farrokhdad and Biru and Gushnay the sons and daughters of Shelta, Yes, (8) Amen Amen Selah, Hallelujah. **ʾbgd hwz ḥṭy klmnn sʿpṣ qrštt**. Amen, Amen, Selah.

ʾbgd hwz ḥṭy klmnn sʿpṣ qrštt, Amen, Amen, Selah. (9) (*magic characters*) You, too, spirits, pebble spirits, liliths, male idols and female goddesses. (10) Bound and sealed is the house and its men, who come in through his door and go up his roof, his fruit (?), his field, his well, and his possessions.

May it be bound and sealed by the seal by which the heaven and the earth are sealed, and by the seal by which Noah sealed his ark, and by the seal of Solomon, (11) by which the demons and the dēws are sealed and by the great seal. May there be sealed, sealed, girded and scattered these amulets that were written for the healing and the preservation of Khusrau son of Qaqay and Shelta daughter of Qayumta and Farrokhdad and Biru and Gushnay the sons and daughters of Shelta.

ʿlʾ ʾsr gws. (12) Bind bindings, tie tyings. Amen Amen Amen Selah Hallelujah. By your name, living god, the god who annuls all demons and dēws. Healing, health, cure, sealing, existence, and the preservation of life (13) from heaven. I have written and God cures. Amen. Now and forever. Yes, and Amen, Amen, Amen, Selah.

Commentary

For access to a photograph of this bowl we are indebted to Dr. Gus W. van Beek (see commentary to Bowl 25).

The bowl measures 17.5 cm. in diameter. Two concentric circles are drawn on its surface. The innermost circle contains a cross, showing it to be of Christian origin. The next one separates one section of the inscription from the other, dividing line 8 in half.

The script of the bowl is Estrangelo. It makes a somewhat peculiar use of *siyāme*, putting it not only over nouns but also over plural verbs and pronominal suffixes, much more than is warranted by general usage (cf. Nöldeke 1898, pp. 10f., §16).

1 קמט is a verb which means to hold fast, draw together, clasp, contract.

חרשׄא ושאׄדין is a combination of a determined and an absolute form of the plural.

2 דיתבין (דו)כ(י)א: Although the letters seem relatively clear (with the exception of the last but one letter, which is written as ***nun***, and should actually be read דוכנא), the reading and the translation are uncertain. Another possibility to be considered is דתכין דוכנא "who cause harm", assuming that דוכנא is an error for תוכנא, the verbal noun from the root תכן, which is the verb perhaps used under the form תכין.

רטן is a verb which is used for alien prayers, e.g. for the manner in which the Zoroastrian priests pray (cf. Greenfield 1974). Here it may allude to the formulae used by sorcerers.

עשף is a verb which is attested in Mandaic as an equivalent of אשף, one of the verbs which designate the typical action of magicians. It is derived from Akkadian *ašpu*. Cf. B 23.

שוחדא and קורבנא, if the reading is correct, seem to form a pair of near synonyms. For קורבנא in the sense of "present, gift" cf. Matth. 15:5, where κορβᾶν occurs, while in the parallel text, Mk. 7:11, δῶρον occurs. On this cf. Fitzmyer 1959, but see Greenfield 1976, p. 60, for the interpretation of the ossuary inscription discussed by Fitzmyer.

3 ובעקא: The *ʿayin* in this word seems to have been added as an afterthought.

4 פוׄרׄהיא: Apparently an error for פוׄרׄהזא.

5 The name אלפישרא may contain the word אלפרא "captain of a ship", since he is said to be the lord of the sea.

6 קניא ... לאגמא: A reed grows naturally in an אגמא, "marsh" or "lake". Cf. קטלי קני באגמא "those who cut reeds in the marsh", Bavli Sanhedrin 33a.

7 להׄוׄן is an error for לה.

8 The alphabet, in its two occurrences, has two *nuns* (one for the final form of the letter) and two *taws*. A similar use of the alphabet for magical purposes is in B 24.

9 אבאה — if the reading is right — is a somewhat strange form for אבה "his (or its) fruit". It is alternatively possible to assume that the first letter is an *ʿayin*, and that the whole word should be read (ע)ב(ור)ה "his crop".

10 לכיולה: This is an unusual spelling of the word. The common spellings are כוילא, כאוילא, כולא, כאולא.

13 כתבתי is an irregular form of the first person singular; see above, Commentary to B 25:7. It is interesting to note that this occurs in Syriac, and in a regular verb (despite the remark of Rossell 1953, p. 47f).

Bowl 27

Protection for Berikhishi (?) son of Aḥata
Leonard A. Wolfe Collection, Jerusalem
Plate 32

(1) בישמך (א)[ני עושה] חתי(ם) ביתיה ודירתיה (2) דברי(כישי בר אחתא) [...]אנוש
ברי (ל)ישמך (3) {מה((ו))ד} מהודענא [...] בישמיה דסימיאל (4) מלאכה ובישמיה
ד[... ובישמיה] דמיכאל מלאכה ובישמיה (5) דרפאל (אסיא רבה) [...] מלאכין
קדישין וחסידין חתמו (6) ואסורו הדין ביתיה ודירתיה [...] דבריכישי בר אחתא מן
כל (כ)איבאי (7) ומרעי ומן כל חומרי זידניתא ומן [...] ומן אישתא ומן ערויתא
ומן רוחא (8) בישתא מן שידא בישא מן דיוא (בישא) ומן סטנא [...] (9) ומן עינא
בישתא ומן כוחתא בישתא [...]

Translation

(1) By your name [I act]. May there be sealed the house and dwelling (2) of Berikhishi (?) son of Aḥata [...]-anosh (his) son (?). By your name ... (3) I announce ... in the name of Simiel (4) the angel and in the name of [... and in the name] of Michael the angel and in the name (5) of Raphael the great healer [...] holy and pious angels, seal and bind this house and dwelling [...] of Berikhishi (?) son of Aḥata against all pains (7) and illnesses, and against all wicked pebble-spirits and against [...] and

against fever and hectic fever and against evil (8) spirit and against evil demon and against evil dēw and against [evil] satan (9) [...] and against the evil eye and against the evil breathing ...

Commentary

In the centre of the bowl there is a drawing of a human figure, perhaps female, holding a stick (which could be interpreted as a sceptre or mace). Part of the surface of the bowl is effaced and illegible.

2 Berikhishi: The composition of this name is unclear, and its vocalization is uncertain. It seems to be written once, further in this line, without a final *yod*.

Aḥata: The name of the mother means "sister".

ברי (ל)ישמך: This sequence of words is difficult, and the translation offered is not certain. ברי may be taken to be an error for בריה. On the other hand it is possible to think of reconstructing the reading as follows:]אנוש ברי(כ)יש מר "...anosh Berikhish son [= an error for בר] of <Aḥata>"; according to this reconstruction, the name of the mother was omitted by mistake.

3 מה((ו))ד מהודענא: The scribe may have attempted to write מהודענא, but having committed an error he started all over again.

6 כאיבאי: If the plural is intended, as seems likely from the following מרעי, the second *alef* is superfluous. The writer may have meant to write a singular form first, then perhaps added a *yod* for the plural without crossing out the *alef*.

9 כוחתא: This seems to be the most probable reading of the word, although the third letter could also be a *samekh*. The form כוחתא is unattested, but it could be a verbal noun from a verb כוח or כחח "to cough". The verb, however, is only attested in Hebrew, not in Aramaic. In Syriac כח means "to breathe, exhale breath", the verbal noun is כחתא.

III. Amulets and Fragments of Magic Books from the Cairo Geniza

Geniza 9

T-S K 1.15

Four pages from a book of magic recipes
for easy birth, hatred, and other purposes

Plates 33-34

[1]

אשר יצר את האדם בחכמה וברא
בו נקבים נקבים חללים חללים
שאם יסתם אחד מהם אינו
מתקיים ברוך אתה ייי יוצר האדם
(*magic characters*) בחק אדם אמסך אדם
לעסר אלולד
יקאל וירדו כל עבדיך אלה אלי
והשתחוו לי לאמר צא אתה וכל העַ[ם]
אשר ברגלך ואחרי כן אצא וי(צא)
צא אצא ויצא: לשנאה
תכתב עלי כתף כלב בדם חמא[ר]
ותדפן אלכתף תחת ראס אלדי תח(ב)
אן יקע בינהם אלבגצ̇ה פאן לם תצ(ל)
אלי דלך תכתבה פי גצארה ותגסלה
במא ביר ליס יראה שמס והדא אלדי
תכתב עלי אלכתף
אגריפוס אסימון / אסימור פסכרבואל
אורפניאל אתון מלאכיא רברביא
הבו שנאה בין פ̇ בןֿ פ̇ ובין פ̇ בןֿ פ̇

[2]

כשנאת אמנון לתמר וכסנאת
כלב בפני חתול וכשנאת <כ>לב בפני חזיר
והדא אלדי יכתב עלי אלגצארה
הללויה מן אול אלהלל אלי אן ינתהי
אלי ישראל בטח בייי יקטע ענד
אנתהאה אליה ויכתב אלאסמא אלדי
פוק ויקול אתון אתיא רברביא

8 אלי אכרה וירש אלמא אלדי יגסל בה
9 הדה אלכתבה מן אלגצארה פי אלמוצע
10 [אלד]י יכון פיה אלמבגיצין אן שא אללה
11 לאהבה
12 [א]בג|יתץ|בייץ אתון שמהאתא
13 דחיליא ותקיפיא הבו אהבה רבה בין
14 פ בן פׂ ובין פ בן פ כי כאשר ידבק
15 האזור אל מתני איש כן תדבק אהבת
16 פ בן פ בלב פ בן פ אמן סלה صمت
17 כבוש גיד ליס מתלה אכתבהׄ פי טאס
18 אנך ואגעלה תחת רגלך וקול
19 הֵךְ דִכְּבַשׁ אלָהָא עָלְמָהּ מִן תְחוֹת
20 יְדֵיה וְאִסכּוּפְתַה דְאַרְעָא תְחוֹת

[3]

1 שְׁמַיָא כְדֵין יִתְכַּבְשׁוּן קֳדָמַי כָּל אָמְרֵי
2 בִישְׁתִּי ו‹כ›ל אנְטִידִיקִי דִידִי זַזבְזַז
3 ויתכַבְשׁוּן קֳדָמַי בשם שְׁמוֹת שְׁמִיתָא
4 אִלין כויר בכויר בקה כור בניכויר
5 בניכויר אִילֵין שְׁמָהָתָא דְיָתְבִין עַל רוּחָתָא
6 וכָבְשִׁין יָתְהוֹן דִלָא יִפְקוּן ויזִיעָן עָלְמָא
7 כֵּן יִתְכַבְּשׁוּן כל אמרי ביש עלי אָנָה
8 זָזבזז ויִתְכַבְשׁוּן קֳדָמַי בשם
9 כבשיאל כבשיאל כבשיאל דִכְבַשׁ (ע)[למא]
10 תְחוֹת רגְלי כֵן יִתְכַבֹשוּן קֳדָמַי
11 אָמְרֵי בִישְׁתִי ואלין
12 כלקְטִירִיָה כתב בְקֵלֶף اكتب هذه القلقطيرات ((فى رق))
13 (*magic characters*)
14 (*magic characters*)
15 וכד תלת חצי ואגעלהא עלי אלכתא[ב]
16 ואעקדהא עליה וארמיה פי אלבחר
17 אלכביר אן שא אללה על שמך חייה וקיימה
18 (*magic characters*)
19 (*magic characters*)

[4]

1 بسم الله الرحمن الرحيم على (الله توكلت)
2 باب بهج
3 ليس لاهل الهند امضا منه
4 فاذا اردت العمل به فابدا على بركه الله وعونه
5 فتطهر و(لا تلبس؟) شي فيه روح ولا شى خرج
6 من روح واجلس على شى مرتفع من
7 الارض فان قمت فهو خير وانت تنجو بمقل
8 [العيـ]ـن يليه (؟) (غير) مرة فاذا فرغت فاختم
9 [قـ]ـعودك وانصرف الى خلف وهذا كلامها
10 تقول اهططو طامها طوطا وهطاطا
11 اطا اطا لهلطوطا مهطوط وطواط
12 مهلاط لفط وطمعطوط مهو مهرور
13 مهرور اندود سامهك شا اشا مقيشا
14 شا اقشا مقشليشا وشاشا قرطينشا
15 وارطيشا قفليشا ( ) مقلميشا وشا ارشا
16 عرس وسر وسواس مقشليش
17 وشلوشا مشا اسلوشا راحميشا

Translation

page 1

(1:1) He who created man in wisdom and who placed (1:2) in him several apertures, several hollow areas. (1:3) If any of those is blocked, the man cannot (1:4) survive. Blessed are You, God, the creator of man. (1:5) « By the right of Adam, hold Adam (?). »

(1:6) « For difficulty at childbirth. (1:7) It is said: » "And all these servants of yours will come down to me, (1:8) and prostrate themselves to me saying, Go out, you and all the people (1:9) who follow at your heels, and after that I will go out. And he went out" (Ex. 11:8). (1:10) Go out, I shall go out, and he went out.

For hate. (1:11) « You shall write on the shoulder of a dog with the blood of a donkey, (1:12) and you shall bury the shoulder under the head of the person(s) you wish (1:13) hate to fall between them. If you do not manage to get (1:14) to that, you shall write it in a bowl, which you should wash (1:15) with the water of a well which has not seen the sun. This is what (1:16) you should write on the shoulder:» (1:17) Agripus, Asimon, Asimor, Paskarbuel, (1:18) Orpaniel, you, the great angels, (1:19) place hatred between N. son of N. and N. son of N.

page 2
(2:1) like the hatred of Amnon for Tamar and like the hatred of (2:2) a dog in front of a cat and like the hatred of a dog (?) in front of a swine. (2:3) «This is what he should write on the bowl: (2:4) Hallelujah, from the beginning of the *Hallel* until he reaches (2:5) "Israel trust in the Lord" (Ps. 115:9). He should stop when (2:6) he reaches that and should write the names as (2:7) above, and say: You, great symbols, (2:8) to the end. He should sprinkle the water with which he washes (2:9) this writing of the bowl in the place (2:10) where the haters are found, God willing.»

(2:11) For love. (2:12) **abg ytṣ byyṣ**. You fearsome (2:13) and mighty names! Place great love between (2:14) N son of N and N son of N. "For as the girdle (2:15) cleaves to the loins of a man" (Jer. 13:11), so shall the love of (2:16) N son of N cleave to the heart of N son of N, Amen Selah. «Silence.»

(2:17) A good subduing, there is none like it. «Write it on a plate (2:18) of lead, place it under your foot and say,» (2:19) Just as God subdued the world under (2:20) his hand, and the threshold of the earth under

page 3
(3:1) the heaven, so shall all those who speak evil (3:2) against me and all my rivals [, I,] NN, (3:3) be subdued before me, in the name of these names, (3:4) (*magic names*). (3:5) These are the names that sit over the winds (3:6) and subdue them so that they should not come out and shake the world, (3:7) so shall all those who speak evil against me, I, (3:8) NN, be subdued. And may those who speak evil against me be subdued before me in the name of (3:9) Kabšiel Kabšiel Kabšiel, who subdued the world (3:10) under his feet. Thus will be subdued before me (3:11) all those who speak evil against me. These (3:12) characters write on parchment (3:13-14) (*magic characters*). (3:15) «Take three pebbles and put them on the writing (3:16) and tie them to it, and throw it into the great

(3:17) sea, God willing,» by Your name, the living and the existent. (3:18-19) (*magic characters*).

page 4
(4:1) «In the name of Allah the Compassionate, the Merciful. I put my trust in Allah. (4:2) Chapter on joy (?), (4:3) there is none more efficacious than it (even) among the Indians. (4:4) If you wish to use it, start with the blessing and help of God. (4:5) You should clean yourself, and do not put on (?) anything in which there is spirit, nor something which derives (4:6) from a spirit. Sit on something elevated above the (4:7) ground, but if you stand up, it is better. You will be saved in a twinkling (4:8) of an eye (?) ... more than once (?), and when you finish, seal (4:9) your sitting (?) ... and withdraw backwards, and this is the wording of it: (4:10-17) (*magic words*)»

Commentary

1:1-4 This text is taken from the prayer said after discharging one's bodily needs (Bavli Berakhot 60b); it occurs also in other prayers (cf. Bar-Ilan 1985). An early formulation of this blessing, quite close in wording to the one given here, is in *Siddur Rav Seʿadya Gaʾon*, p. 88. Cf. also Bar-Ilan 1985.

1:11 The use of a shoulder bone for magic is quite well-known. See for Greek magic (omoplatoscopy) in Bouché-Leclerc 1879/1882, I, pp. 180-181; Fahd 1966, pp. 395ff.

2:4 The *Hallel* is used here as a magic instrument. The *Hallel*, which forms part of the prayers said in the synagogue on festive days, consists of Ps. 113-118.

2:10 "The haters": One might have expected to have a passive participle "the hated ones", but it seems that in this context the terms are regarded as interchangeable.

2:12 The letters in this case are an anagram of אנא בכוח גדולת ימינך תתיר צרורה.

2:17ff. See above A16.

3:5 "Sit over", i.e., rule.

3:12 Repeated in Arabic characters.

4:1-17 The whole page is written in Arabic characters, in the Arabic language. The formulae at the beginning are Islamic.

4:5-6 The meaning does not seem quite clear.

Geniza 10

T-S K 1.18 + T-S K 1.30

Amulet on paper for a pregnant woman, Ḥabiba daughter of Zahra

Plates 35-36

[1]

T-S K 1.18, recto

בשם היה הוה ויהיה השבעתי
וגזרתי עליך אתה מזל אריה שתעמוד
בכל עז ותגבורת ועוצם ותוקף להתגבר
נגד כל המזיקין והמכאיבים והמחלי
אים את האשה חביבה בנת זהרא {ו}
ותעמוד בעדה בתפילה ובאקשה
לפני מלך מלכי המלאכים הק׳ב׳ה
להברייח מיעליה כל מיני שידין ושיד
תין ולילין ולילתין ומרעין בישין ומזיקין
ומאזיקתין ורוחין בישין דכורין ונקבין
וכל מיני פחד ורעד ומורך ליבב וחלשת
הלב וחטיפת הלב וכל מיני מכאוב שיש
באיבאריה או בגידיה באופן שתהיה בא
ריאה ושמורה מכל דבר רע כל הימים
ובפרט אם יש בה מיאותם השבעה רוחין
די עאילין במְיעיהון די נשייא ומעַאכְרן
זרעיהו ושלא תפיל את פרי בטנה על הכל
משביע וגוזר אני עליך שלא תפיל דבר
מכל הכתוב כאן להתפליל עליה בשם
שדי צבאות אדני ובכוח הצירוף
הקדוש הזה שהוא יבע בשיא
למ וא אב כהום ומה
ביל וכת צוא לת מל מיי מכי

מיצ ימאו מאלי רבת ורת כׄ
אימ שלא תעבר על שבועתי זאתׄ
בכוח המלאך הממונה הממונה עליך שהוא
סרביאל ובכוח שבעת המלאכׄים האלה
הממונים על שבעת ימי השבוע שהם
מיכאל גבריאל סמאל רפאל
צדקיאל עניאל קפציאל {ש}
שתיתין כבוד לייי אלוהי ישראל

[2]

T-S K 1.30

ולשמותיו הקׄדושים אשר השבעתי עליך
בהם וקיים אתׄ כל הכׄתוב כאן ועליך {ת}
תבא ברכתׄ טוב אמן -- עוד אני {מ}
משביע וגוזר עליכׄם אתון כל מני
שידׄין ושידׄתין ולילין ולילתׄין ורוחין בישין
ומזיקין ומזיקתׄין דׄכורין ונוקבין דׄי מן
אשא ודׄי ((מן)) מיא ודׄי מן רוחא ודׄי מן עפרא
ובׄפרט אתון שבעה רוחין דׄי אוליף {אש}
אשמדי מלכא דשידׄין לשלמה מלכא דׄי
עאילין במעיהון דנשאיה ומׄעאכׄרן זרעיהוׄ
ואוף הכׄי <מ>ומינא וׄגזרנא עליכׄו אתון כל
מיני מרעין בישין וׄכאיבין בישין וכׄל מני
קאה ושלשול ומיחוש וצער ורפיון שיש
בגׄויתׄ האשה חביבה בתׄ זהרא בשם
אל שדי דׄי מיניה אתון זאייעין {ו}
ודׄאחלין וׄבשם מיכׄאל ריבכׄון
ובשם אשמדי מלכׄכׄון ובשם כל
ממוׄנן דׄי שאלטין עליכׄון דׄי תיטלון
ותׄהכׄון ותערקוׄן ותׄרחקון מעל האדׄין
איתתׄא ולא תוספון למקרב לה לעאלמין
טולו טולו מיעאליה לאתׄרא אחרונה ולה
לא תׄקרבון בחילא דׄי האדׄין צרוׄפא {ק}
קדישא שהוא סס צמ טאת
צמה נכי באופן שלא יהיה לה
שום כאב לא בעתׄ נדתׄה ולא בעתׄ
טהרתׄה ותׄהיה באריאה כל הימים אמן

ואי עברתון על מומאתׄי הדׄא אנא מחינא
לכון בחטרין דׄי פרזלא דאינון ארבע
אמהתא קדישתׄא בלהה רחל זלפה
ליאה בגׄין כׄן קיימו יתׄ מומתׄי הדׄא
ועליכם תבא ברכתׄ טוב אמן

[3]

T-S K 1.18, verso (Fig.18)

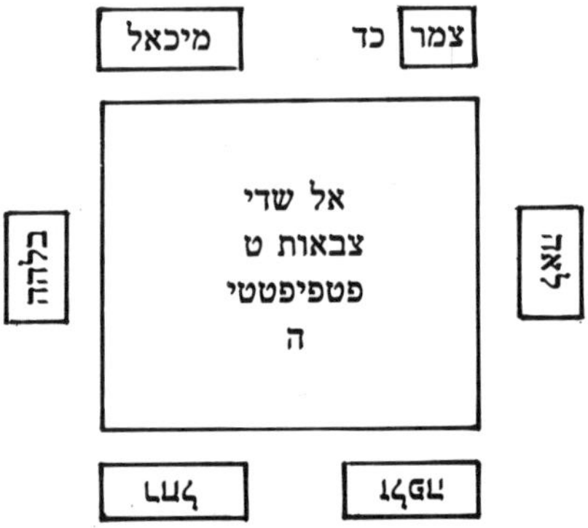

Fig. 18. Geniza 10, page 3

Translation

page 1

(1:1) In the name of He who was, is and will be. I adjure you (1:2) and command you, you the (Zodiac) sign of Leo, that you should stand (1:3) with all (your) might and power and strength and solidity to withstand (1:4) all those who damage and pain and cause illness (1:5) to the woman Ḥabība d. of Zahra, (1:6) and that you should stand and pray and beseech for her (1:7) in front of the King of all kings, the Holy, blessed be His name, (1:8) so that all kinds of demons, male and female, be driven away from her, (1:9) as well as male and female liliths, evil illnesses, male and female (1:10) causers of harm, male and female evil spirits, (1:11) all kinds of fear and trembling, cowardice, weakness (1:12) of heart, terror, and all kinds of pain that there (1:13) are in her limbs or sinews, so that she should be (1:14) healthy and preserved from any evil thing all days, (1:15) and especially if she has any of those seven spirits (1:16) that enter into the entrails of women and spoil (1:17) their offspring, and that she should not abort her foetus.

For all this (1:18) I adjure you and command you, that you should not omit anything (1:19) that is written here from (your) prayer for her. In the name of (1:20) Shaddai Sabaoth Adonai, and with the power of this (1:21) holy combination, which is **ybʿ bšyʾ** (1:22) **lm wʾ ʾb khwm wmh** (1:23) **byl wkt ṣwʾ lt ml myy mky** (1:24) **myṣ ymʾw mʾly rbt wrt k** (1:25) **ʾym**, that you should not trespass against this adjuration of mine, (1:26) by the power of the angel who is appointed over you, who is (1:27) Sarbiʾel, and by the power of these seven angels (1:28) who are appointed over the seven days of the week, who are (1:29) Michael, Gabriel, Samael, Raphael, (1:30) Ṣidqiʾel, ʿAniʾel, Qafṣiʾel, (1:31) that you may render honour to God, the Lord of Israel,

page 2

(2:1) and to His holy names, by which I adjured you, (2:2) and that you should fulfil everything that is written here, and you (2:3) should receive a blessing of goodness, Amen.

Further, I (2:4) adjure and command you, you all kinds of (2:5) male and female demons, male and female liliths, evil spirits, (2:6) male and female causers of harm, those (who come) from (2:7) the fire, and those (who come) from the water, and those (who come) from the wind, and those (who come) from the earth, (2:8) and in particular you, the seven spirits, concerning whom (2:9) Ashmedai, the king of the demons, instructed King Solomon; (spirits) that (2:10) enter the entrails of women and spoil their offspring.

(2:11) I further adjure and command you, you all kinds of (2:12) evil illnesses and evil pains, and all kinds of (2:13) vomiting, diarrhea, pain, unease, and weakness that exist (2:14) in the body of the woman Ḥabība d. of Zahrā. In the name of (2:15) El Shaddai, of whom you shudder (2:16) and fear, and in the name of Michael, your master, (2:17) and in the name of Ashmedai your king, and in the name of all (2:18) those who are appointed, who have power over you, that you may move, (2:19) and go, and flee, and keep away from this (2:20) woman, and that you should no longer come close to her for ever. (2:21) Go away, go away from her to another place and (2:22) do not come near her. By the power of this holy (2:23) combination, which is **ss ṣm ṭ'ʾt** (2:24) **ṣmh nky**, (may she live) in such a manner that she should have (2:25) no pain, either during her menses or during the period of (2:26) her cleanness, and that she should be in good health all days, Amen.

(2:27) And if you transgress against this adjuration of mine, I shall strike (2:28) you with iron rods, that are the four (2:29) holy mothers, Bilhah, Rachel, Zilpah (2:30) Leah. For this reason observe this adjuration of mine (2:31) and you shall have a blessing of goodness, Amen.

Commentary

The amulet, written on one side of the paper, has been pieced together from two different fragments in the Cambridge Geniza Collection. On the back of one of the two fragments, T-S K1.18, a diagram of "names" is drawn, all enclosed within rectangular boxes.

The incantation consists of a number of formulae, which are somewhat repetitive, a phenomenon that is not infrequent in magic texts.

The orthography is remarkable for the fact that it contains in several places *alef* as a *mater lectionis* internally, in words such as **wbʾqšh** (1:6), **wmʾzyqtyn** (1:10), **bʾybʾryh** (1:13), **wmʿʾkrn** (1:16); *yod* is also used more than is usual, e.g. **lhbryyḥ** (1:8), **lybb** (1:11), **myʾwtm** (1:15). It is also noteworthy for the fact that it contains a number of diacritical devices, chiefly a slanted bar over certain letters to indicate the -u- vowel (cf. e.g. lines 1:10, 11, 15); and a dot over the letters BGD KPT to indicate that they are "soft", i.e. fricative. The use of the latter device is sometimes at variance with the rules; it is often used in this text to mark the *dalet* of the pronoun **dy**, even when this follows a consonant, perhaps under the influence of Arabic *alladhī*.

1:4-5 והמחלי/אים: Written first והמאחלי/אים, with the first *alef* crossed out.

1:12 חטיפת הלב means "terror", cf. e.g. II Targum Esther 1:2 (p. 7): למחטף לבהון דסהדיא דלא יסהדון סהדותא שיקרא "to scare the witnesses, so that they should not give a false testimony". Jastrow 1903, p. 450, s.v. **ḤṬP**, seems to have failed to notice the precise meaning of the expression.

2:18 תיטלון, and in line 21 טולו, means "move, go". In Targum Gen. 20:1 נטל translates Heb. נסע.

2:19 ותהכון: From הלך, or an error for ותהפכון. האדין comes here instead of the expected האדא.

2:21 אחרונה: for אחרנה, "another".

2:29 This seems an early attestation of the mediaeval explanation for the efficacy of iron (*barzel*) by deriving it from an anagram of the names of the four wives of Jacob. Cf. *AMB*, p. 121 n. 23.

3 This is arranged as a diagram. The above arrangement renders its lay-out, although the words לאה and בלהה are written vertically, and the words רחל and זלפה are written upside down in the original. For a commentary see Naveh 1989a, p. 303. The sequence צמרכד represents the last letters of the words in Gen. 1:1-5.

Geniza 11

T.-S. K 1.19

Four pages from a book of magic recipes: for a barren woman, for opening locks, and for other purposes

Plates 37-38

[1]

כה אמר ייי יושב הכרובים יושב ערבות
יֹהֹוֹהֹ על סיבנת קמסונות קרוסית כסוד
מצולה פאוסין אלין ניכתב בים כתיב על
קדירה חדשה שלחרש ושבר(ה) על שני
חרשים והשלך חצי מצד אחד וחצי מצד
אחד: הדין קמיעא לאיתתא עקרה כתֿ
בקלף דצבי ותלי עלה כד תדמיך עם בעלה
יהוי תחות ראשה וכד תסחי במיא תטעון
יתיה בדכין. ואלין שמהתה כתֿ אלאהה

יבילה	ההרטה	באטהי	מוזט	כלטל	
אלמא	יסד לי	לדי	ולן	ובנתנ	ותהי
המוטה	ויקרא	הטי	ומל	משכני אחריך	

נרוצה הביאני המלך חדריו נגילה ונשמחה
בך נזכירה דדיך מיין מישרים אהבוך:
כול אתון אתיא קדישיא נטרון זרע פלֿ בֿ
פלֿ לחיי ולקיום עד גמרא אמן אמן סלה
דבעי למפתח כל מסגר בעלמא לימא
הלין שמהתא לכון אנא קרי מלאכיא קדישיא
קדישי עליונין עניאל פתחיאל קמסניאל

[2]

גדגדיאל וצפצפיאל קנקניאל ממליאל נריאל
לוחיאל מישאל ברכיאל תניאל אתון קדישיא
מלאכיה הוו בסעדי הוו לי חיי לי וחיי והבו לי
גבורא דנפתח תרעא הדין בשם ברכיאל
דקאים וממונה על רקיע השלישי ((בֿ)) בשם
ספסקיאל דקאים וממונא על רקיע החמשי ((הגֿ))
בשם חוריאל דקאים וממונה על רקיע
הרביעי בשם ברוכיאל דקאים וממונה

על רקיע החמישי בשם סעדיאל דקאים
וממונה על רקיע הששי אתון מלאכיה
קדישיא פתחו לי תרע הדין והך קופל
בריגלך ותאמר האי פסוקא כי הנה הלכו
משד מצרים תקבצם מף תקברם מחמד
לכספם קמוש יירשם חוח באהליהם
בשמהו בשמא | רבא אמור רבתא בבתא
בשמא רבא אמור בבתא רבתא מנזוף
די אלהא חייא דעזיז קליה אספהום
בדקום אימא לה עד ז̇ זמנין o
לעקרב

[3]

אל על עוקציך מיכאל רברבן על קרנתיך
גבי שמיא על מתנתיך אלהא אסריך
ואנא טעין לך: לוא לאו לחיויא דבראך
מלכא דבראך אלאה אדם אסריאל גנתא
דעדן אי גינתא דעדן: o לעקרה o
דלא ילדה כ̇ת̇ כי עם בציון ישב בירושלם
בכו לא תבכה חנן יחנך לקול זעקך כשמעתו
ענך בשם ייי צבחך הודך והדרך אל חונן יה
חי אל ישים שומך אמונה אזמר לך אשיר לך
אנא נ̇א̇ ח̇נ̇ך̇ י̇ה̇ ח̇ייי י̇א̇ו̇ י̇א̇י̇ י̇א̇י̇ י̇א̇י̇ י̇א̇י̇ י̇א̇י̇ י̇א̇י̇ י̇א̇י̇
י̇א̇י̇ י̇א̇ו̇ כתוב יתיה בטס והוי להון בנין ב̇
<u>ברוך מגן אברהם (*magic characters*)</u>
לאיתתא דלא תפיל כ̇ת̇ במגלת צבי ותלי
בדרעה דשמלא י̇א̇ו̇ י̇א̇ו̇ י̇א̇ו̇ א̇ו̇ י̇א̇
א̇ו̇ י̇א̇ י̇א̇ י̇א̇ י̇ו̇ ה̇י̇ ו̇ה̇י̇ ו̇י̇ו̇ ו̇י̇ו̇ י̇א̇ו̇ אמן א̇
אמן תצליח o לאתתא דמקשיא
למילד o

[4]

טול קליפא דלאבטיח ושחוק יתה יפה יפה
ועריב יתה במעט דבש ותשתה ותלד o
למאן דמידחל ומרתת כתוב ותלי עליה
אנטאל צעתיאל ננתאל עמיתאל צענתאל
שמנאל אתון אתיא נטרון למאן דילבש

6 הדין מן הא שעתה אמן o
7 לפתיחת לב ולשכחה
8 כתוב על ז̇ טרפין דהדס ומחוק יתהון
9 בחמר וישתי וישקי ניסטוקוס o o
10 בא בא בא תרמיוס ללסמס ארי גסף o
11 אתיהבית חוכמתא לחכימיא ואוריתא
12 לסוכלתן ובה נהרא עיני חשיכיא ואתפתח
13 לב כסילא כן ינהר ויתפתח ליבא דילי אנא
14 פל̈ ב̇ פל̇ שאלמוד תורה ואיתעסק בחוכמתא
15 שאלמוד תורה ולא אשכח בשמך אני קורא
16 מיטטרון שר הפנים שהוא שר שלתורה
17 עמיאל שמך כניניא שמך מיקון איטמון
18 פיסקון סטגרון שמך ששמך כשם רבך

Translation

page 1

(1:1) Thus said God, who sits among the cherubim, who sits in the ʿ*aravot*, (1:2) YHWH on (*magic names*). (1:3) These (words) should be written in the sea (?). Write upon (1:4) a new earthenware bowl, break it in two sherds, (1:5) throw one half in one direction and another half in the (1:6) other direction.

This amulet is (designated) for a barren woman. Write (1:7) on the hide of a deer and suspend it upon her. When she sleeps with her husband, (1:8) it should be under her head. When she washes in water she should place (1:9) it on a stand. These are the names that you should write: (*magic names*) (1:12-14) "Draw me, we will run after you. The king has brought me into his chambers, we will be glad and rejoice in you, we will remember your love more than wine, the upright love you" (Cant. 1:4). (1:15) All you holy characters, preserve the seed of N daughter of (1:16) N for life and duration until the end, Amen Amen Selah.

(1:17) One who wishes to open anything that is closed in the world should say (1:18) these names: "You I invoke, holy angels, (1:19) holy of the superior ones, ʿAniʾel, Paṭhiʾel, Qamsaniʾel,

page 2

(2:1) Gadgadiʾel, Ṣafṣafiʾel, Qanqaniʾel, Mamliʾel, Neriʾel, (2:2) Luḥiʾel,

Mishael, Berakhiʾel, Ḥaniʾel. You holy ones, (2:3) angels, come to my aid, give (?) me power and life, and give me (2:4) strength so that I should open this gate. In the name of Berakhiʾel (2:5) who stands and is appointed over the third firmament; in the name of (2:6) Sepasqiʾel who stands and is appointed over the fifth firmament; (2:7) in the name of Ḥuriʾel, who stands and is appointed over the fourth (2:8) firmament; in the name of Berukhiʾel, who stands and is appointed (2:9) over the fifth firmament; in the name of Saʿdiʾel, who stands (2:10) and is appointed over the sixth firmament, you, holy (2:11) angels, open for me this gate". Beat the lock (?) (2:12) with your foot, and say this verse: (2:12-14) "For lo, they are gone because of destruction. Egypt shall gather them up, Memphis shall bury them, the pleasant places for their silver, nettles shall possess them, thorns shall be in their tabernacles" (Hos. 9:6). (2:15) (*magic names*). (2:16) By the great name, say, the great pupil of the eye, to reprimand, (2:17) of the living God, whose voice is strong, **ʾsphwm** (2:18) **bdqwm**. Say it up to seven times.

(2:19) For a scorpion.

page 3

(3:1) El is upon your stings, Michael the great is upon your horns, (3:2) ponds of heaven (?) are upon your loins. God is your bonds, (3:3) and I carry you. Loops (?) to the serpent that created you. (3:4) The king that created you, **ʾlʾh** Adam Asriʾel, the garden (3:5) of Eden, O the garden of Eden.

For a barren woman (3:6) who has not given birth. Write: (3:6-7) "For the people shall dwell in Zion at Jerusalem. Thou shalt weep no more. He will be very gracious unto you at the voice of your cry. When He shall hear it, (3:8) He will answer you" (Is. 30:19). In the name of God. Your brightness (?), your glory and majesty. God give mercy, Yah (3:9) the living, El, (*magic words*), I shall make music for you, I shall sing to you. (3:10) (*magic letters*). (3:11) Write it on a plate and there will be to them sons. (3:12) Blessed be He who protects Abraham.

(3:13) For a woman, so that she should not have an abortion. Write on a scroll (from the hide) of a deer, and suspend it (3:14) on her left arm (*magic syllables*), (3:15) Amen (3:16) Amen. May she be successful.

For a woman who has a difficult (3:17) childbirth.

page 4
(4:1) Take the rind of a melon and pound it well, (4:2) and mix it with a little honey. She should drink it and give birth.

(4:3) For someone who has fears and shakes. Write and suspend upon him: (4:4-5) (***magic words***). You symbols, preserve him who wears (4:6) this from this hour (on). Amen.

(4:7) For the opening of the heart (i.e. for memory and understanding) and for (i.e. against) forgetfulness. (4:8) Write on 7 leaves of myrtle and wash it away with (4:9) wine, and let him drink it and give to drink. (4:9-10) (***magic words***). (4:11) Wisdom has been given to the wise and the law (4:12) to the intelligent. By it will the eyes of the luckless be illuminated, and (4:13) the heart of the fool will be opened. So will my heart be illuminated and opened, I, (4:14) N son of N, so that I may study the Torah and busy myself with wisdom, (4:15) that I may study the Torah and not forget. By your name I invoke, (4:16) Metatron the prince of the countenance, who is the prince of the Torah, (4:17) ʿAmiʾel is your name, Keninya is your name, Miqon, Iṭmon, (4:18) Pisqon, Saṭgaron is your name, for your name is the same as that of your lord.

Commentary

1:1 The epithet יושב הכרובים is attested several times in the Bible (e.g. 1 Sam. 4:4; Ps. 80:2). יושב ערבות seems to be a modification of רוכב בערבות (Ps. 68:5). The traditional Jewish understanding of ערבות is "heaven" (thus for example Ibn Ezra), and it is reasonable to assume that our writer took the phrase to mean someting like this. Modern commentators, following Ugaritic usage, understand the word to mean "clouds".

1:3 ניכתב בים is not clear. The whole sequence from כסוד מצולה may be a scribal corruption of a phrase.
כתיב is probably a corruption of כתוב.

1:9 דכין signifies a raised surface or stand in a kitchen or bath-house; cf. Tosefta Kelim Bava Qama 5:7, etc. (Jastrow, 306).

1:17 מסגר denotes "enclosure", but here it surely designates a locked-up room or the like.

לימא: For the form, which is Jewish Babylonian Aramaic, cf. Epstein 1960, p. 65.

2:3 הוו בסעדי: literally: "Be helpful to me"; in הוו לי *חיילי, הוו is evidently a mistake for הבו. חיי לי is wrongly divided for חיילי.

2:4 דנפחת is first person singular; see G6, p. 3:7, and commentary ad loc.

2:5f. The numbers given to the heavens are somewhat confused, and they are corrected by superlinear glosses. The translation gives the text as it stands, without the corrections.

2:11 והך קופל. If the translation is correct, *qufl* is Arabic "lock". As an alternative to the translation given, *qupal* could mean "scraping"; one might then possibly translate: "and as (you make a) scraping with your foot, you should say..."

2:12 האי פסוקא is written as one word.

2:18 אימא: For the form, which is again Jewish Babylonian Aramaic (cf. above p. 1:17), cf. Epstein 1960, p. 65.

3:1ff. Similar spells are in G14, p. 2; G24, p. 2:3ff. For אל the fuller expression אל שדי occurs in G14. The functions of Michael and Gabriel are reversed here in comparison to G14. The name Gabriel is distorted in our text to read גבי שמיא; it occurs as כפי שמיא in G24.

3:3 לוא לאו may be a corruption of לולאי or the like, but this is far from certain.

3:5 אי גינתא: Written as one word.

3:8 צבחך may be an unattested word meaning "brightness", perhaps by influence of Arabic *ṣubḥ*. Alternatively it could be viewed as a corruption of שבחך "your glory" or as a mistake for צבתך; *ṣibtā* means "cosmetics, beauty outfit".

3:12 ברוך מגן אברהם is one of the blessings of the ʿ*Amida* prayer.

4:1 דלאבטיח: Written דלא בטיח.

4:3 עליה: This form for the masculine is Babylonian usage, as opposed to עלוי in Palestinian Aramaic.

4:17 For מיקון איטמון פיסקון cf. G 14, p. 1:5ff. מיקון איטון איטימון רוחה פסקנית, where further references are given.

Geniza 12

T-S K 1.42

Amulet against ʿAlī b. Nūḥ the Ishmaelite

Plate 39

בשם שדי דברא שמיא
וארעא משביע אני עליכון
מלאכיא קדישיא שתבואו
ותסעדוני ותסמכוני ותחזקו
אותי ולא תעכבוני לעשות
עקירה וגרישה ונתיצה
ולשמיד ולאבד לעלי בן נח
שהו מדת הישמעאלי
בזו השעה הוא וכל העוזרים
לו o—o דׄ [בשם אהי יהא ה[ ]]
או (כאב) אמן o—o זה בשם רואה נסתרות
הוא רואה ועושה רצון יריאיו בשם נורא
נורא נורה נרור נורא נור יקף יקוף יקפיל
יקפואל יקוף יקף אתון השמות
הממונים על הרעה ועל כל דבר פשע
גרשו וטורדו והפרישו מכל בני אדם
וחוה מזכר ועד נוק(י)בה מזו המקום
לעלי הישמעאלי מזו האתר ולא יראה
לעולם בראיית אהבה כי אם בשנאה
גדולה ידחה ויוטרד מזו הבקעה
אשר הוא בה יקד יקוד וקד נור
בליביה כד יחזי זו המקום שידור
בו עלי הישמעאלי בׄאׄהׄוׄהׄ
באדירירון אמן ואמן ((נצח)) (סלה) למחר
במהרה אמן מזומן הדין כתבא
לעלי הישמעאלי דיהי מקולקל

27 ומטלטל ממקום למקום ולא יהיה
28 לו לעלי זה תקומה ולא יהי לו
29 קורות רוח ב<ז>ו הדירה אשר הוא
30 לתחת ולמקום אשר לקחו בגזלה
31 עד שילכו ויפלו במטה בחולי כל
32 ימיהם שהו יושב במקום אשר
33 גזלו במתיים בארבעים ושמנה אברים
34 שבגופו של עלי זה בשם שמ̅ע̅ מא̅ו̅ת
35 אב̅ר̅ מרא̅ו̅ת אמו̅מ̅ילות של צמ̅א̅ות
36 שפר̅מ̅ו שמר̅ו̅מ̅ה שלב̅א̅ות אבר̅ו̅מ̅ות
37 שלמ̅ו̅ת̅ה שלשיותה אתון שמיא
38 מפאריא רבא ותקיפא גרשו וטרדו
39 לעלי הרע הזה משכונתי ולא ישב
40 בו שעה אחת אלא יפול בחולי גדול לא
41 יאכל ולא ישתה ולא יישן עד שיצא
42 מן הדא אלאצטבל ואלמסנד באמ((ת))
43 שמה הגדול עקרוהו משכונתי
44 (*magic characters and figures*)
45 אמן ואמן
46 סלה

Translation

(1) In the name of Shaddai who created the heaven (2) and the earth. I adjure you, (3) holy angels, that you should come (4) and help me, and support me, and fortify (5) me, and not hold me back from doing (6) an uprooting, a chasing away, a crushing, (7) destroying, annihilating, of ʿAlī son of Nūḥ, (8) who is of the Ishmaelite religion, (9) at this hour, him and all those who help (10) him. In the name of ʾ**hy yh**ʾ **h...** (11) ... Amen. This is by the name of He who sees hidden things, (12) he sees and does the will of those who fear him. In the name of the fearsome, (13) fearsome, (*magic names*). (14) You, the names (15) that are appointed over evil and over all criminal things, (16) expel, banish and separate from all sons of Adam (17) and Eve, whether male or female, from this place, (18) ʿAlī the Ishmaelite, from this place. May he never (19) see love, but only great (20) hatred. May he be pushed away and expelled from this valley (21) where he is. May conflagration be made to burn (22) in his heart, when he sees this place where ʿAlī (23) the Ishmaelite resides (*magic words*) (24) Amen, Amen, Neṣaḥ Selah, tomorrow, (25) fast. Amen.

This writing is appointed (26) for ʿAlī the Ishmaelite, so that he may be cursed (?) (27) and wander from one place to another, and that there should be (28) no standing to this ʿAlī, and that he should have (29) no comfort in this dwelling which he has (30) taken (?), and the place which he has taken by robbery (31) until they go and fall to bed, in illness, all (32) the days of their lives, when he sits in the place which (33) he has robbed, with the 248 limbs (34) that are in the body of this ʿAlī. In the name of (*magic words*). (37) You glorified (38) names (?), great and mighty, expel and banish (39) this evil ʿAlī from my neighbourhood, so that he should not stay (40) there even one hour, but that he may fall ill with a serious illness, that he should not (41) eat or drink or sleep until he goes away (42) «from this stable and throne». By the truth (43) of his (?) great name, move him away from my neighbourhood. (*magic characters*). (45) Amen, Amen, (46) Selah.

Commentary

26 מקולקל: Probably an error for מקולל.

30 לתחת: Apparenly a mistake for לקחה.

37 שמיא: Probably a mistake for שמהתא.

38 רבא ותקיפא: Inconsistenly written in the singular, rather than in the plural.

43 שמה: For שמו, apparently by confusion of Hebrew and Aramaic.

Geniza 13

T-S K 1.57

Fragment from a book of magic recipes: For entering the presence of a sultan and for a safe journey

Plates 40-41

[1]

אי	ייי	ואו	אאי	אאו	זה	ווא	הה	הה

אמן אמן סלה תם: ללדכול עלי אלסלטאן

תקול ז̇ מראת ויעזרם ייי ויפלטם וג׳ אריא נהים

שליטא כביש אָסָאן אָסָא וּבִיסָא מלכיאל בלום
אמן אמן סלה תם: תפילת הדרך יהי רצון
ורחמים מלפניך ייי אלהי ואלהי אבותי שתוליכני
לשלום ותסמכני לשלום ותחזירני לביתי לשלום
לי אני פּבּפּ ותצילני מכף אויב ואורב בדרך
ותנני ותתניני לחן ולחסד ולרחמים בעני כל רואי
ברוך אתה ייי שומע תפילה בשם עיר מגדל שופט
מלך מסתיר יוצר בורא גואל רוגע קורא ייי ייי ייי
אלהים ויעבור ייי על פניו ויקרא ייי ייי אל רחום
וחנון ארך אפים ורב חסד ואמת נוצר חסד לאלפים
נושא עון בּ אֹ ייי הרוצה בתפילה גְבָר דִי פֶּלֶךְ
הְפַלְתִיאֵל ועליך (ג)רַא טוֹפָר גְדִיאל הְיָה ויה
יה אהיה אשר אהיה בשם אכתריאל יהיה
יה צבאות קדוש וישר שמו אברוּנָה אֲבַרְגוּנָה

[2]

שמו אֲבַרְגוּרְנָא שמו באילו השמות משביע
אני עליכם אתם מלאכים הקדושים שתטריחו
עצמכם בשבילי אני פּבּפּ ותעורון ותשגעון
ותסמון עין כל האנשים הרואים אותי תפל
עליהם אימתה ופחד בגדול זרועך ידמו כאבן
עד שאעבור אני פּבּפּ אעבור בשלום מעם זו
קניתה קניתה זו עם בשלום אעבור אני פּבּפּ
יעבור עד כאבן ידמו זרועך כגדול ופחד
אימתה עליהם תפל יבוש וזרועו תיבש ועין
ימינו כהה תכהה אמן אמן סלה אתון אתיה
אתיא קדישיא ושמהתא מפרשתא גמלון חינא
וחיסדא לי אני פּבּפּ באנפי כל דחזון יתי וש(ירו)ן
יתי בכל אתר דאנא אזיל מן בוש ומן ע(קא)
ומ(ן) שנ(אין) ומן שלט(נין) ומכל מזיק ומכל מילא
בישא דאית בעלמא מעתה ועד עולם
אֹאֹאֹסֹסֹ הללויה ויגב אן תאכד מעך
זֹ חציאת (ותכון קד) [   ] (מאשך ווגהך)

Translation

page 1

(1:1) (*magic words*). (1:2) Amen Amen Selah, end. «For entering into the presence of the sultan. (1:3) You should say seven times:» "And the Lord shall help them and deliver them" etc. (Ps. 37:40). The lion roars, (1:4) the ruler subdues. (*magic words*) (1:5) Amen, Amen, Selah, end.

Prayer for (setting out on) a journey. May there it be your will (1:6) and mercy, God, my lord and the lord of my ancestors, that you may guide me (1:7) in peace and that you may support me in peace and that you may bring me back to my home in peace, (1:8) me, N son of N, and that you may save me from the hand of an enemy and anyone who lurks on the way, (1:9) and that you may make me have grace, mercy and pity in the eyes of all those who watch me. (1:10) Blessed are you, God, who listens to prayer.

In the name of a fortified town, judge, (1:11) a king who puts in hiding (?), creator, fashioner, saviour, calmer, caller. YYY YYY YYY (1:12) the Lord. "And the Lord passed by before him and proclaimed, YYY YYY, God mercifdul (1:13) and gracious, longsuffering and abundant in goodness and truth. Keeping mercy for thousands, (1:14) forgiving iniquity" (Ex. 34:6-7). Blessed are you, who desires prayer. Gevar di Pelekh (1:15) Hapalti᾿el, and upon you, Gera Topar Gedi᾿el, HYH WYH (1:16) YH, I-am-that-I-am. In the name of Akatriel YHYH (1:17) YH Sabaoth, holy and righteous is his name, Abruna Abarguna

page 2

(2:1) is his name, Abargurna is his name. By these names I adjure (2:2) you, holy angels, that you should trouble (2:3) yourselves on my account, me, N son of N, and blind, drive mad, (2:4) and shut the eye of all people who see me. "May (2:5) fear and dread fall upon them; by the greatness of your arm they shall be as still as a stone" (Ex. 15:16) (2:6) till I pass, (I), N son of N, I pass in peace, of "the people that you have purchased" (*ibid.*). (2:7-8) (*The words of the whole passage are repeated backwards.*) (2:9) May he dry up, and may his arm dry, and his right (2:10) eye become dim, Amen, Amen, Selah. You holy (2:11) characters and outspoken names, cause grace (2:12) and mercy to me, I, N son of N, in the eyes of all who watch me and who observe (?) (2:13) me in every place where I am going, from sickness and from trouble (2:14) and from haters and from <evil> rulers and from every causer of harm, and from all evil (2:15) thing that is in the world from now to eternity (2:16) Amen Amen Amen Selah Selah Selah Hallelujah. «You should take with you (2:17) seven pebbles and ... and your face ...»

Geniza 14

T-S K 1.58

From a book of magic recipes: For shutting the mouths of enemies, for repelling scorpions

Plates 42-43

[1]

1 אְלֹהָיו
2 לסיכור ד(פ)[ומה]
3 אמור זמנין ג̄ על תרעה
4 כד בעית תיעול
5 מִיקוֹן אִיטוֹן אִיטִימוֹן
6 רוּחָה פְּסַקְנֵית̄ זֵיָן[ ]
7 רַבָּה פְּרַנגל(ף) אתון
8 שמהתָה קדישָׁיָּה
9 (סכורו) פמיהון דכָ̄ל מן
10 דעלל באלֵין תרעייה
11 תמת

[2]

1 לטרד אלעקרב תקול
2 עַקְרבָּ̄ה עַקְרבֿונִיתָה
3 אֵל שָׁדָי עַל עוֹקְצָיִךְ̄
4 וגַבְרִ̄יאַל עַל קַרְנֹתַיִךְ̄
5 וְמִיכָ̄אֵל עַל מַתְנֹתַיִךְ̄
6 מִן כְּדֹוֹן ועַד̄ לְעוֹלָם
7 אָמֵן אָמֵן סֶלָה
8 חורן לרחשה תקול
9 חור צמיד̄ צַמִיד̄ חור
10 חור כוכֿב חוורַן

[3]

1 ממעיף מעופפת (הן) הן
2 סב מנגיח קדוש קדוש
3 יחושים הן הן שניתן
4 לרפואה לכל בשר ודָם
5 אמן אמן סלה
6 והוּ יכתב פי גאם וימחא
7 ויסקא לצאחב אלוגע מן
8 אי אלאוגאע כאן יִברַא

9 וללמגנון ואלמצדוע
10 והדא לאבטַאל אלסחר
11 נאפע מגרב תכתב

[4]

1 (מפר אותות) [בדים] וקוסמים
2 יהולל משיב חכמים אחור
3 ודַעְתָּם יְסַכֵּל: ותקל בה
4 אחסיה יחוש זׂא יפף
5 אחסיה יחש כבגז
6 אחס(יה יחוש (*magic characters*)
7 אחסיה יחוש ف غر نح
8 והו יכתב פי גאם וימחא
9 באלמא וישרב ויגֿסל
10 וגהה ובדנה מנה תֿם
11 יכתב ויעלק עליה מגרב
12 נאפע גיד תם

Translation

page 1

(1:1) … (1:2) For shutting (someone's) mouth. (1:3) Say thrice over his gate (1:4) when you wish to enter: (1:5-7) (*magic words*) You (1:8) holy names, (1:9) shut the mouth of every one (1:10) who enters these gates. (1:11) «End.»

page 2

(2:1) «To expel a scorpion say:» (2:2) "Scorpion, female scorpion, (2:3) El Shaddai over your stings, (2:4) Gabriel over your horns, (2:5) Michael over your loins, (2:6) from now to eternity. (2:7) Amen, Amen, Selah."

(2:8) Another one, for a reptile. «Say,» (2:9-3:3) [*Untranslatable formula.*]

page 3

… (3:3) that was given (3:4) for remedy for every human being, (3:5) Amen Amen Selah. (3:6) «It should be written on a cup and washed, (3:7) and be given to drink to a patient (3:8) of any ailment whatever, and he will heal, (3:9) as well as to a madman and one who suffers from headache.»

(3:10) «And this, for annulling the effect of magic, (3:11) is useful, well-tried, you should write:»

page 4
(4:1-3) "That frustrates the tokens of the liars, and makes diviners mad, that turns wise men backward and makes their knowledge foolish" (Is. 44:25). «And you should say over it:» (4:4-7) (*magic words*) (4:8) «He should write (it) on a cup, wash it (4:9) with water, drink it, and wash (4:10) his face and body with it, and then (4:11) write and suspend over (himself). Well-tried, (4:12) beneficial, effective. Finished.»

Commentary

1-2 Several words have Arabic equivalents written over them in Arabic characters.

1:5-6 מיקון איטון איטימון רוה פסקנית: Cf. T-S K 21.95 L, published in Schäfer 1984, p. 136, 2a:10-12, ובא מיטטרון שניקרא שמו איטמון פיסקון רוח פיסק(ונ)ית סנגרון סיגרון מיקון מיטון אסטס הסטס הסקוס (to be read thus). Somewhat more explicit is the explanation offered to these words in another fragment: [א]ני הוא סניגרון פיסקון איטמון סניגרון שני סוגר דברים מלמעלן ואני הוא פסניק פיסקון שני פוסק דברין כסנהדרין אטמון שהכל נאטמין מלפני (T-S K 21.95 A, published in Schäfer 1984, p. 177. Our reading deviates in some points from the printed edition). The speaker is apparently רוח פיסקון "the spirit of Pisqon", mentioned earlier, and it says, among other things: "I am Sanigron, Pisqon, Iṭmon, Sanigron, who [read: *še-ani*] closes things from above, and I am Pasniq Pisqon, who decides in matters like the Sanhedrin, [and I am] Aṭmon, i.e. everyone is closed up in front of me". The etymological interpretations given to these words fit in with their invocation here, where they are meant to "shut the mouth" of one's opponent. In Bavli Sanhedrin 44a we have פסקון איטמון סיגרון. Cf. also *Tan ḥuma Vezot* 6. Similar names occur also in Schäfer 1988, p. 142, §628, to which cf. the notes on p. 128.

2:9 This is a palindrome; cf. Naveh 1988, pp. 40-41.

Geniza 15

T-S K 1.80

Formulae for overcoming one's enemies, for divination, and for other purposes

Plates 44-45

[1]

1 ויעשו ודבר אותו בשם אדוני {משב[יע]}
2 משביע אני עליכם עבדיאל דעבוד
3 מורא דימא רבא כטריאל דעבוד
4 כרם דגהינם רהטיאל דמרהט
5 כוכבי שמייא אשביעת עליכון
6 שתעבדון ותאסרון ותרהטון ותהפכון
7 ותי(כ)בשון ית כל אויביי ושונאי אנא
8 פל ב פ דלא יקומון ולא יהלכון ולא יאמרון
9 ולא יחשבון ולא ימללון עלי מילה בישה וכל
10 חרשיהון יתבטלון ואין בעיתה מלחוש
11 על משחא דמיא וחמר ויהמון מיינוקייא
12 גנבתא דאתגנבתה והנון (ח)מיי לך בן]   [
13 ומן גנסה ואן על בעל דבבה]   [
14 להלוך הרבה
15 כתוב ותלי על רגל ימין ואן]   [
16 תמוניאל (*magic characters*)]   [
17 חודש ימים]   [

[2]

1 יתן על פבפ ובשם מיכאל וגבריאל
2 ורפאל ונוריאל ואוריאל כבשיאל
3 יה יה יה יה יה יה
4 יהו יהו יהו יהו יהו יהו
5 (*magic characters*)

אהה אהה
אהה אהה
אהה אהה
אהה

6 אתון מלאכייא קדישיא וכל קיטרייא
7 ושבחיא (!) הבו חינא וחיסדא לפבפ
8 באפי כל שולטנין ורברבין גוברייא
9 [ונש]ייא ויכבשון קדמי כל בני אדם

10 [וכל בנ]ת חוה ולא ימללון עמי פתגם
11 [ביש אמן אמן] סלה הללויה ותלה אותו
12 [ ] קמיע זה
13 [ ](ד) המזוזה

Translation

page 1

... (1:1) and they shall do, and you should talk to him. In the name of Adonai, (1:2) I adjure you, ʿAvdiel, who made (1:3) the fear of the great sea, Kaṭriel, who made (1:4) the vineyard of Hell, Rahaṭiel, who causes (1:5) the stars of the sky to run, I adjure you (1:6) that you should work and bind and cause to run and overturn (1:7) and subdue all my enemies and fiends, I, (1:8) N son of N, that they should not stand up and not walk and not speak (1:9) and not think and not utter against me one evil word, and all (1:10) their magic be annulled.

And if you wish to say a spell (1:11) over an ointment of water and wine, and the children (1:12) will see the theft that was stolen from you, and they will be seeing (things) for you in the[ ] (1:13) and from his family (?). And if [...] against the enemy [...].

(1:14) To walk much. (1:15) write and suspend from the right foot and ... (1:16) Temuniel (*magic characters*) (1:17) a month.

page 2

(2:1) And he should put it on N son of N, and in the name of Michael, Gabriel, (2:2) Raphael, Nuriel, Uriel, Kabshiel, (2:3) YH (7 ×), 'HH (7 ×), (2:4) YHW (7 ×) (2:5) (*magic characters*). (2:6) You, holy angels and praised (2:7) characters, give grace and favour to N son of N (2:8) in the eyes of all the rulers, the grandees, men (2:9) and women, that they may subdue before me all sons of Adam (2:10) and all daughters of Eve, and that they should not speak to me an evil (2:11) word, Amen Amen Selah, Hallelujah, and suspend it (2:12) ... this amulet ... (2:13) the door-post.

Commentary

The text is badly written, and contains numerous mistakes.

1:10–13 This passage deals with a divination by means of water and oil, in which a young child is used as a medium who is capable of seeing the person responsible for a theft. See שרי מים ושרי שמן in Daiches 1913.

2:7 ושבחיא for משבחיא.

Geniza 16

T-S K 1.91 + K 1.117
(Pp. 1-4 are from T-S K 1.91; pp. 5-8 are from K 1.117)
Formulae for healing, for sleep, for making peace between a man and his wife, etc.
Plates 46-48

[1]

1 קדישתא ואתון מלאכיא מיכאל וגבריאל שימו בגופו
2 ובכל איבריו רפואה ובירא [ב]שם מרירירין
3 בניו נביב גבר גביב ברורידין דלהב לביב
4 הסר הביב גיבוריירון וסב נביב מפ מפירין
5 תפתפירין צב צביב תב תביב הסירו ממתים
6 וארבעים וש[מונה] אברים כל כאב וכל צער וכל מרעין
7 בישין באהיה אשר אהיה באל יהוה שדי ייי צבאות
8 עמנו משגב לנו אלהי יעקב סלה ייי צבאות עמו אלהי
9 יעקב סלה o לשינה
10 קח ביצה בת יומה וכ[ת] עלה | אופיה | אופיה |
11 | ומזם ימום | והב תחות ראשון וכן אמ רבו
12 שנתיה לפ בר פל דידמוך בפריע
13 אאס o
14 לעשות שלום בין איש לאשתו כתוב על קלף צבי
15 ועלקה ללרגל עלי עצדה אלימין וללמרה עלי אל[ ]
16 והא ה(דא) אכתב | יתירים | יכבש | [ ]כיכון |
17 | בשמא | יאר | אמיר | [ ]אור | כתתו | כבוס |
18 | אמיה סוף | אסס יהה | *(three "seals of David")*
19 *(six "seals of David" and another magic symbol)*

[2]

1 לולד ימות במעי אימו כת עלי טאס דנחשא

2 או דהבֿ או אנכֿ צא צא אנא ויצא ויצא

3 ולדודיתא זזוזיתא פוק פוק באלין שמהתא

4 הֿבֿהֿרֿוֿרֿיֿרֿיֿתֿאֿ באלין אותואתא בלא

5 לעכב בלֿ לעֿ בלֿ לעֿ

6 בפריע בפֿ ש׳ד׳ [ ]שדודיתא

7 אמן אמן סלה וקיטוריה ואי זרעא

8 כ(מ)ונא דכורתא

9 דאוכמא דלפתורא

10 ודמנהון

---

12 לאיתתא דיתעכב שליתה

13 מומי אנא מלך שליתא דתיתשדי מְמְעַיָהָ

14 דאנתתא דא פלֿ ב פֿ בשמא הדין

15 [ ]תיאל ואומותיאל ופופותיאל

16 באן [ ] באה וה באה וה קינולגיה

17 אמן סלה בפריע ו[קי]טוריה לבונה או מיעה

18 ואב(ק)ה כתֿוֿ [י]תיה בזכוכיתא או בנחשא

19 ותמחוק יתיה ותשתי מעט מעט o

[3]

1 ל(ח)ל אלמעקוד

2 יכתב עלי ורק נאר וישרב בנביד והדא אלדי

3 תכתבה (*magic figures*)

4 (*magic figures*) יֿאֿוֿ יֿאֿוֿ יֿהֿ הֿוֿהֿ הֿאֿ

5 מֿאֿ הֿאֿ אֿהֿ לֿהֿףֿ אתון אתיא קדישיא וכל

6 קטיריא שרין וכשרין לגידא רביא דפל׳ בן פל׳

7 דמשמש בין עטמתה אֿאֿסֿ

---

8 למסכר פומא

9 משבע אנא ואסרנא ובלימנא ומסכרנא ומטרשנא

10 לבהון דכל בני אנשא וחוה דלא ינזקון יתי אנא

11 פלֿ בן פלֿ להקיאל המלאך הגדול שהוא ממונה

12 על אהבה הוא יחוס על פלֿ בן פלֿ בצאתו בבואו

13 בשכבו ובקומו בשם שם רב אגוקט

14 טגאט פגאט דהוא אחד ושמו כתוב

15 אתן אץ שמו עלא אבגדהוזחטיכך

16 למסנןסעפףצץקרשת . תץ שמו ובשם

[4]

Page seems to be erased

[5]

פתיחת לב אמור על כָּסָא דהבדלה
גֿ פעמים ושתה אותו אֿדֿרֿנֿוֿסֿ אֿבֿרֿינֿוֿסֿ
חֿיֿקֿקֿאֿל פֿתֿחֿיֿאֿל חֿוֿקֿקֿיֿאֿל דחקק אלין[ ]
באוריתא פֿתֿחֿיֿאֿל דפתח מילי אוריתא
פתחון לבי אנא פֿ בן פֿ ל(תו)רה לחכמה ולבינה
וכל מה שאשמע אלמד במהרה וכל שאלמד
לֹא אשכח לעולם ברוך אתה ייי למדני חקיך.
אדא האגֿ אלבחר תכתב הדה אלאסמא אלמקדסה
פי אנא פכֿאר גדיד ותטרחה פי אלבחר והדה
אלאסמא: | דג | קפילמציה | בוקטו | יופים |
| דג | קפי | מציה | בוקטו | יופים |
ללסע אלעקרב אכתב עלי אלוגע
אקרוס
קרוס
רוס
וס
ס

[6]

Most of the upper part of the page was erased

ללצדאע
אבלה בלא אבלה בלא בלא אבלה לא בלה
אבלא אבלא בלא אבלא לא אבלא א אבלא אבלא
אבלא לפֿ בן פלֿ בלא לא וא סלה : о

[7]

שלוח אש.
כתוב בדם עוף על שמך חייא וקיימא בשמך
דברת רוח סערה בימא וביבשתא קֿוֿרֿ קֿרֿ קֿיֿרֿ
צֿיֿרֿ צֿרֿ בשם חי ייי צבאות ייי יֿהֿ יושב הכרובים
שלח זיקין מן זיקך ונור מן נורך ככתוב
בתורה יככה ייי בשחפת ובקדחת ובדלקת
ובחרחור וגֹ כן יכה את פֿ בן פֿ כמה שנ׳
ארבעים יכנו לא יוסיף פן יוסיף להכותו על אלה

מכה רבה וג׳ כתוב על פומא דקוניצא יעני
ראס ⟦קצבה⟧} בניקה דלך אלרגל וטמור יתיה
בקבר או קדם תרעיה דבית שנאך. יוכתב
פי קמיץ עדוה בדם טיר.

לחסד ולשלטון
חסד ואמת נפגשו צדק ושלום נשקו. כתוב
והב בשמאלך. כי ארך ימים ושנות חיים ושלום
יוסיפו לך. כי לוית חן הם לראשך וענקים לגרגרותיך
כי בי ירבו ימיך ויוסיפו לך וג׳ ושמר ייי אלהיך לך וג׳

[8]

The writing that was on this page has been erased

Translation

page 1

(1:1) holy [...] and you angels, Michael and Gabriel, put in his body (1:2) and in all his limbs cure and heal[th. In the] name of (*a sequence of magic names*) (1:5) remove from the two hundred (1:6) forty eight limbs all pain, all affliction and all bad (1:7) illnesses. By I-am-who-I-am, by the God YHWH Shaddai YY Sabaoth (1:8) is with us, the God of Jacob, Selah (Ps. 46:8, 12). YY Sabaoth is with him, the God (1:9) of Jacob, Selah.

For sleep. (1:10) Take an egg which has been laid on the same day, and write on it: (*magic names*), (1:11) and place it under his head, and say thus: "Increase (1:12) the sleep of N son of N, so that he may sleep at once, (1:13) Amen, Amen, Selah, Selah.

(1:14) To make peace between a man and his wife. Write on the hide of a deer (1:15) «and hang it on the man on his right arm, and on a woman on her [...]. (1:16) And this is that which you should write: » (*magic words*).

page 2

(2:1) For a child who dies in his mother's belly. Write «on» a plate of copper (2:2) or gold or lead: Go out, go out, please, and he has gone out, he has gone out (2:3) (*magic words*). Go out, go out by these names (2:4) (*magic names*) by these symbols without (2:5) delay (*repeated in abbreviated form two times more*), at once, at once, at once (2:7) Amen,

Amen, Selah. (2:7-10, ***in two columns:***) And its perfuming is (by means of) black cumin, [... ?], or the seed of ... (?).

(2:12) For a woman whose afterbirth is delayed. (2:13) I adjure the angel of the afterbirth, that you should be ejected from the belly (2:14) of this woman, N daughter of N, by this name: (*magic names, ending with* **qynwlgyh**), (2:17) Amen Selah, at once. Its perfuming is frankincense or «desiccated (2:18) intestines» (?). Write it on a glass or copper (2:19) and wash it off, and she should drink a little at a time.

page 3
(3:1) «To release someone who is bound. (3:2) Let him write on a leaf of a pomegranate, and drink in wine. This is what you should (3:3) write:» (*magic figures and letters*) (3:5) You, holy symbols and char(3:6)acters, loosen and make fit the big (?) sinew of N son of N (3:7) that performs among his bones. Amen Amen Selah.

(3:8) To shut (someone's) mouth. (3:9) I adjure, bind, restrain, shut, and obstruct (3:10) the heart(s) of all sons of man and (daughters of) Eve, that they may not harm me, I, (3:11) N son of N. Lahaqiʾel, the great angel who is appointed (3:12) over love, may he have mercy on N son of N as he goes out and comes in, (3:13) as he lies down and stands up. In the name of the great name (*magic names*), (3:14) who is one, and whose name is written (3:15) (*magic names, including the full sequence of the alphabet*), (3:17) and in the name ...

page 5
(5:1) Opening of heart. Say over a cup of *Havdala* (5:2) thrice, and drink it. (*magic names, including*) Petaḥiel, Ḥoqeqiel, for (he?) has carved ... (5:4) in the Torah, Petaḥiel, for he has opened the words of the Torah, (5:5) open my heart, I, N son of N, for Torah, wisdom, and understanding. (5:6) May I learn quickly every thing that I shall hear, and may I (5:7) never forget that which I shall learn. Blessed are you, God, teach me your decrees.

(5:8) «If the sea is swollen, write these holy names (5:9) on a new earthenware vessel, and throw it into the sea. These are the (5:10) names:» (*magic names*).

(5:12) «For the stinging of a scorpion, write over the pain(ful spot)»:

(5:13-17) (***magic names, consisting of the word ʾ*qrws *in five lines, in each successive line one further letter being omitted***).

page 6

(6:1) «For a headache.» (6:2-4) (***magic names***) to N son of N, (***magic names***) Selah.

page 7

(7:1) Causing fire. (7:2) Write with the blood of a fowl: "By your name, the living and the existent. By your name, (7:3) (you) who have created stormy wind on the sea and on dry land (***magic names***). (7:4) In the name of "As the Lord of Hosts lives" (1 Kings 18:15, etc.), Yah who dwells between the cherubim, (7:5) send off sparks from your sparks and fire from your fire, as it is written (7:6) in the Torah: "The Lord shall smite you with a consumption and with a fever and with an inflammation (7:7) and with an extreme burning" etc. (Dt. 28:22), so shall he smite N son of N as it is written: (7:8) "Forty stripes shall he give him, and shall not exceed, for, if he should exceed and beat him above these (7:9) with many stripes" etc. (Dt. 25:3). Write on the edge of a ...(?), «i.e. (7:10) the head of the ["reed" *crossed out*] gore of the shirt of that man,» and bury it (7:11) in a tomb or in front of the gate of the house of your enemy. «It should be written (7:12) on the shirt of his enemy with the blood of a chicken.»

(7:13) For (finding) grace and for (achieving) authority. (7:14) "Mercy and truth are met together. Righteousness and peace have kissed each other" (Ps. 85:11). Write (it) (7:15) and put (it) on your left (hand). "For length of days and long life and peace (7:16) shall they add to you" (Pr. 3:2). "For they shall be an ornament of grace unto your head, and chains about your neck" (Pr. 1:9). (7:17) "For by me your days shall be multiplied, and the years of your life shall be increased" (Pr. 9:11). "And the Lord your God shall keep unto you (the covenant and the mercy)" (Dt. 7:12), etc.

Commentary

1:2 ובירא: Evidently an error for ובריאות.

1:11 ראשון is an error for ראשו.
רבו is an error for הבו.

2:1 עלי: The scribe slips into Arabic in the middle of a Hebrew phrase, and moves over to Aramaic. Among other instances of a confusion of languages, דהב in line 2 is an Aramaic form, but one would expect דהבא. The writer may have been influence by the Arabic word, which has the same graphic appearance.

2:7-10 The recipe given here is hard to understand. It seems that the scribe did not understand the recipe in the *Vorlage* from which he copied and treated it as a sequence of magic words.

2:13 מלך could alternatively be "king".

2:16 קינולגיה: Cf. note to G22, 1:15, where the text is קינו קינו אמן. G18, 9:5 has קני as a magic word.

3:1 מעקוד, literally "bound", may signify "one who is under a sorcerer's spell", cf. Dozy 1927, II, p. 148b s.v. *ʿaqada siḥran*, and perhaps even more specifically "impotent because of a charm", as an abbreviation of the expression *maʿqūd ʿani-l-nisāʾ*, cf. Dozy 1927, II, p. 151b. The second possibility may be supported by the expression גידא רביא in 3:6; cf. the note there.

3:2 נאר: written seemingly like גאר.

3:6 שרין וכשרין: An error for שרון וכשרון.
גידא רביא: The translation offered is based on the assumption that רביא is an error for רבא; however, if the spelling is correct, the expression may mean "the sinew that grows". This could be a reference to a specific organ. Cf. note to 3:1.

3:9 בלימנא: Cf. for this verb G19, 1:3.

5:1 The expression "opening of heart" refers to the ability to study and retain the Torah.
"A cup of *Havdala*" recalls the various magic formulae connected with the idea of the *Havdala* (the blessing which marks the end of the Sabbath, and which serves to distinguish the Sabbath from weekdays). For a prominent example of this kind of magical composition cf. Scholem 1980/1.

7:3 דברת seems like a badly written דבראת.

7:9 קוניצא: The word is so far unattested. Assuming that this is not a miswritten קמיצא, which is unlikely (קמיץ is an Arabic, not an Aramaic word), one may think of a word like קינסא (apparently a variant of קיסא)

"piece of wood, chip", which may have been initially in the mind of the glossator who wrote קצבה "reed". He then crossed it out to write בניקה instead.

Geniza 17

T-S K 1.132

Recipes for divination, for being influential, for ease of learning, and for other purposes

Plates 49-52

[1]

1 פתיחת לב כתוב ומחוק במים
2 ותלוש באותם המים קמח שעורים
3 ותעשה ממנו שלוש עוגות ותאכל
4 מהם בכל יום עוגה אחת בכל יום
5 קודם הלימוד וזה אשר תכתוב
6 אַסְסְתוֹן קַטְרְ(.)וֹן פַּטְרְסוֹן
7 מַטְרִירוֹן שטוטירון חנונירון
8 [...] קַמְסָא טַנְמְרוּקִין

---

9 [לאה](בה)
10 קח עלה תאנה וכתוב עליה ותשרה
11 אותו במים ותשקם לשניהם וזה אשר
12 תכתוב אענונון אמנונין
13 אמסתא קמסתא גנדודין אש((ב))עית
14 עליכון אתון מלאכין קדישין שתתנו

In the margin:

15 אהבת פל' הנולד מן פל' בלב פל' הנול<ד> מן פל' ואם לא תוכל להשקותם
16 שפוך אותו על אם דרך שהם עתידין לעבור

[2]

1 פתיחת לב
2 קח קערה חדשה ותכתוב
3 ג' ימים בכל יום אלו השימות

4 ותרחוץ אותו במים ותשתה
5 וזה אשר תכתוב

6	אשדרון	אשקרון	אשקטרון
7	חנטתא	טנמירא	[ ]
8	שנמא	אתמנא	[ ]

9 לשנאה
10 כתוב על ביצה בת יומה ותשרה אותו
11 במים ותשפוך אותו על אם הדרך
12 שהם עתידין לעבור. וזה אשר
13 תכתוב אַסְמְסָא שַׁצְצָסָא קַצְטְרָא

In the right-hand margin:

14 עזבובון טראובון אשבעית עליכון אתון
15 שדין ואלילין במה דאתון דחלין מניה דתשרון
16 סנאה ואבה וריב בין פל ובין פל אאס ס

Between lines 1 and 2, in a different direction:

אשרי האיש / אשר לא הלך / בעצת רשעים / ובדרך חטאים / לא עמד ובמושב

In the margin above:

גם יו׳ הסיר חטאתך / לא תמות

[3]

1 אם בקשת לדע[ת]
2 אם תתעבר האשה
3 ואם לא כתוב בקלף
4 צבי עדנאל סרבנאל
5 ( )נמניאל רחמיאל יהביאל
6 שעמאל חנמאל אשבעית
7 [ע]ליכון אתון מלאכין
8 קדישין שתודיעוני רזא
9 הדין: ותשים אותו
10 בחיק האשה ולא תרגיש היא
11 ואם תצחוק עד חצי שעה דע כי
12 תתעבר ואם לאו לא.

[4]

1 בשם גׄנׄבׄ צׄוׄבׄיׄהׄ צׄחׄבׄיׄןׄ נׄיׄגׄבׄ צׄתׄיׄןׄ יׄהׄ צׄבׄאׄ חׄיׄ יׄהׄ
2 הׄוׄהׄ הׄוׄאׄ ברוך שם כבוד מלכותו לעולם ועד אתון

3 שמהתא קדישא אסרון לי עיניהון דכל בני אנשא
4 מלמחזי יתי אנא וכל אשר עמי יפלו במכמריו
5 רשעים יחד עד שאעבור בשלום תפול עליהם
6 אימתה ופחד אימתה עליהם תפ((ו))ל מזומן הדין קמיעא
7 לאצלא מן לסטיא ומן כל אינש ביש ומן אריותא ומן
8 חיותא בשיא ומן כל מדעם ביש בשם ס̇ט̇ מ̇ח̇ ב̇ה̇
9 אדרירון ה̇ה̇ ס̇ל̇ מ̇ח̇ ש̇ש̇ ה̇י̇ח̇ ב̇ה̇ ה̇ה̇ ב̇א
10 ה̇כ̇ס̇א̇ נ̇ו̇ך̇ א̇ו̇י̇ב̇ ה̇ב̇ה̇ ב̇א̇ה̇ב̇ה̇ צ̇י̇( ) ב̇י̇ה̇ ב̇ה̇
11 נ̇צ̇ב̇י̇א̇ ה̇ה̇ה̇ א̇ל̇א̇ל̇ אמן אמן סלה
12 אכתובהא פי רק אלגזאל
13 וחטהא פי עוד אללוז

[5]

1 [...]
2 לאהבה (...)
3 (.)ן תבוא [...] שם אדם ותעשה (ובבית)
4 (י)ש בה ד̇ פתחים ותיכנס עליהם (...)ל [...]
5 [...] וכן [...]
6 לעשות ביניהם אהבה מבגדיהם ומש(ער)
7 ראשיהם או מצפרניהם או מן הע(ו)ר [...]
8 ותחיל ותאמר על אלו הרוחות של ספרן[...]
9 (ובתוך) דבריך תאמר שמעיני אש ולהבה [...]
10 (בן) (פלוני) [ב פל] לפל̇ ב̇ן פל̇ [...]
11 [...] שלהם ו(ת)זכיר
12 [...]בה בתוך דבריך שתתע(...)
13 (והיב) [...] על (פלוני בן פלוני ותא[...]
14 [...]
15 בידיך [...]לם
16 מאכלם [...] הם
17 או באחריהם [...] שתהיה אהבה [...]
18 עד שימותו זה על אהבה. ותולה [...]

[6]

1 תאמר א̄י̄ ס̄ר̄כ̄ג̄ וא[י] (חנ)סא אלו̄ח̄א̄ [אל]ו̄ח̄א̄ אנ̄ה̄
2 [ ] אואנה בוקץ ואנה [...]קשא [...]ה שמרון
3 אשביעת עליכון בנקנא ו(חוחת) ו[מר]קת שתביאו לי
4 כעת [...אם] (הוא) [י](ש)ן

5 הקיצוהו ואם הו יושב העמידוהו והביאוהו אלי
6 ואל תסירו את דעתו מיעליו ותרצה שתאמר אותו
7 שלשה פעמים ותשים על הגחילים את הקטורת
8 עם סמרטוט מבגדיהם או ש(ע)ריהם כול והזכר
9 [דבר]ים של הב׳ בדבריך ואם יבאו [ ] באותה
10 שעה דע כי בא דעתו מ(בולבל)ת [...] כחפצך
11 ואם תרצה לאחזרו ה[ ]
12 (לא י)בוא לך כבה את הגיח(לין)[...]
13 שתר(צה) והם יבואו א[ליך ...] לברנש
14 [...]
15 [...] או מהלך
16 [...] יונית
17 [...] הנדי וקחיהו
18 [...] (לפתיחת חלום) [...] חצות

[7]

1 ועמוד כנגד השמש שיהייו אחוריך אל השמש
2 והמראה בידיך ופני המראה כנגד השמש
3 ותביט בה בעיניך בחזק והשמר וחזה
4 בכל כחך שלא תעצם עיניך ולא תסתמם
5 והתחזק יפה יפה בכל כחך ואפלו אם יורדות
6 דמאעות מעיניך אל תעצומם ואל תסתמם
7 כי אמנם מצהיבות {המארה} המראה ומכוח
8 (כ)זוהר השמש יתפחדו עיניך ויתבלבלו אלא יתחזק
9 כי איש חיל שכן צוה מר והתחזקך להביט בה
10 אז תראה האיש אשר תתאוה ותבקש ותראה
11 כל מ[ה שבקש]ת עושה כך בתחלה תשביע על המ((ר))אה
12 ותאמר [ ] השטן שתראה לי פלוני בן פלונית
13 ואז תביט בשעה אחת ותראיהו וזה הו מקיים:
14 אם בקשתה שיהייו דבריך נשמעים לפני העם
15 או לפני {ש}שר {ושופט} ושופט אמור אלין פסוקי
16 האזינו השמים וג יערף כמטר וגם כי שם
17 ייי אקרא ואמור משביע אני עליכם שמות
18 הקדושים שבהם הוכיח משה את בני ישראל
19 במדבר שתעשו את דברי נשמעים בעיני העם

[8]

הזה או בעיני פל̇ ויהיו דברי נראים בשם | הִי | אף | זי
יר | נס | וא | הץ | שר | ((מא)) | יה | מע | וס | [ ] | אש | דת | בו
רה | ובשם | יי | עת ((דר)) | פס | כא | מל | טט | רב | לל | קז
חית | כבר | שש | סע | יד | דל | כם | מע | עם | לי | יב | די
שב | אר | זכ | ובשם | כו | יז | שי | מה | יהוה | אל | קא
דל | אל | הד | בוג
קולי אל אל ייי אקרא ויענני מהר קדשו סלה בׄשׄכׄמׄלׄוׄ
אׄאׄאׄ סׄסׄסׄ הללויה: סלה: קיבוץ שידים קטר לבונה

Translation

page 1
(1:1) The opening of the heart. Write and wash off with water, (1:2) and in the same water you should knead a dough of barley, (1:3) and make three cakes from it, (1:3) and eat from them every day, a cake a day, (1:5) before studying. This is what you should write: (1:6-8) (*magic names*).

(1:9) [For love.] (1:10) Take a leaf of a fig tree, write on it, immerse (1:11) it in water, and let both of them drink from it. This is what (1:12) you should write: (*magic names*), (1:13) I adjure you, (1:14) you, holy angels, that you should give (1:15) love for N born of N in the heart of N born of N. If you cannot let them drink it, (1:16) pour it over the road through which they are about to walk.

page 2
(2:1) (For) opening of the heart. (2:2) Take a new bowl and write (2:3) for 3 days, every day these names, (2:4) wash it with water, and drink. (2:5) This is what you should write: (2:6-8) (*magic names*).

(2:9) For hate. (2:10) Write on an egg laid on the same day, immerse it (2:11) in water, pour it over the road (2:12) where they are about to pass. This is (2:13) what you should write: (2:13-14) (*magic names*). (2:14) I adjure you, you (2:15) demons and idols with that of which you fear, that you should place (2:16) hatred, enmity and strife between N and N, Amen, Amen, Selah.

(2:*between lines 1 and 2*) "Happy is the man that does not take the wicked for his guide, nor walk the road that sinners tread, [nor take his] seat..." (Ps 1:1).

(2:*in the margin above*)... "The Lord has laid on another the consequences of your sin. / You shall not die" (2Sam 12:13).

page 3
(3:1) If you wish to know (3:2) whether a woman will get pregnant (3:3) or not, write on the hide (3:4) of a deer: ʿAdnaʾel, Sarbanaʾel, (3:5) ...niʾel, Raḥmiʾel, Yahbiʾel, (3:6) Šaʿmaʾel, Ḥanamʾel. I adjure (3:7) you, you holy (3:8) angels, that you should divulge this (3:9) secret to me. You should place it (3:10) in the lap of the woman without her noticing. (3:11) If she laughs within half an hour, know that (3:12) she will get pregnant. If not, no.

page 4
(4:1-2) (*magic names*) (4:2) Blessed be the name of his kingship for ever. You (4:3) holy names, bind for me the eyes of all people, (4:4) so that they should not see me, me and all those who are with me. "Let the wicked (4:5) fall into their own nets together" (Ps 141:10), whilst I go through in safety. "Fear and dread (4:6) shall fall upon them" (Ex 15:16) (*The same words are repeated in inverted order*). This amulet is designed (4:7) to save from robbers and from every evil man and from lions and from (4:8) evil beasts and from all evil things. By the name of (4:8-11) (*magic names*). Amen, Amen, Selah. (4:12) «Write it on the hide of a deer, (4:13) and place it in (a piece of) almond wood.»

page 5
(5:2) For love ... (5:3) [... to a house where there is no] person and you will do (?), and in the house (5:4) there are four doors, and you will come in through them ... (5:5) ... [of the people] (5:6) whom you wish to connect with love, from their garments, from the hair of their (5:7) head or from their nails or from the skin (?) ... (5:8) and you will begin and say concerning the spirits of the book ... (9) and you will say among your words: Listen to me, fire and flame, [make love between N] (5:10) son of N and N son of N ... (5:11) ... their ... and you will mention (5:12) ... among your words ... (5:13) concerning N son of N ... (5:14-16) ... (5:17) or at their back ... that there should be love ... (5:18) until they die. This is (an amulet) for love. He hangs ...

page 6
(6:1-2) (***magic names, in which the Arabic word:*** al-waḥā ***"speed", is included twice.***) (6:3) I adjure you, ... that you should bring me (6:4) now ... [If he is asleep] (6:5) wake him, if he is sitting, make him stand and bring him to me, (6:6) and do not cause his mind to be taken from him. Be willing and say it (6:7) three times. Put the incense on the embers (6:8) with a piece of cloth from their garments or their hair. ... and mention (6:9) ... in your words, and if they come ... at that (6:10) time know that ... his mind is disturbed ... as you wish, (6:11) and if you wish to bring him back ... (6:12) ... [will co]me to you, extinguish the embers...

page 7
...(7:1) and stand against the sun so that your back should be towards the sun (7:2) while the mirror is in your hand, with the mirror facing the sun. (7:3) Look at the mirror strenuously with your eyes, but take care and *be *strong (7:4) with all your might so that you should not shut your eyes and not block them. (7:5) Be strong very much, with all your might, even if tears drop (7:6) from your eyes do not shut them and do not block them, (7:7) for indeed, because of the yellowness of the mirror, and of the power of (7:8) "like the brightness of" the sun, your eyes will be frightened and disturbed. But he should be strong (7:9) like a man of valour, for thus did Mar (?) command. (When) you are strong to look at it (7:10) you will see the man you wish and seek, and you will see (7:11) everything t[hat... And you should] do thus. First you should adjure the mirror (7:12) and say: [I adjure you,] Satan, to show me N son of N. (7:13) And then you will look within an hour and you will see him, and this is valid (?).

(7:14) If you wish your words to be heard by the people (7:15) or by a prince or a judge, say these verses: (7:16) "Give ear, o ye heavens" etc. (Dt 32:1), "My doctrine shall drop as the rain" etc. (Dt 32:2), "When I call (7:17) the name of the Lord" (Dt 32:3), and you should say: I adjure you, holy (7:18) names, through which Moses admonished the Children of Israel (7:19) in the desert, that you should cause my words to be heard by this

page 8
(8:1) people or by N, and that my words should be acceptable. By the name of (8:1-6) (***magic names***). (8:7) "I cried unto the Lord with my

voice and He heard me out of His holy hill, Selah" (Ps 3:5). Blessed be the name of His kingship for ever and ever (8:8) Amen, Amen, Amen, Selah, Selah, Selah, Hallelujah. Selah.

The gathering of demons. Burn frankincense...

Commentary

The order of the pages is not entirely certain. This group of pages seems to contain two different handwritings: Scribe A wrote pages 1-3; Scribe B wrote pages 4-8. The writing on pages 5-6 is very faint, and their reading is uncertain.

2: ***in the margin above*** גם יו' הסיר חטאתך / לא תמות: The text in 2Sam 12:13 is גם יהוה העביר חטאתך לא תמות.

7:3 וחזה: Read וחזק.

7:8 (כ)זוהר השמש: The first letter seems crossed out or uncertain. The expression is in imitation of Dan. 12:3 כזהר הרקיע.

יתפחדו עיניך ויתבלבלו: Rather than "your eyes will be frightened and disturbed" some physical reaction may be meant, such as "your eyes will blink and flutter".

ויתבלבלו: At first ויתפלפלו was written, and this was written over as transcribed here.

7:9 שכן צוה מר is obscure.

7:14 שר ושופט: Compare Ex. 2:14.

7:16 וגם: This is probably an error for וגו' "etc."

8:1-6 The words written in boxes are vowelled, but the vowels have not been reproduced in the transcription.

Geniza 18

T-S K 1.143

"The Book of Guidance": a twenty-page fragment of a magic book

Plates 53-62

[1]

1 (חסמון דשמר)
2 אלעגלה אלעגל (...)[
3 האדא כיתב אלהודה
4-7 (*magic names in Arabic and magic characters*)
8 באליל עטיל עזיל עזיל

[2]

The page is filled with magic figures and drawings. In the margin:

1 ימינה וקדיב אלדי פי יסרה ואעזום
2 עלכון ותרהבון בן חויא מבן עינ(י)[ה]
3 ותטכלון פי עקהא

[3]

1 אעזמ(ת)[כם איהא אסבעה]
2 אלאכוה א(עז)מת(כם) [ ]
3 (י)א מועז תדק יא( )
3a ... ש
4 יא (קדו)ש בחק [ ]
4a בחק מומ( )
5 [אסמך] אלכביר ובחק אבר[א]ס[כס]
6 אלגיב אלמוע(ק)ה פי א[ ] (אלתי)
7 תע(ל)יפו בהא (ק)דא חוו(יג) בני (אדם)
8 (וחווה) והיא סבעה א(כווה) אמת[ ]
9 [אעזמתכם] איהא אסבעה אלאכוה
10 [ ] היאתום לי (סו)נה [ ] (אעתוב)
11 (..) מן עינהא וטעם ושרב מן
12 ..א ודכרתוהא אסמי אנה
13 ... ע(ס)י הדה אל(וחא)

[4]

1 [ ](אסעה א)[ ]אאא

2 [ ](תכוד)[ ]

3 [ ](דרב... ותכונו)[ ]

4 [ ]הדה אלאסמ(י) ולע[ ]א

5 [ ]הא פי בית לא יס[כנה]

6 (א)[נ]סן סוף ותבכירה ב[דלך]

7 [אלוקת] אטיב ותצירהא [ ]

8 ... פי אנבובת קצ[ב]

9 ... יתכול דאליך

10 אליום [ ] והוא (ולד) לאבו. פרוך[ ]

11 תלא אתלי פי א(לאחרוף) חתא א[ ]

12 תלא קולת להום א(פ)רע(ון) א( )[ ]

13 [ ] אכולכום (פי) אדהים א( )

14 (...) בכרוה גיר ציחיב הד[א]

[5]

1 להא[ ]

2 כת על גרים ((עצם)) ד[ ]

3 דבעי ל(בעירה) א[ ]ה ( )[ ]

4 דאינון עלין ונפקין בה אלין[ ]

5 הוי יהיה יעף איל מי בן[ ]

6 (יד יי) הו׳יה׳ בפבפ אין בין[ ]

7 (אמור) אמן אמן סלה

8 (ל)[ ]המלאל

9 (מרעין ט)מין מנוי דמן אתבעי

10 [ ](ת) (עלוי) אלין מלאכיה לׄהׄמׄלׄאׄל

11 [אבר]אסכס אלהות כתות יואל פולי

12 הביקמות אטא בי יהוה יהוה

13 [ ]ל ר(מכ)י יהוה המרמה רגל אתון

[6]

1 [ ]ון רבא

2 [ ]תיזלון ותיתון לפבפ

3 [ ]ות(...) יתה מן אבוה ומן

4 [י]הוי (כפן) ל(א י)כל וצהי ולא שתי
5 [נאים ולא י](דמו)ך ויהוי צהיל בתר פבפ
6 (בתר) [ ](ר)יה ובתר חלקתיה ובתר
7 (תר.)יה אמן סלה
8 לאיתה דתהוי
9 [ ](גמי)לה חסד באפי בעלה כת̇ מן [ ]
10 ויה(ון רחמוי) עליה (*magic characters*)
11 (בא)(*magic characters*) הגמ (*magic characters*)
12 אמן (*magic characters*)

[7]

1 ניבעי מינכון כ(לק)[טיריא]
2 תהוי גמיל חסד (וא)[מת באפי]
3 בעלה מן יומה הדין ול[עלם]
4 א א ס
5 שרוי לכל מילה (ד)[ ]
6 סב עפר מן תחות רגלך [ ]
7 עלוי (ז̇) כ̇(א̇) עוצו עיצה ותופר דברו
8 דבר ולא יקום כי ע(מ̇ אל יי הפיר עצת)
9 גוים הניא מחשבות עמים כ(מה)
10 דבטלת עצתהון ד(דריה) דפלגתה
11 (כמה) דבטלת (עצתיה) דאחיתופל
12 [הי]כדין יתבטלון כל חרשין וכל אסרין
13 [ ]ין וכל פיג(ע)ין דמתעבדין
14 לפ׳ בן פ׳ אמן סלה

[8]

1 [ ](נ)יתה באלהא
2 [צ]באות יושב הכרובים
3 [ ]ין ומחמיין לי שאילותי
4 [ ]אבעי מנכון בשם
5 [כל] קטירייה (*magic characters*)
6 (*magic characters*)
7 (*magic characters*) אתון כל קטירייה
8 קדישייה אודעון יתי וגלון לי אנה פ̇ב̇פ̇
9 אין אתלי קני לוגייה ה̈
10 סב חימר כ̇ן כלבני רכיכה כ̇ן כצווה

11 ת(ר)ב דחמר ודל דוהון בלסם ופת[ת]
12 כולהון בדוהנה והב בקדיר(ה) [ ]
13 וארתח יתהון ציבחד וסב עמר צ[ ]

[9]

1 ועבוד עורדין [ ]
2 כד סאובתה קיימה יו [ ]
3 יטוש גברה בריתה (ח)[ ]
4 נושרה (ק)לילה במיי פשור(י) [ ]
5 א(י)ז ויועך ערבני קדם סני קני (ל)[...]
6 אמאנאמאנוס
7 מאנאמאנוס
8 אנאמאנוס
9 נאמאנוס
10 אמנוס
11 מנוס
12 נוס
13 וס
14 ס

To the left of lines 6-8: Magic characters; to the left of lines 10-13, the following four lines are written:

10a אתון אתייה קדישייה
11a וכל קטירייה קדישייה
12a ברחמי אב הרחמין
13a אסון רישה דׄןׄ ס אמן סל(ה)

The last two lines of the page are written over its whole width:

15 בשם יהוה נעשה ונצליח על חסדך
16 ועל אמיתיך אׄחׄסׄ אׄחׄסׄ אׄחׄסׄ

[10]

1 [ ] אׄחׄסׄ אׄחׄסׄ אׄחׄסׄ
2 [ ] מׄכׄתׄמׄ מׄכׄתׄמׄ מׄכׄתׄמׄ
3 [מׄכׄ]תׄמׄ מׄכׄתׄמׄ מׄכׄתׄמׄ מׄכׄתׄמׄ
4 [אל]יׄהׄ אׄלׄיׄהׄ אׄלׄיׄהׄ אׄלׄיׄהׄ
5 [ ] אׄלׄיׄהׄ אׄלׄיׄהׄ אׄלׄיׄהׄ אׄלׄיׄהׄ
6 [אׄלׄיׄהׄ] אׄלׄיׄהׄ רׄדׄ הׄנׄץׄ רׄדׄ הׄנׄץׄ רׄדׄ הׄנׄץׄ
7 רׄדׄ הׄנׄץׄ רׄדׄ הׄנׄץׄ רׄדׄ הׄנׄץׄ רׄדׄ הׄנׄץׄ

8	רֹד הֹנֹץ וֹסֹמֹכֹיֹהֹוֹ וֹסֹמֹכֹיֹהֹוֹ
9	וֹסֹמֹכֹיֹהֹוֹ וֹסֹמֹכֹיֹהֹוֹ וֹסֹמֹכֹיֹהֹוֹ
10	וֹסֹמֹכֹיֹהֹוֹ וֹסֹמֹכֹיֹהֹוֹ וֹסֹ<מֹ>כֹיֹהֹוֹ
11	וֹדֹחֹפֹיֹהֹוֹ וֹדֹחֹפֹיֹהֹוֹ וֹדֹחֹפֹיֹהֹוֹ
12	וֹדֹחֹפֹיֹהֹוֹ וֹדֹפֹפֹיֹהֹוֹ (!) וֹדֹחֹפֹיֹהֹוֹ
13	וֹדֹחֹפֹיֹהֹוֹ וֹדֹחֹפֹיֹהֹוֹ וֹדֹחֹפֹיֹהֹוֹ
14	הִיתֹגֹ<עֹ>רִי הִיתֹגֹעֹרִי הִיתֹגֹעֹרִי
15	הִיתֹגֹעֹרִי הִיֹדֹחֹפִי הִיֹדֹחֹפִי
16	הִיֹדֹחֹפִי הִיֹדֹחֹפִי נֹוֹסִי נֹוֹסִי נֹוֹסִי (נֹוֹסִי)

[11]

1	ואין מדליקין א[ת]
2	אבל מערין את (ה)[ ]
3	וטמנין בחמין [ ]
4	לוחשה לאדמ[ה]
5	אמור זמ ג או ז אין [ ]
6	איסטפי
7	לוחשה לאדמ[ה]
8	אמור זמ׳ ג או ז איסט[פי]
9	אמומה פרוטי לולו בני (ס)דום
10	אשבעת עליך בשם יה יה יי צבֹ(א)
11	תטוף דם אברהם מ(ש)ה פסק
12	ויהוה הוא חתומה ○

[12]

1	[ ] סב פתה נגיבה
2	[ ](ק)ה ותתן יתהון בדב[ש]
3	[ ]דדה וכד היא דכייה
4	[ ](תה ו)תֹ לֹהֹ וישמע אליה
5	[אלהים] ויפתח את רחמה יה יֹה יה
6	[יה יה] יה אה אה אה אה אה אה
7	[ ]ע לעולם הלוליה ○
8	[לוחש]ה למכנשה כל עמה גבך
9	[ ]ך כתוב בֹז בירחה בקלף
10	טבני ו[ח]תלי באדרעך דסמלה
11	ואלין כת׳ או או או א אות יהוה
12	אדוני צבאות יה אלהים אה

אה אה אה אה אה מר
מראות מר מר אורי בר ברית

[13]

רבות משבע אנ[ה יתכון]
מלאכיה הבו חנה ו(חסדה)
ות((י))שבחתה לי אנה (פ ב)[ב]
דאלהא עילאה ד[ית]יב ע[ל כורסה]
מלכותה היבו באפי חנה ו[חיסדה]
ותישבחתה ושיפרה קודם [כל דחמי]
לי ושמע ממללי אׄ אׄ סׄ [כתוב]
על כף ומחוק במשח דוורד
ותהוי טייש אפיך ניפש (לקום)
עמנואל סוריאל לם מריא
אתון אתייה קדישייה
היבו לי חנה וחנה (!) ושיפרה
באפי כל מן דחמי לי ושמע קל
מימרי אׄ אׄ סׄ הללויה (סל)א

[14]

[ ]סב זרע אטטא
[תרנ]גולה אכומא
[ ] ויתאסי ○ לעשו[ת]
[שלום] בן גבר לאנתיה יכ בדהב
[או בכ](ס)ף ית[ל]י יתה בכרעה דכרס(ה)
[ ] מיכאל | אמבאל | אות
[עשו] שלום בן פ׳ב׳פ׳ לבן פ׳ב׳פ׳
ממממממממממ אן כן
שכן תכן הכן נכן רכן ○
לראשה ולמקרניה בקלף דטוי
כתׄ (ר)יקורגוס יקורגוס קורגוס
ורגוס רגוס גוס וס ס. לכבוש
משבע אני עליך סמאל
המלאך ועל כל החבירים

[15]

שיש לך בשם אבא[ל]

2 כל בריות עולם ות[ ]
3 וכל החבירים ש[ ]
4 אל הארץ ותסתום כל פה [ותשפיל]
5 כל קומה ותפר כל מחשבה [ ]
6 אני פ׳ב׳פ׳ ויהיו כ(ת)ועים ומ(ט)[עים]
7 מאיש ועד איש ומיעולל ועד [יונק]
8 בשם (*magic characters*)
9-10 (*magic characters*)
11 שששששששששש צצ[צ]
12 צצצצ קקקקקק
13 עעעעעע אאאאאא

[16]

1 אתון כבשו לי
2 עלמה באיסרה
3 היך מה דשמיה קודם
4 שמי שמיה וימה
5 קודם בני ישראל
6 דעברו בגוה וחלה
7 קודם ימה וימה קודם
8 אלהא ובני נשה קודם
9 מותה ומותא קודם
10 אלהא (ודקי) עופה קודם נישרה כן
11 יהוון כל בני אנשה קודמי אנה פ׳ב׳פ׳
12 מעתה ועד עולם הללויה א׳א׳ס׳ צלח צלח
13 וצלח על חסדך ועל אמיתיך אמת
14 שמושיה צום חד יום וחתר מאכך
15 בההוא יומה ג׳ זמנין וכת׳ יתה בטס
16 דאיבר במחט דפרזל חדתה וקפל
17 עלוי מרטוט מטכסין ותנן יתה
18 ותהוי קרץ בצפרה ונסב ליה בידך

[17]

1 ויהב ליה על עינך ונ[ ]
2 יתה והוא טב רב ותק[יף]
3 לאתה דלא תרמ[י]
4 ות׳ עליה בשם נוכ[ ]

אבֿאל רפֿאל צורֿיאל מ[ ]
אתון מלאכ׳ קדיש׳ ית [פלנית דלא]
תפל ולדה עד זמן דישלמון [ט׳ ירחיא]
שומר פתאית (!) יי דלותי ולי (י)הוש[יע]
למחזרה גבר על אנתתה כ[תוב]
על חסף דלא אזי וטלק לאתונ(ה)
או לנורה והדן כתב בשם תֿץֿן וף
תץן ון ופ ון וף נסס פוכת כיה אי( )
בירחה אאסה ○ לאנש דיהווי ((חביב)) ורח[ים]
באפי כל מן דחמי יתה כתֿ ותלי באד[רעה]
דסמאלה (*magic characters*)

[18]

(*magic characters*)
[את]ון אתייה קדישייה וכלקטיר[יה]
[משבחיי]ה הבו חן וחסד ורחמה לפ׳ב׳פ׳
[באפי] כל מן דחמי יתה ושמע ברת קלה
[אא](ס)ה ○ אסו לכל מחוש כת׳ בגלד
[ד](ת)ור והב יתה תחות ראשה דביישה
[והו]א מנשם בשם אשכון אשכון
[סרג]ון סרגון מיכאל מיכאל רפאל
רפאל עניאל עניאל אוריאל אוריאל
אתון אתייה מלאכייה קדישייה אסון
לפ׳ב׳פ׳ מן כל מחוש אמן עיני דאבה
מני עוני וגו׳ רפאני יי וגו׳ ○ לאתה
דלא תרמי כת׳ בקרטס ות׳ עליה בשם
נוריאל סרטיאל אביאל רפאל צוריאל
מיכאל גבריאל אתון מלאכייה

[19]

קדיש׳ ית פלנית דלא יפל [ולדה עד זמן]
דישלמון ט׳ ירחייה שומר [פתאים]
יי דלותי ולי <י>הושיע: לאת[ ]
סב ז׳ לבלובין דארז מן ז׳ ארזין ופרטין [ ]
ופיגם ותום ועפר מן זו(ו)יתה דבייתה ומס[...]
דתורה נוקבה ותקטור יתה קדמוי לעל מן [ ]
ותהוי כקבלה תננה יומין ז׳ וסד אדם מן פרי(ג)

8 חוור ותשחוק אליך עקרייה ותגבול בה ה[דה]
9 מררתה ואדמה ותתן עליה בציף דלא (מ)[תבלי]
10 והוא טב קמיע לכלה כתוב בשם יהוה צב[אות]
11 ובשם מלאכייה האליין קדוש ג׳ בשם צ(ד)ק[יאל]
12 ועזריאל ופקמיאל וצפייאל בשם יה(ס)
13 דמרבי עויתיה דכרמה ד<ת>פתרון ותשרון
14 ותעקרון כל רוחין בישין דיכרין וניקבן רוח
15 שועלה רוח כנפרה רוח משק רוח מחבל רוח
16 דפרח ר׳ דשכן רוח צנתה רוח תרעי לבה רוח
17 אוסטומכה רוח צפר נפשה רוח דמזיק ועיין
18 ברייה וכל רוח וצער ומכאוב מן גופה דפ׳ב׳פ׳
19 מן ת(רתי)ן מאוון וארבעין ותמניה
20 אברין (דא)י(ת) בה אמן
21 אמן (סלה)

In the margin:

הללויה בדוק

[20]

1 [ ] הד(ר)ך תכתוב בגל[ד]
2 (וגד) כאתב סוני וסוסונאוס
3 [ ]וס לעל ו(כיפיה) וניסגאת
4 [ ] נהרי ( ) כתוב
5 [ותלי באד]רעך דסמאלא אסו בפ(ל̇)ו̇ מן
6 [ ] (...) דתבעי
7 (לחנותא) חסד חסד חסד חסד
8 [חסד חס]ד חסד לחנ(ו)תא דפ׳ב׳פ׳ דתהוי
9 [לי חנו]תא וחסדא ויהוון בני אנשא
10 [ ] ורהטין גברייא ונשייא ועלו
11 [...] ולגין דיהוי לי אני אכר בשם
12 [אבר]סכסיה | אברסכסיה | אברסכסיה

Translation

page 1

(1:2) «Haste, haste. … (1:3) This is the book of guidance … (1:8) at night.» …

page 2
(2:1) «[in] his right hand, and a rod that is in his left hand, and I adjure» (2:2) you and you shall frighten the serpent's son (?) from between his eyes (?) (2:3) «... in ...»

page 3
(3:1) «I invoke [you, the seven] (3:2) brothers, I invoke [you] (3:3) O mighty one, ... (3:4) O holy one. By the power (3:5) [of your] great [name] and by the power of Abras[ax] (3:6) the hidden one, mighty (?) in ... by (3:7) which you feed (?) carrying out the needs of the sons of Adam (3:8) and Eve. These are seven brothers ... (3:9) I invoke you, the seven brothers (3:10) ... [may you] prepare for me a way ... I reprove (?) (3:11) [sleep?] from her eye and food and drink from (3:12) ... and may you mention to her my name, that is ... (3:13) ... Haste.»

page 4
(4:1) «... now. ... (4:3) ... and you will be ... (4:4) ... these names ... (4:5) in a house in which no person (4:6) except you resides. And you shall perfume it with incense at that (4:7) good [time], and you shall place it ... (4:8) in the pipe of a reed (4:9) ... he will bode well (?) on that (4:10) day [ ] and it belongs to Abu Farrukh (4:11) in the characters until ... (4:12) I said to them: "Hurry towards (4:13) ... I shall bestow upon you (?) in misfortune ... (4:14) Make incense, except the owner of this...» (***In lines 11-12 there are some magic words enclosed in a box.***)

page 5
(5:1) For ... (5:2) Write on the bone of ... (5:3) that he wants to ... (5:4) for they enter and go out in it ... (5:5) **hwy yhyh yʿp ʾyl my b**[... "Behold,] (5:6) the hand of the Lord is upon" N. son of N. ... (5:7) ... Amen, Amen, Selah. (5:8) For ... (5:9) Impure diseases ... from him who is requested (?) (5:10) ... may those angels enter (?) ... (5:11) [Abr]asax **ktwt ywʾl pwly** (5:12) **hbyqmwt ʾṭʾ by yhwh yhwh** (5:13) ...

page 6
(6:1) ... great (6:2) ... (may you) go and come to N. son of N. (6:3) [and take] her from her father and from (6:4) ... [may he] be hungry without eating, thirsty without drinking, (6:5) [drowsy without] sleeping, and may he be lusting after N. son of N., (6:6) after his..., after his share, after (6:7) his ... Amen, Selah.

(6:8) For a woman, that she may be (6:9) full of charm in the eyes of her husband. Write from: (6:10) And God had mercy on her ... (6:12) Amen.

page 7
(7:1) I desire of you, the [holy] charac[ters, that N. daughter of N.] (7:2) may find grace and truth in the eyes of (7:3) her husband from this day to eternity. (7:4) Amen, Amen, Selah.

(7:5) Loosening for every matter which ... (7:6) Take (some) dust from underneath your feet ... [say?] (7:7) over it eleven times ... "Make your plans, but they will be foiled; speak (7:8) the word, but it will not stand, for God is with us" (Is. 8:10). "The Lord brings the plans (7:9) of nations to nothing, he frustrates the counsel of the peoples" (Ps. 33:10). Just as (7:10) you cancelled the counsel of the people of the generation of the Tower of Babel; (7:11) as you cancelled the counsel of Ahitophel, (7:12) just so may there be cancelled all spells, incantations, (7:13) ..., and all afflictions which may be done (7:14) to N. son of N. Amen Amen Selah.

page 8
(8:2) ... [God Lord of H]osts, who sits among the cherubim, (8:3) ... [you inform] and show me my desires, (8:4) [those that] I beg of you, in the name of (8:5) [the char]acters (*magic characters*). (8:7) You, holy (8:8) characters, inform me and divulge to me, I, N. son of N., (8:9) if I have ...

Formula (?) five. (8:10) Take clay, either like soft bricks, or like chips (?), (8:11) the fat of a donkey, and, if (this is) not (available) (?), balsam oil. Cru[sh them] (8:12) all in the oil and put (them) in a pot ... (8:13) and boil them a little. Take wool ...

page 9
(9:1) and make reeds (?) ... (9:2) while the impure woman is standing ... (9:4) small (?) dropping in tepid water ... (9:6-13) Amanamanus (*the letters of this name are reduced successively*).

(9:10a) You holy symbols (9:11a) and holy characters. (9:12a) By the mercy of the Father of mercy, (9:13a) heal the head of such-and-such. Amen Selah.

(9:15) By the name of God we shall act and succeed. "For your mercy (9:16) and for your truth's sake" (Ps. 115:1; 138:2). Amen, Neṣaḥ (?), Selah (*repeated 3 times*).

page 10
(10:1-16) (*magic words*)

page 11
... (11:1) and one should not light t[he candles...] (11:2) but one should *separate the *tithe (?)... (11:3) and one should place the hot water ...

(11:4) A spell for ... (11:5) Say three or seven times ... (11:6) **ʾysṭpy** (11:7-8) (*same as lines 4-6*). (11:9) (*magic words*) the sons of Sodom (11:10) I adjure you in the name of **yh yh** God of Ho[sts]. (11:11) May you cause the blood of Abraham to drip, Moses decides (in legal matters?) (11:12) and God is the undersigned (witness).

page 12
(12:1) ... Take a dry loaf of bread (12:2) ... and put them in hon[ey] (12:3) ... and while she is pure (12:4) ... and you shall say to her (?): "and [God] hearkened (12:5) to her and opened her womb" (Gen. 30:22). **yh yh yh** (12:6) **[yh yh] yh ʾh ʾh ʾh ʾh ʾh ʾh** (12:7) [...] to eternity, Hallelujah.

(12:8) A spell for causing all people to assemble around you (12:9) [and to follow you?]. Write on the 7th day of the (lunar) month on (12:10) the skin of a deer, and hang it from your left arm. (12:11) And these are the things that you shall write: **ʾw ʾw ʾw ʾ ʾwt** YHWH (12:12) Adonay of Hosts, **yh** Elohim **ʾh** (12:13) **ʾh ʾh ʾh ʾh ʾh ʾh ʾh mr** (12:14) **mrʾwt mr mr ʾwry** son of the covenant

page 13
(13:1) ... I adjure [you] (13:2) angels, give me grace and charm (13:3) and praise, to me [...] (13:4) of the supreme God who sits o[n the throne] (13:5) of His kingship. Give to my countenance grace and [charm] (13:6) and praise and beauty in front of [everyone who looks] (13:7) at me and who listens to what I say. Amen amen selah.

[Write] (13:8) on the palm of a hand and wash it away with rose oil (13:9) and you shall smear (it) over your face. ... (13:10) Emmanuel, Suriel ... (13:11) You, holy characters, (13:12) give me grace and *charm and beauty (13:13) in the eyes of all those who look at me and who listen to the voice (13:14) of what I say, Amen Amen Selah. Hallelujah. Selah.

page 14

(14:1)... Take the seed of a box-thorn (14:2) ... a black hen (14:3) ... and he will be healed. To ma[ke] (14:4) [peace] between a man and his wife. Let him write (?) with gold (14:5) [or si]lver, let him suspend it from the leg of the chair (14:6) [ ] Michael Amba᾿el Ot, (14:7) [make] peace between N. son of N. and N. son of N. (14:8-9) (*magic letters and words*). (14:10) For his (her?) head and the crown of his head with the hide of *deer. (14:11-12) Write: Rikorgos (*the letters of this name are reduced successively*).

For a subduing. (14:13) I adjure you, Sama᾿el (14:14) the angel, and all the friends

page 15

(15:1) that you have, in the name of Aba᾿e[l...] (15:2) all the creatures of the world, and [ ] (15:3) and all the friends that [you have...] (15:4) to the earth and you will shut everyone's mouth, [and you will cause] (15:5) every stature [to be low] and you will annul everyone's thought [from me,] (15:6) I, N. son of N., and they will be like people who have lost their way and [are being led astray] (15:7) "whether a man or a *woman, whether an infant or a [suckling]" (1Sam 15:3; 22:19), (15:8) in the name of (15:8-13) (*magic characters and letters*),

page 16

(16:1) you, suppress for me (16:2) the world by the spell. (16:3) Just as the sky (is suppressed) before (16:4) the highest sky, and the sea (16:5) before the Children of Israel (16:6) who passed through it, and the sand (16:7) before the sea, and the sea before (16:8) God, and human beings before (16:9) death, and death before (16:10) God, and small (?) winged creatures before the eagle, so (16:11) shall all human beings be before me, I, N. son of N., (16:12) from now to eternity, Hallelujah, Amen Amen Selah, Success, success, (16:13) and success. "For the sake of your mercy and your truth" (Ps. 115:1). Truth.

(16:14) The praxis belonging to it: Fast one day, and rub your *teeth (16:15) on that day three times. Write it on a plate (16:16) of lead with a new iron pin, and fold (16:17) over it a silken rag. Smoke it, (16:18) rise in the morning, take it in your hands,

page 17
(17:1) and put it over your eye, and [...] (17:2) it. It is effective, great and mighty.

(17:3) For a woman, that she should not abort. (17:4) [Write] and suspend it from her: In the name of **nwk**[...] (17:5) Abael, Raphael, Ṣuriel, M[ ]. (17:6) You holy angels. <Preserve > [N. so that she should not] (17:7) abort her foetus before she has completed [nine months]. (17:8) "The Lord preserves the simple-hearted. I was brought low and he sav[ed me]" (Ps. 116:6).

(17:9) For a man to return to his wife. Wr[ite] (17:10) on an unbaked piece of clay, and throw it into an oven (17:11) or fire, and this is what you shall write: In the name of **TṢN WP** (17:12) (*further magic words*) (17:13) in the month, Amen Amen Selah.

For a man to be liked and loved (17:14) by every one who looks at him. Write, and suspend from the left arm: (*magic characters*).

page 18
(18:1) You, holy letters and [praised] (18:2) characters. Give grace, charm and love to N. son of N. (18:3) in the eyes of every one who looks at him and who hears his voice. (18:4) Amen Amen Selah Hallelujah.

Healing for every ailment. Write on a hide (18:5) of an ox and place it under the head of the patient (18:6) [...] (*magic names*) (18:7) Sargon, Michael, Raphael, (18:8) 'Aniel, Uriel (*each name repeated twice*). (18:9) You, letters, holy angels, heal (18:10) N. son of N. from every ailment, Amen. "My eye mourns (18:11) by reason of affliction" (Ps. 88:10) etc. "Heal me, o Lord" (Jer. 17:14; Ps. 6:3) etc.

For a woman, (18:12) that she may not abort. Write on a sheet (of paper), and suspend it from her. In the name of (18:13) Nuriel, Sarṭiel, Abiel, Raphael, Ṣuriel, (18:14) Michael, Gabriel. You, holy

page 19
(19:1) angels, <preserve > N. so that her foetus should not abort before

(19:2) it completes nine months. "God preserves the simple-minded. I was brought low, and He helped me" (Ps. 116:6).

For [...] (19:4) Take seven blossoms of a cedar tree, from seven cedars, and grapes fallen off, [...], (19:5) and rue, and garlic, and dust from the corner of the house, and the [gall] (19:6) of a female ox, and burn it as incense in front of him (?) above [...], (19:7) and she should *receive the smoke for seven days. *Take blood from a white young (19:8) chicken, pound these roots and mix with it t[his] (19:9) gall and blood, and put over her in a mat which is not [worn out], (19:10) and it will be good.

An amulet for a bride. Write: In the name of YHWH Sabaot (19:11) and in the name of these angels. Three times Qadosh. In the name of Ṣadqiel, (19:12) 'Azriel, Paqmiel, Ṣafyiel. In the name of **yh(s)**, (19:13) who increases the convulsion of the *bone (?). May you disperse and loosen (19:14) and uproot all evil spirits, male and female; the spirit of (19:15) the fox (?), the spirit of the gang (?), the spirit of the noisy movement (?), the spirit of he who causes damage, the spirit (19:16) that flies, the spirit that dwells, the spirit of the chill, the spirit of the gates of the heart, the spirit of (19:17) the stomach, the spirit of the breastbone, the spirit of he who harms and the eye (19:18) of (any) creature, and all spirits of pain and suffering from the body of N. b. N., (19:19) from the 248 (19:20) limbs that are in her. Amen (19:21) Amen Selah (*Margin:*) Hallelujah. Tested.

page 20

(20:1) [ ] ... «Write on a hide... (20:2) ... a writer» **swny wswswnʾws** (20:3) ... (20:4) Write (20:5) [and suspend from your] left arm: Heal N. from (20:6) ... that she may desire.

(20:7) For (finding) favour. Kindness (*seven times*). (20:8) For the favour of N. son of N. May I (20:9) have grace and favour, and may all human beings ... (20:10) and that men and women should run... (20:11) ... That I may have, I, ..., in the name of (20:12) Abrasaxia (*three times*).

Commentary

Fragment from a book of magic recipes, written on parchment. The extant fragment contains 20 pages, not all of them clearly legible. The text is in Judaeo-Arabic, Hebrew, and Aramaic. The handwriting varies, although this does not necessarily mean that the book was written by different hands. It could possibly be written by the same person over a long period of time. Several ink marks by a much later user of the text can be discerned. These are characterized by black ink, with which the headings of new spells are distinguished by means of a curved line above the heading or a line separating a new section from the preceding one.

The Judaeo-Arabic portions of this text are written in the archaic spellings typical of early Geniza documents (cf. Blau and Hopkins 1984). The language is not very clear, the writing contains many errors, and as the state of preservation of some of the pages is bad, the translation is in many cases tentative.

2:2 בן חויא: Perhaps an error for מן חויא.

2:3 ותטכלון פי עקהא: This is unclear.

3:7 תעריפו: Apparently written תעליפו.

3:10 עתב seems to be used here in a sense similar to גער in Aramaic.

5:2 גרים: Above the line, עצם

5:6 יד יי הויה: Cf. Ex. 9:3.

5:9 מנוי: A wrong form for מניה, perhaps by analogy with עלוי.

6:4–6 For this sequence cf. A7:17ff.

6:4 By a scribal error, apparently, we have למיכל for ולא אכל.

6:5 צהל, in the sense suggested here, is attested only in Syriac.

6:9 The expression גמל חיסדא usually means "to be charitable", but here it seems to have the meaning of "loving, finding someone graceful". גמילה is a passive participle. The same phrase is also used in p. 7:2, but the gender there is masculine, obviously by an error. For this usage cf. the Hebrew phrase לגמילות חסדים, apparently in the same sense, in *Sefer ha-Razim* I:170 (a reference we owe to Menahem Kister). We may note that as in *Sefer ha-Razim*, here too a recipe for finding favour follows on a recipe for love. The Arabic version in *Sefer ha-Razim* (cf. ibid. note to line 168) has a similar injunction that the person concerned should not eat, drink or sleep.

6:10 Moulded after 2Chron. 36:15, and similar verses.

7:1 ניבעי may denote either first person singular or plural. In p. 8:4 the equivalent form is אבעי. Examples are numerous; cf. note to Geniza 6, p. 3:7 (*AMB*, p. 235).

7:2 תהוי גמיל חסד ... [באפי] בעלה the verb and the possessive pronoun of בעלה are in the feminine, but the participle גמיל is masculine, no doubt by an error. Cf. above, p. 6:9, where the participle is in the feminine.

7:5 שרוי is the verbal noun from שרא.

7:6 For the practice of taking dust from underneath someone's feet for a magical purpose see Bavli Ḥullin 7b and the discussion in Lieberman 1962, pp. 85f.

7:7 ז̇: Possibly an abbreviation for זמנין "times".

7:12 Cf. *Havdala de-Rabbi Akiva* 4:13; 6:13-14.

8:9 אתלי: This could possibly be an error for *it li*, "I have". Alternatively it could belong to the verb תלה "to hang", an action often said to be done with amulets and incantations.

קני לוגייה is probably wrongly divided. It seems to represent the Greek word κοινολογία, which serves to denote apparently something like "common magic formula"; the word occurs once in the Paris magic papyrus, cf. Preisendanz 1928, p. 136 (text IV:2079f.). The word means otherwise also "consultation". Cf. also below, 9:5 קני, in G21, 1:15 קינו, G16, 2:16 קינולגיה. It is possible that the same element occurs in the text of Yerushalmi Sanhedrin 27b: המקלל בקסם כגון אילין נפתאי דמקללין לקנייך קיינך קנייך.

ה̈ may be an abbreviation for הדא. We take it however to represent the figure for "five".

8:10 כן כ...: This combination occurs twice here, evidently in the sense of "either ... or".

כלבני רכיכה This is apparently a construct form (unless it is an error for כלבנין רכיכין).

כצווה: This could be a form of the word צבתא "chips, twigs, etc." (Jastrow 1903, p. 1274b), which is however attested mostly in connection with wood chips.

8:11 תרב: Cf. Targum to Lev. 9:10, where Heb. חֵלֶב is translated by תרבא.

ודל seems to represent the contracted form of ודאי לא "for if not"; cf. Jastrow 1903, p. 308a.

דוהון: This spelling is somewhat unusual. The common spellings of this word are דהנא ,דוהנא, and the additional *waw* may represent a popular pronunciation influenced by the dialect of Arabic spoken by the writer.

9:1 עוררדין: This is either two words, עורר דין, "this clepsydra"; or an error for עוזרדין "crab apples", or "reeds".

9:2 סאובתה: Probably "a menstruating woman".

9:13a דְן: This should be an abbrevation for any person's name. One may think of the Greek δεῖνα, which is used in this sense (perhaps in contamination with the Aramaic demonstrative דין?).

9:15-16: See A16:1-2.

11:1ff. The text here seems to be derived from Mishna Shabbat 2:7: ספק חשיכה ספק אין חשיכה אין מעשרין את הודאי ואין מטבילין את הכלים ואין מדליקין את הנרות אבל מעשרין את הדמאי ומערבין וטומנין את החמין. "When there is doubt whether it is dark or not, one should not separate the tithe in that which certainly requires tithing, one should not immerse the vessels in water, and one should not light the candles. But one should separate tithes in that which is doubtful, and one should perform ʿ*eruv* and place the hot water (in the oven)". The relevance of this passage to the magical context here is puzzling.

11:2 מערין is probably an error for מעשרין.

11:3 בחמין seems like an error for את החמין.

11:4-6 The text of these lines is repeated again in lines 7-8.

11:4 לאדמן[ ]: Probably a reference to some illness. One may wonder whether the reference is to "red leprosy", as in Lev. 13:42ff.?

11:11f. The allusions to the circumcision of Abraham and to the fact that Moses decided in legal matters (if this is the sense of the verb *pesaq* in this context) while God endorsed, are phrased in terms that are not encountered in the rabbinical literature, as far as we know.

12:4 ות׳ לה׳ may be an abbreviation for ותאמר לה.

12:9 At the beginning of this line one ought perhaps to read ולמיזל] בתר[ך.

13:8 ומחוק במשח דוורד: Cf. a similar instruction, with wine instead of rose oil, in G11, p. 4:8f.

13:11-12. After אתון and היבו לי there is a magic drawing covering both lines.

13:12 חנה וחנה is an ovious error for חנה וחסדה.

14:1 אטטא, like its variant אטדא, and like Hebrew אטד, is boxthorn, lycium europaeum. Cf. Löw 1928/1934, IV, pp. 69, 76, and the index; Löw 1881, pp. 44-45.

14:10 ולמקרניה: This form is not attested, but it seems close enough to מוקרא to make it possible to equate the two forms. As it seems, מקרנא is perhaps an error for מקדנא or מוקדא "top of the head", which is to be expected as the place where a piece of writing on parchment is to be placed, rather than a word which means "brain". See also B13:8.

דטוי: Evidently an error for דטבי.

15:7 מאיש ועד איש is an error for מאיש ועד אשה.

15:13 The *alefs* are written defectively, without the left leg.

16:1-9 To the right of these lines there is a drawing.

16:3ff. The text is based on four separate cycles: (1) sky—highest sky[—God?]; (2) children of Israel—sand—sea—God; (3) human beings—death—God; (4) winged creatures—eagle. The last sequence stands out as somewhat strange, as it does not seem to lead towards God as the highest of all beings, and it does not seem to be part of a larger cycle. A cyclic saying occurs also in Amulet 16:11-17, where the structure of the cycle is clear and unified. See Commentary there.

16:10 The expression עופה (ודקי), if the reading is right, is unusual. One may however compare the Hebrew phrase העוף הדק (Mishna Ḥullin 3:1). Another reading could be עופה (ובני).

16:14ff. The word מאכך is probably a scribe's error for כאכך; the verb חתר is used for cleaning or rubbing one's teeth. Cf. in Hebrew Bavli Kiddushin 24b.

17:6 The text is supplemented according to p. 19:1, where the same ellipsis occurs.

17:10 אזי is the passive participle of the verb אזה, to which also belongs the form אזה in B 13:9, where the correct translation of ובטילו אזה should be: "and remove heat (i.e. fever?) from..."

18:3 ברת קלה means here obviously not "an echo" or "mysterious voice", but simply "voice".

19:2 ט ירחייה could be "9 months" or "her 9 months".

19:4 פרט is the Aramaic rendering of the second Targum Yerushalmi of the Hebrew פרט in Lev. 19:10.

19:5 זו(ו)יתה: Apparently written זוריתה.

19:5 ומס[ ] may be an error for ומר[רתה] as in line 9. The word should mean "gall", as in Syriac and as its Hebrew counterpart מרה.

19:6 קדמוי written קדמיו.

19:7 כקבלה is probably an error for מקבלה.
וסד seems to be an error for וסב.

19:13 כרמה is probably an error for גרמה.

19:15 שועלה "fox" seems strange in this list. The word could also mean "hollow of the hand", or possibly "cough" (although the latter sense is attested in Hebrew and Syriac, not in Jewish Aramaic).
כנפרה can be explained as badly written for כנ(ו)פיה "gang" or for כופרא "pitch".
משק is apparently borrowed from biblical Hebrew, unless an otherwise unknown Aramaic terms is here attested.

19:16 פרח and שכן seem to form a contrast; cf. A 26:10.

19:17 צפר נפשה is interpreted by Rashi as the "the cartilage which is opposite the heart" (Bavli Bava Qama 90b). Jastrow 1903 s.v. translates "cartilage at the end of the sternum".

19:17-18 עיין ברייה cf. G29, p. 1:10, 17.

19:19 Instead of מאתן, the usual way of designating "two hundred", we have here the combination תרתין מאוון.

20:2 סוני וסוסונאוס: This is the same sequence which is familiar from A15:20f. and the parallel versions; cf. there.

20:7 חנותא is regularly "store, shop". In this context, however, it is possible that it is an unusual form of חנא "grace, favour, loveliness"; cf. G27, 4:7.

Geniza 19

T-S K1.167
Amulet for Sitahm daughter of Sitt al-Ahl
Plate 63

[1]

על שמך
משבענא ואסרנא
ובלימנא ומסכרנא
ומעינא ומטרשנא
לבהון דכל בני אדם
וחוה דלא ינזקון
יתי אנא סתהם
בת סת אלאהל
להקיאל המלאך
הגדול שהוא ממונה
על אהבה הוא יחוס
על סתהם בצאתה
ובבואה בשכבה
ובקומה וישים
אתה לחן ולחסד
ולרחמים בעני
בעלה מוסי בן גאלא
בשם זה שם רב
אגיקט טגאט
פגאט דהוא
אחד ושמו א(חד)
אץ שמו [בץ שמו]

23 גץ שמו דץ שמו
24 הץ שמו (וץ) שמו
25 זץ שמו חץ שמו טץ
26 שמו יץ שמו כץ
27 שמו לץ שמו מץ שמו
28 שמו מץ שמו נץ שמו
29 סץ שמו עץ שמו
30 פץ שמו צץ שמו
31 קץ רץ שץ תץ
32 ובשם עמיאל ומיכאל
33 ובשם אבר[כסס]
34 שר החן[כמה?]

[2]

1 ועליהם שרים אחרים
2 תסכרו פיו משא (מסא)
3 שהן שליטין על פומא
4 דבני אנשא לאפוקי
5 מלין טבין ולא יכלין
6 לאפוקי מילין בישין
7 הא של(חו) מלאכא
8 קדם דניאל כן
9 יכבוש כל בני אדם
10 ויסתכר פמהון
11 דכל בני אנשא
12 ופום מוסי בן גאלא
13 שלא ינזק אותי
14 אני סתהם
15 בשם יה יה יה
16 יהיה א(ח)יה
17 ובשם אל שדי
18 קדוש שמו צבאות
19 הוא יהיה עם
20 סתהם בצאתה
21 ובבואה וציג
22 אעבור ואתן א(ת)
23 סתהם לחסד ולרח(מים)

24 באנפי כל דחזי יתה
25 אמן ואמן

Translation

page 1

(1:1) By your name. (1:2) I adjure and bind (1:3) and restrain and bar (1:4) and investigate and obstruct (1:5) the hearts of all men (1:6) and women, that they should not harm (1:7) me, I, Sitahm (1:8) daughter of Sitt al-Ahl.

(1:9) Lahaqi'el the great angel, (1:10) who is appointed (1:11) over love, will have mercy (1:12) on Sitahm in her going (1:13) and coming, in her lying (1:14) and standing, and will make (1:15) her gain grace and love (1:16) and mercy in the eyes (1:17) of her husband, Mūsā son of Jala.

(1:18) In the name of Ze Shem Rav, (1:19) Agiqaṭ, Ṭagaṭ, (1:20) Pagaṭ, (1:21) who is one and whose name is one. (1:22) His name is Aṣ, [his name is Baṣ], (1:23) his name is Gaṣ, his name is Daṣ (*and so on, through the alphabet*).

(1:32) And in the name of ʿAmiel and Michael, (1:33) and in the name of Abrasax (1:34) the Prince of [Wisdom?],

page 2

(2:1) and over them (there are) other princes. (2:2) Shut his mouth ... (2:3) who have power over the mouth (2:4) of people, that they may utter (2:5) good words, and that they should not be able (2:6) to utter bad words.

(2:7) Here, they sent the angel (2:8) to the presence of Daniel, thus (2:9) shall he overcome all people, (2:10) and the mouths of all (2:11) people should be shut, (2:12) as well as the mouth of Mūsā son of Jala, (2:13) that he may not harm me, (2:14) I, Sitahm.

(2:15) In the name of Yah, Yah, Yah, (2:16) Yah Yah, Aḥya, (2:17) and in the name of El Shaddai, (2:18) holy is his name, Sabaoth, (2:19) he shall be with (2:20) Sitahm in her going (2:21) and coming, and ... (2:22) I shall pass and cause (2:23) Sitahm to find favour and mercy

(2:24) in the eyes of every one who watches her. (2:25) Amen and Amen.

Commentary

1:4 מעינא looks like a participle of עַיֵּן, combined with the pronoun אנא. The sense required here should perhaps be "I blind", but this is not attested for this verb so far. It is possible that this is a corruption of מעיקנא.

1:6 ינזקון is a *pa*ʿ*el* or *af*ʿ*el* form.

1:7 Sitahm (or Sitham?) is not known as a proper name. Sitahm looks like the Persian word for "fury, violence", which in New Persian has the shape *sitam* (Middle Persian *stahm*). It does not seem likely that this name is to be read Sittuhum, literally "their lady".

1:8 Sitt al-Ahl is an Arabic title, meaning "Lady of the family".

1:28 שמו מץ שמו: These words constitute a repetition by mistake.

1:31 קץ רץ שץ תץ: The word שמו, which follows each of the names, is here omitted.

2:7 הא: Used instead of כמא ד- (?).

Geniza 20

T-S 12.41

Imprecations against anyone who unlawfully takes possession of a sacred book

Plate 64

הקדיש זה המצחף מׄ ו׳ פל׳ בר פל׳ חלקו עם שבע כתות של צדיקים בגן עדן וערסו תחת עץ החיים והספר התורה הזה הוא קודש לייׄ אלהי ישראל לא ימכר ולא יגאל והמוכרו או הגונבו או המוציאו על מנת ימכרהו או יגנבהו יהיה בחרם ייי צבאות ובחרם יהושע בן נון שחרם ביריחו ובחרם שחרמו עשרת אחי יוסף והשכינה היתה עמהם ויהיה מחורם בשם אכתריאל יה זה יהוה צבאות ויהיה מחורם מפי יושב הכרובים ויהיה מחורם מכ(סא ה)כבוד

ויהיה מחורם מחיות ואופנים ויהיה מחורם מפי מיטטרון
ויהיה מחורם מפי יפיפייה שר התורה ויהיה מחורם מפי
זגנזאל ויהיה מחורם מפי שבעה מלאכים גבריאל מיכאל
רפאל צדקיאל ענאל אוריאל חסדיאל ויהיה מחורם
משבעה רקיעים ומשבעה ארצות ומשבעים אומות ומישראל
ויהודה וידבקו בו כל הקללות הכתובות בתורה ובנביאים ובכתובים
ויקולל במאה תוכחות פחות שתים לא יאבה ייי סלוח לו והבדילו
ייי לרעה מכל שבטי ישראל ומחה ייי את שמו מתחת השמים יהיו
בניו יתומים ואשתו אלמנה יואבד ויכנע ויושמד וימחה את שמו
מספר חיים כל הגונב וכל המוכר אתו יהי(ה) [ ] (ק)ללות
האלה וכאלה ברם כל ברכן יהיה כגק מר [ ]
כל הברכות הכתובות בתורה ובנביאי(ם) ובכתובים [ ]
נזר ועטרת ותפארת ויבואו על ראש[ ]
אמן ואמ[ן]

Translation

(1) This codex was dedicated by Our Master Rabbi N son of N, may his share be with the seven classes of the righteous (2) in Paradise, and may his place of rest be underneath the tree of life. This Book of the Law is exclusively dedicated to God, (3) the God of Israel. It should not be sold or redeemed. Whoever sells it, steals it, or takes it out (4) in order to sell it or steal it, shall be under the ban of the God of Hosts and under the ban that Joshua (5) son of Nun imposed on Jericho, and under the ban that the ten brothers of Joseph imposed, and the Divine Presence (6) was with them.

He shall be under a ban in the name of Akatriel, Yah Zah. YHWH Sabaoth. (7) He shall be under a ban from the mouth of him who sits among the cherubim. He shall be under a ban from the throne of glory. (8) He shall be under a ban from the living beings and the *ofanim*. He shall be under a ban from the mouth of Metatron. (9) He shall be under a ban from the mouth of Yefefiya, the prince of the Torah. He shall be under a ban from the mouth of (10) Zagnaza᾿el. He shall be under a ban from the mouth of the seven angels: Gabriel, Michael, (11) Raphael, Ṣidqi᾿el, ῾Ana᾿el, Uriel, Ḥasdi᾿el. He shall be under a ban (12) from the seven firmaments and from the seven lands and from the seventy nations and from Israel (13) and Judah. May all the oaths written in the Torah, in the Prophets and in the Ketubbim cling to him. (14) May he be cursed with ninety-eight admonitions. May God refuse to forgive him. May

God (15) separate him for ill from all the tribes of Israel, and wipe his name off from under the sky. May his sons (16) become orphaned, and his wife widowed. May he be lost, subdued, destroyed, and may his name be erased (17) from the book of the living. Any one who steals or sells it shall be ... (18) these curses and (others) like these. However, all blessings shall be (on the head of) the respected, honoured, and revered master ... (19) all the blessings written in the Torah, in the Prophets [and in Ketubbim ...] (20) a crown, a diadem, and an ornament, and may they come to the head of ... (21) Amen Amen.

Commentary

This text does not belong formally to the genre of incantations. It is a dedicatory text written on a codex of the Pentateuch, but since it makes use of detailed imprecations and blessings (the latter much shorter and partly lost), it is close in style and contents to the incantation texts, and gives a good specimen of the absence of clear boundaries between the two types of writing.

Geniza 21

T-S Arabic 1c.36

Verses from the Book of Psalms for a headache, for gaining access to the sultan and for a safe journey

Plate 65

הדא ברסם מן תוגעה ראסה נאפע אן שא אללה תעלי
למה רגשו גוים ולאמים יהגו ריק: יתיצבו מלכי ארץ
ורוזנים נוסדו יחד על ייי ועל משיחו: ננתקה את
מוסרותימו ונשליכה ממנו עבתימו: יושב בשמים
ישחק אדני ילעג למו: אז ידבר אלימו באפו ובחרונו
[יבה]למו: ואני נסכתי מלכי על ציון הר קדשי:
[אספרה] אל חק יי אמר אלי בני אתה אני הי[ום]
[ילדתיך:] שאל ממני ואתנה גוים נחלתך ו[אחזתך]
[אפסי] ארץ: תרועם בשבט ברזל ככלי [יוצר]
תנ[פצ]ם: הדא ברסם קבול ללסלטאן

וללטריק יסלם מן אל(קטא)ע ומן כל מ[ ]
אן שא אללה תעאלי וברסם מן תוגעה
ראסה נאפע אן שא אללה תעאלי:
מזמור לדויד בברחו מפני אבש[לום]
בנו: יי מה רבו צרי רבים קמים
עלי: רבים אומרים לנפשי [אין]
ישועתה לו באלהים סלה: וא[תה]
יי מגן בעדי כבודי ומרים
ראשי: קולי אל [יי אקרא]
ויענני מהר קדשו סלה
אני שכבתי ואישנה הקי[צותי]
כי יי יסמכני: לא אירא
מרבבות עם אשר סביב
שתו עלי: קומה יי הושיעני
אלהי כי הכית את כל
אויבי לחי שני ר[שע]ים
שברת: ליי הישועה
על עמך ברכתך
סלה: נאפע
אן שא
אללה
תעאלי
(...)

Translation

(1) « This is for someone whose head aches. Useful, God willing. » (2-10) [Ps. 2:1-9].

(10) « This is for being accepted by a ruler (11) and for a journey. He will be safe from highway robbers and from all ..., (12) God willing. Also for someone whose head (13) aches. Useful, God willing. » (14-29) [Ps. 3:1-9]. (29) Useful, (30) God (31) willing.

Commentary

An extract from *Shimmush Tehilim*, only partly corresponding to the printed editions.

Geniza 22

T-S Misc. 27.4.11

From a book of magic recipes, with a recipe by R. Shimeon b. Yoḥay

Plates 66-67

[1]

1 אם ביקש שישתעבדו לך כל הרוחות ועושים כל
2 מלאכה שבעולם הזכיר השם הזה בשבועה והם
3 משתעבדים לך ובו היה שלמה משתעבד אותם (ב)ו
4 ועשה בטהרה ואז תצליח מלך אביר ושמך אביר זהב
5 אורביניתייה עגבר חותיפירו צריפתי יהוה אלהי יש
6 ניגתותייה אש צש איתיה עקל מתיוה עקרפתי
7 ניוה זך זך יהיה יהוי אאין והוא וה חי יה יהוה
8 כת על חסף דלא אזי הראות איתבאות קולהון ((קלהון))
9 ספתון ((ספונין)) סוסיג ((סוסגר)) מכמר אתון מלאכיא קדיש
((אשבע[ית] / עליכון / היך / מה)) כמה
10 דהדין חספא יקוד ((בנורא)) כן יקד ליבא דפ בן פל וכוליתיה
11 בתרי ובתר גדי ובתר חלקי ולא ידמוך ליביה
12 ויתהפכון לי ((עד זמן דתיתי [בתרי])) אנא פבפ לאהבה ולרחמה רבא בשם
13 נביאל מלאכה ואנת סמאל סטנא אבצלח ואנת
14 אשמדיי קלילא עבידו לי צביוני בהדא שעתא
15 [ב]מהרה בפריע מעתה ועד עולם קינו קינו אמן
16 [אמן ס]לה הללויה (*magic characters*)
17 [לאתתא דמקשיא למילד טו]ל [ק]ליפה שלאבטיח
18]ה[ ]

[2]

1 לר שמעון בן יוחי ולכל תלמידין צום ג ימים וכת בטרפין
2 דער ומחוק יתיה במי מבוע והב יתיה בכסא והב כסא
3 בארונא ג יומין וביום השלישי שתה אותו ואותו היום לא
4 תיחמי אשה וטהר עצמך מכל דבר רע . oo
5 באדיאב האיי מראות חאמוס אלס
6 אבירי ואנבוכון ברוך שם כבוד מלכותו
7 לעולם ועד
8 אין דורשין בעריות לשלשה ולא במעשה בראשית
9 לשנים ולא במרכבה ליחיד בראשית ראשית

10 בגימטריא נפיק יוד שבאלבם וסלק ליוד שבאלבם
11 הי נפיק מן הו ומן עׂז שבאחס ומן למד שבאלבם וסלק
12 ליוד שבאחס וׂאׂ נפיק מן יוד ומן פי שבאחס וסלק
13 לוא שבאתבש נפיק מן הי ומן אלף שבאחס ומן לאמד שבאלבם וסליק ליוד שבאחס
14 לאשתא יכׂ בקלף
15 אבג יתץ. קרע שטן. נתד יכש. פטר צתג. הקב טנע. יגל פזק. שקוצ[ית]
16 ברוך שם כבׂ מלכותו לעולם ועד. בר[וך ...]
17 שמו לעולם ולעולמי [...]
18 זה המ[...]

Translation

page 1

(1:1) If (you) wish to subdue all the spirits, that they should do (for you) all (1:2) the (various) works in the world, mention this name with an oath, and they (1:3) will be subdued to you. By this (name) Solomon used to subdue them. (1:4) Act in purity and you will succeed. Melekh Abir and your name is Abir. **ZHB** (?). (1:5-7) (*combinations of words and letter.*)

(1:8) Write on an unbaked clay: **hrʾwt ʾytbʾwt qwlhwn ((qlhwn))** (1:9) **sptwn ((spwnyn)) swsyg ((swsgr)) mkmr**. You, the holy angels, ((I adjure you.)) Just as (1:10) this piece of clay burns in the fire, so shall the heart of N son of N and his kidneys burn (1:11) after me and after my fortune and after my lot. His heart shall not sleep. (1:12) They shall turn to me ((until she (!) follows me [me])), I, N son of N, with great love and affection. By the name of (1:13) Nebiel the Angel, and you, Samaʾel the Satan, **ʾbṣlḥ**, and you, (14) Ashmedai the swift, perform my desire at this hour, (1:15) quickly, at once, from now till eternity. **qynw, qynw**, Amen, (1:16) [Amen, Se]lah, Hallelujah.

(1:17) [For a woman who has a difficult delivery. Ta]ke [the p]eel of a melon …

page 2

(2:1) By R. Shimeon ben Yoḥai and his disciples. Fast for three days and write on bay-(2:2)leaves, and wash it off with the water of a spring. Put it in a cup and put the cup (2:3) in a chest for three days. On the third day drink it. On that day you (2:4) shall not look at a woman, and you shall purify yourself from every evil thing.

(2:5-6) (*magic combinations*) Blessed be the name of the glory of His kingdom (2:7) for ever and ever.

(2:8) It is forbidden to study sexual matters in the company of three men, or the story of Genesis (2:9) in the company of two, or the matter of the Chariot in the company of one.

Bereshit is *reshit* (2:10) by *gimatria*. The *yod* of *Albam* goes out and it goes up to the *yod* of *Albam*. (2:11) *He* goes out from **hw** and from **ʿz** of Aḥas and from *lamed* of Albam, and it goes up (2:12) to *yod* of Aḥas and *alef* goes out of *yod* and of *pe* of Aḥas and goes up (2:13) to **w**ʾ of Atbash, it goes out from *he* and from *alef* of Aḥas and from *lamed* of Albam and goes up to *yod* of Aḥas.

(2:14) For fever. Let him write on a piece of parchment. (2:15) (*magic words*) (2:16) Blessed be the name of the glory of His kingdom for ever and ever. Bl[essed ...] (2:17) be His name for ever and ever ...

Commentary

1:1 אם ביקש: An error for **אם ביקשת**.

1:2 הזכיר: This is the imperative form הַזְכֵּר.

1:3 ובו היה שלמה משתעבד אותם: The seemingly passive form **משתעבד** is used in an active sense, a phenomenon which is not rare in rabbinical literature and other writings of the period (see Kutscher 1982, p. 131; Bar-Asher 1983, pp. 91ff.; Yadin and Greenfield in: Lewis 1989, p. 148). The last **בו** is superfluous.

1:4 אביר: Perhaps **אכיר**, the initial letters אמן כן יהי רצון.
זהֹכֹ: Read perhaps זהֹכֹ, for זה הכתוב?

1:8ff. Cf. A 10, which contains essentially the same text, and which is itself a specimen of an unbaked piece of clay, as required by the recipe. The text of A10 can be reconstructed with greater accuracy and confidence on the basis of the present Geniza text as follows:

הראות	אתבאות	קולהון
ספתון	סוסגר	[מכמר]

אתון מלאכיה קד[ישיה...]
[אשבעית] יתכון כמה [דהדין חספא]
[יקוד (בנורא) כן] יקוד לבה דר[חל ברתה]
[דמר]ין בתרי אנה ...[... בר ... ויתהפכון]
[לבה והונה ו]כוליתה [לרחמה ...]
[... ולא י]דמוך [ליבה ...]
[... ואתון סמאל ואשמדי עבידו לי]
ציביוני בהדה [שעתה במהרה בפריע אמן]

1:10 The text formula here is indecisive as to the gender of the two parties, and uses mostly masculine forms for both. Only the gloss in line 12 דתיתי is feminine.

1:11 גדי and חלקי signify approximately the same thing, viz. fortune.

1:17f. Supplemented according to G11, p. 3:16ff.

1:15 קינו seems to be connected to קינולגיה, cf. G16, p. 2:16. Cf. also קני לוגיה in G18, p. 8:9 and possibly 9:5.

2:2 דער is written רעד.

2:8ff. This is the famous text which occurs in Mishna Ḥagiga 2:1.

2:9ff. This is a somewhat unclear set of instructions connected with speculations based on various arrangements of the alphabet. It is translated here without any claim to understanding their precise meaning.

2:15 This is the well-known combination of letters connected with the hymn אנא בכח (for which cf. Schrire 1966, p. 98). There are certain variations here on the traditionally established sequence, and a conscientious editor marked some notes in the text. Over the second letter of נתד יכש there is a ק, as well as over the last but one letter. The traditional sequence is נגד יכש. There is no mark over פטר, which should have been בטר, or over הקב, which should have been חקב. The editor (or the original scribe) marked a dot in the space above every sixth letter of the sequence (in our transliteration the dots have been placed between the words).

Geniza 23

T-S Arabic 44.44

From a book of magic recipes: Formulae against forgetting, for love, and for other purposes

Plates 68-69

[1]

אוכלת אש הוא בֹרשֹכֹמֹלֹו:
בשם אדוניאל שנחקק בקרבו שם
המפורש |אבסכס| הגדול והנורא
שמע ישראל יהוה אלהינו יהוה אחד
ובשם קדוש בְרוּנְיָה אבֶן טפַיָה ופַלי
[ ]שם השם שֹמַסְיֹה הַרֹרֵי רֹוֹן
(אל)הא דישראל

[2]

באב ללנסיאן קח פיולי שלזכוכית וכתוב
עליה האתות הללו ומחוק במים חיים וש(תה)
ועשה [ב]טהרה בשם יֹהֹוֹהֹ בקטור
למרינייה רוקיני צוגייה יֹהֹוֹהֹ צבאות קינו

באב ללקרח	באב לנידה למפסוק
אכשה מבשה	סב חד טרף דערבה וכתֿ
קפוטה	ביה גטבט נוריה כל
באב לשקיקה אכת עלי	טרף לירחא ואין תרי ׳ תרין
ורק קצב ואדעה עלי	ירחין ואי תלת לתלת ׳ ירחין
ראסה פ (8x)	בין בריק ק (9x)
ייה חוד חים	צ (7x)

ייה יה (...) חי וה יהוה נא אל רפא נא אל
כאתם שלמה בן דויד עלקה ע[לי]
דראעך ולא תכאף שי אֹהֹ וֹהֹ יהוֹהֹ הֹו חי חו חי ח[ ]
חו חיחי[ ]
הא מסמיה בשם (*a cross*) צבאות צבאות ממסך
אֹסֹ
לאהבה כאתם (איצא)
כד מסמ((א))ר מן כשבה מצלוב ואעמל מנה כאתם
ואיצא אכר פצֹה ואנקש עליה אורי בלע תלע

20 פאדא ארדת תעמל בה מא   הלע אוריה
21 שית פכוד ... תראב אל אל(י)((כ))לד וכוד דיך אביץ
22 אפרק ואדבחה עלי דלך אלתראב ואגבלהא
23 ואעמלהא טאבע

Translation

page 1

(1:1) "... is a consuming fire", blessed be the name of the glory of His kingdom for ever and ever.

(1:2) In the name of Adoniel, in whom the ineffable name (1:3) was engraved, Absax, the great and awesome. (1:4) "Hear, O Israel. The lord our God is one Lord" (Dt 6:4). (1:5-6) And in the holy name of Berunia, [other *nomina barbara* follow]. (1:7) God of Israel, ...

page 2

(2:1) Chapter for forgetfulness. Take a glass bowl and write (2:2) on it these symbols and wash it off with living water, and drink, (2:3) and act in purity. In the name of YHWH (*magic names*) (2:4) (*magic names*) YHWH Sabaoth, **qynw**.

(*Column 1*) (2:5) Chapter for an ulcer. (2:6-7) (*magic words*). (2:8) Chapter for a (headache of) half the head (?). Write on (2:9) the leaf of a reed, and put it on (2:10) his head (2:11-12) (*magic words*) "Heal her now, O God".

(*Column 2*) (2:5) Chapter for menstruation, that it should cease. (2:6) Take one leaf of a willow and write (2:7) on it (*magic words*) each (2:8) leaf for a month. If it is two, two (2:9) months, and if it is three, for three months, (2:10-11) (*letters and magic words*).

(2:13) The seal of Solomon son of David. Suspend it from (2:14) your arm, and you will not fear anything. (*magic words and letters*). (2:16) In the name of Sabaoth, Sabaoth, **mmsk**. Amen, Selah.

(2:17) For love. A seal, again. (2:18) Take a nail from the wood of someone crucified, and make of it a seal. (2:19) Again, another one, of silver, and engrave on it (*magic words*). (2:20) If you wish, you can make with it what you will. (2:21) Take the dust of ... (?) , and take a white cock,

(2:22) and slaughter it on that earth, mix it with water, (2:23) and make of it an impression.

Commentary

1:1 אוכלת אש הוא: This looks like a corruption of Dt 4:24 אש אכלה הוא.

1:2 ברשכמלו: This is an abbreviation of ברוך שם כבוד מלכותו לעולם ועד.

1:3 Absax is evidently a corruption of Abrasax.

2:5-11 is dividied into two columns.

2:8 שקיקה means in Arabic "half the head", and here apparently an ache in that area is meant.

2:12 נא אל רפא נא אל is based on Nu 12:13 אל נא רפא נא לה.

2:19 אכר is perhaps a corruption of כד, or of אבר<ה> "needle".

2:20 Line 21 continues תעמל בה מא. The letters הלע אוריה seem to belong to the previous line.

2:21 פכוד .. תראב אל אל(י)((כ))לד: This sequence of words is unclear.

2:22 אפרק is another term for "a white cock", already expressed by the words דיך אבין.

Geniza 24

T-S Arabic 44.127

From a manual of magic recipes: For repelling insects

Plates 70-71

[1]

1 לטרד אל[צ]ראציר מן אלבי[ת]
2 אכתב ואחד ועשרין יום פי אל( )
3 או כ̄ב̄ ואג̇עלה פי ד̇ זוא(יא) אלב[ית]
4 (*magic characters*)
5 אתון כלקטיריא תקיפיא ומשבח[יא]
6 אפיקו צרצריה דאית בהדין ביתא

7 דפלב̇ פל̇ א̇א̇ס̇:
8 באב (אכר) לטרב [!] אלצראציר
9 יכתב [ ] חוה חוה אדם
10 קט(ט)[...] יופיאל יפוק כג[....]
11 מן הדין ביתא אמן א̇
12 באב אכר לעק[רב]
13 עקרבה עקרב[וניתה]
14 [ ]חק מסרך א[...]
15 [ ]ח( ) אתא[...]

[2]

1 בחתמה דשלמה ובחוטריה
2 [דא]ברהם: באב אחר
3 (ע)קרבה עקרבוניתה מיכאל
4 על מקרניך ועל קרנותיך כפי
5 שמיה על מתנתיך וכוכבי
6 שמיא אסרין בחרציך אמר י״י
7 לא את מכייה לי ולא אנא מכי ליך
8 באב לשנאה
9 כוד רצאץ ואעמל(ה) צפי(חה)
10 וכוד שמע אביץ וס[ויה] שבה
11 [אלא]תנין אלאנתי ואלדכר
12 [ ] ואכתב בהא עלי

(*magic names in two or more triangles*)

[3]

1 פלא נום יכ[ון לה] ולא הדו ולא [ ]
2 ולא עיש אלא בנטר פל ותו[ ]
3 מע אלסחב תודי ומע אלרי[ ]
4 ואלהרי תדרי ומע אלדיב ת(לד)י ומע
5 אלכלב תעוי כתמ(ת) עלי פל (בר) [פל]
6 בכאתם מוסי על[...]
7 תסמע עלי ב[...]
8 אלי אחד אלא פל̇ ועלי גוארח[הא]
9 וחואסהא ב(זף זף) צאחב אלב[ ]
10 ואלראיאת בין כתפיה חתי יסוא[...]

11 אלי פל̇ יא מ(..) אלקואד [...]
12 אגלבוה ואחמלוה מן משרק אל
13 ארץ̇ ומן מגרבהא וסהלהא
14 וג̇באלהא ובחארהא וברהא מע דלך
15 תכון אלנאר מן תחתהא ומן פוקהא

[4]

1 [ען] ימינהא וען שמאלהא ומן
2 [ורא]הא ומן קדאמהא כתמת
3 עלי קלבהא ועלי גוארחהא ועלי
4 גמיע חואסהא ותגוע ולא
5 תאכל ויעטש ולא ישרב ויכון
6 אחלא (מן) אלעסל ואלד מן אלמא
7 [צח]בתהא לפל בחק הדה אל
8 [א]סמא אל מכזונה אלמטהרה
9 אלמקדסה אלא אטעתם
10 [וא]גבתם וסמעתם וג̇לבתם
11 פלניתא בר פלני לפלני בר
12 פלני בשם אהיה אשר אהיה
13 יה שדי צבאות אלהים רחום
14 ומשוש חתן על כלה אמן סלה

Translation

page 1

(1:1) « For chasing away crickets from the house. (1:2) Write for 21 days in the … (1:3) or 22, and place it in the four corners of the ho[use]. » (1:4) (*magic characters*).

(1:5) You, O mighty and praised characters, (1:6) cause the crickets that are in this house (1:7) of N son of N to go out, Amen Amen Selah.

(1:8) « Another chapter for *chasing away crickets. (1:9) Let there be written » … Eve Eve Adam (1:10) … Yopiel, let him go out … (1:11) from this house, Amen, Amen.

(1:12) Another chapter for sco[rpions]. (1:13) Scorpion, [small female] scorpion, (1:14) … (1:15) … came …

page 2
(2:1) ...by the seal of Solomon, by the rod (2:2) of Abraham.

Another chapter. (2:3) Scorpion, small female scorpion, Michael is (2:4) over your scalp and over your horns, the domes (2:5) of the sky over your waist, the stars of the sky gird your loins. God says: (2:7) You shall not harm me, nor shall I harm you.

(2:8) A chapter for hatred. (2:9) «Take lead and make of it a tab[let]. (2:10) And take white wax and [make it] like (2:11) the two, the male and the female, (2:12) ... and write with it on ... (*magic names*)»

page 3
(3:1) «and no sleep [will be to him] and no peace and no ... (3:2) and no living except through the sight of N ... (3:3) with the cloud you shall perish (?) and with the ... (3:4) and the wicked (?) you shall know and with the wolf you shall give birth and with the dog (3:5) you shall howl. I have sealed N [son of N] (3:6) with the seal of Moses [peace be with him]. (3:7) You shall listen to ... (3:8) to (no) one except to N and over [her] limbs (3:9) and her senses by **zp zp** the master of the ... (3:10) and the banners on his shoulder until he shall be equal to ... (3:11) to N, O ... of the commanders ... (3:12) overcome him and carry him from the easternmost part of the (3:13) earth and from its westernmost part, (from) its plains (3:14) and (from) its hills, (from) its seas and (from) its dry places. At the same time (3:15) the fire should be under her and over her,»

page 4
(4:1) «[at] her right hand side and at her left hand side, at her (4:2) [ba]ck and in front of her. I have sealed (4:3) her heart and her limbs and (4:4) all her senses. She shall be hungry and shall not eat, he (!) shall be thirsty and shall not drink. And there shall be (4:6) sweeter than honey and more delightful than water (4:7) her [friendship] with N. By the power of these (4:8) hidden, pure (4:9) and holy names, may you obey, (4:10) [res]pond, listen, overpower» (4:11) N *daughter of N for N son (4:12) N. By the name of I-am-who-I-am, (4:13) Yah, Shaddai, Sabaot, Elohim, the merciful one, (4:14) and "the bridegroom rejoices over the bride" (Is. 62:5). Amen, Selah.

Commentary

1:8 לטרב is evidently an error for לטרד, perhaps caused by contamination with לצֹרב.

2:2 [דא]ברהם: Although the reading is partly restored, it seems fairly certain. The association of a rod with Abraham, rather than with Aaron, is quite peculiar.

באב אחר presents a mixture of Arabic (or Aramaic?) with Hebrew.

2:3ff. This formula is already familiar from G11, p. 3:1ff.; G14, p. 2:1ff.

2:4 מקרניך: One recalls that מוקדא is "the top of the head" and מוקרא is "brain, marrow"; cf. note to B13:8 (*AMB*, p. 208). The two words appear to have been confused with each other, at least at the late date in which this Geniza fragment may have been copied; it was no doubt phonetically associated with the following word, which designates "horns". The form with a final *-ānā* is not so far attested.

2:5 מתנתיך: This word for "waist", occurring also G11, p. 3:2; G14, p. 2:5, is not attested in this form in the Talmudic literature, but this is almost certainly the meaning required here.

3:3 תוֹדִי The form required here, if this is from the verb **WDY**, is *tūdīna* "to perish", unless the writer wanted to use a grammatically unacceptable passive form, *tūdā* (for the 3rd singular feminine) or *tūdayīna* (for the 2nd singular feminine). In any case the vowel signs do not fully accord with any of these possibilities. The forms תלדי shows that the writer omitted the *-na* ending in the 2nd singular feminine of the imperfect, as is common in dialects.

4:5 ויעטש ולא ישרב: There is here an abrupt change from the use of the feminine to the masculine.

Geniza 25

T-S Arabic 49.54
From a book of magic recipes: For a lame woman, for difficulty in childbirth, and for other purposes
Plates 72-73

[1]

אכר[ ]
[...](..קר) וקול עליה
קרית שמע ז̇ז̇ אלי אכרהא וקול
(ויוש)ע ז̇ז̇ אלי ת(פ)ול וקול אמת ויציב
ז̇ מראר אלי ואין עוד אלהים זולתך
וארמי ד̇ חצ(א)יאת מ(ן) ד̇ ג̇האת
כמא תקדם. וארבט (אלג̇) פי (סלאלך)
(..ב)ה אי(.)ך ואד.... הא)
(...א) קלת (מן אלכלאם) [...]
כרוג̇ך באליל פאדא אצבחת [ ]
אלקול:
באב לטחונה
כוד תוראב מן תחת רג̇לך אליסאר ואלקיה
פי חלקהא וקול בשם אלפונים
לפנונים ואכפונים אתון אתיה קד[ישיה]
ושמהתא (קדישי)ה אסורו הדא (...)
דל[א ... ה]אדא שעתא:

[2]

קול אנפינוס אפנתפינוס
אתון שמהתה קדישיה
שרון הדא טחונתה
ותהלך: מג̇רב
מפר אותות בדים
וקוסמים יהולל משיב
חכמים אחור ודעתם
יסכל:

[3]

1 מקלוב
2 יסכל ודעתם אחור [חכמים]
3 משיב יהולל וקוסמים
4 בדים אותות מפר
5 מגֿרב
6 למרה עסר עליהא אלו(לאד)[ה]
7 כוד כזפה זפת מן אלסוק ואכתוב
8 פיהא: דאין שמא חמש זמנין
9 ודעה עלי בטנהא וכמא תלד ירפע
10 ואלא אנחדר אמעאהא
11 חורי מופוס חמש זמנין זפיר [...]

[4]

1 [   ]פלֿ מן קבילא לנוהרָא
2 [והי]א מצלחא אמן ואמן סלה
3 מגֿרב ללמצורע
4 כוד כוז גדיד ומלאה מא וקול עליה
5 סבע כראת   ויקצוף נעמן
6 וילך ויאמר הנה אמרתי אלי יצא
7 יצוא ועמד וקרא בשם ((ײי)) אלוהיו
8 והניף ידו אל המקום ואסף המצורע
9 (וחדר) ומיתי קרלי וקי ליבנא ולאיש
10 ל[הון] בחדדי במיי רגלין והוא אל
11 (ב)ול דבתולתא (ד)לאמא היא לחיק
12 והוא מ(נש׳) יברא אֿאמן סלה

Translation

page 1

(1:1) «Another one. [...] (1:2) ... and say over it (1:3) the *Shemaʿ* (Dt. 6:4) seven times, up to its end. And recite (1:4) *Wayyošaʿ* (Ex. 14:30) seven times up to *Tippol* (Ex. 15:16). And say *emet we-yaṣib* (1:5) seven times to *we-en ʿod elohim zulatekha*, (1:6) and throw four pebbles from four directions (1:7) as was (said) before. And tie the three (?) in your baskets (?) (1:8) ... (1:9) ... (1:10) your coming out at night, but when you get up in the morning ... (1:11) the speech.»

(1:12) «A chapter for a lame woman (?). (1:13) Take dust from underneath your left foot and throw it (1:14) into her gullet, and say:» "In the name of (*magic* (1:15) *words*). You, holy characters (1:16) and holy names, bind this ... (1:17) that he may not ... this hour".

page 2

(2:1) «Say»: (*magic names*), (2:2) you, holy names, (2:3) release this female lame (?) person (2:4) that she may walk. «Tested.»

(2:5) "That frustrates the tokens of the liars (2:6) and makes diviners mad; that turns (2:7) the wise men backward and makes their knowledge (2:8) foolish" (Is. 44:15).

page 3

(3:1) «Turned (backwards)». (3:2-4) (Is. 44:15 *in reverse order of words.*) (3:5) «Tested.»

(3:6) «For a woman who has difficulty in ch[ildbirth]. (3:7) Take a sherd (?) of pitch from the market place and write (3:8) on it:» **d'yn** name, five times, (3:9) «and place it over her belly, and as soon as she gives birth let it be removed. (3:10) Otherwise, her intestines will go down.» (3:11) (*magic names*) five times. ...

page 4

(4:1) [... bring] N from darkness to light. (4:2) [and it is] successful. Amen, Amen, Selah.

(4:3) «Proven. For a leper. (4:4) Take a new jar, fill it with water, and say over it (4:5-8) seven times:» "But Naaman was wroth, and went away, and said: Behold, I thought He will surely come out to me, and stand, and call on the name of the Lord his God, and strike his hand over the place, and recover the leper" (2 Kings 5:11).

(4:9) And he should again bring ... and frankincense and knead (4:10) them together with urine «that is the» (4:11) «urine» of a virgin that is in her mother's lap, (4:12) and immediately «he will be healed». Amen Amen Selah.

Commentary

1:4 אמת ויציב: Cf. Bavli Berakhot 12a, 13a; Mishna Tamid 5:1.

1:5 ואין עוד אלהים זולתך: Cf. Beer 1937, p. 84 (where this blessing ends אין אלהים זולתך).

1:12 טחונה is an Arabic form of the Aramaic טחונתה in 2:3. The Aramaic word means normally "a miller" (feminine). The context here however indicates that it should mean something like "lame, cripple"; cf. 2:3-4.

3:8 דאין שמא: It is doubtful whether there is a *yod* after the *alef* in **dʾyn**. This "name" brings to mind the mysterious **dʾn** of Amulet 7a:22.

4:9 וחדר: Although this is written with a *ḥeth* it is clear that the word is the same as הדר. The same observation applies to בחדדי in line 10, which clearly corresponds to בהדדי.

קרלי וקי may be some substances that, together with the frankincense mentioned after them, served as ingredients in the preparation described here.

4:10f. והוא אל בול is evidently a gloss in Arabic (although הוא is spelled as in Hebrew and Aramaic) on the expression במיי רגלין.

4:11 (ד)לאמא היא לחיק is quite clearly written, but without any apparent sense. לחיק perhaps signifies "in the bosom, in the lap" of a mother, and the whole phrase therefore probably means "who is (still) on the lap of her mother". This is offered with considerable reservations.

4:12 מנש׳ may be an abbreviation of מן שעתיה "at once". Syriac has מן שלי, מנשל, etc. for expressing the notion of suddenness.

יברא "to be healed, recover" is Arabic.

Geniza 26

T-S Misc. 10.35 + Misc. 10.122

A collection of recipes: For love, for all purposes

Plates 74-75

[1]

T-S Misc. 10.122

1 אלקסם אלתאני והוא

2 לאהבה כתוב יתיה לסמרטוט מבגדו השבעתי

3 עליך אהביאל סרא רבא וזה הוא השם בשם
4 אבא דהת הזי אלד לאן ההע שתתן לי ((אני)) פל ב פ
5 בלביה דפלני בר פלוני אהבה רבה וחן וחסד ורחמנותא בשם
6 ה[ש]ם (ה)זה ותלי על ידיך טוב יהיה ולכל דעבד מכל טוב יועיל על
7 מגילת צבי אמן אמן סלה

(*Verso: Unrelated notes in Arabic script*)

[2]
T-S Misc. 10.35

1 אלקסם לג והוא לכל צורך לביש להרוג ולשלוח אש וגם לשנאה
2 וגם להפריד כתוב על סמרטוט מן בגד מי שתחפוץ וטמון בתר((עיה))
3 ודין תכתוב השבעתי עליכון מלאכיא קדישיא דאנון
4 (ק)מיאל וסרפיאל הפריאל והגזיאל וסטניאל והפכיאל בשם
5 (א)ליסבה. הַרֶיָ הַקָם לֶאַוּדלו שתשלחו אש מאצלכם עלי
6 פל בן פלו׳ אף ואש וחמה וקצף ומשחית ותמחון יתיה מן דארי עלמה
7 ומן תחות שמיא ואם בעת לסנאה אמור
8 שתתנו שנאה ואבה ותחרות לפלוני בר פלוני באנפי פל׳ ב פל מיומא הדין

verso

1 ועד עלמא א אמן סלה

(*The rest of the page contains notes in Arabic script, unrelated*)

Translation

page 1

(1) «The second incantation.» It is (2) for love. Write it on a piece of cloth from his garment. I adjure (3) you, Ahabiel, the great prince, and this is the name, by the name of (4) (*magic names*), may you give me, I, N son of N, (5) great love, charm, grace and affection in the heart of N son of N, by the name (6) of this name. Hang (it) on your hand(s). It will be good, and it will be useful for every good thing that he will do. [Write it] on (7) a scroll (of) deer (hide). Amen, Amen, Selah.

page 2

(1) «The third incantation.» It is meant for every need, for causing disease, for killing, for causing fire, also for hatred, (2) also for separating

(two people from each other). Write on a piece of cloth from the garment of whoever you wish, and hide (it) in his gate. (3) And this is what you should write: I adjure you, holy angels, who are (4) Kamiel, Sarafiel, Hafriel, Hagziel, Sataniel, Hafkiel. In the name of (5) (*magic words*), that you may send forth fire from your quarters against (6) N son of N, anger, and fire, and wrath, and indignation, and destroyer, and that you may wipe him off from amongst the inhabitants of the world (7) and from under the sky. If you wish (to use it) for hatred, say: (8) That you may place hatred, grudge and rivalry towards N son of N in front of N son of N from this day (*verso*) to eternity. Amen Amen Selah.

Commentary

The two fragments brought together in this section seem to be written by the same hand and to belong to the same notebook. In both cases they are written on the length of the paper and in principle on one side of the leaf (though in the case of fragment 2 there was no room on the recto, and the last words were written on the verso). The two pages apparently belong to a loose-leaf notebook of magic recipes, as opposed to a book. The verso side of the individual leaves was subsequently used for commercial notes.

1:1 **אלקסם**: This word, which is used as a title for the second fragment as well, may denote either, as translated here, "incantation" (*qasam*, literally "oath"), or "part, section" (*qism*).

1:6 **ה[ש]ם (ה)זה**: One wonders whether these two words do not reflect, in a mutilated form, the name of the angel Shemḥazai; a *Midrash* Shemḥzai and ʿAzaʾel is edited in Jellinek 1853/1877, IV, pp. 127-128.

2:1 **לביש**: This is obviously a denominative from **בושא** "illness".

Geniza 27

T-S Misc. 29.4

Amulet against Abū l-Karam al-Khazzāz the Christian

Plate 76

1 בשמך רחמנא
2 משביע אני עליכון בשם כבשיאל
3 דכבש ימא בידיה וארעא {בקלל}
4 בקלולותיה כבוש לי בשם דישי בן
5 דישיבין דשובי ייי אלהא דאלהא
6 והוא עילאה ובשם נוריאל
7 ורח(מ)יאל דהוא ממונה על
8 תרעי נהורא ובשם ייי
9 צבאות אל {שדי} שדי ובשם
10 רח(מ)יאל בלום בר בלום מנ[י]
11 אנא הנלום עורו ופשרו
12 ו(ת)לאי (בנ)אי בשמך
13 מידות ביאל חי וגיבר חרש((א))
14 עבדא ופרושא לא מפרשא
15 היא תכבוש את לשון אבו אל
16 כרם אלכזאז אלנצראני אמן ((נצח סלה))
17 קנית זו עם יעבור עד ייי
18 עמך יעבור עד כאבן
19 ידמו זרועך בגדול ופחד
20 אימתה על לשון אבו
21 אלכרם אלנצראני ( )
22 אמן (נצח סלה) בחק (עליון)
23 הנגלה על הר סיני
24 אסאלך בזכות אברהם
25 בזכות יצחק בזכות יעקב
26 בזכות משה בזכות

In the right margin:

27 יהושע בזכות שמואל בזכות (דוד) בזכות דניאל חנניה מישאל ועזריה
28 אכביש (זה) אבו אלכרם אמן נצח סלה

On the back side there are several lines in Arabic characters, apparently unrelated.

Translation

(1) By your name, O merciful. (2) I adjure you, by the name of Kabshiel, (3) who subdued the sea by his hand and the earth (4) by his ...: Subdue for me, in the name of Dishi ben (5) Dishibin Dashubi, YYY the Lord of Lord(s) (6) and He is supreme. And in the name of Nuriel (7) and Raḥmiel, who is appointed over (8) the gates of light, and in the name of God (9) of Hosts, El Shaddai, and in the name of (10) Raḥmiel, Balum bar Balum, from me, (11), I, the Nalum. Rise and melt (?) (12) and ... By your name, (13) Midot Bi El, living and mighty, sorcerer, (14) magician, one who does not make explicit (?), (15) she will subdue the tongue of Abū l-(16)Karam al-Khazzāz the Christian, Amen, Neṣaḥ, Selah. (17-20) "Fear and dread [shall fall] upon them by the greatness of your arm they shall be as still as a stone" (Ex. 15:16), on the tongue of Abū (21) l-Karam the Christian. [Amen] (22) Neṣaḥ Selah. By the virtue of the Supreme One (23) who appears on Mount Sinai. (24) «I beg you» by the virtue of Abraham, (25) by the virtue of Isaac, by the virtue of Jacob, (26) by the virtue of Moses by the virtue of (27) Joshua, by the virtue of Samuel, by the virtue of David, by the virtue of Daniel, Hananiah, Mishael and Azariah. (28) Subdue this Abū l-Karam. Amen Neṣaḥ Selah.

Commentary

4 בקלולותיה: This word should mean something like "foot", but it is not yet attested in Aramaic.

14 ופרושא לא מפרשא: There are several alternative possibilities for understanding this sequence of words: "one who does not separate", "who does not keep off", "who does not explain".

15 Al-Khazzāz: The epithet means a silk merchant.

17-20 Ex. 15:16 is written backwards, with the order of words inverted.

Geniza 28

T-S NS 246.32

Magic recipes for love, for finding favour with people, and for other purposes

Plates 77-78

[3]

[...]ה
[...]ת (הכוז) בער חמאר וחש כדי מן כל
[ ](ט)יפות המנטפות מן הכוז ו(כך) יתחיל
[וי]אמר ז זמנין משבע אנא עליכון
שני הבחורים בשם סמאל ובשם קצפיאל ובשם
רוחיאל שר הרוחות ובשם סורדניאל ובשם
להקיאל טיט שרי טיט לקי להקיאל אתרסיאל
אבריאל באלין שמהתא משביע ומומי
יתכון שתהבו לפבפ קלא דלא פסיק מן
אחורי<ה> על כל טיפה וטיפה דנפיק מן הדין
בקבוקה דהוא כוזא יח((ת))ר פל בפ מתריז
מן חוריה ולא פסיק מן יומא דנן ובשעתא
(ד)א כל זמן דמטיף כוזא דנן על גללי
(ה)חמור אמן אֹסֹ — באב אהבה כתוב על
[ח](ס)ף דלא צלי וטלק לנורא
בשם מיכ̄אל וג̄בריאל ורפ̄אל וענ̄אל וחס̄דיאל
ונת̄ניאל וכב̄שיאל אתון מלאכיא קדישיא
בעי אנא מנכון דתוקדון ליבה ד(פל ב פ)
בתר פל̄ב̄פ̄ ואן הוות כפנא לא תיכול

[4]

[...]
בשם [ ]
[ ]
(ואל)היבו (לי)בה וכולייתה פ בן פ כמה הדה [חספא]
יוקדא כן תוקיד ליבה וכוליתיה דפ ב̄ פ ב[תר]
פב(פ)   ותטרח פי תנור פי נאר אותון //
[ל](זבינו) לחנותא כת׳ על קלף צבי

8 אשבעית עליכון רחמ̄יאל וחס̄דיאל וחנ̄יאל וכפ̄ש[יאל]
9 תנו חיל וחסד לפ בר פ̄ קדם כל בני אדם וחוה
10 ויתכנשון <ג>(ב)יה כל הרוצה ליש<א> וליתן לקנות
11 ולמכור כל דבר שבעולם ולא יהיה רשות לכל
12 בני אדם וחוה לפתוח פה לדבר ולענות לזה
13 פ ב̄ר̄ פל בשם ברקיאל ובשם קדושיאל ובשם
14 חסין יה שתתנו לפל בר̄ פ חן וחסד ולרחמים
15 לפני כל ראיו וימצא כקן ידו לחיל העמים
16 וימצא יוסף חן בעיניו וישרת אותו ויפקדהו
17 על ביתו וכ[ל י]ש לו נתן בידו וישרת בעיניו
18 (חן) יוסף וימצא ויהי יהוה את פל בר פ ויתן לו חן
19 וחסד בעיני הכל בשם כרוביאל המלאך על
20 [ ] ונח מצא חן בעיני יהוה (כן י)מצא פ [בן פ]
21 [ח]ן וחסד בעיני אלהים ואדם אמן אמן סלה

Translation

page 3

... (3:2) the jug «the dung of wild donkeys, thus:» From all (3:3) [...] the drops that come down from the jug and thus he should start (3:4) and say seven time: I adjure you, (3:5) the two youths, in the name of Samael, and in the name of Qaṣpiel, and in the name of (3:6) Ruḥiel the prince of the winds, and in the name of Surdaniel, and in the name of (3:7) Lahaqiel, (*magic words*) Lahaqiel, Atarsiel, (3:8) Abriel. By these names I adjure and invoke (3:9) you, that you should give N son of N a noise that does not stop from (3:10) his back. For every drop that comes out of this (3:11) pitcher, which is a jug, N son of N shall be discharging (3:12) from his back, and he shall not stop from this day and this (3:13) hour, as long as this jug drips over the excrements (3:14) of the donkey, Amen Amen Selah.

Chapter for love. Write on a (3:15) pottery (sherd) that has not been baked, and cast it into the fire: (3:16) In the name of Michael, Gabriel, Raphael, ʿAnael, Ḥasdiel, (3:17) Nataniel, Kabšiel. You holy angels! (3:18) I beg you that you should set the heart of N daughter of N on fire (3:19) after N son of N. If she is hungry, she should not eat, [...]

page 4

(4:1-3) [...] (4:4) and [make] the heart and kidneys of N daughter (!) of N burn. As this [sherd] (4:5) burns, so shall the heart and kidney of N daughter of N burn after (4:6) N son of N. It shall be cast into an oven, in the fire of a furnace.

(4:7) For commerce (and) for (finding) grace. Write on the hide of a deer: (4:8) I adjure you, Raḥmiel, Ḥasdiel, Ḥaniel, Kafšiel. (4:9) Give power and grace to N son of N in front of all sons of Adam and Eve, (4:10) and may there assemble in his prsence every one who wishes to conduct a bargain, to buy (4:11) and sell any thing in the world. None of the sons of Adam and Eve (4:12) shall have the authority to open the mouth, to speak or to answer this (4:13) N son of N. In the name of Barqiel and in the name of Qedušiel, and in the name of (4:14) Ḥasin Yah, may you give N son of N beauty and grace and mercy (4:15) in the eyes of all those who see him, and "his hand has found as a nest the riches of the people" (Is. 10:14), (4:16) "And Joseph found grace in his eyes, and he served him. And he made him overseer (4:17) over his house, and all that he had he put into his hand" (Gen. 39:4) (4:17-18) (*part of the verse repeated backwards*). And may God be with N son of N and may he give him grace (4:19) and mercy in the eyes of all. In the name of Kerubiel the angel (who is appointed) over (4:20) ... "And Noah found favour in the eyes of God" (Gen. 6:8), so shall N son of N find (4:21) [grace] and mercy in the eyes of both God and Man. Amen, Amen, Amen, Selah.

Commentary

Pages 1-2 of this fragment contain a portion of *Sefer ha-Razim* as reconstituted by M. Margalioth (1966). The text contained in these two pages corresponds in Margalioth's text to IV:29-52, and the variants are given marked as ג2 (please note that the shelf-mark as quoted in Margalioth 1966, p. 48 and p. 97, n. to line 29, is erroneous). Since the text given by Margalioth is on the whole accurate, we see no point in reproducing it here.

3:5 The notion of "the two youths" has so far no parallel in our texts.

3:11 בקבוקה דהוא כוזא: The gloss uses an Aramaic word that was probably more familiar than בקבוקה, also an Aramaic word.

יח((ת))ר: Probably an error for יהה.

מתריז is unattested in Aramaic. The Hebrew word means "to squirt, splash, have diarrhoea".

4:4 בן: This is obviously an error for בת.

4:5 ליבה וכוליתיה The spelling is erratic, but it seems that in both nouns the writer meant to refer to a possessive pronoun in the third person singular feminine.

4:6 אותון probably stands for אתון.

4:7 זבינו signifies literally either "purchase" or "sale".

4:9 חיל וחסד: One should have expected חן וחסד, and it is possible that this is what the writer had in mind. The confusion could have occurred by the fact that biblical Hebrew חיל was taken to mean "material success". In Prov. 31:29, רבות בנות עשו חיל, the Targum renders the word by עתרא; Rashi similarly seems to take it as meaning wealth.

4:11 ולא יהיה רשות: Cf. A 18:3 ולא תהי לך עוד מכען רשו בה.

4:14 חסין יה (Ps. 89:9) "a strong God".

Geniza 29

Or. 1080.6.19
Amulet to heal Saʿīda daughter of Sitt al-Ahl
Plates 79-80

[1]

בשם רחום ו(חנון) ארך אפים מוחץ
ורופא נעשה ונצ[לי]ח לישועתך קויתי ײײ
ײײ ײײ אלהים אל רחו[ם] וחנון ארך אפים
ורב חסד ואמת בשמך אל אלהים האל
הגדול הגבור והנ(ו)רא בשמה דמיכאל
ובשמה דרפאל ובשמה דגבריאל
דהינון אינון שליחוי ומהיימנוי דאלהא
חיה רבון כל העולם ובשמה דרעמיאל
ובשמה דפניאל הינון יבערון רוחה
בישה ועינה דברייתה ומסקוריתה
וסכל(ת)ה סעידה בנת סת אלאהל בשם

12 אתייה האילין פּטֿ פּטֿ צֿ צֿ צֿ צֿ צֿ צֿ צֿ צֿ
13 טֿן כֿו פֿוס ולֿן לֿן חֿז חֿז אתון אתיא קדישיא
14 ומלאכיא משבחיא אסון לכל מי שיהיה
15 עליו זה הכתוב (יע)ברון מיניה כל רוחין
16 ומזיקין וסכלתה בישתה וכל עין בישה
17 וכל עין בריה וכל צער ביש דאית ביה
18 וכל מילה בישת(ה) דאית בעלמה דיהוה
19 צבאות {עם ((סעידה)) ס(ת) אלאהל בנת} עם סעידה
20 בנת סת אל[אהל מש]גב לה אלהי יעקב
21 סלה אסותא [מן ש]מיא תהי לסעידה
22 בנת סת אלאהל ב[מ]אתים וארבעים
23 ושמונה אברים (מ)כף רגל(ה) ועד
24 קדק<ד>ה עתה מ(הר)ה אשבע(ית) יתייך
25 גופה דשמך [רו]חתא באו(רת)א בשם
26 אל אל אל אלהים (ב)[...] (יהוה) [צב]אות
27 צבאות צבאו[ת ...] ית סעידה
28 בנת סת אלאה[ל] בשם אל קנא (אל ק)נא אל קנא
29 הנגלה למשה ב[ס]נה שתזוז (מן) סעידה
30 בנת סת אלאהל[...] יהי יהי יהי יהי
31 יהי יהו יהו יהו [ ] יהי יהי יהי יהי
32 (ב)יה היה צ[באות ...]

[2]

1 הקדושים והנכבדים בראש אל מלך
2 חי וקיים שתגערו בכל {בכל} רוח ושיד
3 וזיק ומזיק וחומתא וכאב וצינים מן
4 {סת אלאהל} סעידה בנת סת אלאהל ומן
5 א((י))ברים איברים שיש בה בשם האל
6 הנשגב והנאמן אמן אמן סלה בשם

שדי	צבאות	יה	אה	אהיה	אל	אלהים
שדי	צבאות	יה	אה	אהיה	אל	אלהים
שדי	צבאות	יה	אה	אהיה	אל	אלהים
מא	כא	כיא	כא	כא	כא	כא

7 אסותא לסעידה בנת סת אלאהל בשם חננאל
8 המלאך ובשם מיכאל השר הגדול
9 סכמואל טמיאל קנטיאור קנטיאור
10 הבו אסותא לסעידה בנת סת אלאהל
11 ותנשם מן כל צער ומחוש אמן סלה

12 (*magic symbols*)
13 בשם לך טמיאל (*magic symbols*)
14 קורא אני למלא[ך] (שהו) ממונה על
15 מחוש ראש וגו[ף] שישלח אס<ו>תא
16 לסעידה בנת סת [אל]אהל ואתון אתיא
17 ומלאכיא וקטיריא (מ)שבחיא בבקשה
18 מכם (הצ)ילו סעיד[ה] בנת סת אלאהל מכל
19 צער ומחוש ומכא[וב בגו]פה אמן אמן אמן
20 סלה (הללויה)

Translation

page 1

(1:1) In the name of He who is merciful and full of pity, forbearing, smiting (1:2) and healing, we shall act and succeed. "I have waited for your salvation, O Lord" (Gen. 49:18). (1:3) "God, God, Elohim, merciful and gracious, long-suffering (1:4) and abundant in goodness and truth" (Ex. 34:6). By your name, El Elohim, (1:5) the great, the mighty, and the fearsome God. By the name of Michael, (1:6) by the name of Raphael, by the name of Gabriel, (1:7) who are the messengers and the confidants of the living (1:8) God, the master of the whole world, and in the name of Ra῾amiel, (1:9) and in the name of Paniel. They will remove the evil (1:10) spirit and the eye of people and the envious eye, (1:11) and gaze <from> Sa῾īda daughter of Sitt al-Ahl.

In the name of (1:12-13) these characters (*combinations of characters*). You holy characters (1:14) and praised angels. Heal every one who will wear (1:15) this (piece of) writing. May be removed from him all spirits (1:16), harmful spirits, evil gaze, any evil eye, (1:17) the eye of all creatures, any evil pain that is in him, (1:18) and any evil thing that is in the world of YHWH (1:19) Sabaoth, with Sa῾īda (1:20) daughter of Sitt al-[Ahl]. "The God of Jacob is her refuge (1:21) Selah" (Ps. 46:8).

May there be healing from heaven to Sa῾īda (1:22) daughter of Sitt al-Ahl, in the two hundred and forty (1:23) eight limbs of her body, from the sole of her foot to (1:24) the skull, now, fast.

I adjure you, (1:25) the body, whose name is The Spirits at Night (?). In the name of (1:26) El El El Elohim, YHWH Sabaoth (1:27) Sabaoth Saba[oth, heal] Sa῾īda (1:28) daughter of Sitt al-Ahl. In the name of El

Qana, El Qana, El Qana, (1:29) who appeared to Moses in the bush, that you may move away from Saʿīda (1:30) daughter of Sitt al-Ahl YHY YHY YHY (1:31) YHW (*repeated several times*) (1:32) BYH HYH Sabaoth ...

page 2

(2:1) holy and fearsome, (and) at the head God, king, (2:2) living and existent. May you chase away every spirit and demon (2:3) and blast demon and destroyer and fever and pain and shivering (?) from (2:4) Saʿīda daughter of Sitt al-Ahl and from (2:5) the limbs that are in her.

In the name of the (2:6) exalted and trustworthy God, Amen, Amen, Amen, Selah. In the name of Shaddai Sabaoth Yah Ah Ehye El Elohim (*repeated three times, followed by several combinations of letters*) (2:7) healing to Saʿīda d. of Sitt al-Ahl.

In the name of Ḥananʾel (2:8) the angel, and in the name of Michael the great prince, (2:9) Sakhmuel, Ṭamiel, Qantiur, Qantiur. (2:10) Give healing to Saʿīda d. of Sitt al-Ahl (2:11) and may she be healed from every pain and affliction, Amen Selah. (2:12) (*magic symbols*).

(2:13) (*magic symbols*). In the name of you, Ṭamiel, (2:14) I invoke the angel who is appointed over (2:15) headache and body-ache that he may send healing (2:16) to Saʿīda daughter of Sitt al-Ahl.

And you, praised symbols, (2:17) angels and *qeṭirayyā*, (I) request of you, (2:18) [save] Saʿīda daughter of Sitt al-Ahl from all (2:19) pain, affliction and suffe[ring in her bo]dy... Amen, Amen, Amen (2:30) Selah Hallelujah.

Commentary

1:10 עינה דברייתה Cf. below 1:17 עין בריה. See also G18, p. 19:17-18 and A1:17.

1:11 סכלתה stands parallel, here and in the following, to עינה, hence the preferred translation should be "gaze" (although the form is not attested) rather than "understanding" or "foolishness".

1:17 צער ביש or בוש could also mean "the pain of illness".

1:20 משגב לה adapted consciously, it seems, from Ps. 46:8.

1:25ff. These lines were torn along the middle and the two parts were joined in a manner that makes the left-hand half of the page lower than the right-hand part.

2:11 ותנשם: *ithp.*

2:17 קטיריא, literally "knots", is here taken to be an independent noun designating some kind of celestial agents. It is, in fact, historically an error for כלקטיריא "characters".

Abbreviations, Bibliography, Glossary and Indices

ABBREVIATIONS

AASOR	*Annual of the American Schools of Oriental Research*
AMB	*Amulets and magic bowls*, see Naveh and Shaked 1985
BASOR	*Bulletin of the American Schools of Oriental Research*
BJPES	*Bulletin and Journal of the Palestine Exploration Society*
BT	Babylonian Talmud
CIJ	Frey 1936/1952
CIS	*Corpus inscriptionum semiticarum*
HUCA	*Hebrew Union College Annual*
IEJ	*Israel Exploration Journal*
JAOS	*Journal of the American Oriental Society*
JBL	*Journal of Biblical Literature*
JNES	*Journal of Near Eastern Studies*
JRAS	*Journal of the Royal Asiatic Society*
LSJ	Liddell and Scott 1976
OLZ	*Orientalistische Literaturzeitung*
PGM I,II,III	Preisendanz 1928, 1931, 1941
PSBA	*Proceedings of the Society for Biblical Archaeology*
PT	Palestinian Talmud
RB	*Revue Biblique*
REJ	*Revue des Études Juives*
WZKM	*Wiener Zeitschrift für die Kunde des Morgenlandes*
ZAL	*Zeitschrift für Arabische Linguistik*
ZPE	*Zeitschrift für Papyrologie und Epigraphik*

BIBLIOGRAPHY

Albright, William F.

1937 "A biblical fragment of the Maccabean age. The Nash papyrus", *JBL* 56, pp. 145-176

Alexander, P.S.

1986 "Incantations and books of magic", in: E. Schürer, *The history of the Jewish people in the age of Jesus Christ (175 B.C.—A.D. 135)*, English version revised and edited by G. Vermes, F. Millar and M. Goodman, vol. III, part I, Edinburgh, pp. 341-379

Allbutt, T. Clifford

1921 *Greek medicine in Rome* (The Fitzpatrick Lectures on the History of Medicine), London

Altmann, Alexander

1946 "שירי קדושה בספרות ההיכלות הקדומה", מלילה ב, עמ' 8–10

Attal, Robert

1984 *Ketoubot d'Afrique du Nord à Jérusalem, collections de l'Institut Ben-Zvi, de la Bibliothèque Nationale et Universitaire et du Musée d'Israël*, Jerusalem

Avigad, Nahman

1976 *Beth She'arim*, III, Jerusalem

Baer, Seligmann (Isaac Dov)

1868 סדר עבודת ישראל, Redlheim [Re-issued: Berlin: Schocken, 1937]

Baillet, Maurice

1963 "Un livret magique en christo-palestinien à l'Université de Louvain", *Le Muséon* 76, pp. 375-401

1982 *Qumran Grotte 4*, Part 3 (4Q482-4Q520), in: *Discoveries in the Judaean Desert*, 7, Oxford

Bar-Asher, Moshe

1977 מחקרים בסורית ארץ-ישראלית, ירושלים

1983 ״נשכחות בלשון התנאים״, מחקרי לשון מוגשים לזאב בן-חיים, ירושלים, עמ׳ 83–110

Bar-Ilan, Meir
1985 ״ברכת ׳יוצר האדם׳ — מקומות הופעתה, תיפקודה ומשמעותה״, *HUCA* 56, pp. ט–כז
1987 סתרי תפילה והיכלות, רמת גן

Barkay, G.
1986 *Ketef Hinnom*, Israel Museum Catalogue No. 274, Jerusalem

Bedjan, Paul
1895 *Histoire de Mar Jabalaha, de trois autres patriarches, d'un prêtre et de deux laïques Nestoriens*, 2nd ed., Leipzig

Ben-Zvi, Izhak
1976 ספר השומרונים, ירושלים

Betz, Hans Dieter (ed.)
1986 *The Greek magical papyri in translation, including the Demotic spells*, vol I: Texts, Chicago and London

Beyer, Klaus
1984 *Die aramäischen Texte vom Toten Meer samt den Inschriften aus Palästina, dem Testament Levis aus der Kairoer Genisa, der Fastenrolle und den alten talmudischen Zitaten*, Göttingen

Blau, J., and S. Hopkins
1984 "On early Judaeo-Arabic orthography", *ZAL* 12, pp. 9-27

Blau, Ludwig
1898 *Das altjüdische Zauberwesen* (Jahresbericht der Landes-rabbinerschule in Budapest für das Schuljahr 1897/8), Budapest

Bouché-Leclercq, Auguste
1879/82 *Histoire de la divination dans l'antiquité*, 4 vols., Paris [Reprinted, New York: Arno, 1975]

Canova, R.
1954 *Iscrizioni e monumenti protocristiani del paese di Moab*, Roma

Cantineau, J.
1930/1932 *Le nabatéen*, 2 vols., Paris

Cohen, Shaye J.D.
1987 "Pagan and Christian evidence on the ancient

synagogue", in: Lee I. Levine (ed.), *The synagogue in Late Antiquity*, Philadelphia, Pa., pp. 159-181

Cook, S.A.
1903 "A pre-massoretic biblical papyrus", *Proceedings of the Society of Biblical Archeology* 26, pp. 34-56

Daiches, Samuel
1913 *Babylonian oil magic in the Talmud and in the later Jewish literature* (Jews' College, London, Publication No. 5), London

Danby, Herbert (tr.)
1933 *The Mishnah*, Oxford

Deshen, Shlomo
1980 ״חידת ׳כל נדרי׳: בירור אנתרופולוגי והיסטורי״, פרקים בתולדות החברה היהודית בימי הבינים ובעת החדשה מוקדשים לפרופ׳ יעקב כ״ץ במלאת לו שבעים וחמש שנה, ירושלים, עמ׳ קלו-קנג

Dornsieff, F., and B. Hansen
1978 *Rückläufiges Wörterbuch der griechischen Eigennamen / Reverse-Lexicon of Greek proper names*, Chicago

Dozy, R.
1927 *Supplément aux dictionnaires arabes*, 2 vols., 2nd ed., Leiden-Paris

Drower, E.S., and Rudolf Macuch
1963 *A Mandaic dictionary*, Oxford

Elbogen, Ismar (Isaac Moses)
1972 התפילה בישראל בהתפתחותה ההיסטורית, תרגום י׳ אמיר, בעריכת י׳ הינמן, תל אביב [translation of: *Der jüdische Gottesdienst in seiner geschichtlichen Entwicklung*, Leipzig 1913]

Enoch III, see Odeberg 1928

Epstein, J.N.
1921 "Gloses babylo-araméennes", *REJ* 73, pp. 27-58
1922 "Gloses babylo-araméennes", *REJ* 74, pp. 40-72
1960 דקדוק ארמית בבלית, ירושלים
1964 מבוא לנוסח המשנה, מהדורה ב, ירושלים

Even-Shoshan, Abraham
1966 המלון החדש, (הדפסה שביעית), ירושלים

Fahd, Toufic
1966 *La divination arabe. Études religieuses, sociologiques et folkloriques sur le milieu natif de l'Islam*, Leiden

Faraone, C.A.

1988 "Hermes but no marrow. Another look at a puzzling magical spell", *ZPE* 72, pp. 279-286

Fitzmyer, Joseph A.

1959 "The Aramaic qorbān inscription from Jebel Ḫallet eṭ-ṭûri and Mark 7^{11} / Matt 15^{5}", *JBL* 78, pp. 60-65 [Reprinted in: J.A. Fitzmyer, *Essays on the Semitic background of the New Testament*, London 1971]

Fitzmyer, Joseph A., and Daniel J. Harrington

1978 *A manual of Palestinian Aramaic texts* (Biblica et Orientalia, 34), Rome

Franco, Fulvio

1978/9 "Five Aramaic incantation bowls from Tell Baruda (Choche)", *Mesopotamia* 13-14, pp. 233-249

Frey, Jean-Baptiste

1936 *Corpus inscriptionum iudaicarum*, I, Europe, Rome [Reprinted, with "Prolegomenon" by B. Lifshitz, New York 1975]

1952 *Corpus inscriptionum iudaicarum*, II, Asie-Afrique, Rome

Gaster, Moses

1896 "The Sword of Moses. An ancient book of magic published for the first time from an unique manuscript (Cod. Heb. Gaster 178), with an introduction and translation", *JRAS*, pp. 149-198, I-XXXV [Reprinted in Gaster 1928, I, pp. 288-337; III, pp. 69-103]

1900 "Two thousand years of a charm against the child-stealing witch", *Folk-Lore* 11 (46), pp. 129-162 [Reprinted in Gaster 1928, II, pp. 1005-1038]

1928 *Studies and texts in folklore, magic, mediaeval romance, Hebrew Apocrypha and Samaritan archaeology*, 3 vols., London [Reprinted with a "Prolegomenon" by T. Gaster, New York 1971]

Gawlikowski, Michel

1988 "Une coupe magique araméenne", *Semitica* 38, pp. 137-143

Geller, Markham J.

1980 "Four Aramaic incantation bowls", *The Bible world. Essays in honor of Cyrus H. Gordon* (ed. by J. Rendsburg et al.), New York, pp. 47-60

1986 "Eight incantation bowls", *Orientalia Lovaniensia Periodica* 17, pp. 101-117, pl. IV-X

Ginsburger, Moses

1899 *Das Fragmententhargum (Thargum jeruschalmi zum Pentateuch)*, Berlin

Goldschmidt, D.

1969 הגדה של פסח, מקורותיה ותולדותיה במשך הדורות, מהד׳ ג, ירושלים תשכ״ט

Gollancz, Hermann

1898 "A selection of charms from Syriac manuscripts", *Actes du onzième congrès international des orientalistes, Paris 1897*, 4e section, Paris, pp. 77-97

1912 *The Book of Protection, being a collection of charms...*, London

Goodenough, Erwin R.

1953 *Jewish symbols in the Greco-Roman period*, II (Bollingen Series XXXVII), Chapters 6 and 7, pp. 155-295

Goodblatt, David

1976 "*ʾypr*ʾ *hwrmyz* mother of King Shapur and *ʾpr*ʾ *hwrmyz* mother of Khusro: A note on the name *ʾypr*ʾ / *ʾpr*ʾ *hwrmyz*", *JAOS* 96, pp. 135-136

Gordon, C.H.

1934a "An Aramaic incantation", *AASOR* 14, pp. 141-143

1934b "Aramaic magical bowls in the Istanbul and Baghdad museums", *Archiv Orientální* 6, pp. 319-334

1941 "Aramaic incantation bowls", *Orientalia* 10, pp. 116-141, 272-284, 339-360

1978 "Two Aramaic incantations", in: Gary A. Tuttle (ed.), *Biblical and Near Eastern studies. Essays in honor of W. S. LaSor*, Grand Rapids, Mich., pp. 231-244

1984 "Magic bowls from the Moriah Collection", *Orientalia* 53, pp. 220-241

1989 "Targumic ʿdy (Zechariah XIV 6) and the not so common cold", *VT* 39, pp. 77-80

Gottheil, Richard, and William H. Worrell

1927 *Fragments from the Cairo Genizah in the Freer Collection* (University of Michigan Studies, Humanistic Series, XIII), New York

Greenfield, Jonas C.

1974 "רטין מגושא", *The Joshua Finkel Festschrift*, New York: Yeshiva University Press, pp. 63-69

1976 [Review of J.A. Fitzmyer, *Essays on the Semitic background of the New Testament*, London 1971], *JNES* 35, pp. 59-61

Greenfield, J.C., and J. Naveh

1985 "קמיע מנדעי בעל ארבע השבעות" ("A Mandaic lead amulet with four incantations"), *Eretz Israel* 18 [Avigad Volume], pp. 97-107

Halperin, David J.

1988 *The faces of the chariot. Early Jewish responses to Ezekiel's vision* (Texte und Studien zum Antiken Judentum, herausg. von Martin Hengel und Peter Schäfer, 16), Tübingen

Harviainen, Tapani

1981 *An Aramaic incantation bowl from Borsippa. Another specimen of Eastern Aramaic "koiné"* (Studia Orientalia, ed. by the Finnish Oriental Society, 51:14), Helsinki

Havdala de-Rabbi ʿAqiva, see Scholem 1980/1

Heinemann, Joseph

1966 התפילה בתקופת התנאים והאמוראים, טיבה ודפוסיה, מהדורה ב, ירושלים

Heller, B.

1908 "Le nom divin de vingt-deux lettres dans la prière qui suit la bénédiction sacerdotale", *REJ* 55, pp. 60-71

Hippocrates

Oeuvres complètes, ed. & transl. E. Littré, 10 vols., Paris 1839-

1953 With an English translation by W.H.S. Jones, London and Cambridge, Mass., vol. IV (The Loeb Classical Library)

Hyvernat, Henri

1885 "Sur un vase judéo-babylonien du musée Lycklama de Cannes (Provence)", *Zeitschrift für Keilschriftforschung* 2, pp. 113-148

Ilan, Zvi

1983 "מקומה של מרות — יישוב מבוצר בגבול הגליל", קדמוניות טז, עמ' 83-85

Ilan, Zvi, and Emmanuel Damati

1985 "חפירת בית הכנסת של מרות", קדמוניות יח, עמ' 44-50

1987 מרות, הכפר היהודי הקדום. חפירות בית הכנסת ובית-המדרש, תל אביב

Isbell, Charles D.
1975 *Corpus of the Aramaic incantation bowls* (Dissertation Series 17, Scholars Press), Missoula, Montana
1976 "Two new Aramaic incantation bowls", *BASOR* 223, pp. 15-23

Jastrow, Marcus
[1903] *A dictionary of the Targumim, the Talmud Babli and Yerushalmi, and the Midrashic literature*, 2 vols., New York [Reprint: New York 1950]

Jellinek, Adolph (אהרן יעללינעק).
[1853-1877] בית המדרש [Bet ha-Midrasch], 6 vols., 3rd ed., [Reprint: Jerusalem 1967]

Jeruzalmi, Isak
1963 *Les coupes magiques araméennes de Mésopotamie*, thèse pour le doctorat du troisième cycle présentée à la Faculté des Lettres et Sciences Humaines de l'Université de Paris (unpublished), Paris

Justi, Ferdinand
1895 *Iranisches Namenbuch*, Marburg [Reprint, Hildesheim, 1963]

Kaplan, J.
1967 "Two Samaritan amulets", *IEJ* 17, pp. 158-162

Kasher, M.M.
1967 הגדה שלמה, מהד׳ ג, ירושלים תשכ״ז

Kimelman, Reuven
1987 "The *Šema*ᶜ and its blessings: The realization of God's kingship", in: Lee I. Levine (ed.), *The synagogue in Late Antiquity*, Philadelphia, Pa.: American Schools of Oriental Research, 73-86

Kloner, Amos
1990 ״חורבת קצרה — מערת הקפלה״, עתיקות י, עמ׳ 129-139

Kotansky, Roy
1991 "Two inscribed Jewish Aramaic amulets from Syria", *IEJ* 41, pp. 267-281

Kotansky, R., J. Naveh and S. Shaked
1992 "A Greek-Aramaic silver amulet from Egypt in the Ashmolean Museum", *Le Muséon* 105, pp. 5-26

Kraemer, C.J.
1958 *Excavations at Nessana, III: Non-literary papyri*, Princeton
Krauss, S.
1908 "Note sur le nom divin des vingt-deux lettres et sur le démon de l'oubli", *REJ* 56, pp. 251-254
1937 תוספות הערוך השלם להרב ח.י. קהוט. *Additamenta ad librum Aruch Completum Alexandri Kohut*, congessit, scripsit, edidit S. Krauss, adiuvantibus B. Geiger, L. Ginzberg, I. Löw, B. Murmelstein, Vienna [Reprint, New York 1955]
Kropp, A.M.
1931 *Ausgewählte koptische Zaubertexte*, 3 vols., Bruxelles
Kutscher, E.Y.
1971 "Aramaic", *Encyclopedia Judaica* III, cols. 259-287 [Reprinted in Kutscher 1977]
1976 *Studies in Galilean Aramaic*, tr. by Michael Sokoloff, Ramat-Gan
1977 *Hebrew and Aramaic studies*, ed. Z. Ben Ḥayyim and others, Jerusalem
1982 *The history of the Hebrew language*, ed. R. Kutscher, Jerusalem
Levy, Jacob
1867/8 *Chaldäisches Wörterbuch über die Targumim und einen grossen Theil des rabbinischen Schrifttums*, 2 vols., Leipzig
Lewis, Naphtali
1989 *The documents from the Bar-Kokhba period in the Cave of Letters. Greek papyri*, Jerusalem
Liddell, Henry George, and Robert Scott.
1976 *A Greek-English lexicon*, Revised by H.S. Jones and R. McKenzie, with a supplement 1968. Oxford: Clarendon Press
Lidzbarski, Mark
1902 *Ephemeris für semitische Epigraphik*, I, 1900-1902, Giessen
Lieber, E.
1991 "An ongoing mysterty, the so-called Book of Medicines attributed to Assaf the Sage", *Bulletin of Judaeo-Greek Studies* 8, p. 18-25
Lieberman, Saul
1942 *Greek in Jewish Palestine. Studies in the life and manners*

of Jewish Palestine in the II-IV centuries C.E., New York: Jewish Theological Seminary

1962 — יוונית ויוונות בארץ־ישראל, ירושלים

Lifshitz, B.

1962 — "Beiträge zur palästinischen Epigraphik", *ZDPV* 88, pp. 64-88

1967 — *Donateurs et fondateurs dans les synagogues juives*, Paris

Löw, Immanuel

1881 — *Aramäische Pflanzennamen*, Leipzig

1928/1934 — *Die Flora der Juden*, 4 vols., Wien [Reprinted: Hildesheim 1967]

Mann, J.

1931/1935 — *Texts and studies in Jewish history and literature*, 2 vols., New York [Reprinted: New York 1972]

Manns, F.

1979 — "Nouvelles inscriptions grecques de Palestine", *Liber Annuus* 29, pp. 238-243

Margalioth, M.

1966 — See *Sefer ha-razim*

Melamed, E.Z.

1945 — "שנים שהם אחד(ἕν διὰ δυοῖν) במקרא", תרביץ טז, עמ׳ 173–189 [= ע״צ מלמד, מחקרים במקרא, בתרגומיו ובמפרשיו, ירושלים תשמ״ד, עמ׳ 142–159]

1961 — "Break up of stereotype phrases as an artistic device in biblical poetry", *Scripta Hierosolymitana* 8, pp. 115-153

Milik, J.T.

1959/60 — "Inscription araméenne christo-palestinienne de 'Abûd", *Liber Annuus* 10, pp. 197-204

1972 — "4Q Vision de 'Amram et une citation d'Origène", *RB* 79, pp. 77-97

1976 — *The books of Enoch. Aramaic fragemnts of Qumran Cave 4*, ed. by J.T. Milik with the collaboration of M. Black, Oxford

Mittwoch, Eugen

1902 — "Hebräische Inschriften aus Palmyra", *Beiträge zur Assyriologie* 4, pp. 203-206

Montgomery, James A.

1912 — "A magical bowl-text and the original script of the Manichaeans", *JAOS* 32, pp. 434-438

1913 *Aramaic incantation texts from Nippur* (University of Pennsylvania, The Museum, Publications of the Babylonian Section, vol. III), Philadelphia

Muntner, Suessman

1957 מבוא לספר אסף הרופא, הספר הרפואי הקדום ביותר, ירושלים

Naveh, Joseph

1970 "The ossuary inscriptions from Giv'at ha-Mivtar", *IEJ* 20, pp. 33-37

1978 על פסיפס ואבן. הכתובות הארמיות והעבריות מבתי הכנסת העתיקים, ירושלים

1985a "כיבוש טוב, אין כמוהו", תרביץ נד, עמ' 367–382

1985b "Another Jewish Aramaic tombstone from Zoar", *HUCA* 56, pp. 103-116

1988 "Lamp inscriptions and inverted writing", *IEJ* 38, pp. 36-43

1989a "הכתובות הארמיות והעבריות מבתי הכנסת העתיקים", ארץ ישראל כ (ספר ידין), עמ' 302–310

1989b "Did ancient Samaritan inscriptions belong to synagogues?", in: R. Hachlili (ed.), *Ancient synagogues in Israel, third-seventh century C.E.* (BAR International Series, 499), 61-63

1992 על חרס וגומא, כתובות ארמיות ועבריות מימי בית שני, המשנה והתלמוד, ירושלים

Naveh, J., and S. Shaked.

1985 *Amulets and magic bowls. Aramaic incantations of Late Antiquity*. Jerusalem-Leiden [Second edition, Jerusalem 1987. Quoted *AMB*]

Negev, A.

1981 *Greek inscriptions from the Negev*, Jerusalem

Newsom, Carol

1985 *Songs of the Sabbath Sacrifice: A critical edition* (Harvard Semitic Studies 27), Atlanta

Nitzan, Bilha

1986 "שירי שבח מקומראן 'לפחד ולבהל' רוחות רשע, 4Q510 ו-4Q511", תרביץ נה, עמ' 19–46, [Comments by I. M. Ta-Shma, *Tarbiz* 55, pp. 440-442; J.A. Baumgarten, ibid., pp. 442-445; a rejoinder by B. Nitzan, ibid., pp. 603-605]

Nock, Arthur Darby
1972 *Essays on religion and the ancient world*, ed. Z. Stewart, 2 vols., Oxford

Nöldeke, Theodor
1888 "Persische Studien", *Sitzungsberichte der philosophisch-historischen Klasse, K. Akademie der Wissenschaften*, Wien, Bd. 116, pp. 387-423
1898a *Kurzgefasste syrische Grammatik*, 2nd ed., Leipzig [Reprinted with an Appendix by Anton Schall, Darmstadt 1977]
1898b [Review of Pognon 1898], *WZKM* 12, pp. 141-147, 353-361

Odeberg, Hugo
1928 *3 Enoch or the Hebrew Book of Enoch*, ed. and translated by H. Odeberg, Cambridge [Reprinted, with "Prolegomenon" by Jonas C. Greenfield, New York 1973]

Oelsner, J.
1989 [Review of Naveh and Shaked 1985], *OLZ* 84, pp. 38-41

Oppenheimer, Aharon
1983 *Babylonia Judaica in the Talmudic period*, in collaboration with Benjamin Isaac and Michael Lecker (Beihefte zum Tübinger Atlas des Vorderen Orients, Reihe B, Nr. 47), Wiesbaden

Pape, W.
1863/1870 *Handwörterbuch der griechischen Sprache. III. Wörterbuch der griechischen Eigennamen*, 3. Auflage, neu bearbeitet von G.E. Benseler, Braunschweig

Payne Smith, J.
1903 *A compendious Syriac dictionary*, Oxford

Payne Smith, R.
1879/1901 *Thesaurus syriacus*, 2 vols., Oxford

Peterson, Erik
1926 Ἑις Θεός. *Epigraphische, formgeschichtliche und religionsgeschichtliche Untersuchungen* (Forschungen zur Religion und Literatur des Alten und Neuen Testaments, N.F. 24 [=41]), Göttingen

Polotsky, H.J.
1937 "Suriel der Trompeter", *Le Muséon* 49, pp. 231-243 [Reprinted in Polotsky, *Collected papers*, Jerusalem 1971, pp. 288-300]

Preisendanz, Karl
1928 *Papyri graecae magicae. Die griechischen Zauberpapyri*, I, Leipzig-Berlin
1931 *Papyri graecae magicae. Die griechischen Zauberpapyri*, II, Leipzig-Berlin
1941 *Papyri graecae magicae. Die griechischen Zauberpapyri*, III, Leipzig-Berlin [Index, unpublished]

Preisigke, Fr.
1922 *Namenbuch*, Heidelberg

Preuss, Julius
1923 *Biblisch-talmudische Medizin. Beiträge zur Geschichte der Heilkunde und der Kultur überhaupt*, 3. Auflage, Berlin

Pummer, Reinhard
1987 "Samaritan amulets from the Roman-Byzantine period and their wearers", *RB* 94:251-263

Quecke, Hans
1963 "Zwei koptische Amulette der Papyrussammlung der Universität Heidelberg (Inv. Nr. 544b und 564a)", *Le Muséon* 76, pp. 247-265

Reeg, Gottfried
1977 *Die samaritanischen Synagogen* (Frowald Hüttenmeister and Gottfried Reeg, *Die Antiken Synagogen in Israel*, 2; Beihefte zum Tübinger Atlas des Vorderen Orients, Reihe B, Nr. 12/2), Wiesbaden

Reich, R.
1985 "A Samaritan amulet from Nahariya", *RB* 92, pp. 383-388

Rossell, William H.
1953 *A handbook of Aramaic magical texts* (Shelton Semitic Series, 2), Skylands, Ringwood Borough, N.J.

Schäfer, Peter
1981 *Synopse zur Hekhalot-Literatur*, in Zusammenarbeit mit Margarete Schlüter und H.G. von Mutius (Texte und Studien zum Antiken Judentum, 2), Tübingen
1984 *Geniza-Fragmente zur Hekhalot-Literatur* (Texte und Studien zum Antiken Judentum, 6), Tübingen
1987 *Übersetzung der Hekhalot-Literatur*, II, in Zusammenarbeit mit H.-J. Becker, K. Herrmann, C. Rohrbacher-Sticker und S. Siebers (Texte und Studien zum Antiken Judentum, 17), Tübingen

1988a *Konkordanz zur Hekhalot-Literatur*, in Zusammenarbeit mit Gottfried Reeg, II (Texte und Studien zum Antiken Judentum, 13), Tübingen

1988b *Hekhalot-Studien* (Texte und Studien zum antiken Judentum, 19), Tübingen

Schiffman, L.H.

1982 "Merkavah speculation at Qumran: The 4Q Serekh Shirot ha-Shabbat", in: J. Reinharz and D. Swetchinski (eds.), *Mystics, philosophers and politicians: Essays in Jewish intellectual history in honor of Alexander Altmann* (Duke Monographs in Medieval and Renaissance Studies, 5), Durham, N.C., pp. 15-47

1987 "The Dead Sea Scrolls and the early history of Jewish liturgy", in: Lee I. Levine (ed.), *The synagogue in Late Antiquity*, Philadelphia, Pa.: American Schools of Oriental Research, pp. 33-48

Scholem, Gershom G.

1965 *Jewish Gnosticism, Merkabah Mysticism and Talmudic Tradition*. (Second Edition), New York

1980/1 ״הבדלה דר׳ עקיבא — מקור למסורת המאגיה היהודית בתקופת הגאונים״, תרביץ נ, עמ׳ 243–281

Schrire, T.

1966 *Hebrew amulets: their decipherment and interpretation*, London

Schulthess, Friedrich

1903 *Lexicon syropalaestinum*, Berlin

Schwab, Moïse

1890 "Les coupes magiques et l'hydromancie dans l'antiquité orientale", *PSBA*, April 1890, pp. 292-342

Schwabe, M.

1947 ״שתי כתובות קבר מאשקלון וצורתן הארכיאולוגית״, ידיעות החברה לחקירת ארץ ישראל ועתיקותיה יג (תש״ז), עמ׳ 149–153

Schwabe, M., and B. Lifshitz.

1967 בית שערים, ב. הכתובות היווניות, ירושלים

Schwabe, M., and A. Reifenberg.

1945/6 ״קמיעה יהודית-יוונית מסוריה״, ידיעות החברה לחקירת ארץ ישראל ועתיקותיה יב, עמ׳ 68–72

Seder Rav 'Amram Gaon

סדר רב עמרם גאון, מהד׳ ד׳ גולדשמידט, ירושלים 1971

Sefer ha-razim.

ספר הרזים, ההדיר מרדכי מרגליות, ירושלים 1966

Shachar, Isaiah

1981 *Jewish tradition in art. The Feuchtwanger Collection of Judaica*, Jerusalem: The Israel Museum

Siddur Rav Se'adya Ga'on

סדור רב סעדיה גאון. כתאב ג׳אמע אלצלואת ואלתסאביח, מהד׳ ש׳ אסף, י׳ דוידסון, י׳ יואל, הדפסה רביעית, ירושלים 1978

Smelik, K.A.D.

1978 "An Aramaic incantation bowl in the Allard Pierson Museum", *Bibliotheca Orientalis* 35, pp. 174-177

Smith, Morton

1979 "Relations between magical papyri and magical gems", *Papyrologica Bruxellensia* 18 (Brussels, Actes du XVe Congrès Int. de Papyrologie, 3e partie), pp. 129-136

1981 "The hymn to the Moon, PGM IV 2242-2355", *Proceedings of the XVI International Congress of Papyrology*, Chico, pp. 643-654

1982/3 "How magic was changed by the triumph of Christianity", in: V. Christides and M. Papathomopoulos (eds.), *Graeco-Arabica. Papers of the first International Congress on Greek and Arabic Studies*, Athens, vol. 2, pp. 51-58

1983 "On the lack of a history of Greco-Roman magic", *Althistorische Studien Hermann Bengtson ... dargebracht*, ed. H. Heinen, Wiesbaden, pp. 251-257

Sokoloff, Michael

1982 קטעי בראשית רבה מן הגניזה, ירושלים

1990 *A dictionary of Jewish Palestinian Aramaic of the Byzantine period* (Dictionaries of Talmud, Midrash and Targum, II), Ramat-Gan

de Sola Pool, David

1909 *The Kaddish* (Inaugural-Dissertation zur Erlangung der Doktorwürde der hohen philosophischen Fakultät der Ruprecht-Karls-Universität Heidelberg), Leipzig [3rd printing, New York 1964]

Sperber, D.
1977 "Greek and Latin words in rabbinic literature. Prolegomena to a new dictionary of classical words in rabbinic literature", *Bar-Ilan* 14-15, pp. 9-60

Stark, Jürgen Kurt
1971 *Personal names in Palmyrene inscriptions*, Oxford

Steinschneider, M.
1872 "Assaf", *Hebräische Bibliographie* 12, pp. 85-88
1879 "Zur medizinischen Literatur. 4. Assaf", *Hebräische Bibliographie* 19, pp. 35-38, 64-70, 84-89, 105-109

Strugnell, J.
1959 "The angelic liturgy at Qumrân: 4Q Serek širot ʿolat haššabbat", *Supplements to Vetus Testamentum* 7, pp. 318-345

Stübe, R.
1895 *Jüdisch-babylonische Zaubertexte*, Halle a/S

Sword of Moses, see Gaster 1896

Ta Shma, I.M.
1986 Cf. Nitzan 1986

Tal, Shelomo
1984 סדור רנת ישראל נוסח הספרדים ועדות המזרח, second edition. Jerusalem

II Targum Esther
= *Das Targum Scheni zum Buche Esther*, ed. Moritz David, Krakau 1898

Trachtenberg, Joshua
1939 *Jewish magic and superstition. A study in folk religion*, Cleveland, New York, Philadelphia [Reprint: New York 1970]

Unvala, J.M.
1953 "An Aramaic incantation vase from Susa", *Indica. The Indian Historical Research Institute Silver Jubilee Commemoration Volume*, Bombay, pp. 410-414

Urbach, E.E.
1990 "The role of the Ten Commandments in Jewish worship", in: B.Z. Segal (ed.), *The Ten Commandments in history and tradition*, Jerusalem, pp. 161-189

Venetianer, Ludwig
1915/1917 *Assaf Judaeus. Der älteste medizinische Schriftsteller*

in hebräischer Sprache (38., 39., 40. Jahresbericht der Landesrabbinerschule in Budapest), 3 parts, Budapest

Weinfeld, Moshe

1976 "עקבות של קדושת יוצר ופסוקי דזמרה במגילות קומראן ובספר בן סירא", תרביץ מה, עמ' 15-26

1979 "התפילות לדעת, תשובה וסליחה בתפילת שמונה־עשרה. אופיין של התפילות, מקבילותיהן בקומראן ושורשיהן במקרא", תרביץ מח, עמ' 186-200

1982 "לגלגוליה של משאלה בישראל ובעמים", ארץ ישראל טז (ספר אורלינסקי), עמ' 93-99

1990 "ברכות השחר במגילות קומראן ובתפילה היהודית המקובלת", סיני קה, עמ' 72-82

Wertheimer, Shelomo Aharon

1980 בתי מדרשות, עשרים וחמשה מדרשי חז"ל על פי כתבי יד מגניזת ירושלים ומצרים. מהדורה חדשה עם הוספות מכתבי יד, מלואים ותיקונים מאת אברהם ורטהימר, 2 כרכים, ירושלים

Yadin, Yigael

1969 "תפילין של ראש מקומראן", ארץ ישראל ט, עמ' 60-83

Yahalom, Joseph

1978 "'אזל משה' בפפירוס", תרביץ מז, עמ' 173-184

1987 "Piyyûṭ as poetry", in: Lee I. Levine (ed.), *The synagogue in Late Antiquity*, Philadelphia, Pa.: American Schools of Oriental Research, pp. 111-126

Yamauchi, Edwin M.

1967 *Mandaic incantation texts* (American Oriental Series, 49), New Haven, Conn.

Yāqūt b. ʿAbdallāh al-Ḥamawī al-Rūmī, Shihāb al-Dīn Abū ʻAbdallāh *Muʿjam al-buldān*, 5 vols., Beirut n.d.

Yardeni, Ada

1991 "Remarks on the Priestly Blessing on two ancient amulets from Jerusalem", *Vetus Testamentum* 41, pp. 176-185

Youtie, H.C., and Campbell Bonner

1937 "Two curse tablets from Beisan", *Transactions and Proceedings of the American Philological Association* 68, pp. 43-77

Zadok, Ran

1989 "Zur Struktur der nachbiblischen jüdischen Personennamen semitischen Ursprungs", *Trumah*

(Hochschule für Jüdische Studien, Heidelberg) 1, pp. 243-343

Zertal, A.
1977 ״טבעת שומרונית וזיהויה של עין כושי״, קדמוניות 38-39, עמ׳ 86-84

GLOSSARY

In the following, all the words and names occurring in the Amulets and Bowls published in this book are indexed. Restored words have mostly been ignored; when they are given, they are usually in parenthesis. Words occurring in the Geniza texts have not been incorporated in the Glossary.

The main Glossary is followed by an index of divine names, names of angels and *nomina barbara*, and by an index of personal names of clients and adversaries. Names of biblical figures and geographical names are in the main Glossary. Biblical quotations are listed in a separate index. The individual words in such quotations are not included in the Glossary.

Numbers in italics indicate that the reference is to a text in Syriac (this applies to B *16*, B *17* and B *26*) or in Christian Palestinian Aramaic (A *32*).

Verbs are placed under their root forms. Nouns are arranged in principle according to their spelling, usually in the definite form. *Matres lectionis* are ignored in the alphabetical arrangement, unless they form part of the root or of the basic nominal form. This rule has not been strictly observed in foreign words.

H = Hebrew, A = Aramaic (not indicated except in special cases).

אבא father, ancestor. אבהתנא B 19:8
אבנא stone B 24:4
אברא limb. אברוי A 19:6,27
אברהם Abraham A 27:10; 31:3
אגמא marsh B *26:6*
אגנא bucket B 21:12
איגרא roof. איגרה B *26:10*
אדון (H) lord A 24:8
אהרן Aaron A 17:4; 27:1
או or A 22:3
אוקינוס ocean A 22:13
אות (H) letter A 28:23. אתות A 19:15. See also אתא
אזל to go B *26:6*. תיזלון B 25:11. זה (*imper.*) B *16:1*
אחד (H) one A 22:5; 28:(29). (א)חד ומיוחד one and only A 22:2
אחד to seize A 23:2
אחורי behind. מאחורה B 22:3
אילנא tree. אילנייה A 16:7
אין yes B 19:7; *26:7,13*
איש (H) man A 26:2
אית there is/are A 19:33; B 23:5; 25:1
אל (H) God A 16:3; 19:17; 21r:5,9,10; 22:4,7; 24:9; 27:21; 28:10,23,25; 29:8; B 14:5; 19:9; 24:5,6

* Prepared by Yuval Harary.

אל שדי B 18:5; 20:10
אלא except, but A 30:2; B *26:5*
אלהא God A 16:12,17; 25:7; 27:4,20; B 19:9; *26:12,13*. אלהה A 22:4a; B 25:6. אלה A 21(left):2. אלהי B 23:8
אלהים (H) A 28:19,28; B 22:4. אלוהים A 28:19,20. אלוה A 22:4. אלוהי A 28:10
אלהים חיים A 17:9
אלהים צבאות B 20:10
אלהותא deity B *16:1*
אלין see הדין
אלמא see על מא
אם mother. אימם A 29:4
אמין see אמן
אמן A 16:24,25; 17:19,32; 19:28,33; 21(left):7; 22:14; 24:26; 27:8; 29:5,7,9; B 14:5,7; 15:8; 18:2,6; 19:5,9,11; 20:10; 21:13; 22:6; 23:11; B 24:6 25:4,7,11; *26:13*. אמין B *16:8*; *26:6,8,12,13*
אמר (H, A) to say, speak A 22:1; B *17:3,4*; 21:13. אמרה B 21:5. אמרין B 21:12. מאמר B 21:12
אנה I A 16:23; 19:10,30,34; 30:4,5; B 21:13; 23:5. אנא B 21:13; *26:13*
אני (H) I A 26:1; B 15:1
אנפא face. אנפה B *17:5*. אנפוהי B 21:11
אנשא man, individual. איניש B 23:11. אניש 16:6. אינשי (pl.) people B 18:5. אנשיה B *26:10*. See also בני אנשא (s.v. ברא)
אנת, אנתי, אנתון see את you
אנתתא see אתתא
אסותא healing B 18:5; 19:1; 20:1,7; 25:1. אסותה A 21(left):3; 31:4; B 20:10. אסיותא B *26:12*. אסיותה B *26:11*
אסי *pa.* to heal. אסי A 19:31; 31:4. נאסא B *26:12*. אסו A 22:2. מאסין A 24:27; 28:2. למאסיה A 24:25. למסיה A 19:7. *itp.* יתסון B 19:2. יתסי B 25:2. תתסי B 19:11. תתאסי A 23:2
אסיא healer B 27:5
אסיותא see אסותא
אסר to bind B 21:10; B *26:12*. יאסר B 21:11. תאסרון B 14:(1). אסורו B 27:6. אסרנה A 28:35. אסיר A 18:3; B *16:2,4,5,8*; 23:9; *26:10*. אסירא B *16:7*. אסירין B 14:1; 23:1,10; *26:1,12*. איסרין B 23:7. אסיריתון B 14:4. *pa.* אסורי (*inf.*) B 14:1. *itp.* ניתאסרון B 20:6. ליתאסרון B *26:4*
אסרא binding, knot, bond B *26:4*. אסרה B 20:2. אסורא B *16:4*. אסורה B *16:4*. אסור B *16:5*. אסרי B 14:3. איסורה B 18:2
איסקופתא threshold. איסקופתיה B 19:8. איסקופתהון B 15:7
איסתרתא goddess. *pl.*: B *16:6*; 22:8; 23:2,8; *26:9*
אף also B *26:9*
ארבעא four B 25:11. ארבעתי A 30:3
ארחא road. ארחתה A 19:38
אריא lion B *16:4*
ארעה earth A 16:5,8,13; B 14:7; 21:13. ארעא B *26:10*
ארעאי lower A 17:7
ארץ (H) land A 22:4; B 24:5
אשתה fire, fever A 19:1,13,25. אישתא B 27:7. אשא A 17:1,(18),31. אשה A 24:11. אשת A 19:2
אשה (H) woman A 26:3
אשלמתא spell, magic rite B 14:4; 15:6; 19:5
אשתיתאה see שת
את you A 16:6; 18:3; 19:31; 22:8; 24:10. אנת A 22:8
אתי (fem.) A 26:13. אנתי B 25:9
אתון (pl.) B 25:10. אנתון B *26:9*

את (H) acc. particle A 22:2; 24:10
אתא letter. אתיה A 19:9. אתיתא B 15:8
אתי to come. אתא B *26:6*. אתת B *16:3*. יתון B 25:4. תיתון B 25:7
אתרא place. אתר B 25:11. See also סלהתר
אתתא woman. אנתתא B *17:5*. אינתתיה B 19:1,8. נשין (pl.) A 29:4
-ב (prefix) at, by, in, over, with. בה A 17:5; 18:3; 23:3,4; 24:4; B 21:9; *26:10,11*. ביה B 19:9. בהון A 26:13; B *26:7*
בבא door. בבה B *26:10*
בדק to prove. בדיק A 24:1
בדר *pa.* to scatter. מבדרין B *26:11*
בוא (H) to come. לבוא A 26:4
בודינה sorcery (?) A 23:4
בורכתא blessing B 23:6
בושה illness, sickness A 19:13. בוש A 17:(2),18,31
בטל *pa.* to annul. בטיל B *26:12*. מבטילנא B 19:6,7. *itp.* נתבטל B *17:5*
בטנא pregnant (?) B 21:14
בין between B 19:8. בינגא B 19:7
בירא well. בירה B *26:10*
ביש evil A 18:6; 27:6; 29:3; B 25:(6); B *26:4*. בישא B *16:2,6*; 25:3,4; 27:8. בישה A 19:26; 23:3,(5); 27:5. בישתא B 14:3; *16:1,7*; 19:4,7,10; 23:3,10; 25:2; 27:8,9. בישתה A 19:25,37; 25:5; 26:10; 27:5,19. בישין A 25:9; B 14:4; 15:6; 19:10 19:3,4,5; 25:9,10. בישן B 15:4
בית house. B 20:7; 25:9. ביתא B *16:2,4,6,7*; *26:6,10*. ביתיה B 14:2; 19:8,9; 20:7,9; 25:11; 27:1,6. בתה (?) B 23:9. ביתיהון B 14:3. בתיהון B 15:4,7; 18:5
בן (H) son A 24:11. See also ברא
בסם to sweeten, make fragrant. בסים B 24:5. לביסומיה B 24:1

בעקא convulsion B *26:3*
ביעותא fright, scary thing. בעותין B 25:10
בעתה egg B 21:3,5,7
ברא son. בר ,-ד ברה *passim*. בנין (pl.). בני B 19:2. בניהון B 15:4,7. בנה B *26:4,6,7,11*
בני אדם וחוה B 21:14,15
בני אנשא people A 26:13. בניאנשא B *26:7*. בני אנשה A 16:13,14. בני אינשה B 23:6; 25:10
ברתא daughter. ברת A 23:1; 30:1,2,4,6,6c,9. בת B 14:2; 15:3; 18:4; 19:1,8; 21:2,3,8; 22:8. 23:9. -ברתה ד A 17:17,30; 18:2; 25:6; 27:6,18,22,27; 28:(3),38. בנתה B *26:4,6,7,11*. בנתהון B 15:4,7
בנת חוה daughters of Eve A 30:9
ברא external. דברי B 14:5
ברא (H) create B 25:6
בריה creature A 24:9
ברך to bless. בריך A 24:10. *Hebrew*: ברוך A 16:3; 17:19; 28:32 B 25:5. ברוכה A 16:4. *pu.* מבורך A 28:27; B 24:2
ברקתא cataract B 25:2,5,7. ברקתי B 25:9
בשר (H) flesh, living being. כל בשר A 28:10
בת גודא (?) B 21:14
בתולתא virgin. בתול(אתא) A 29:4
בתר after. בתרי B 21:5,8. בתרך B 21:6. בתרהון B 21:13
גאוה (H) haughtiness. גוה A 24:7
גבר man. גברין A 29:4
גיבור (H) mighty A 16:3
גבורה (H) might. גברות (?) B 25:5
גדא fortune. גדיה B 23:9
גדול (H) great A 22:8; 24:13
גוא inner. מן גו B *26:6*. בגוה B *16:2,7*. דגוי B 14:(6) לגו A 27:23
גודיה troops (?) A 22:2

גוה see גאוה
גוי (H) gentile A 26:3
גופא body. גופה A 17:17,30; 19:5,13,26; 27:6; 28:2 29:3
גזי *pa.* to remove (?). מגזא B 24:4
גזר to determine, decree. גזרנא B 19:5
גיתא world B 23:4
גלי to reveal A 24:2. *itp.* אתגלית A 30:(4),5. נגלה (H) A 28:26
גולית Goliath B 21:10
גלל to unroll. גליל A 17:(4)
גער to rebuke, expel, drive out (away), exorcise A 20:3. גוער (H) A 27:16. געור 27:12. גערורו A 25:5. יגעור A 27:18. למגעור A 19:1. *itp.* יגערו A 22:4. תגער A 18:2. יתגערון A 19:24; 27;4. יתגערין A 27:15
גרש (H) to stir up. *hitp.* מתגרשים A 26:4
דויד David A 27:3; B 21:10
דון to judge. *itp.* מתדנאן B 21:12
דוש to thresh. דישין B 23:1
דוכיא purity B *26:2*
דיוא dēw, devil, demon B *16:1,7*; 20:3,8, 25:3; *26:11*; 27:8. דיוין B 15:5. דיואין B *26:12*. דיוי B 14:3; 19:3; 25:6.
דיזא village B 24:2
דין (H) judge A 24:8.
דין (Syr.) but, then B *17:4*
דין see הדין. See also כדין, הכדין
דירא inhabitant. דיארא B *16:2*
דירתא residence, dwelling, living quarters. דירתהון B 14:3. דירתיה B 14:2; 19:8; 25:11; 27:1,6. See also מדירתא
דכר to remember. *itp.* אדכרי A 26:14
דכר male A 24:12,22; 27:29. דכרא B *26:9*. דיכרא B *16:3*; 20:3-5; 25:2,5,7,9. דיכרין B 19:4. דיכרי B 22:8; 23:2

דמא blood B 21:12
דמותא form, likeness, appearance. B 25:10. דמון A 26:12. דמואתה B 18:1
דימינא appearance. דימינין B 25:3,9
דמי *itp.* to be like, take on a form, appear as. תידמון B 25:10. תדמין A 26:12. מדמיה A 26:13. מידמין B 25:9. מיתדמיה B 18:1; 25:2. מיתדמין B 25:10
דעתא mind. דעתך (?) B 21:4
דקיק hectic (fever). דקיקה A 17:(1),18,31
דרגא ladder. דוריגי B 23:2
דרמנא cure B *26:12*
הדא see הדין
הדין this A 30:8; B *16:3*; 18:4; 19:9; 20:2; 21:1,8; 22:1; 23:8; 24:1; 27:6. הדן A 19:5,10,14,18,27,31. דין B 18:2; 19:1,9. דנין B 25:4,7
הנא B *16:2,6,7*. הנה B 18:1
הדא (fem.) B *16:7*; 21:13. הדה A 16:18; 17:7; 27:19
אלין (pl.) A 19:8; 26:9. איליהן B 15:8
הלין (pl.) B 26:11
הדר see מהדר
הדרא glory B 21:11
הוא he, it A 17:3,(5),6,7,(19); 19:12; 21(left):2; 24:(10),19; 28:32; B 21:11; 25:5. הו A 27:17; 28:10; B *17:5*
הי she B *17:1*
אינון they B 15:3; 23:6,7
הוי to be. הוה A 17:3,5; B 19:7; 23:5. הוין B *26:7*. יה B 24:2. יהווי A 16:10. יהוון A 16:17. ייהון A 24:4. ניהא B 24:5. תהוא B *26:7*. תהוי B 20:7. תהי A 18:3. תיהוי B 18:5. תיהי B 25:8
היך as A 16:4,6. איך B *26:6*. הך A 16:11

הכדין thus, so B 21:8. בהיכדין B 21:8
הכנא so, in this manner B *17:5*; *26:7*
הלין see הדין
הללויה A 16:26; 24:26; B 19:5,9; 24:6. הללוהי B *26:8,12*
הנא see הדין
הפך to return, invert. *itp*. ליתהפכון B *26:5*
הרהורא thought. הרהרין B 25:10
הש see השעתא
השעתא now B *17:4*. הש B *26:13*
ולדא child. ולדה A 30:(9). ולדהין A 30:9
זבד to equip. זבדין B 14:6
זוח *af*. to remove. לאזחא B 20:3. יזיחון B 15:7
זויתא corner. זוית B 25:11
זוע to move. תזוע A 18:2
זידן wicked, malicious, impious. זידנין B 15:6. זידניתא B 19:7; 23:3,10; 27:7
זיוא splendour B *26:5*
זיפא forgery, falseness. זיפין B 19:6
זיקא blast demon B 25:4. זיקי B 22:7. זיקין B 19:10. זעקא B *16:5*
זכי to win B *17:4*
זכר (H) male A 26:2
זמן *pa*. to designate. מזמן B 21:1 (?); 24:1
זמנא time. זמנה A 30:6
זני to fornicate. זניא B 20:9
זעקא see זיקא
זרז to gird. זריזין B *26:1*. *pa*. מזרזין B *26:11*
זרק to spill (?). ניזריק B 24:5
חברון Hebron A 31:3
חדר to go back, return. ניחידרון B 23:8
חוש quick (?) A 18:9
חזוא vision. חזויא A 20:3
חזי *itp*. to appear. מיתחזיא B 18:1
חזק (H) strong A 16:3

חטרא rod. חטרה A 27:1
חיותא vitality B *26:7*
חיי to live. חיה A 27:4. חיא B *26:12*. חי (H) B 24:6. *pa*. יחיה A 28:10
חיין life A 31:8. חיא B *26:7*
חילא power. חילה B *17:6*
חכם wise. חכמיא B 21:13
חלמא dream. חילמי B 18:1
חולמנא health B *26:12*
חלץ to girt. חליצין B *26:1*
חמא heat (?) B 14:6
חמי *itp*. to become visible. תיתחמון B 19:9
חמיטריטין semi-tertian (fever) A 19:3
חמימתה fever A 19:32
חמר to ferment, become hot. חמרת B *17:3,4*. לחמריה B 24:1
חמרא wine. חמריה B 24:1,3,5
חומרא pebble spirit, charm B *16:6*; *26:9*. חומרי B 23:3,10; 27:7. חומרין B 15:6. חומרתא B *16:3*; 20:5,8
חמש five. חמישאה fifth B 14:6
חנון (H) merciful A 24:9
חסיד (H) pious B 27:5
חפר to be ashamed (?). יחפרו A 22:4
חקלא field. חקלה B *26:10*
חקק (H) to engrave. חקוקה A 19:15
חרם (H) *ḥerem*, ban B 21:13
חרשא sorcerer, sorcery, witchcraft B 24:4; *26:1,7*. חרשי B 15:5; 25:6. חרשין B 14:4; 19:4,6,7
חשב *pa*. to think, plan. מחשבת B 21:7
חתם to seal. חתמו B 27:5. חתמנא B 22:(1). חתמה B *26:10*. חתים B 14:5; *16:4,5,8*; 19:9; 20:9; 23:9; *26:10*; 27:1. חתימא B *26:10*. חתימה A 18:6. חתימי B 15:8. חתימין B 14:1,6; 15:1; 23:10; *26:1,4,11*. חתימיתון B 14:4. *pa*. מחתם B 14:5; 20:9. מחתמין B 15:2. חתומי B 14:1. *itp*. יתחתמון B 19:2.

תיחתמון B 14:1. ניתחתמון B 20:6

חתמא seal, sealing B *16:4*; 18:4; 19:9; 20:7; *26:10,11*. חתמה B *16:4* 20:2,10. חתמיה B 23:11. חתמין B 14:5. חתמתא B 18:4; *26:12*

טב proper, good A 19:1; 23:1; 24:1. טביא A 30:7. טבתא B 18:5

טופא sailing (?) A *32:3*

טלניתא shadow spirit. טלני A 22:3; 24:12. טלנית A 24:(20). טולנין B 15:6. טלנין A 24:2. טולין B 25:3

טנף filthy. טנפא B 24:4

טעי to err. טעין errant (spirit)s B 15:6

טרטיה tertian (fever) A 19:2,25

טתלתולה excrescence (?) A 23:2

יד (H) hand. ביד B 21:10,11. See also מיד

ידי *af.* to admit. מודין B 21:12

ידע *haf.* to announce. מהודענא B 27:3

יהב to give, place A 30:5. הב A 31:8

יהושוע בר נון Joshua son of Nun B 21:11

יומא day B 18:2,9; 25:5,7. יום A 16:7,8. ימאמא B *26:2*. ימאמה B 25:8

יומדן today A 17:32; 27:(7)

יונתן Jonathan A 31:1

יוסיף Joseph B 21:11

יחד *pu.* to be specially designated. (א)חד ומיוחד one and only A 22:2

ילד to give birth. יליד B *17:5*

ילדותא childhood. ילדותיה B 25:2

ימה sea A 16:5. ים (H) A 27:16

ימאמא see יומא

ימי to swear. *af.* to adjure, beswear. אומית 25:5. אומיתי B 25:7. מומי A 19:34. מומינא B 19:5

ימין right. ימינה B 22:2. ימיניה B 25:9

יצב (H) *hitp.* to stand. מתיצב A 24:14

ירושלים Jerusalem A 28:23

יריחו Jericho B 21:11

ירח (H) moon A 22:10

ירת to inherit. ירתי B 23:9

ישב (H) to sit, to reside A 24:6. יושב A 27:11

ישע (H) *hif.* to save. הושיע A 24:17,27

ישראל Israel A 16:22; 24:5; 26:3; B 25:6

ית acc. particle A 27:14; 31:4,7; B 19:6. יתיך A 19:13; 27:14. יתה A 19:7. יתיה B 25:9. יתהון B 19:7,8

יתב to sit A 19:35,38,39,40; 28:23. תיתבון B 25:9. יתבין B *26:2*

כאיבא pain. כאיבאי B 27:6

כבד (H) *nif.* נכבד glorious A 24:(17,27)

כבוד (H) glory A 24:7. כבודו A 22:2.

כבש to suppress, press down, subdue. כבשה B 21:10. כבשת A 16:4. תיכבשון B 25:8. כביש A 16:16. כבישה A 16:13. כבישין A 16:12,14,15 B 23:1. *pa.* מכבש A 16:6. מכבשין B 21:8. *itp.* ניתכבשון B 20:6. מיתכבשה B 21:9

כיבשא subduing B 21:1

כהן priest. כהנה רבה high priest A 17:4; 27:2

כוחתא breathing, coughing B 27:9

כיולה ark B *26:10*

ככבא star. ככיבי B 22:7

כדין so, thus A 16:8,17

כל, כול all, any, each, every, whole *passim*. כוליה B 14:3; 18:5; 20:7,9. כולה B 14:3. כולהון B 20:6. כלהון B 25:6

כלה total (?) B 21:14

כלילה wreath A 17:4

כני to nickname. כנאו (?) A 28:25

כנש to collect. כנישין (?) B 21:12

כסא cup, fate (?). כסי B *17:2*

כסא (H) throne A 24:17

כסי to cover, hide. כסה A 24:2. כ(ס)י B 15:8

כסס to beat, blow, strike. כיס B *17:2,3*. כיסין B 19:6. כיסי B 19:9.

מכים B *17:2*
כען now A 18:3
כפת to tie up. תכפתוהי B 25:7
כרוב (H) cherub. כרוביה A 28:24. כרובים A 17:19. יושב הכרובים enthroned among the cherubim A 17:19
כרסיא throne. כ[ר]סיה A 28:(23-24)
כתב to write A 19:11,31. כתבתי B *26:13*. כתוב A *32:2*. כתיב A 17:3. כתיבין A 19:9; B *26:4*. *itp.* אתכתבו B *26:11*
-ל acc. particle, or prefix: unto, to, toward, for. *passim*
לי B 21:5; 21:13; 23:5. לך A 18:3; B 21:7. ליך A 28:35. ליה B 20:7; 24:3; 25:2,8,9,10. לה A 26:12; 23:(2); B *16:7*; *26:3,7*. לכון A 30:7. להון B 18:5; 19:9; *26:7*
לא no, not *passim*. לה A 26:11; 28:(38)
ליבא heart B 21:(7). לבה A 23:4
לות by, near B *26:5*. לותה B *16:6*
לחש to charm. לחושי לח[ישי]ן B 14:1
לטבא no good, no good spirit B *16:1,3,6*. לטבי B 22:7
לוטתא curse B 14:4; 15:6; 19:4,6; 23:2-4,6-8
ליליא, ליליה night A 22:3; B 25:8; *26:2*. לילא B 21:5
ליליתא lilith B 14:3; 19:4; 20:5,9. ללִיתא B *16:3,6,7*; *26:9*. לילין B 15:6
לית there is (are) not B 21:7
לכן therefore A 24:10
לקט to gather. לקיטין B *26:1*
מאתה town B 24:2
מבכלתא tormentor B 15:5; 18:1; 20:5,9
מבלעא gullet. מבלעיה A 27:14
מגנא magic craft (?) B 24:4
מדבחה altar A 27:3
מדון (H) strife. מדינ (?) B 23:7
מדירתא residence, dwelling, living quarter. מדירתהון B 15:4,7
מה what A 26:14. היך מה as A 16:6. הך מה A 16:11. על מא why? B *17:2,3*
מהדר splendid A 17:29,34 מהודר (H) A 17:29
מובלא load B *16:5*
מוכנתא (?) B 21:14
מום blemish A 25:(8)
מור to change. תימירון B 25:8
מותה death A 16:15,16. See also מיתותא
מזונא sustenance. מזוניהון B 18:5
מזיקא doer of harm, evil destroyer, harmful spirit B 25:4. מזיקין B 15:6; 19:3,5,10. מזיקי B 19:7
מזלא zodiac sign. מזלי B 22:7
מחוש pain A 29:7
מחי to hit, smite. מחתה B *17:1*. *itp.* נתמחא B *17:5*. תיתמחא B *17:1*
מטי to arrive, come. ימטי A 30:6
מי (H) he who A 22:8
מיא water, river B 21:9,10; *26:3,5*
מיד at once B 21:13 (?)
מידעם anything B 19:10; 25:4. מידיעם B 14:4
מיוחד (H) see יחד
מימר word A 18:6; B 22:3. מימרי A 16:11
מכון (H) abode. מכונם A 21m
מין (H) kind. מיני B 19:6
מית dead B *17:4*
מיתותא death. מתות(א) B 21:9
מלא *pa.* to fulfil. למלאה A 17:(5)
מלאכה angel A 16:21; 19:17; 24:3; 25:7,8; 26:8; 31:2,6 B 21:14; 23:5,10; 27:3. מלאכין B 27:5. מלאכיה A 26:9,15; 27:25; 30:3,7. מלאכוי A 18:1-2; 25:(8).
מלך to rule. מוליך (H) ruler A 24:6
מלך (H) king A 24:9 28:11 31:6.

מלכי A 28:11. מלכים A 28:11. מלך מלכי המלכים A 28:11; B 25:5
מלכותא kingdom B 21:11. מלכו B 21:10. מלכותך (H) A 16:4
מלל to speak. מללת A 30:5
מללא spell, (magical) word. מללתא B 19:6,9; 23:4
מן who. מנו B *17:5*
מן from *passim*
מני A 30:10,11. מנך A 18:6. מנה A 17:7; 18:4; 19:36. מיניה B 20:6; 23:7; 25:10. מנכון B 21:13. מינהון B 15:7.
מנא whence? מנא לי B 21:(5),6
מני *pa.* to appoint. ממני A 19:12. ממנין A 27:25-26
מסיק (=מציק) oppressor. מסיקי B 21:9. מסיקייהו B 21:8
מסנא shoe. מסנך A 16:6
מסקור (evil) gaze A 19:4. מסקוריתה A 26:15
מסר *itp.* to be surrendered. ניתמסרון B 20:6
מסר denunciation (?) B 21:12
מעבד magicl act. מעבדי B 19:7. מעבדין B 19:9
מעי belly A 30:5. מעיה A 27:7,23,28; 28:3,38-39; 30:4
מעלנא entrance. מעלוניה B 25:8,11
מעסה see מעשה
מעשה (H) action. מעסים A 24:8
מפואר (H) glorious, magnificent A 17:23,34
מפקנא exit. מפקוניה B 25:8,11
מצרים Egypt B 21:11
מרדותה rebellion (?) B 21:12
מרוביא educator(?). מרובין B 15:6
מריא lord. מרי B 14:5. מריהון B 20:1,10.
מרי שמיא Lord of Heaven B 19:7. מרי ארעא Lord of the Earth B 19:7. מרי רזיה lord of mysteries B 21:10
מרעא sickness, illness. מרע A 17:2,18,32. מרעי B 27:7
משה Moses A 27:1; 28:26; B 21:10
משיחא Christ B *17:6*
משל (H) to rule. מושל A 22:(5),6,8,9,10,13
משמע obedience. משמעי A 16:11
משמתתא ban B 15:5
משפט misfortune (?) A 19:4
משרת (H) servant A 22:2. משרתו A 22:4a,5,7,8,10,(13)
מתותא see מיתותא
נאמן (H) faithful A 24:26
נדר to pour down (?). נדרין B *26:3*
נידרא vow. B 19:4; 25:3,6. נידרי B 15:5; 19:6,10; 23:2,4,7
נהרה river B 21:9
נוד (the land of) Nod B 24:5
נוח Noah B *26:10*
נורא (H) awesome A 28:16
נזק *pa.* (or *af.*) to cause harm. תנזקון B 19:8
נחירין breathing (?) A 25:(9)
נחלה river A 19:36
נחת to descend, go down A 17:5. ניחת B 24:5. נחתין B *16:8*
נטר to protect, guard, keep A 31:7. טור A 29:6,(8). טרו A 27:(22). יטרון A 25:9. נטירי B 15:8. למנטרה A 19:7. למנטרנותיה B 24:1
נטרתא protection, preservation B 18:4; 20:7; *26:12*. נטרתה B *26:11*
נידא uncleanness B 25:3
נכי (H) *hif.* to smite. מכה A 24:9
נסב to take. נסיב B *26:2*
נפח to blow. לפחון B *26:5*
נפל to fall. נפילין A 16:19
נפק to emerge, go out A 19:36; 30:10,11. יפוק A 30:2; *32:2*. תיפקון B 25:8. יפקון B 15:7. *af.* to drive out. לאפוקא B 20:3

נפשא tomb. נפשתה A 31:3
נקבה female A 24:12,22; 26:2; 27:29. נוקבתא B 19:4; 20:4-5. ניקבתא B *16:3*; 22:8; 23:2; 25:2,5,7,9,10; *26:9*
נקט to seize. נקיטין B 23:1
נקש to knock. נקיש B 21:13
נשמה (H) soul A 24:8
נתן to give. יתן A 21(left):3. יתין (H) A 24:19
סבל to carry A 17:6
סיהרא moon B 14:6
סוסיא horse. סוסיך A 16:5
סחף to sweep, pour. סחפין B 21:12
סטן Satan, enemy. סטנא B 20:4; 27:8. סטני B 19:(6). סטנין A 28:4; B 15:5; 19:3,10. שטן B 22:4
סימן sign A 16:23
סכר to shut. סכרא B 21:14. סכרן B *17:4*. סכורא he who shuts (?) B *17:3*
סלה A 16:25; 17:19,33; 19:28,33; 27:8; 29:5,7,9; B 14:5,7; 15:8; 18:2,6; 19:5,9,11; 20:10; 22:6; 23:11; B 24:6; 25:4,7,11. סלח B *26:8,12,13*. סלחה B *26:8*
סלהתר B 23:11
סלק to go up. סליקין B *26:10*
סנה burning bush A 28:26
סני to hate. סניא B 14:4
סניא enemy. סנייהו B 21:8
סעי to assail (?). סעיא A 27:(5)
ספף to burn. *itp.* ניסתפף B 24:5
סקר to cast a glance, gaze. סקרה A 23:3. See also מסקור
סר prince A 24:13
סיתבה winter A 16:7
סתם to block. סתמה A 27:(13)
עבד to make, perform A 16:23; B 21:10. עבדין B *26:7*
עבד slave B 21:10
עבר to transgress (against). נעברון B *26:4*
עד until A 30:6
עדילתא accusation B *26:3*
עדנה time. A 30:(2). עדניה chronic (?) A 19:2
עובדא deed, act. עובדין B 14:4; 19:(4)
עוד more, also A 18:3,6
עולה foetus A 27:7,12,16,19,23,28; 28:3,7,38; 30:(1),2,(4),5
עולם see עלמא
עוף bird A 22:3
עור to become awake B *17:6*
עזק to bind. תיעזקון B 25:6
עזקתא signet, seal ring B 14:6. עזקתה A 27:2. עיזקתא B 15:8; *26:10*. עיזקתה B *26:10*
עין eye A 29:3,4. עיין A 19:4. עיני A 31:3; B 21:(6),7. עינך B 21:4
עינא בישתא B *17:1*. עינא בישא B 27:9
עירא awake B *16:1*
על upon, over, in, against, at, to *passim* עלי B *17:2,4*; 21:4,7. עלייך A 19:12. עלך B 21:6,14. עלכי A 26:9. עלהי B 25:4. עלוהי B 25:7. עלוי A 19:33. עלה B 23:9. עליכו B 25:5,7. עליהון A 16:11; B 21:12. עלהון B 21:12
על מא why?. אלמא B 21:3-5
מעל above. מעליה B 22:(2)
עלא high. לעלא above B *26:6*
עליא supreme A 25:7. עלאי (*pl.*) A 17:6
עלל to enter, come in. תיעלון B 19:8. תעלון B 25:8. אילין B *26:10*.
עלמא, עלמה world A 18:6; B 25:6. עלם A 24:8
לעלם, עד לעלם to eternity, for ever A 17:32; 27:8; B 25:4,7; *26:13*
לעלמא ולעלמי עלמיא for ever and ever B 24:2-3
לעולם (H) forever B 18:2; 20:3

צור העלמים (H) the Eternal Rock A 22:1
עם with A 26:2,3; 30:5. עים B 23:6,7
עמה people, inhabitants A 16:17
עמד (H) to exist. עומדין B 20:2
עננא cloud. ענני B 21:13
ענקתא necklace-charm B 19:6,10
עסי see עשה
עסבה grass A 16:7
עקבא heel. עוקבי B 21:13
עקר to eradicate, to uproot. יעקור A 19:12. עקור A 17:17,30
עקרתא spirit of barrenness B 15:5
ערבות (H) clouds A 22:5
ערויתא hectic fever, shiver B 27:7. ערוי A 24:11
עשה (H) to do, to act. עושה B 15:1. עסא A 24:17. נעשה A 16:2
עשיה (H) act. עשיות (?) B 25:5
עשף to exorcise. עשיפין B 23:1. עשפן B *26:2*
עשפא exorcism B *26:2*. עושפא B 23:3. עישפא B 23:4
פאר (H) see מפואר
פגע harm, affliction, trouble A 25:8; B 22:4. פגעא B 25:3. פגעין A 28:4; B 15:5. פגעי B 19:3
פוג to cool. יפוג A *32:4*
פומא mouth. B 21:6,(7); B 21:14. פומך B 21:3
פורהיא (for פורהזא ?) warning B *26:4* (*pl.*)
פיקדא commandment. פיקדי B 22:7
פלקטון phylactery A *32:1*
פנים (H) countenance, front. ביפני in front of A 28:24. מלפנה B 22:2
פרח to fly. פרחא A 26:10
פרעה Pharao B 21:10
פרק to redeem. פרוקו A 27:27
פרש *pa.*; *af.* to distinguish, separate. פריש B 24:3. מפריש B 24:3. מפרשא B 24:4. מפרשה B 24:4. מפרשין B 24:4
פתח to open. פתחת B 21:3,7. פתחנא B 21:(6)
פתכרא idol B *16:6*; 20:9; *26:9*. פתכרין B 15:6. פתכרי B 14:3; 22:8. פתיכרי B 23:1
צבא (H) army A 22:2
צבו thing B 25:10
צורתא form, figure B 14:6. צורתיה B 19:9
צילמא figure B 18:1
ציצה front plate (of the high pries) A 17:3; 27:1
צלח to succeed. *hif.* נצליח (H) A 16:2
צלח success A 16:23,24
צמד to bind, attach. צמידין B 23:1
צמידא binding B 23:4
צעקתא cry B 23:5
צערא pain, torment, suffering A *32:2*. צער A 29:7
קבורתה burial A 31:3
קבל *pa.* to accept. מקביל B *26:2*
קבל against. קיבלה B *17:5*. קבליה 21:10(?)
קיבלא charm B 23:5. קבלאתא B 23:3
קבר to bury. קביר B *16:7*
קדוש (H) holy A 17:22,35,36; 22:3; 28:7,16,26; B 24:2,6. קדושים A 17:29
קדיש holy A 18:6. קדישה A 30:7. קדישוי A 25:(8). קדישיה A 18:2; 19:9; 30:(3). קדישין B 27:5
קדיש עלמה the holy one of the world A 18:6
קדמאה first, primordial B 14:(5); 19:7
קודם before A 16:10,12,13,15,16, 20,22
קום to stand, exist, rise. נקום B *17:5,6*. קאים B *17:5*. קימה A 27:4. קימין B 20:3; 23:6. *af.* אקימית B *17:4*. אקים B *17:3*
קטר to tie B *26:12*. קיטרין (for קטירין)

B 14:1. *pa.* קטורי *(inf.)* B 14:1. *itp.* ליתקטרון B *26:4*
קטרא knot, tying. קטרין B 19:6; *26:12*. קיטריה B 23:11
קייטה summer A 16:8
קימתא existence B *26:12*
קלקלא destruction B 21:14
קמט to clasp. קמיט B *26:4*. קמיטין B *26:1*
קמיעה amulet A 19:10; 30:8; B 22:1; 24:1. קמיע A 19:1; 23:1; 24:(1). קמעיא B *26:11*
קניא reed B *26:6*
קנינא possession. קיניניהון B 18:5. קנינה B *26:10*
קרא, קרי to call, name. קורא (H) A 28:16. *itp.* מתקרי B 25:1
קרב to approach, come near, touch. תקרובין A 26:11. תיקרבון B 19:9. ניקרבון B *16:7*. קרבה A 23:4
קרוב (H) near A 28:16
קריב near, kinsman. קריביהון B *26:5*
קורבנא offering, present B *26:2*
קרביל Qarbil (name of a village) B 24:2
קריתא misfortune, accident, calamity B 14:4; 19:4,6,10. קיריתא B 23:4,6-8. קיריא B 23:4. קירין B 19:3
קרנא horn, corner. קרנתה horns (of the altar) A 27:3
קרתה town A 16:18
ראשא head. ראשי B 21:13
רב great A 21(left):2. רבא B *16:5*; 24:2; 25:5; *26:5*. רבה A 19:18; 21(right):(1),2-12;22:(14); 27:20; B 14:7; 19:11; 20:10; *26:11*; 27:5. רבתה A 19:2. רברבין B 14:(5)
רבא prince. רב A 31:4
רגלא foot. רגלי B 21:6. רגליך B 21:5. ריגלי B 21:7
רדף to chase. ירדפו A 22:4
רהט to run. רהטת B 21:6,7
רוגזא anger. רוגזה B *17:5*
רוחא spirit A 19:24; 26:10,14; 27:15,19; B *16:7*; 20:5,8; 25:2,6; *26:9*; 27:7. רוחה A 18:1,8; 25:5. רוח A 19:3,26; 21(left):4; 23:3; 24:20; 27:12,29; 29:7; B 20:9; 25:3. רוחין B 15:4; 25:6. רוחתא A 19:36. רוחי B 19:(6),7; 23:3,10 רוחא דקודשה B 20:10
רוסתקא village B 24:2
רזא secret, mystery B 19:1; 21:1. ראזא B *16:7*. ראזה B 14:7. רז B 15:8; 21:10. רזי B 19:6. ראזי B 14:6; 15:8
רחום (H) compassionate A 24:10
רחמין mercy. רחמי B 19:2
רחץ to trust. רחיצנא B 21:14
רחק to keep away, remove. תרחק A 18:2. תירחקון B 14:2. מרחק A 18:3
רטן to mumble. רטנן B *26:2*
ריטנא mumbling B *26:2*
רכב to ride. רכיבין B *17:3*
רם (H) lofty A 24:6
רמז to wink. רמזת B 21:7. מרמזת B 21:4
רמי to cast. לרמון B *26:5*
רעד to tremble. רעדין A 17:(7)
רעה (H) evil A 24:20. רעות A 26:2
רפא (H) to heal. רפה A 24:10. רופה A 24:9,10
רפואה (H) healing. רפואתו A 24:19
רקיעה firmament, sky B 14:7; 21:10,13
רקע to stamp. רקעת A 16:5
רשו power A 18:3; 28:(6)
שאול Sheol A 22:6
שאר remaining, other B 25:6
שבטא plague. שבטין B 15:4. שיפטין B 23:9. שיבטי B 19:3
שבע *af.* to adjure, invoke. אשבעית A 26:9; B 25:5,7. אשבעת A 27:14.

אשבעתיך A 26:14. משבע A 19:10,30,34. משבענא B 19:5. משבעת A 18:1. משביע (H) A 26:1
שבעה seven B 14:4. שבע B 15:7. שביעאה seventh B 14:6
שד demon A 21(left):5. שיד A 24:20; 29:7. שידא B *16:5,6,7*; 20:3,8,9; 25:3; 27:8. שאדא B *26:11*. שידין B 15:4; 23:9. שאדין B *26:1,12*. שידי B 14:3; 19:3; 25:5
שדר *pa.* to send. משדריניהון B 23:9. משדרניהון B *26:5*
שודשידא (=שורשירא) chain B 15:8
שוחא pit. שוחין דשוחין (?) B 21:12
שוחדא gift B *26:2*
שורא wall B 21:11. שורין B 14:5
שטן see סטן
שיר (H) song A 25:7; B 25:4
שיכבא asleep B *16:1*
שכינה Shekhina. שכינת אל B 22:3
שכן to rest, dwell. שכנא A 26:10
שלח to send. ישלח A 24:25. *itp.* אשתלח A 16:22.
שולטנא dominion B 21:10
שלל to chain. תשלילוהי B 25:8
שלמה Solomon A 27:2; B 20:8. שלמא B 18:4. שלימון B *26:10*
שם name A 19:15; 22:5; 24:17; 28:25,29. שום B 25:1. שמא A 17:21. שמה A 17:6; B *16:6*. שמו A 22:9; 27:17; 28:16,27,34. שמיה B 23:9; 24:2. שמך A 16:3; 19:30; 24:26; B *26:12*; 27:1,2. שמהתה A 19:8; 30:7
בשם, בשום *passim*. בשמה A 18:1,4,5,6; 19:17; 27:(3),20; 30:1; B 20:10. בשמיה B 14:5; 19:11; 21:(15); 24:6; 25:5. בישמיה B 23:10; B 24:2,4. בשמך B 15:1
שמאל left. שמאלה B 22:2; 25:9
שמיא sky, heaven B 18:5; 19:2; *26:10,12*. שמיה A 16:12; B 21:10; 24:4; 25:1
שמים (H) sky, heaven A 22:5
שמש *pa.* to serve. משמש A 17:5
שמש (H) sun A 22:8
שימשא sun B *26:5*
שיקופתא mishap, afflication B 14:4; 19:5. שיקופיתא 23:2,3,8
שמת *pa.* to ban. משמיתנא B 19:6
שיפטא see שבטא
שפף to bow. שפיפת B 21:7
שרי (1) to exist, to dwell. שרא B *16:8*. שריא B *16:7*. שרין B *16:2*; 23:7. שרת B *16:3*
שרי (2) to loosen, untie B 23:11
שרירא firm B 18:4
שרת see משרת
שת six. אשתיתאה sixth B 14:6
שתי to drink. שאתא B *26:3*
תבר to break B 23:11. תבירין A 16:(19)
תברא misfortune B 25:8
תגא crown B 21:10. תגיה B 21:11
תוב further B 19:5; *26:6*.
תוך (H) inside. מתוך from inside A 28:26
תור to confound. תיתור B *17:1*
תחות underneath B 21:9
תכלתא spirit of abortion B 15:5
תלי to suspend. תלא A 30:7
תלתא three B 14:5
תמרורתא exchange, place of change (?). תמרורתיה B 25:8
תינינא second B 14:5
תנינא dragon B *16:4*
תקיף strong, mighty B *26:4*. תקיפין B 14:4; 19:(5),10
תרי two A 28:24. תרי עשר twelve B 15:8
תרנגולתה hen B 21:3
תרפיה healing (?) A 22:3
תשבחות (H) praise A 25:7; B 25:5

Proper Names of Gods, Angels, Demons and Nomina Barbara

אשמאזה A 17:24
את A 22:7
את בש גר דק הצ ופ זע חס טנ ים כל A 28:21-22
אתא A 22:4
א(ת)בן A 24:16
ב(× 3) A 22:8; ב(× 7) A 19:29
בא A 18:11
באדות A 30:8
[ב]אל A 27:10
בא(פ)יה A 24:16
בביאל A 22:6
בגדנא B 16:5,8
בדיה A 30:11
בדרך A 30:12
בהנאל A 20:2
בוחר A 22:6
בוניון A 31:8
בחור A 22:6
ביגריא B 21:13
ביה A 27:10. See also יה ביה
במון A 18:11
בן A 22:8
בסלר A 24:13
בסמאל A 18:5
בפגיאנגאה B 21:12
ברוריאל A 25:3
בריאל A 30:3
ברכיאל A 25:3
גבריאל A 24:3; 30:10; 31:5; B 18:2
גגראים B 23:7
גוס B 26:11
גור A 18:12
גניאל A 20:3
גנניאל A 22:10
גסת A 18:12
גתבינן A 22:6
דאות A 25:8
דאיה A 24:2
דביר B 14:5
דד A 18:6
דוקון A 26:5
דיאס A 28:22
דימין B 21:12
דימר A 18:11
דלל A 24:23
דנחיש B 20:9
דנתי B 21:12
דרהי A 24:23
דרקון A 26:5
ה(4) A 24:16; ה(× 7) A 19:29
הא A 17:26
הגיז B 21:14
הוא A 17:2
הויה A 28:22
הי A 21r:6
המון A 21r:10
המשל A 22:3
הסא A 17:28
הסונה A 28:17
הקהק A 19:22
השם A 17:28
השני A 22:6
ואל A 21r:7-10
וו A 19:22
זא A 17:28
זהיאל A 21r:6
זובה A 18:12
זוזעיה A 30:12
זזזז A 17:9
זיבה A 31:7
זיגוריתא B 23:2
זתבדי A 18:11
חבה A 24:23
חח A 21r:4; 22:6; ח(× 3) A 21r:4; ח(× 4) A 19:22; ח(× 7) A 22:13; 29:2
חונא A 22:7
חוסא A 22:7
חזק A 28:18
חחף A 22:14
חטועע A 16:21
(ח)נאל A 21r:3
חניאל A 21r:4

חס A 18:6
חצץ A 22:3
חצרות A 22:2
חקק A 18:7
חרביאל B 22:2
חרסיאל B 21:11
חרפיאל B 21:9
טביאל A 21r:5
טוריאל A 18:5
טמנואל A 19:35
טסיריס A 24:21
טרחיאל A 25:1
טרסוס A 22:14
י(× 4) A 24:6,16; 27:17; 28:15,24,33; 30:4; י(× 7) A 19:30; 29:2
יא A 22:8; 24:6,15
יאל A 21r:3-7,10
יאסיה A 22:9
יה A 17:2,(3),11-16,25; 18:10; 22:9; 24:6,8,23; 25:2,6; 27:27; 28:16,17, 20-22,25; 29:6,8; B 18:3; 24:2,3,6
יה ביה A 22:5; 24:16; B 20:10
יהא A 24:15
יהו A 25:2,3; 28:27; 29:6,8; B 18:3; 24:6
יהוה A 16:2; 17:18; 28:27,28; 29:7; 31:6; B 18:3; 20:10
יחוש A 28:17,18
יואל A 21r:6
יויאל A 21r:7
יזות A 17:2
יזיד מחדט B 23:5,10
יללוס A 18:12
ינה A 24:23
יעל A 24:25
יקהרי A 24:22
יקומיאל A 19:37
יקר(ס)נא A 22:7
ירפא A 17:8
ישר A 19:35
כדאיא A 27:21
כדרקר A 31:2
כוכביאל A 26:8
כנפיאל A 28:25
כפויאל A 18:5
כרביאל A 21r:8
כשיאל B 21:9
כתראת A 18:11
ל(× 7) A 29:2
לאלא A 31:7
לבטירות A 24:5
לגלל A 24:22
להטט A 24:5
לוליאל A 21r:9
לוס A 22:9
ללוזבה A 19:19
למן A 22:7
מדות A 27:25
מה A 17:25
(מ)וריאל A 30:10
מזה A 17:24
מיכאל A 18:5; 31:5; B 22:2; 26:4
מיקון A 18:12
מכיאל A 22:14
מלאיתגה A 22:14
מלל A 22:10
ממר A 22:9
מן A 22:7
מנין A 18:11
מסא A 17:27
מסוס A 24:15
מסס A 24:15
מעוף A 22:3
מפריאל A 18:4
מר A 22:1
מראה A 24:22
מראות A 19:20
מראפו(ת) A 19:19
מרותה A 22:11
מ(רי)ה A 21r:7 (מ)ריה A 22:1
מרכביאת A 17:9
מרמ(וי) A 22:3
נא A 22:9
נגג A 22:14

נותביאל A 19:24
נג A 18:7; נגג A 18:6
נגע A 24:22
נדא B 15:8
נדבך A 30:12
נדבאל A 18:5
נהריאל A 19:(39)
נובס B 21:13
נוריאל B 18:2
נותיאל A 20:2
נחומיאל A 19:18
נטתא B 15:8
ניחות B 21:14
ניטרואל B 23:6
ניפש B 21:13
נתנאל A 27:10
ס(×7) A 29:2; ס(×21) A 19:20-21
סבר A 32:3
סגי B 21:14
סוסגד A 30:3
סוסיאל B 22:2
סימיאל B 27:3
סין A 24:23
סלדאקליף A 26:7
סליחות A 29:8 סלי(ח)ות A 29:6
סמך B 18:6
סנבאותתייך A 17:25
סנגין in סנג(י)ן אגגן בר פרגגוס A 22:11;
סנג ופרנגיס A 25:8
סננתיאל A 25:4 ס(נג)תיאל A 25:2
סנר A 24:13
ססח B 24:3
סעצכקסס A 18:7
סעקצסכרד A 18:7
ספיני A 22:7
ספנייאל A 22:7
סקופק A 26:6
סרגינוס A 24:21
סרדיאל B 21:11
סריפון B 21:12
סרמון A 31:1
סתריאל A 25:2

עאות A 22:11
עברי A 18:8
עדה B 22:6
עוזאל A 19:23
עותיאל A 20:3
עזריאל A 31:5
עליזא A 17:10
עליך A 24:23
עלילאל B 22:6
עמיאל A 18:5
ענאל A 30:11
פ(×7) A 29:2; 29:2
פאלרצות A 31:2
פגע A 18:7
פיתיה A 17:27
פלאות A 31:6
פנואל A 28:34
פנותה A 30:8
פנחתיאל A 25:4
פניאל A 31:2
פנייס A 22:8
פנרוס A 22:8
פקידאל B 23:6
פקרון B 26:5
פרנגיס, פרגגוס see סנגין
פרחיאל A 30:11
צ(×7) A 29:1; צ(×19) A 19:16
צבאות A 27:17; 28:28; צבאו(ת) A 28:15
צבאו[ת] A 28:33 צבואות A 22:1
ציצלי B 15:8
צביאל A 22:6
צפירים A 24:6
ק(×3) A 19:22; ק(×7) A 19:23
קדדך A 17:26
קדישאל B 22:3
קותא A 32:1
קירחא B 21:13
קסיה B 24:3
קרבתיאל A 25:4
קתר A 18:11
רב A 22:10
רבא A 22:8

רביבאות A 17:27
רבתה A 22:6
רדביאל A 20:2
רושי A 24:23
רזאל B 21:9
רפאל A 18:4; 22:1; B 26:5
ררקותא A 32:3
שאל A 29:6
שבעואות A 22:14
שדאי B 24:6
שדי A 28:22; B 19:9
שווי A 28:18
שוי A 28:18
שומרך A 17:8
שוקוי B 21:14
שותא B 21:14
שותקאניה B 21:14
שיתקא B 21:14
שלום A 22:4
שלוש A 22:8
שמא A 17:25
שמאות A 29:6
שמאריה A 17:10
שמושנאות A 22:11
שמעלל A 24:13
שמרות A 29:8
שמשא A 22:7
שמשיאל A 19:19; 30:10; 31:5
ש(נ)קק A 26:7
שרם A 17:28
תה ובה A 25:6
תהריאל A 28:34
תומיאל A 19:40
תיאון A 22:8
תמב A 18:12
תפנט A 22:7
תקשפרה B 15:8
תרדו A 29:6,8
תרמ(ון) A 31:1

Personal Names of Clients and Adversaries

אברהם B 21:2
אברוי B 20:2
אחתא B 27:2,6
אחתימא B 23:9
איכומא B 14:3
אינה A 17:17,30
איפראהורמיז B 15:3
אמא B 14:2,3; אימא B 19:2; 25:1,4,7,9,11
אימי B 21:2,3,8
ארו B 21:2
בורזבהרם B 24:1,3,5,6
בפתוי B 18:4
בירו, ברו B 26:6,7,11
ברזאנדוך B 15:2
בריכישי B 27:2,6
ברנדוך B 23:5,8-10
ברשבתי B 19:2
ברשותי B 25:1,11
גוזו A 21(left):6
גוריי B 15:2,3
גושנאי B 19:1,2,8,9; גושני B 15:3; 26:4,6,7,11
גיורגיס A 29:3,6
גיות B 18:4
גש B 21:3
דאטי B 20:7-9
דבארה B 14:2
דדי B 19:1,8
דודא B 22:8
דודי B 21:2,8
דותאי B 24:1,3-6
דמטיה A 31:4
זינביה A 16:10,20
זעירתי A 17:1,17,31
חביבי A 26:4,11

חרתה, חירתה A 26:5,12
טיו A 23:1
יויעא B 16:2; 17:2,4
יוסי A 16:10,20
כוסרו B 26:3,(5),7,11
כוסתי B 18:4,5
מגאותיס A 29:3
מגלי A 25:6
מהאדרגושנצף B 20:6,8,9
מחוי B 25:1,4,6,7,9,11
מטרונה A 23:1
מיהרוי B 19:1,8,9
מכסימיון A 20:4
מלבונאי B 19:2
מלך A 21(left):3
מקריא A 32:1
מרותא B 22:8
מרין A 27:6,12,15,18,22,27; 28:6,38
נונה A 25:(5)
סוניונא B 21:8,11,12,15
סוסיה, סוסיא B 21:2,8
סורה A 30:1,2,4,6,9,
סימון A 19:5,14,26,31
סרגיס B 23:5,8-10
סרא B 23:9
סרה A 30:1,2,4,6,6b,9
פדרדוך B 19:1,2,8
פנאחורמיז B 18:4
פרדוך B 15:3
פרוכדעד B 26:(3),6,7,11
פריברד B 21:3
קאקי B 26:3,5,7,11
קדומה A 24:11,18,19,25,27
קטטיה A 19:6,14,27,32
קיומתא B 26:3,6,7,11
קיטין B 21:8,11,13,15
קיראנה A 18:3
קאסיאנוס, קסהיאנוס A 31:4,7,8
קרל, קירל A 24:11,18,20,25
קלארא A 18:2,9
קרקי B 20:1
רדיני B 21:2
רשדינדוך B 16:2
רשנדוך B 18:4
רשנינדוך B 17:2,3,4
שלם B 14:2
שלתא B 26:3,(4),6,117
שרה A 27:18,22,28; 28:3,38
שרשיי B 14:2
תוס (?) B 21:2
תידוסוס A 22:4
תידורא A 22:4

Biblical Quotations in Amulets and Bowls

Ex. 3:14 A 18:1; 28:19,27-28
Num. 9:23 B 22:10
Isa. 51:15 A 27:16-17
Jer. 31:35 A 27:16-17
Ezek. 32:27 B 22:11
Am. 4:13 A 28:32-33
Ps. 115:1; 138:2 A 16:1
46:8,12 A 17:20-21; 29:5
89:8 A 24:7
116:6 A 30:4,5
Dan. 4:10 A 24:4

INDICES

General Index

* Prepared by Yuval Harari .

Index of Personal Names

Names of Gods, Angels and Demons

Index of Quotations

OLD TESTAMENT

QUMRAN, NEW TESTAMENT AND PSEUDEPIGRAPHA

TARGUM

MISHNAH, TALMUD AND MIDRASH

MAGICAL AND HEKHALOT TEXTS

Index of Words

GREEK

Amulet 17

PLATE 2

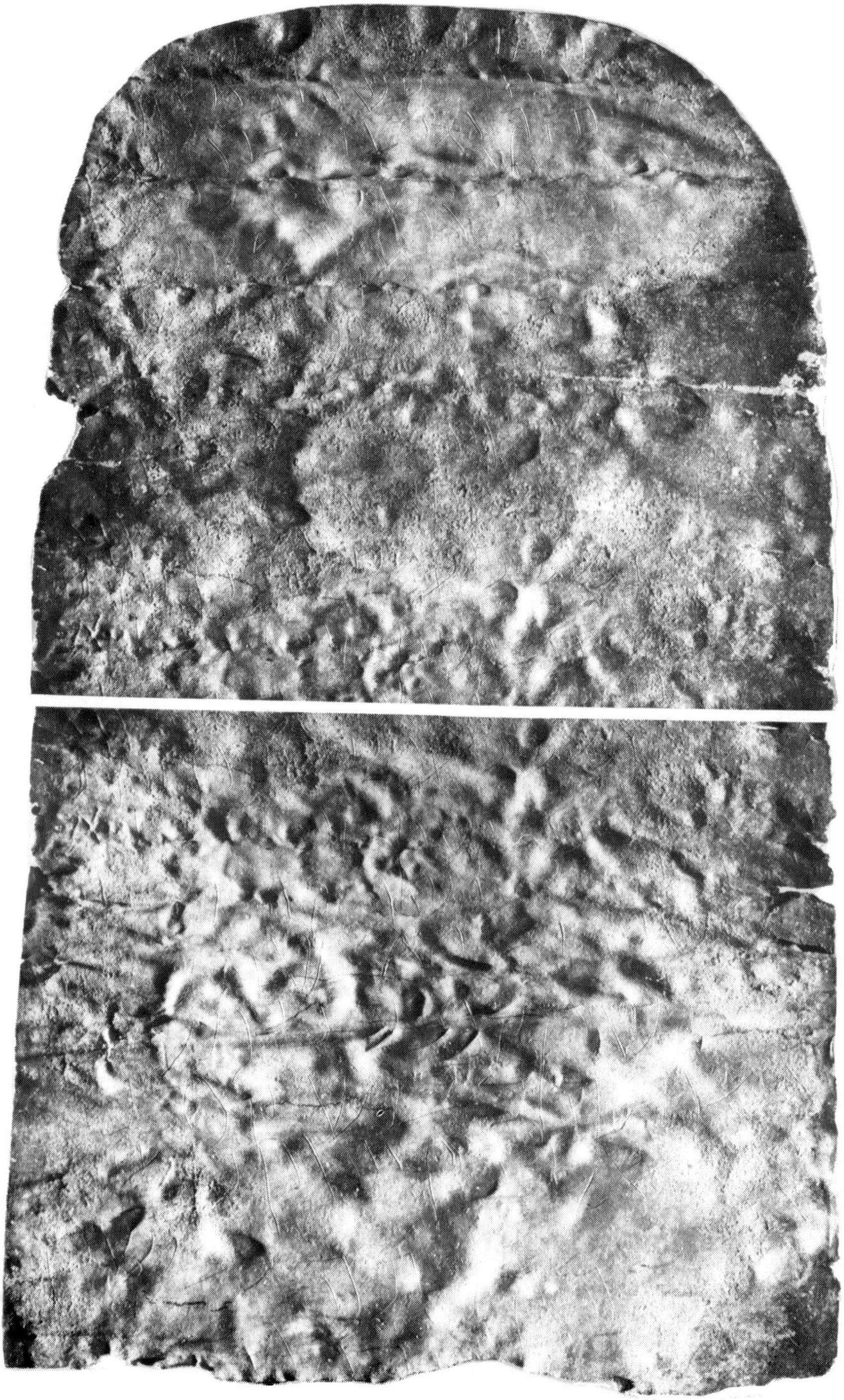

Amulet 16, upper part

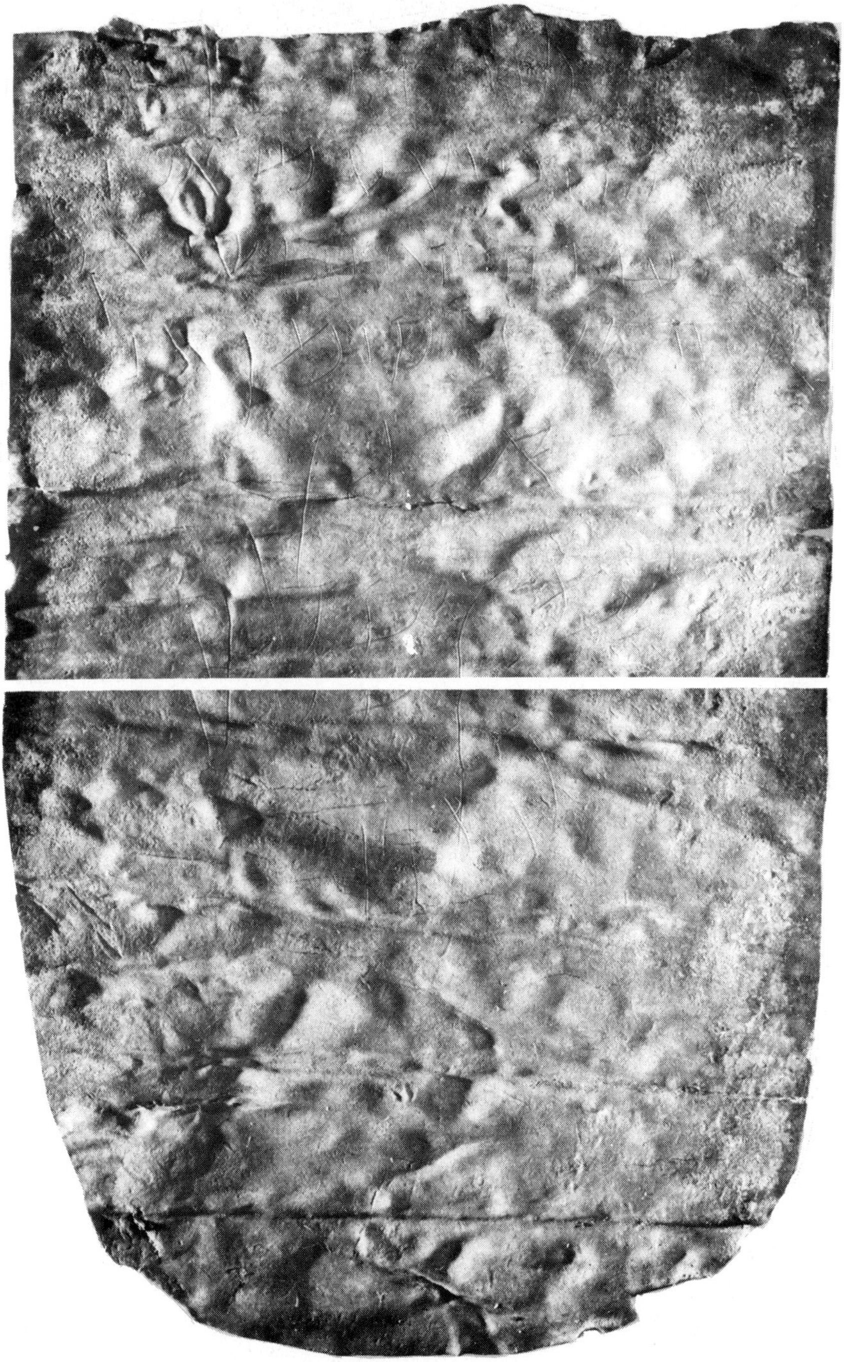

Amulet 16, lower part

PLATE 4

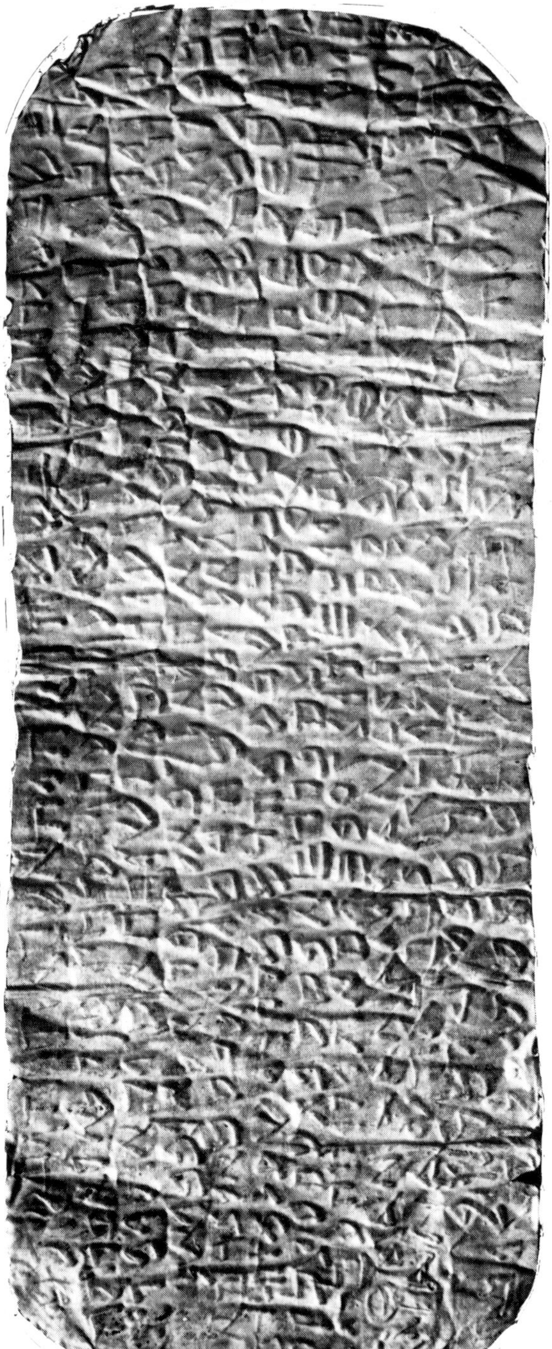

Amulet 18

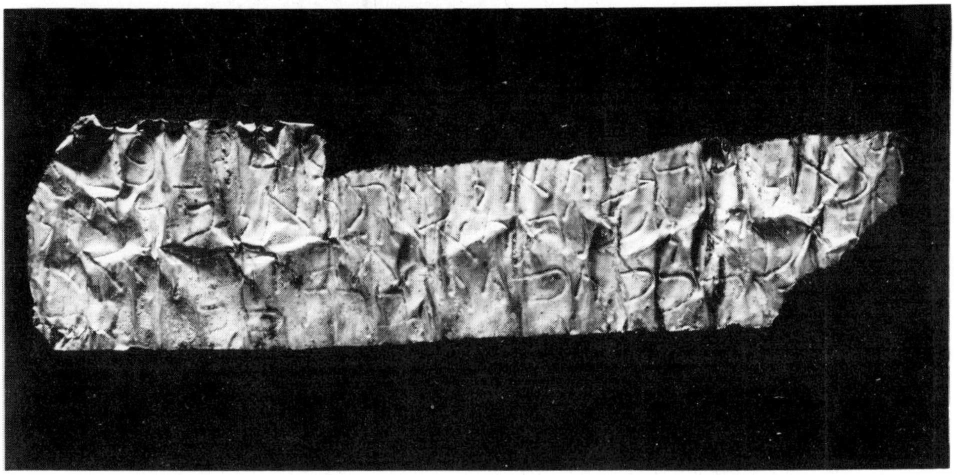

a. Amulet 20

b. Amulet 23

Amulet 19, upper part

Amulet 19, lower part

PLATE 8

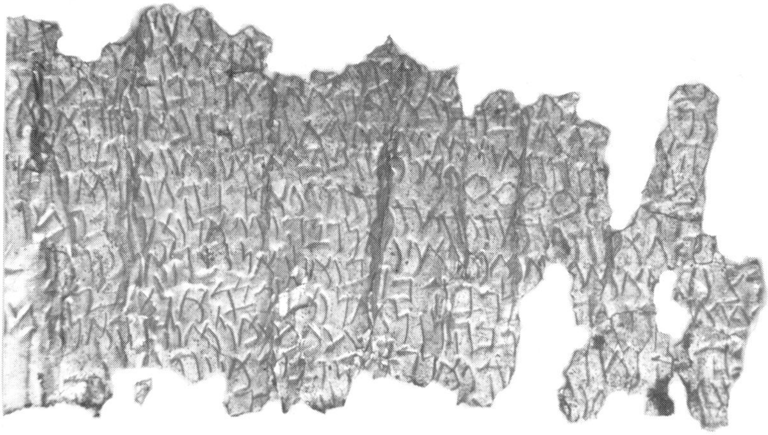

Amulet 21

Amulet 22

Amulet 24

Amulet 25

PLATE 12

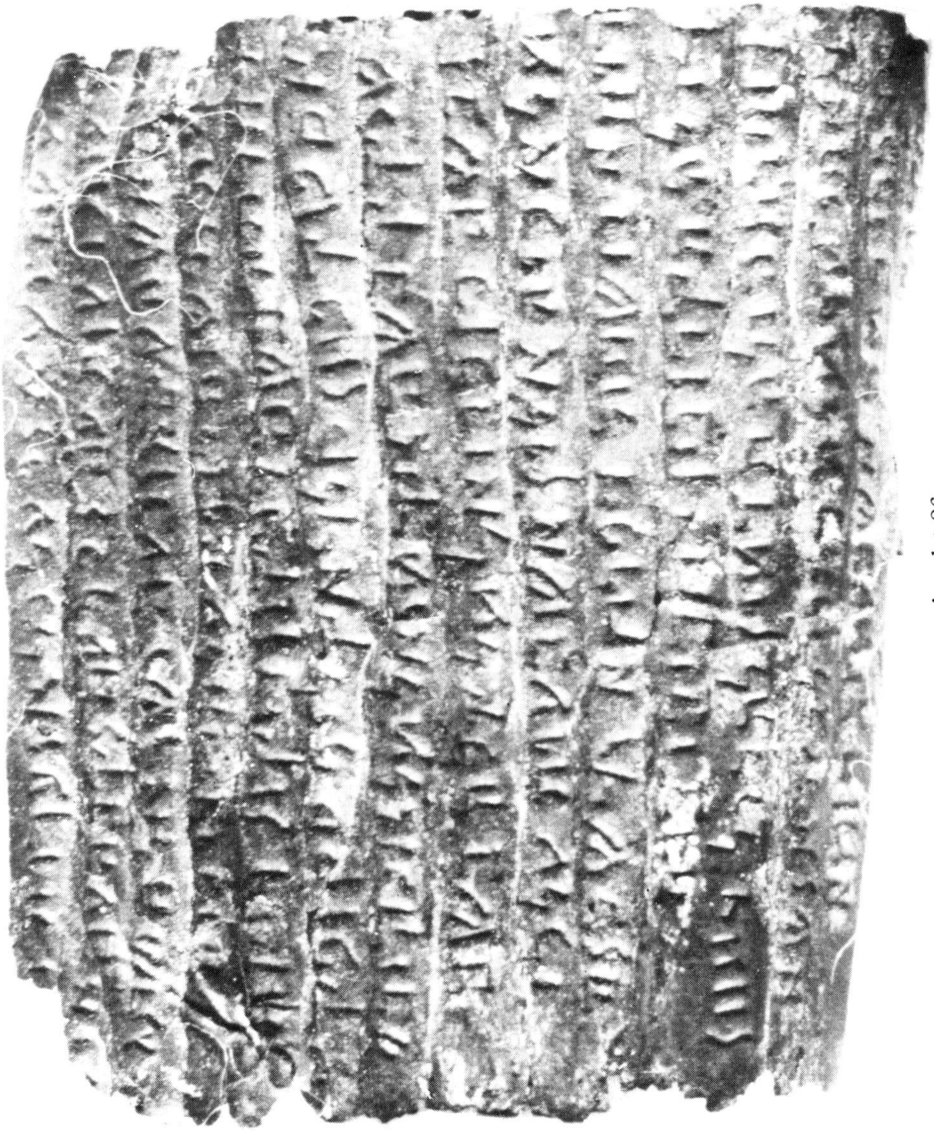

Amulet 26

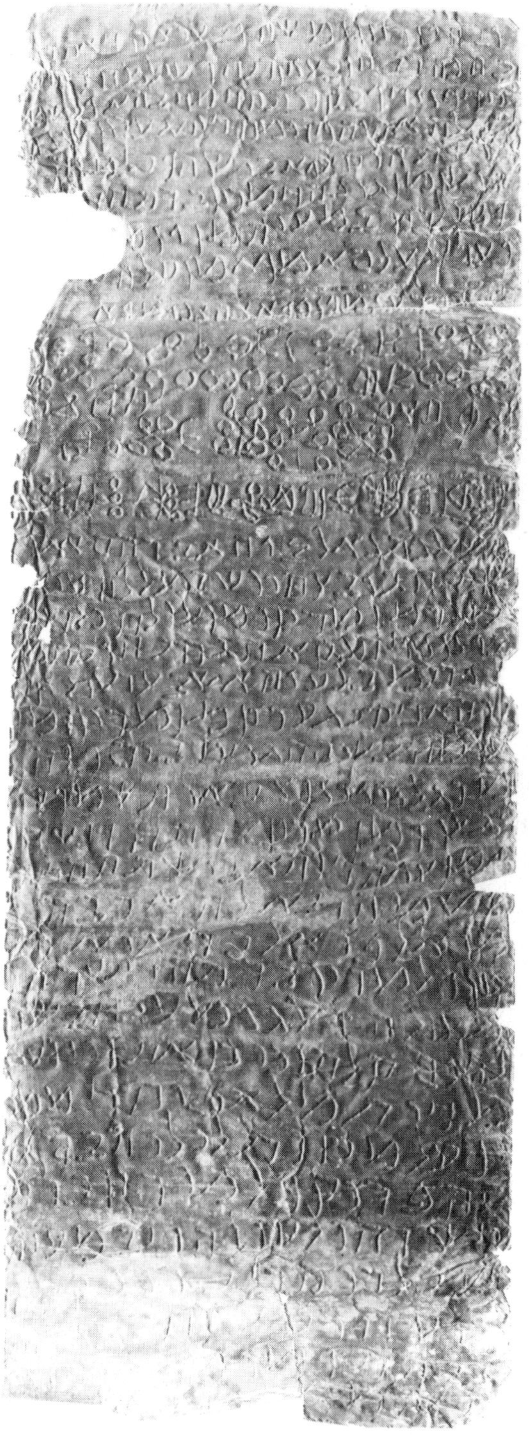

Amulet 27

PLATE 14

Amulet 28

Amulet 29

Amulet 30

PLATE 17

Amulet 31

PLATE 18

Amulet 32

Bowl 14

Bowl 15

Bowl 16

Bowl 17

Bowl 18

Bowl 19

Bowl 20

PLATE 26

Bowl 21

Bowl 22

PLATE 28

Bowl 23

Bowl 24

Bowl 25

Bowl 26

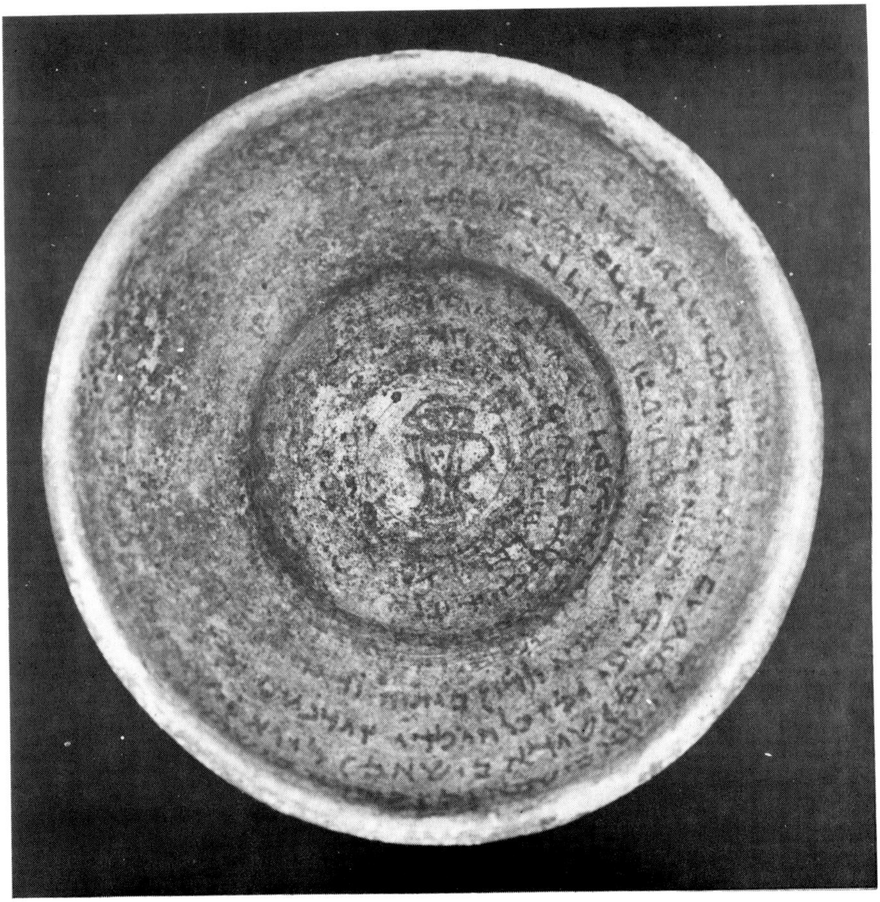

Bowl 27

Geniza 9, pages 1 and 4

Geniza 9, pages 2 and 3

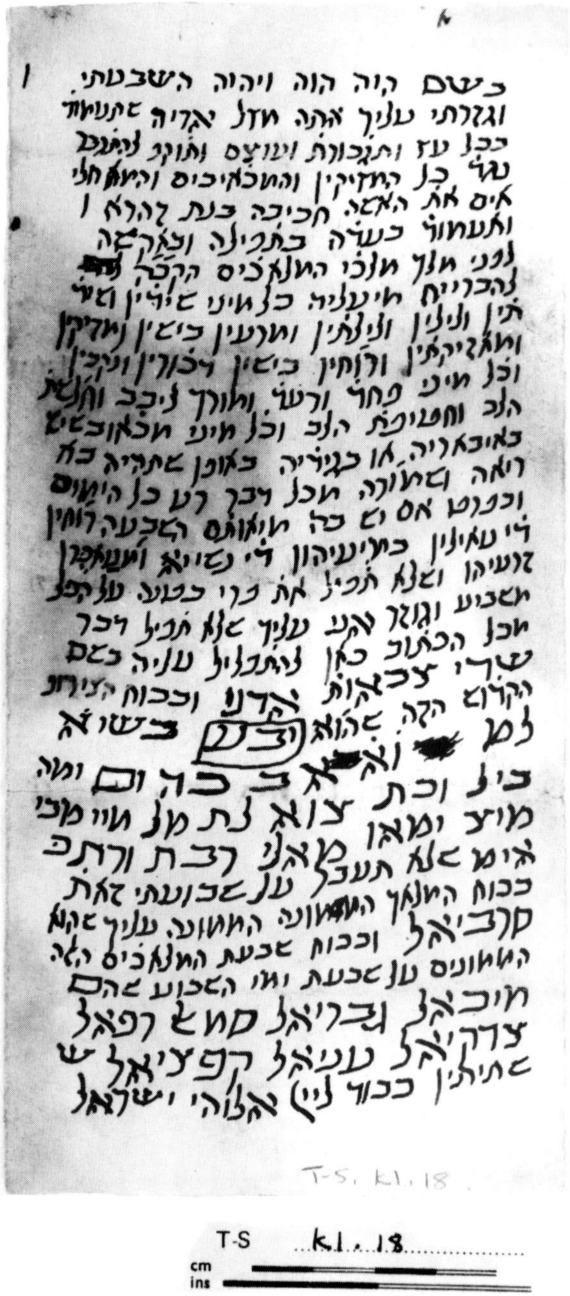

בשם יהוה הוה ויהיה השבעתי
וגזרתי עליך אתה מזל מאדים שתעמוד
בכל עז ותגבורת ועוצם ותוקף להתגבר
על כל המזיקין והמכאובים ותשלח חלי
אים את האשה חביבה בת זהרא
ותעמוד כשרה בתולה ובארשה
לפני מלך מלכי המלאכים הקבה
להבריח מעליה כל מיני שידין ושי
דין ולילין ולילתין ומרעין בישין ומזיקין
ומזיקתין ורוחין בישין דכורין ונוקבין
וכל מיני פחד ורשף ומורך לבב וחלשת
הלב ומפועפעת הלב וכל מיני מכאובים
באיבאריה או בגופה באופן שתהיה בת
ראה ושמורה מכל דבר רע כל הימים
וכרגע אם יש בה מאומה השבעה רוחין
די עאלין במיעיהון די נשיא ומשחבן
זרעיהו ושלא תכיל את פרי בטנה עליהם
משביע וגוזר אני עליך שלא תכיל דבר
מכל הכתוב כאן להתגלגל עליה בשם
שדי צבאות אדני ובכוח הצירוף
הקדוש הקה שהוא [illegible] בשוא
לם [illegible]
בכל ובכת [illegible] כה ום ומה
מיץ ימאו צוא לת מל מוי מכי
אימ שלא תעבל מאני רבת ורתכ
ככוח המלך המשונה על שבועתי זאת
קרביאל המשונה עליך שהוא
ובכוח שבעת המלאכים הלא
המשונים על שבעת ומי השבוע שהם
מיכאל גבריאל סמאל רפאל
צדקיאל עניאל קפציאל ש
שתיתין בכבוד לשם אלוהי ישראל

T-S. K1. 18

T-S K1. 18

Geniza 10, page 1

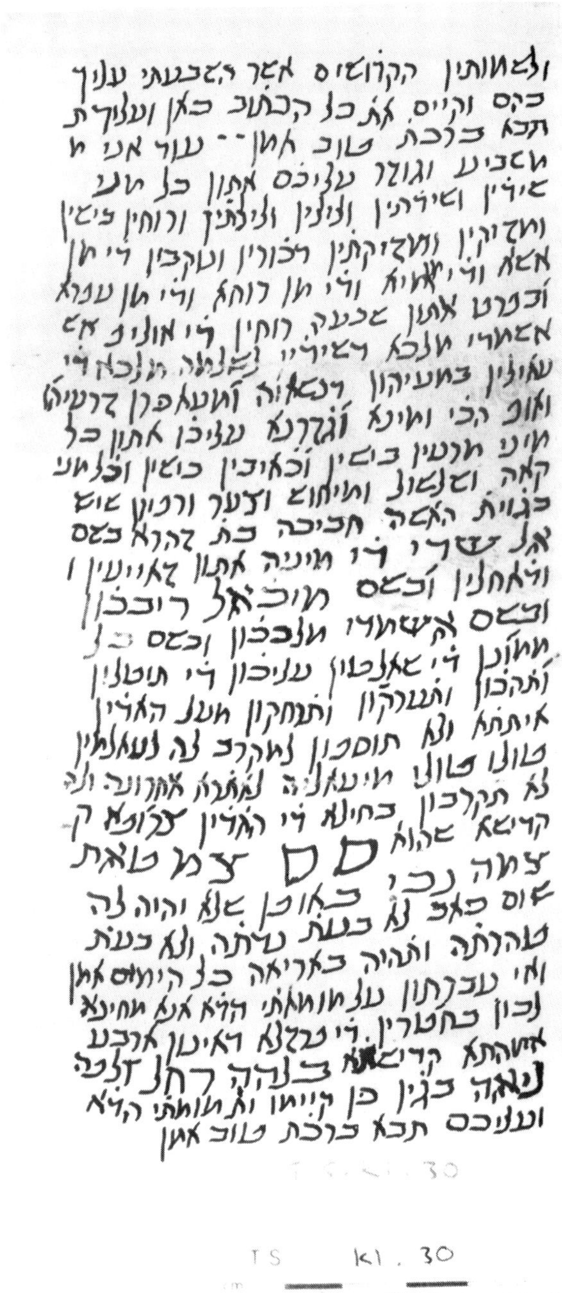
ולשמותיך הקדושים אשר השבעתי עליך
כים וקיים את כל הכתוב כאן ועליך ת
תבא ברכת טוב אמן -- עוד אני מ
משביע וגוזר עליכם אתון כל מזי
שידין ושידתין ולילין ולילתין ורוחין בישין
ומזיקין ומזיקתין דכורין ונוקבין די מן
אשא ודי מיא ודי מן רוחא ודי מן עפרא
ובפרט אתון שבעה רוחין די אוליד אש
אשמדי מלכא דשידין ושלמה מלכא די
שוילין במעיהון דנשיה ומשתפכן דרשיה
ואוף הכי מומינא וגזרנא עליכון אתון כל
מיני מרעין בישין וכאיבין בישין וכל מני
קאה ושעול ומיחוש וצער ורתיון שיש
בגוית האשה חביבה בת זהרא בשם
אל שדי די מניה אתון זאיעין ו
ודחלין ובשם מיכאל ריבכון
ובשם אשמדאי מלככון ובשם כל
מחנין די שלטין עליכון די תיטלין
ותהכון ותערקון ותרחקון מן האדין
איתתא ולא תוספון למקרב לה לעלמין
טולו טולו מיעלניה למתרה אחרנה ולא
לא תקרבון בחילא די האדין צלמא ק
קדישא שהוא
צמה נכי סס צמ טאת
שום כאב לא באוכן שלא יהיה לה
לא כשנת שיתה ולא כשנת
טהרתה ותהיה בבריאה כל היומים אמן
ואי עברתון על מומאתי הדא אנא מחינא
לכון בחטרין די פרזלא דאיתון ארבע
אימהתא קדישתא בלהה רחל זלפה
לאה בגין כן קיימו ית מומאתי הדא
ועליכם תבא ברכת טוב אמן

Geniza 10, page 2

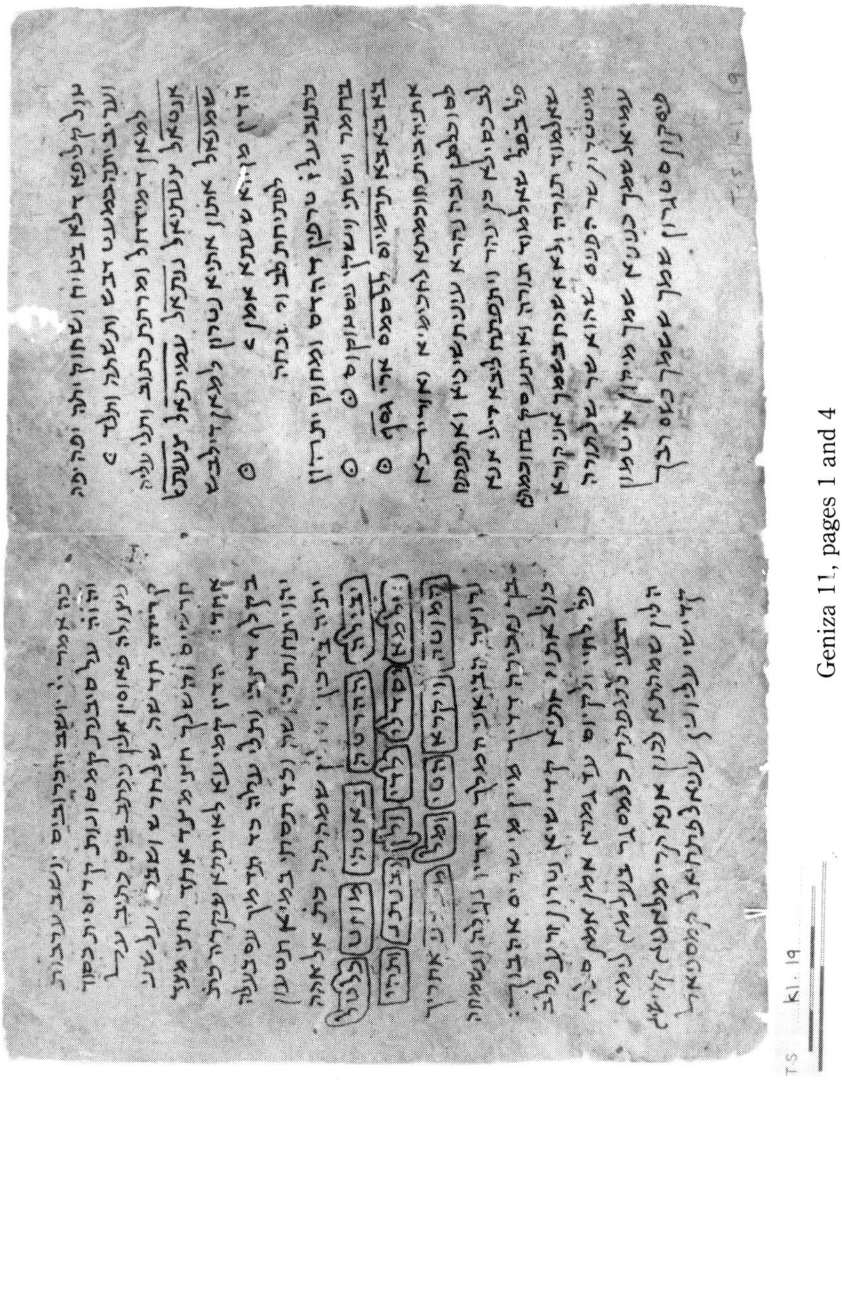

Geniza 11, pages 1 and 4

PLATE 38

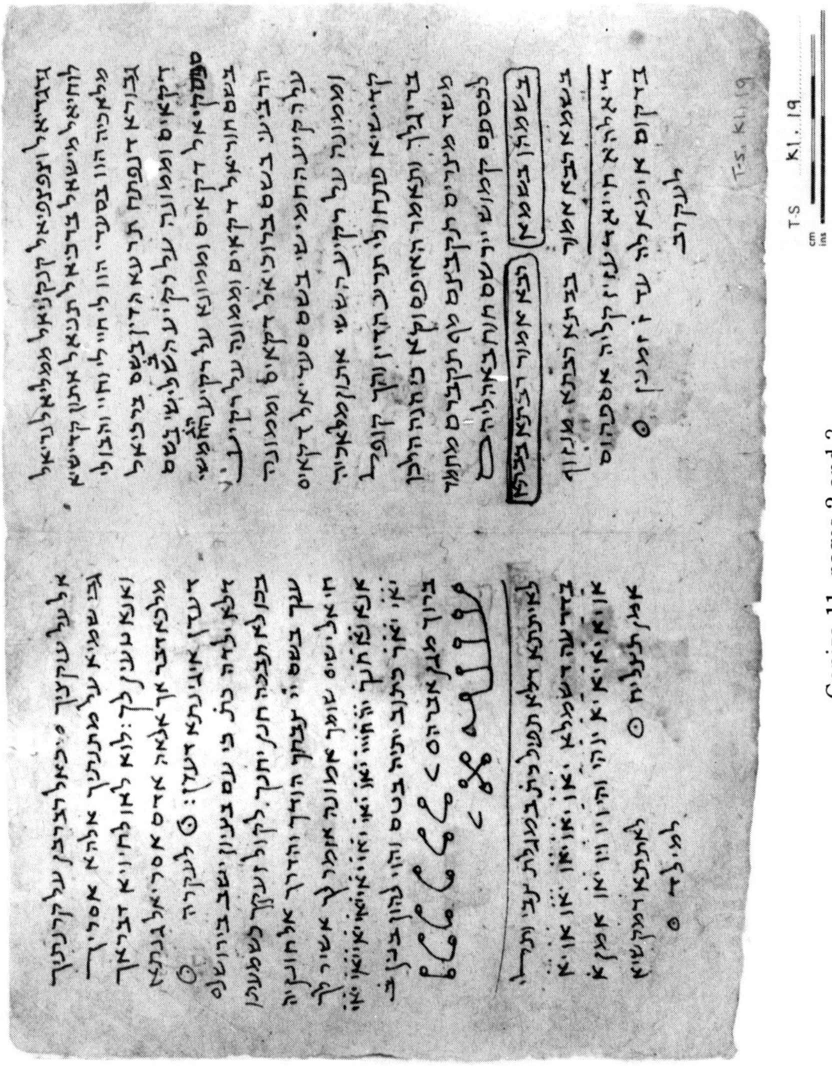

Geniza 11, pages 2 and 3

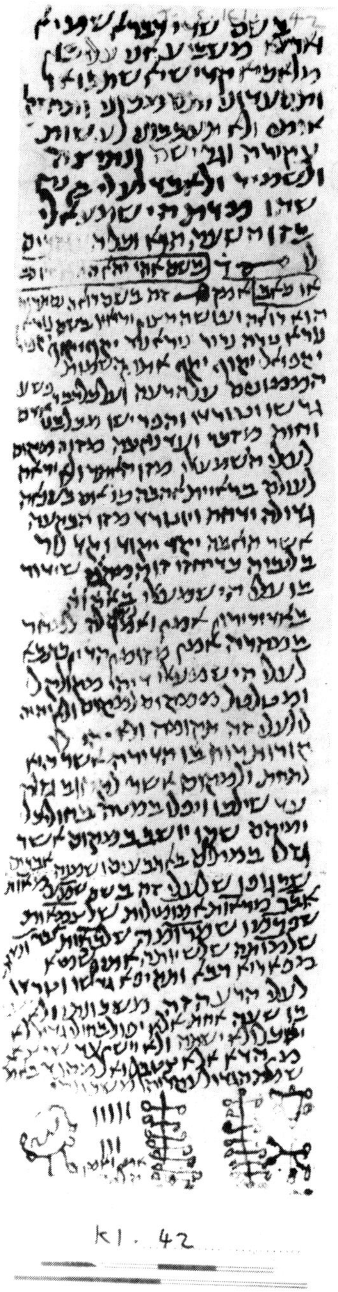

Geniza 12

PLATE 40

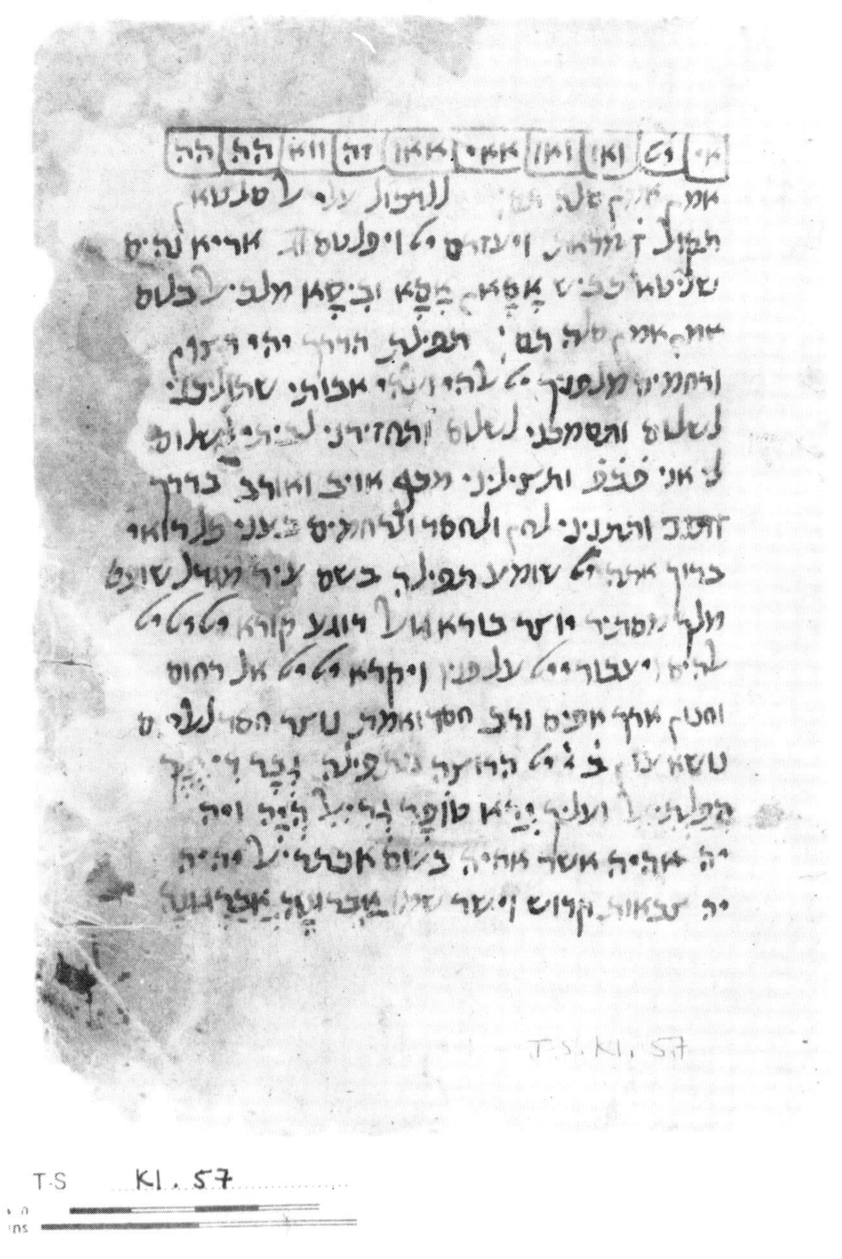

Geniza 13, page 1

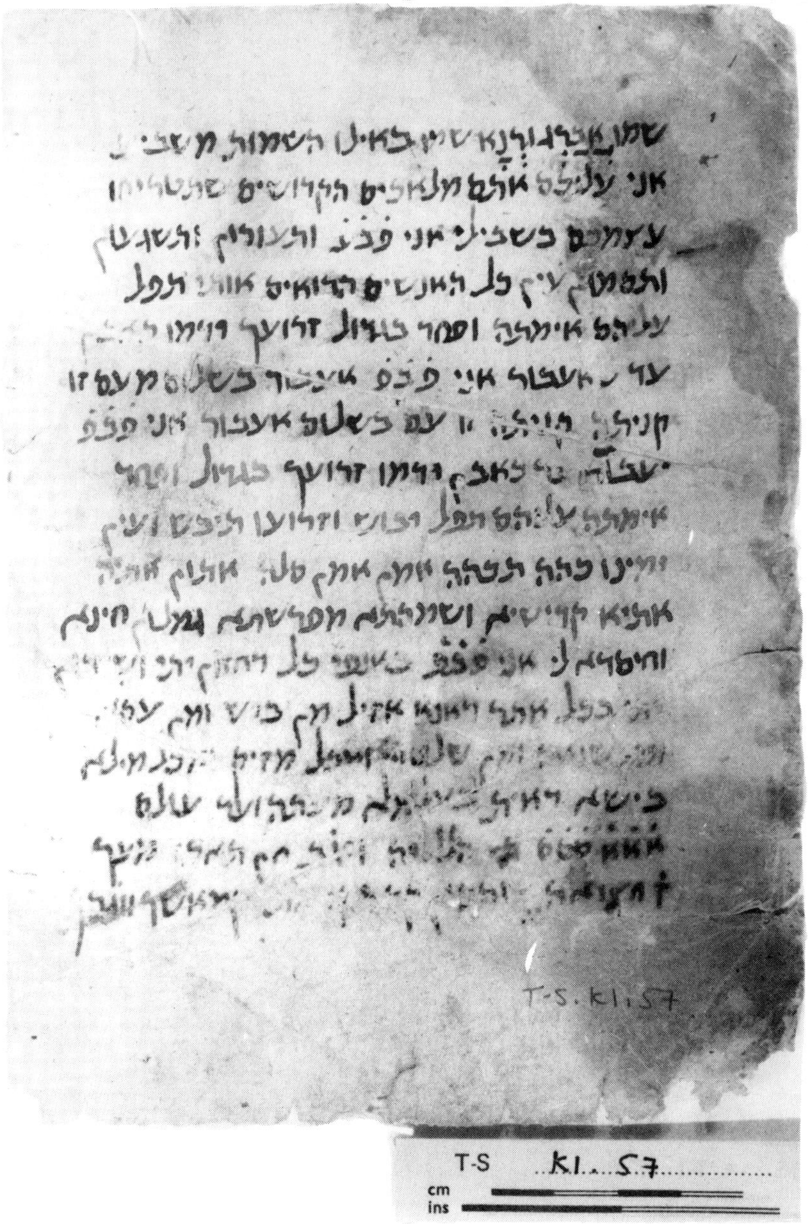

Geniza 13, page 2

PLATE 42

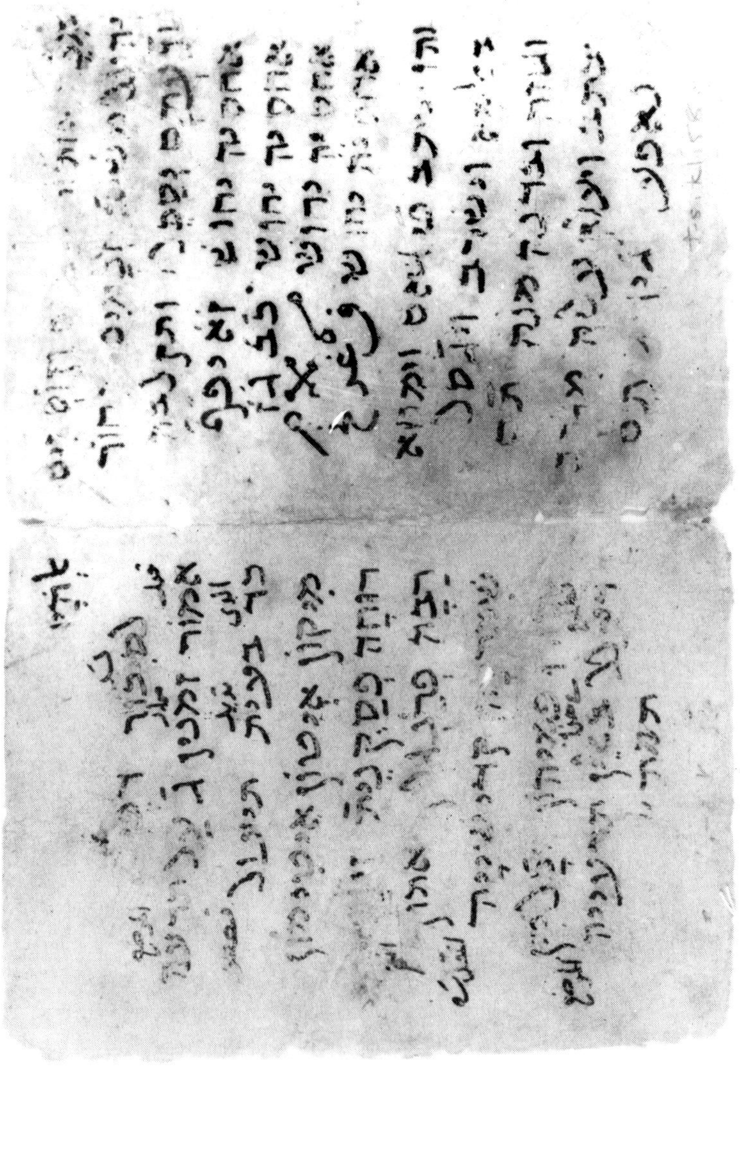

Geniza 14, pages 1 and 4

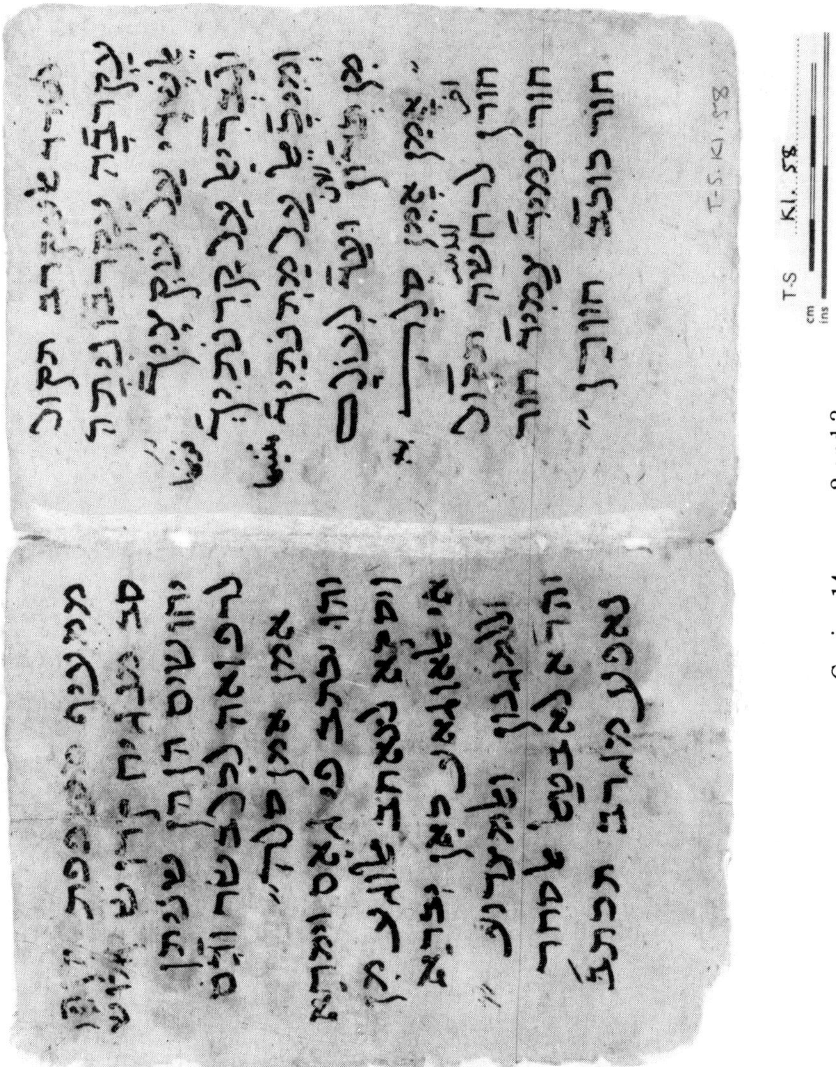

Geniza 14, pages 2 and 3

PLATE 44

Geniza 15, page 1

Geniza 15, page 2

PLATE 46

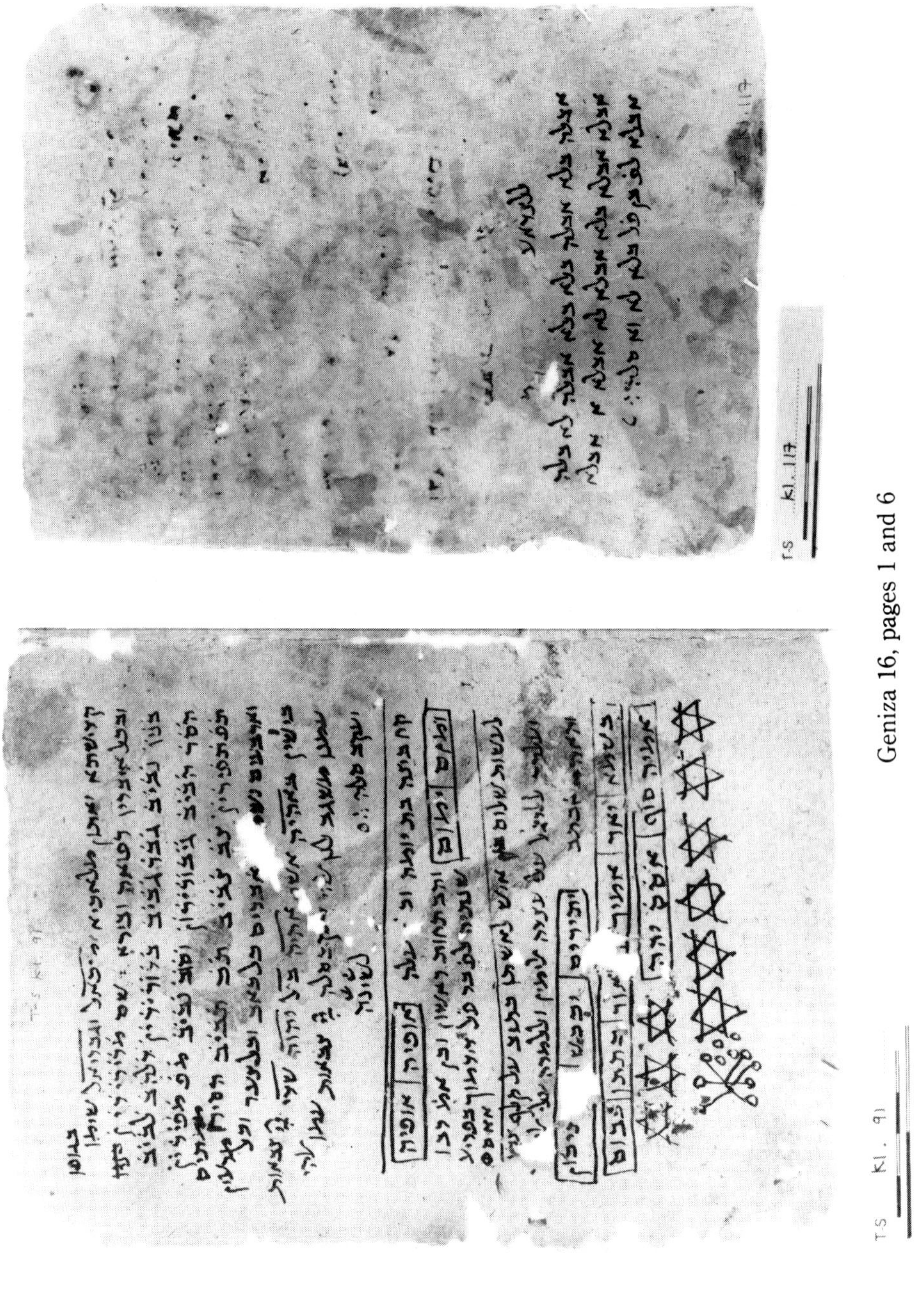

Geniza 16, pages 1 and 6

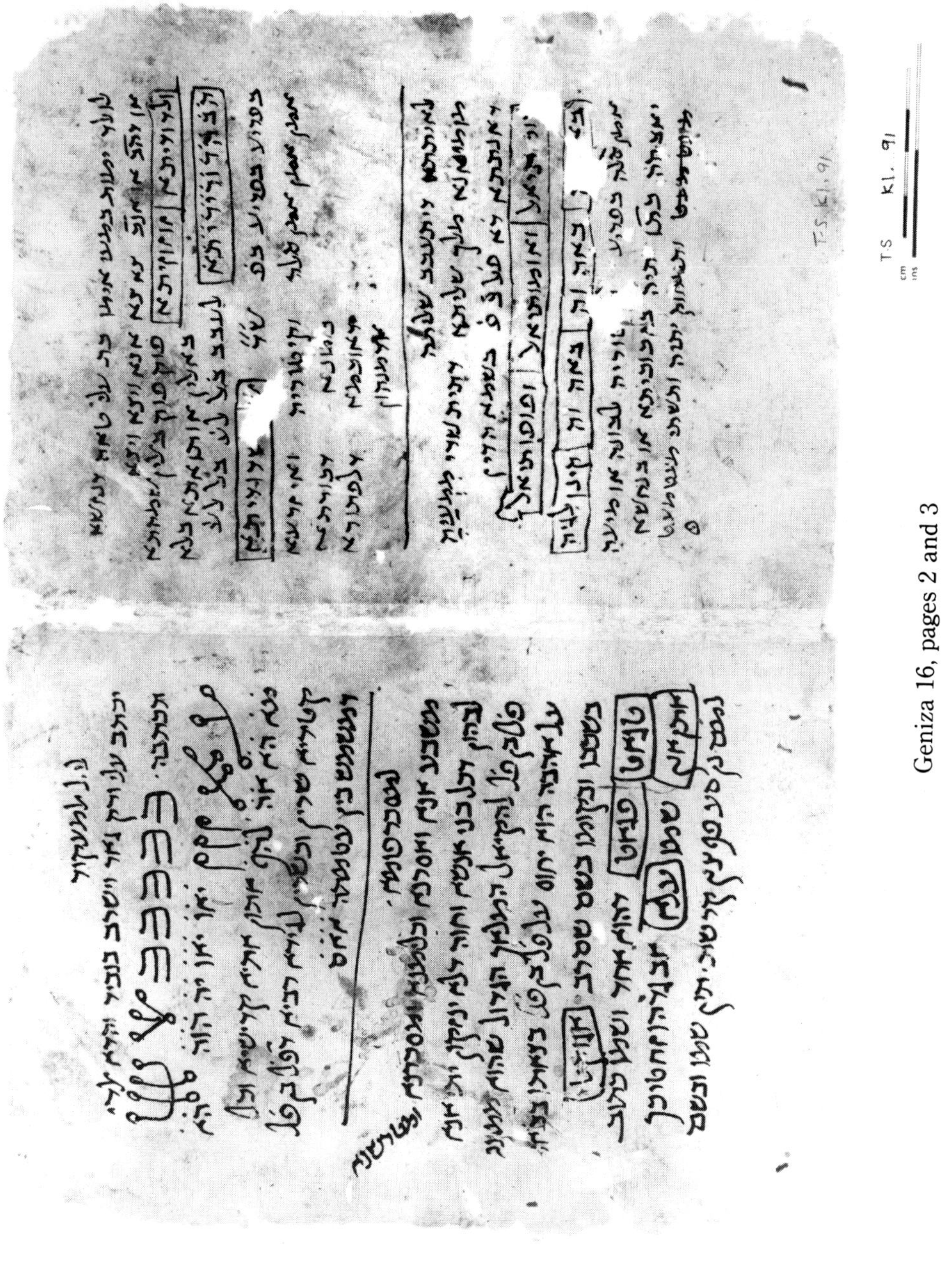

Geniza 16, pages 2 and 3

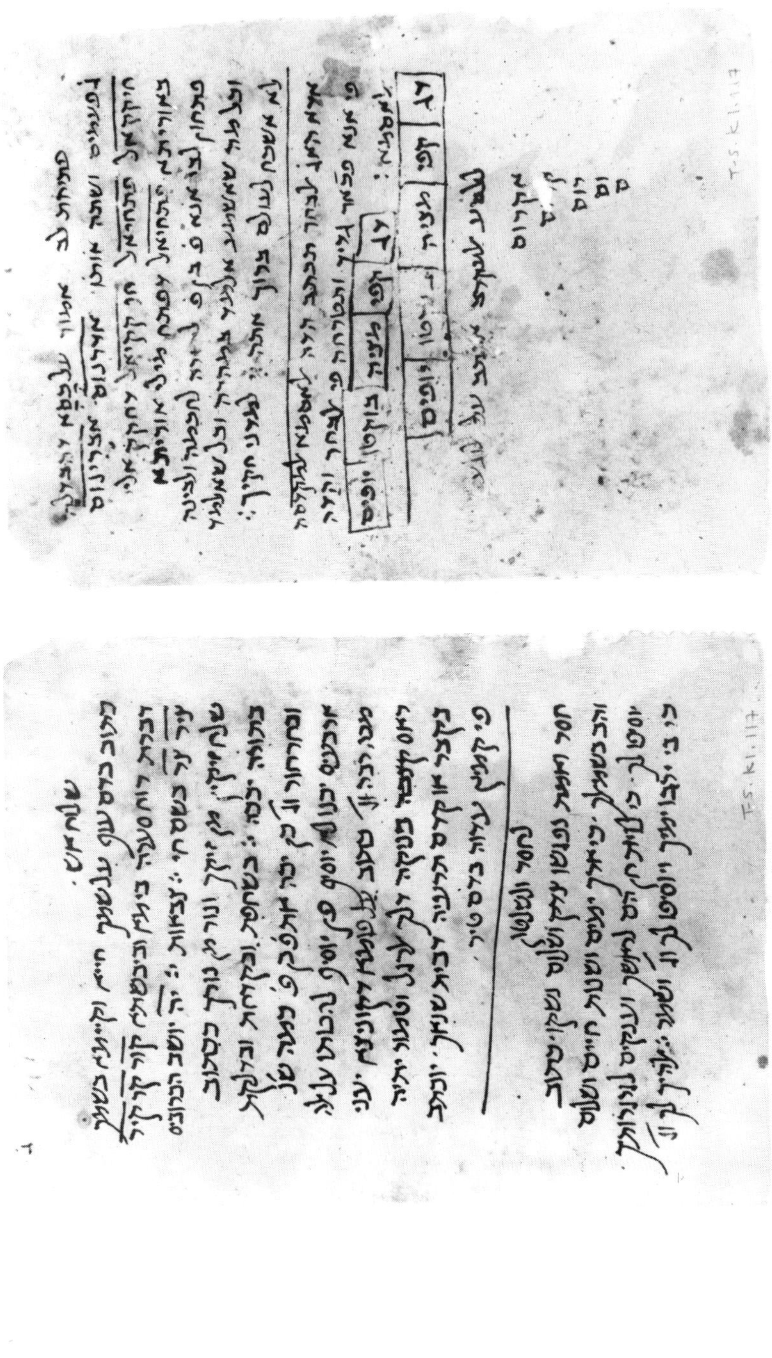

Geniza 16, pages 5 and 7

PLATE 49

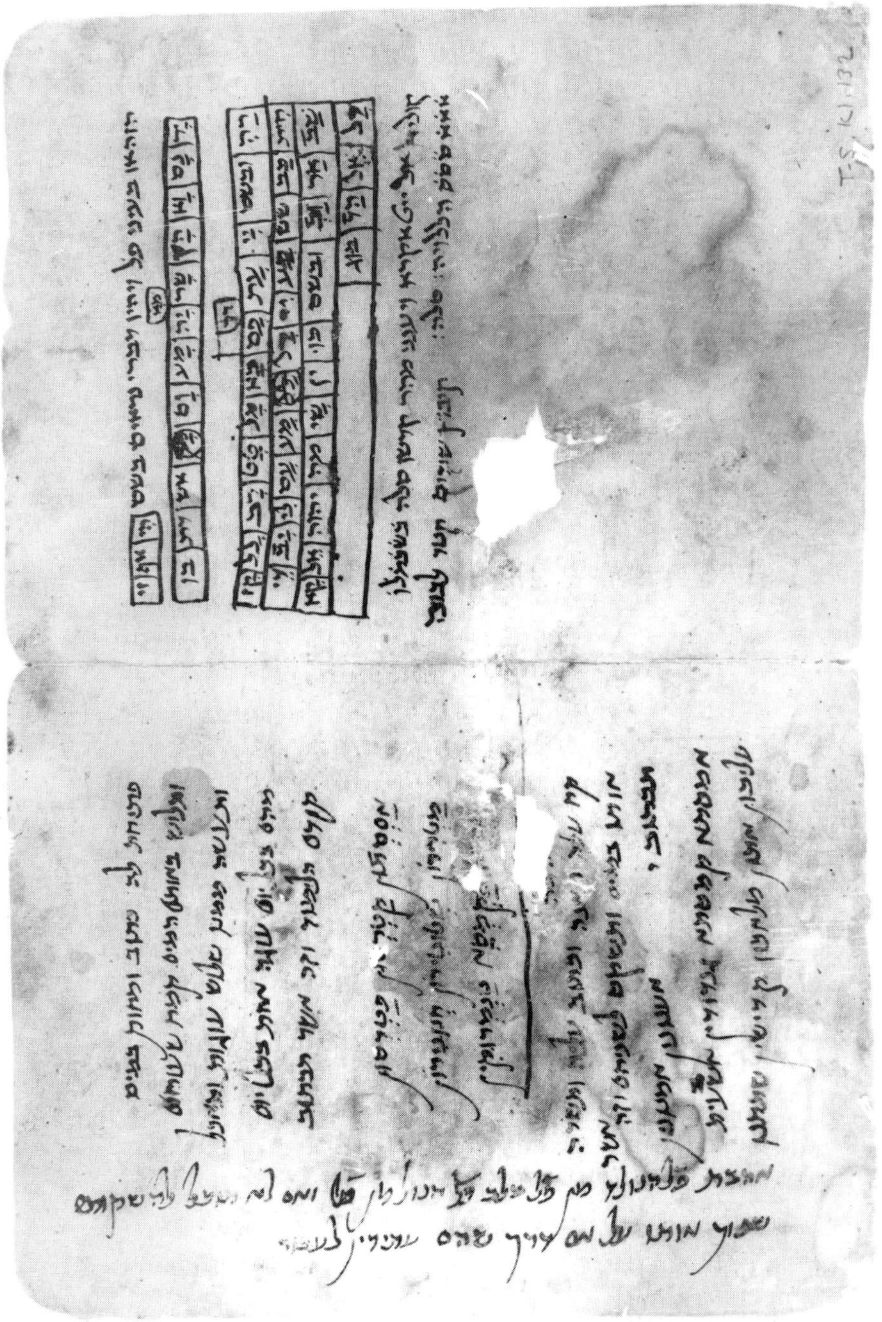

Geniza 17, pages 1 and 8

PLATE 50

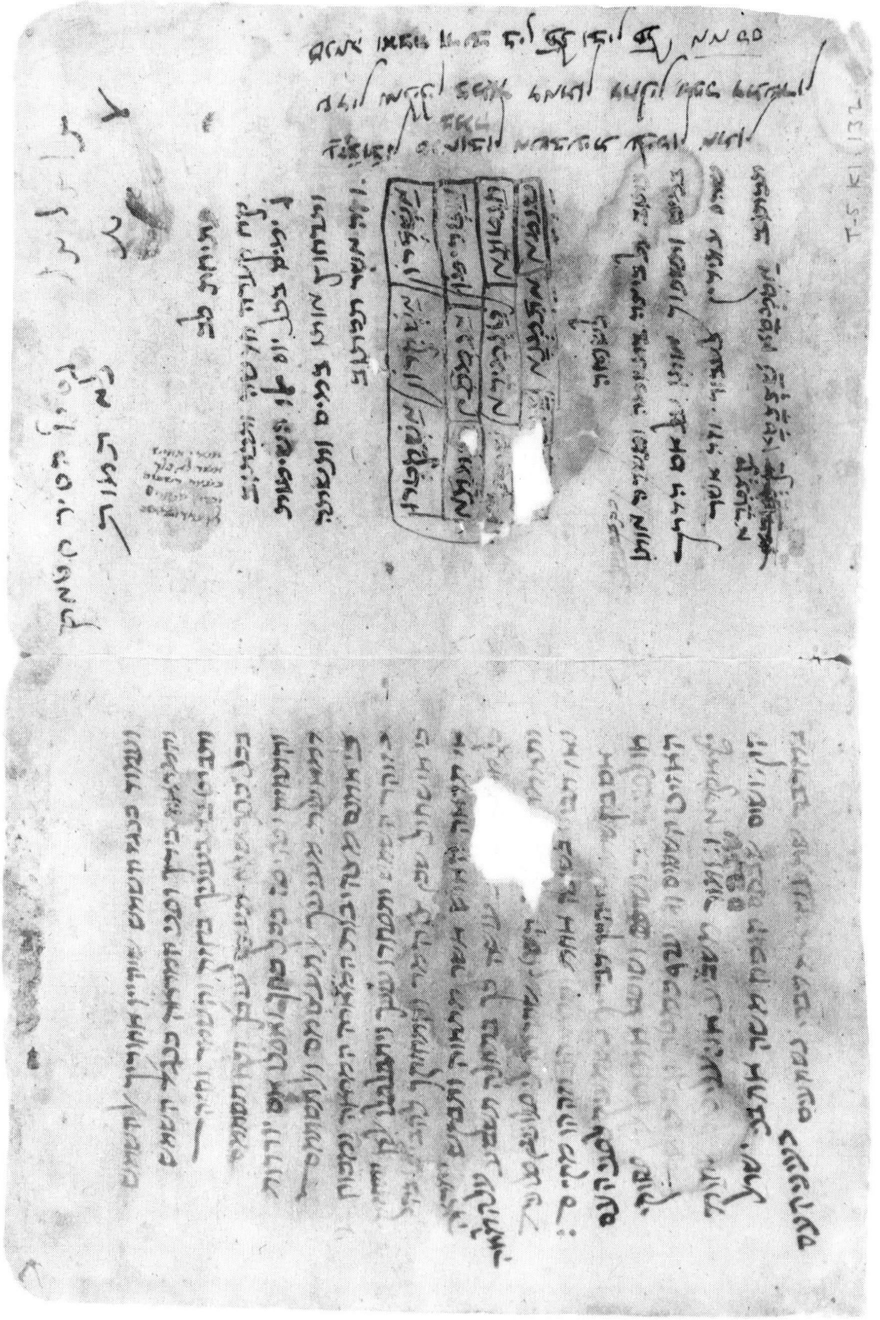

Geniza 17, pages 2 and 7

Geniza 17, pages 3 and 6

PLATE 52

Geniza 17, pages 4 and 5

Geniza 18, pages 1 and 10

PLATE 54

Geniza 18, pages 2 and 9

PLATE 55

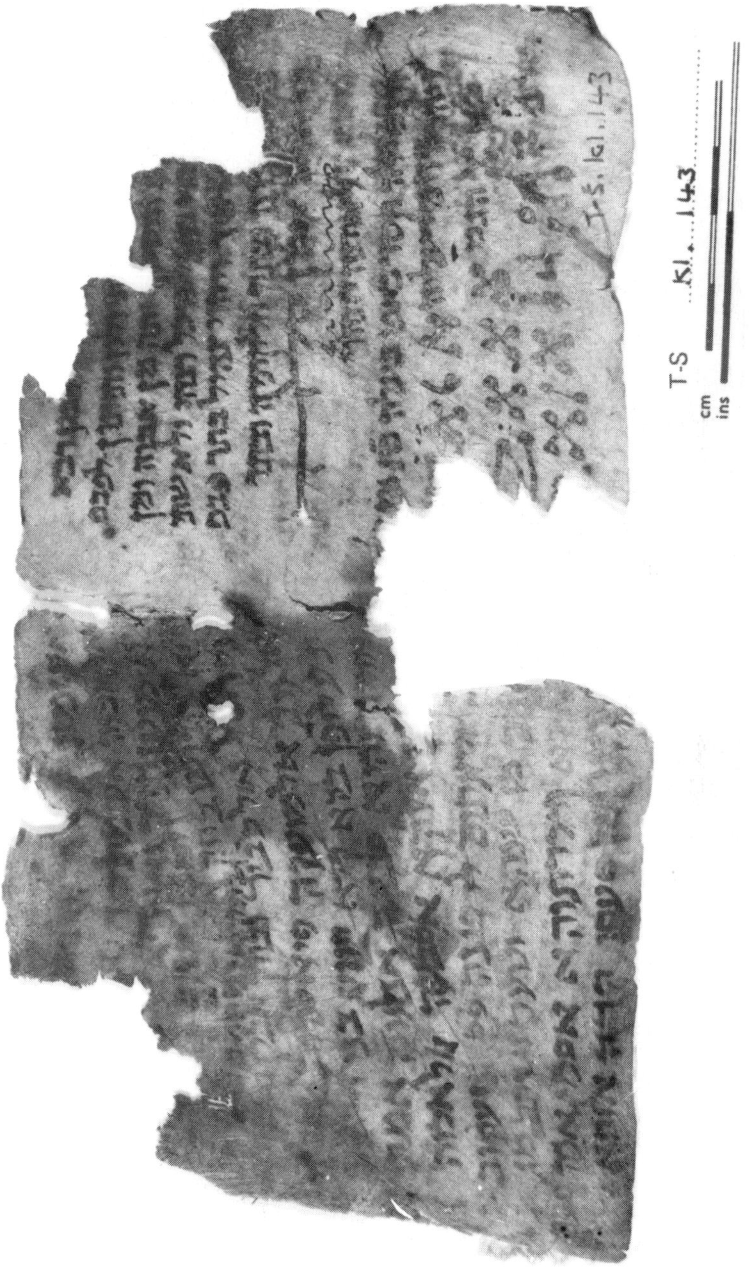

Geniza 18, pages 3 and 6

PLATE 56

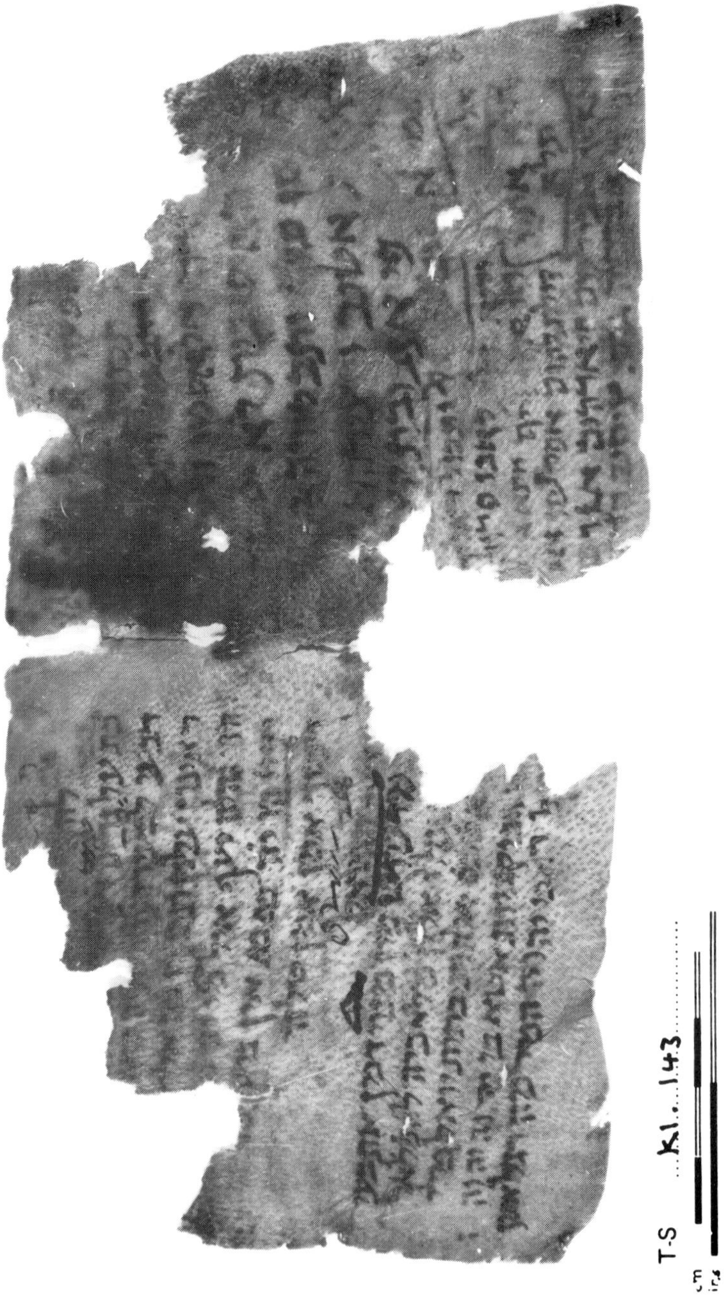

Geniza 18, pages 4 and 5

Geniza 18, pages 7 and 8

PLATE 58

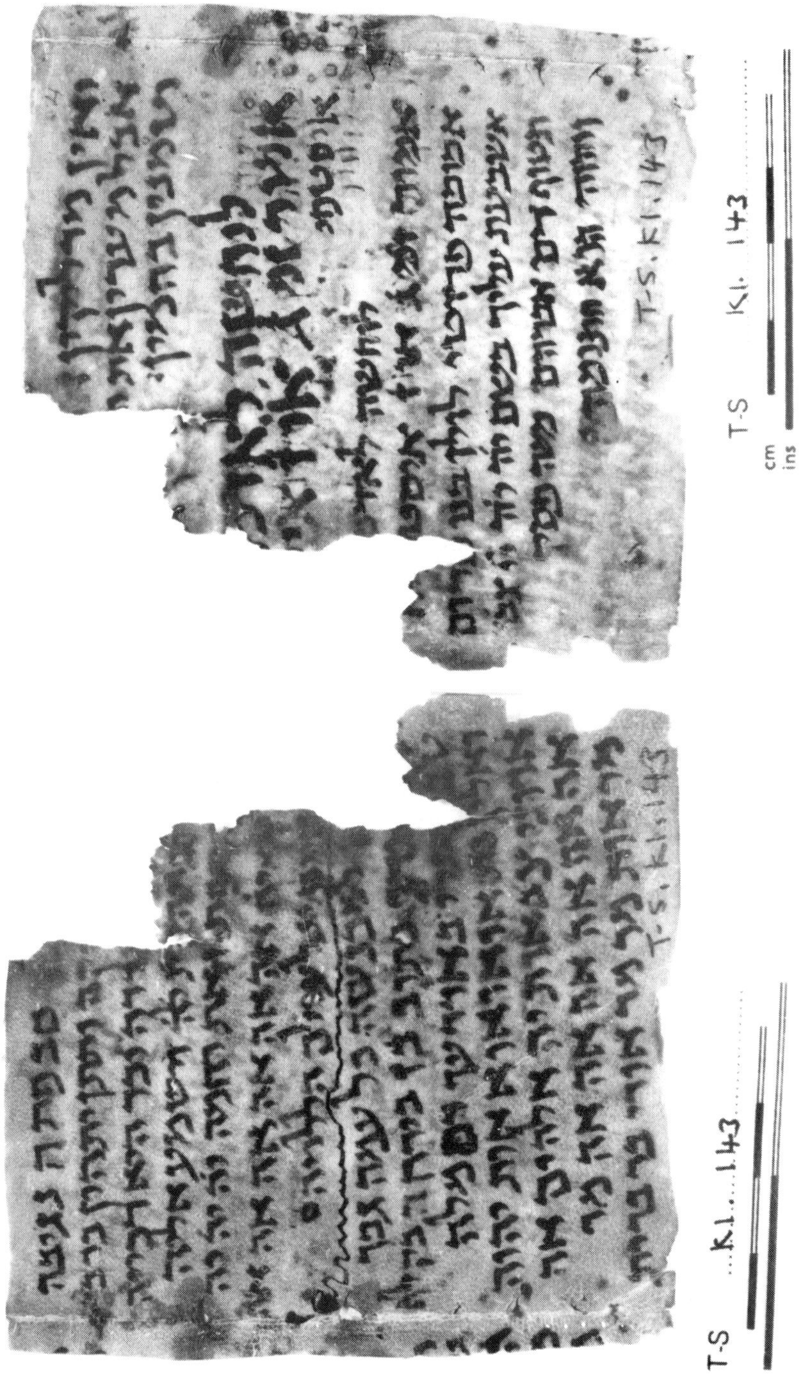

Geniza 18, pages 11 and 12

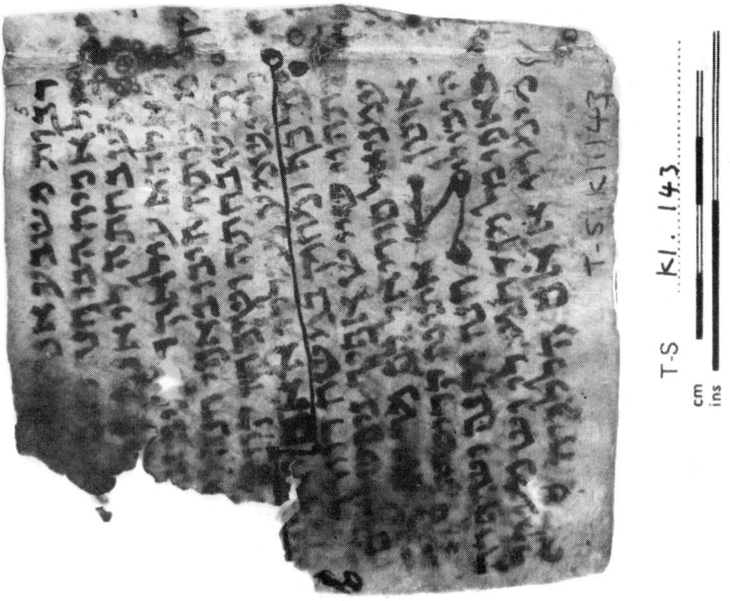

Geniza 18, pages 13 and 14

PLATE 60

Geniza 18, pages 15 and 16

PLATE 61

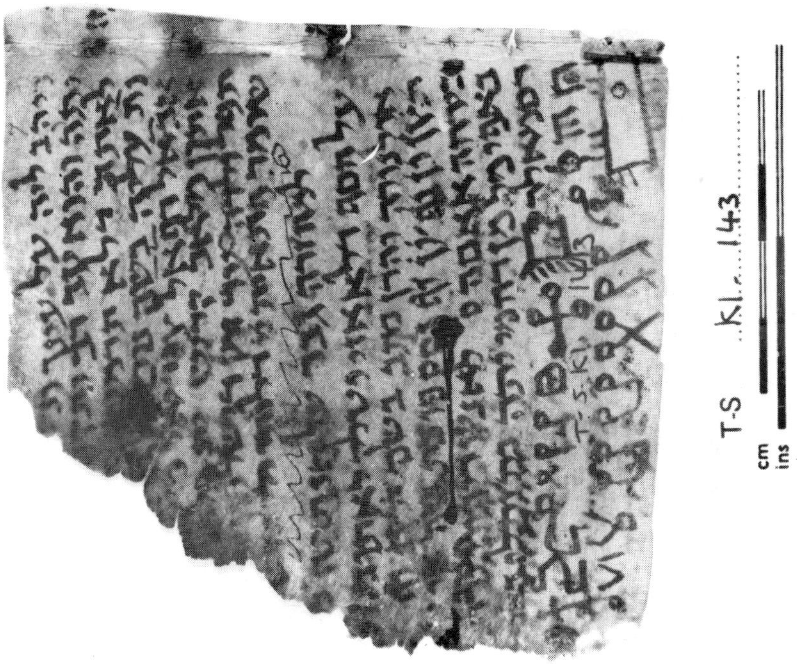

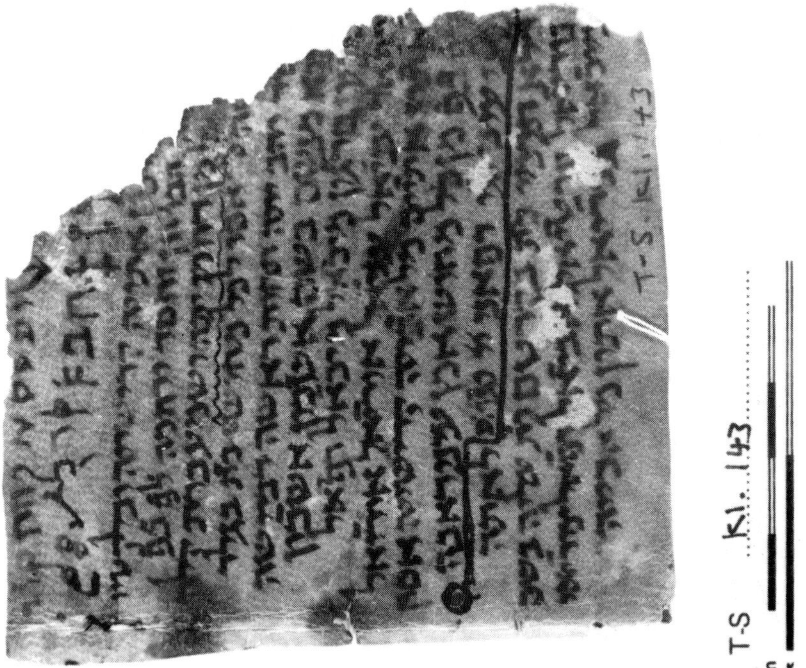

Geniza 18, pages 17 and 18

PLATE 62

Geniza 18, pages 19 and 20

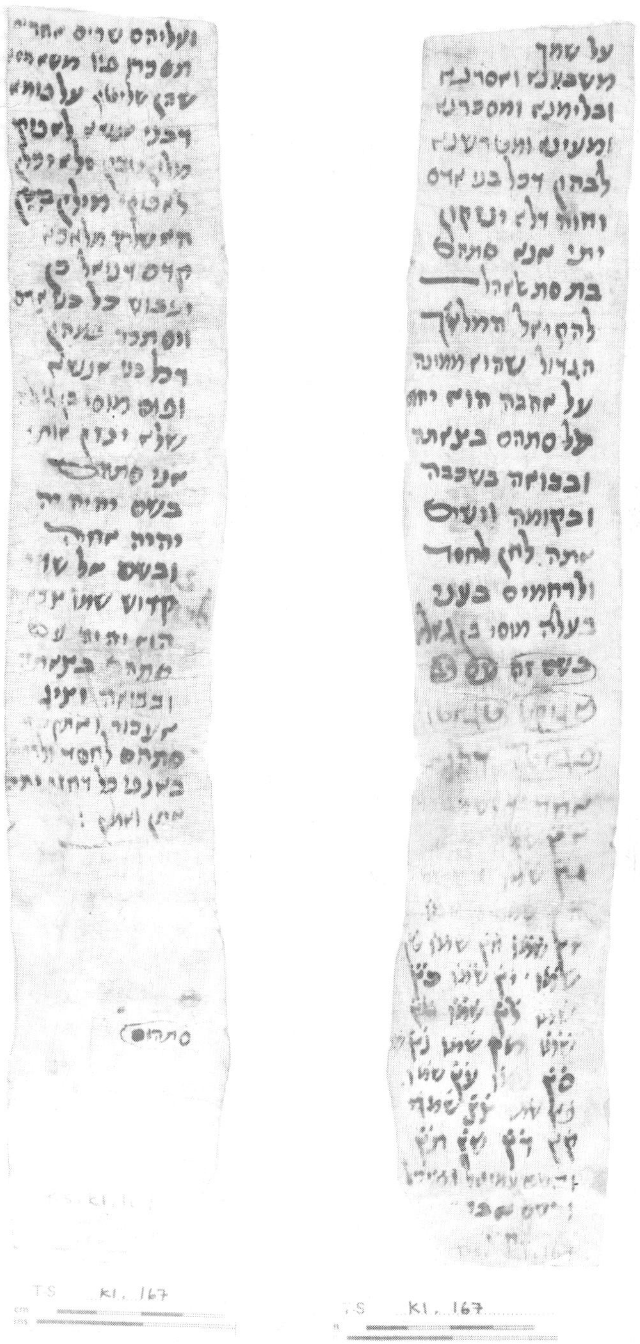

Geniza 19, pages 1 and 2

PLATE 64

הקדיש זה המצחף מ' ור' פל' בר פל' חלקו עם שבע כתות שלצדיקים
בגן עדן ושרשו תחת עץ החיים והספר התורה הזה הוא קדש ל
אלהי ישראל לא ימכר ולא יגאל והמוכרו או הגונבו או המוציאו
על מנת ימכרהו או יגנבהו יהיה בחרם יי צבאות ובחרם יהושע
בן נון שחרם יריחו ובחרם שחרמו עשרת אחי יוסף והשכינה
היתה עמהם ויהיה מחורם בשם אכתריאל יה וה יהוה צבאות
ויהיה מחורם מפי יושב הכרובים ויהיה מחורם מפי [illegible]
ויהיה מחורם מחיות ואופנים ויהיה מחורם מפי [illegible]
ויהיה מחורם מפי יפיפיה שר התורה ויהיה מחורם מפי
זגנזאל ויהיה מחורם מפי שבעה מלאכים גבריאל מיכאל
רפאל צדקיאל ענאל אוריאל חסדיאל ויהיה מחורם
משבעה רקיעים ומשבעה ארצות ומשבעים אומות וישראל
ויהודה וידבקו בו כל האלות הכתובות בתורה ובנביאים ובכתובים
ויבואו בו מאה תוכחות פחות שתים לא יאבה יי סלוח לו והבדילו
יי לרעה מכל שבטי ישראל ומחה יי את שמו מתחת השמים יהיו
בניו יתומים ואשתו אלמנה יאבד ויגוע וישמד וימחה את שמו
מספר חיים כל הגונב וכל המוכר אותו יהיו [illegible]
האלה ובאלה ברם כל ברכו יהיה [illegible]
כל הברכות הכתובות בתורה ובנביאים
נזר ועטרת ותפארת ויבואו על ראש
אמן ואמ

T-S 12.41

Geniza 20

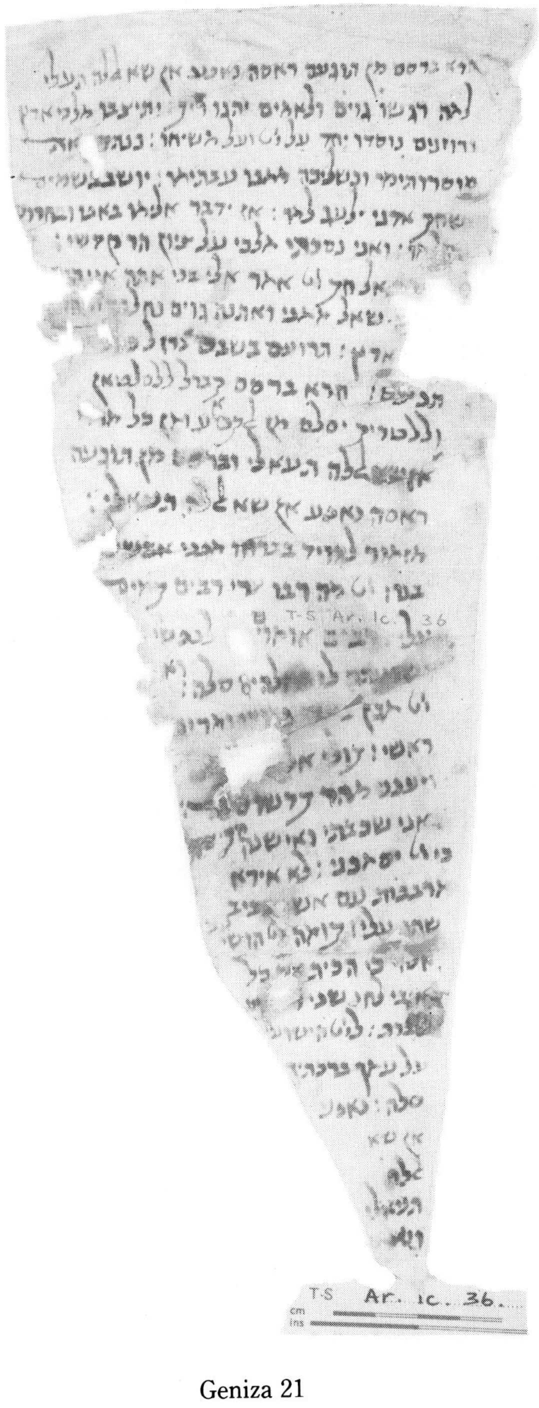

Geniza 21

PLATE 66

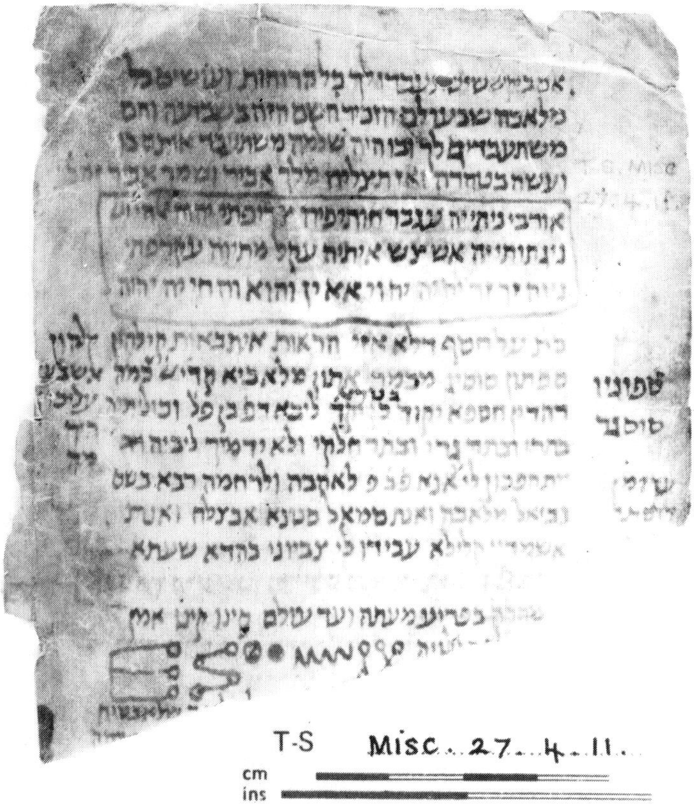

Geniza 22, page 1

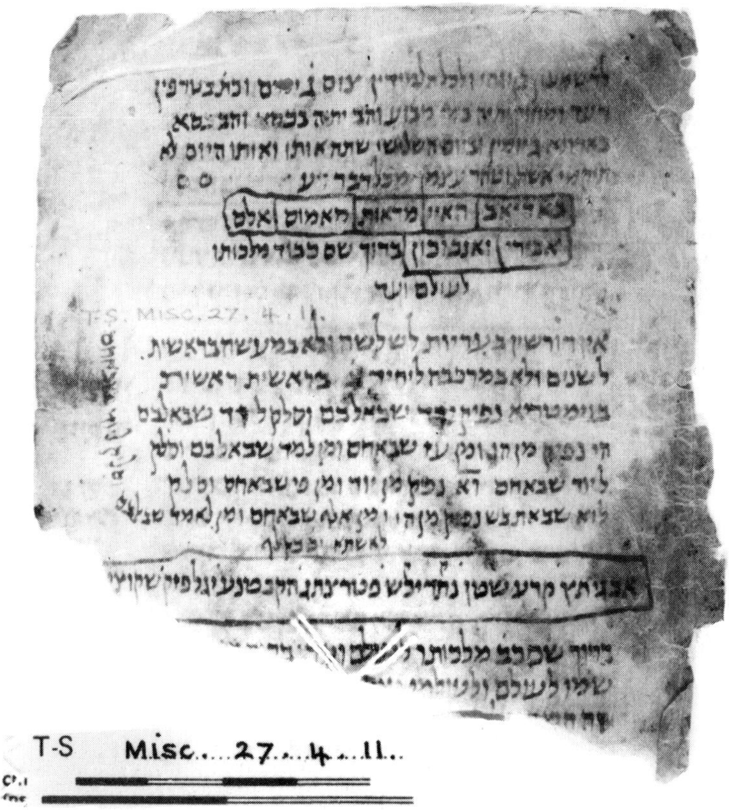

Geniza 22, page 2

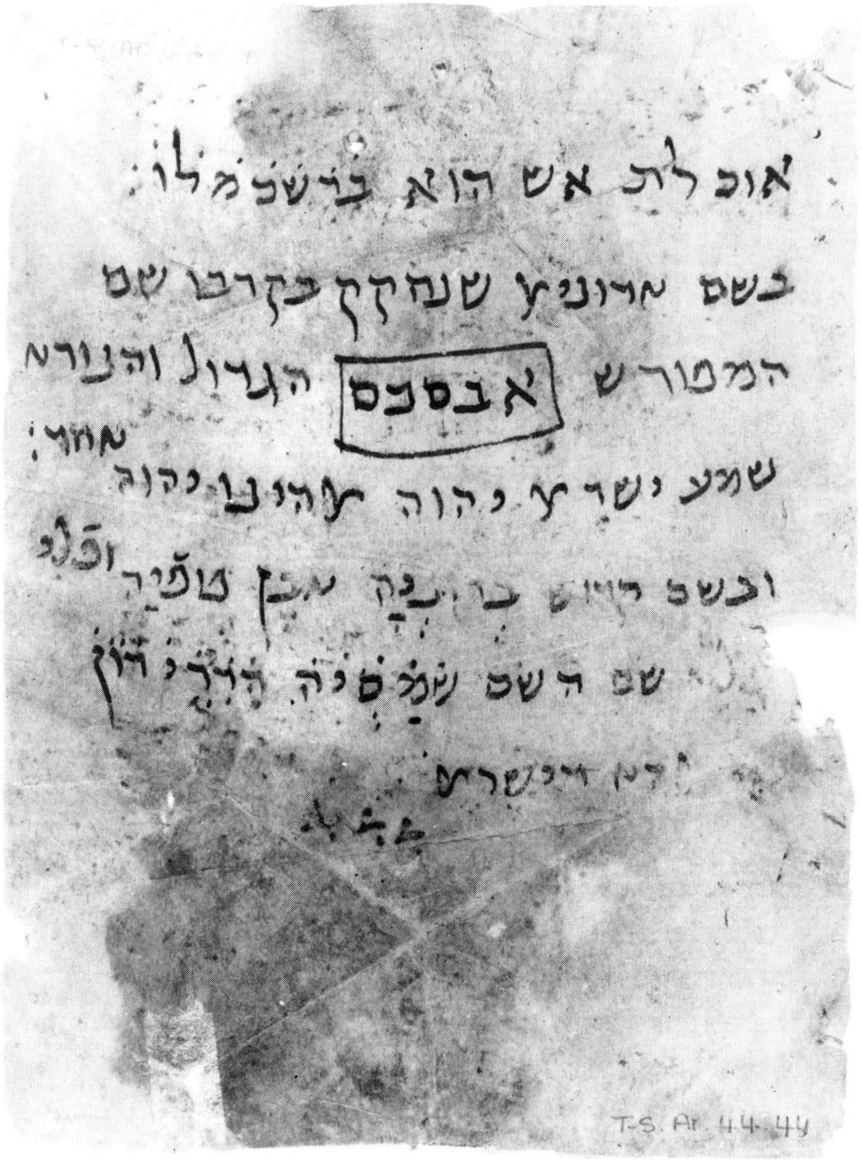

T-S Ar. 44. 44
cm
ins

Geniza 23, page 1

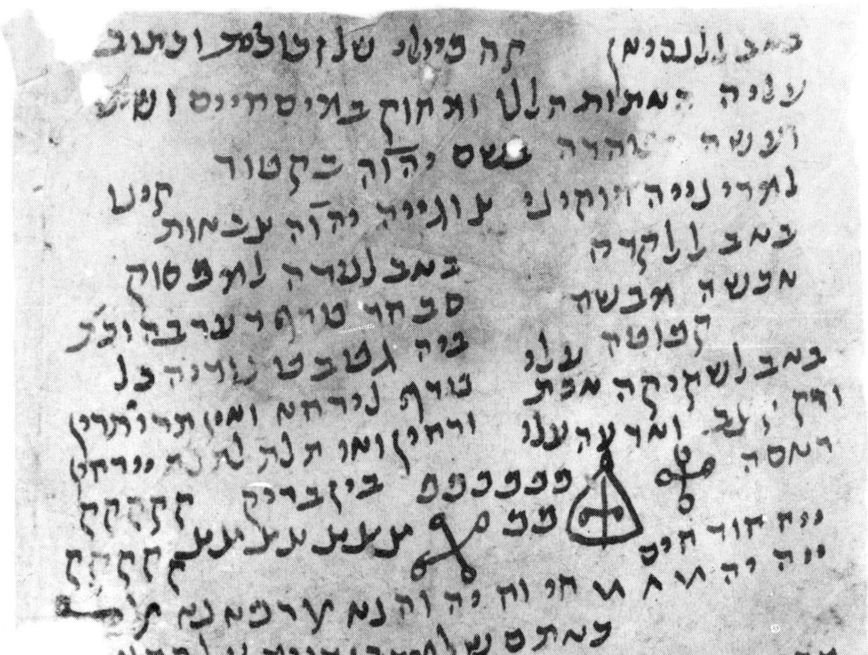

T-S Ar. 44. 44

Geniza 23, page 2

PLATE 70

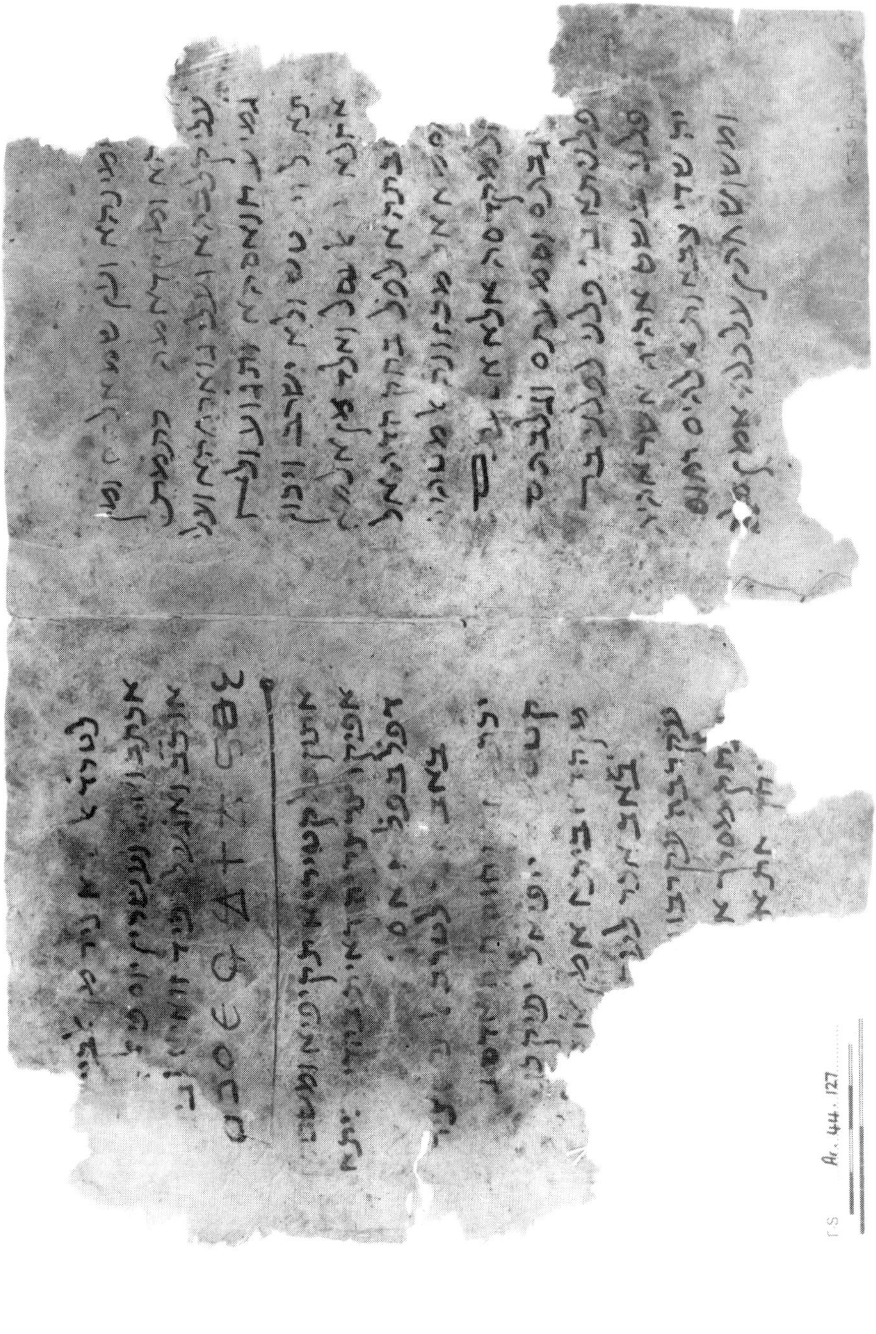

Geniza 24, pages 1 and 4

PLATE 71

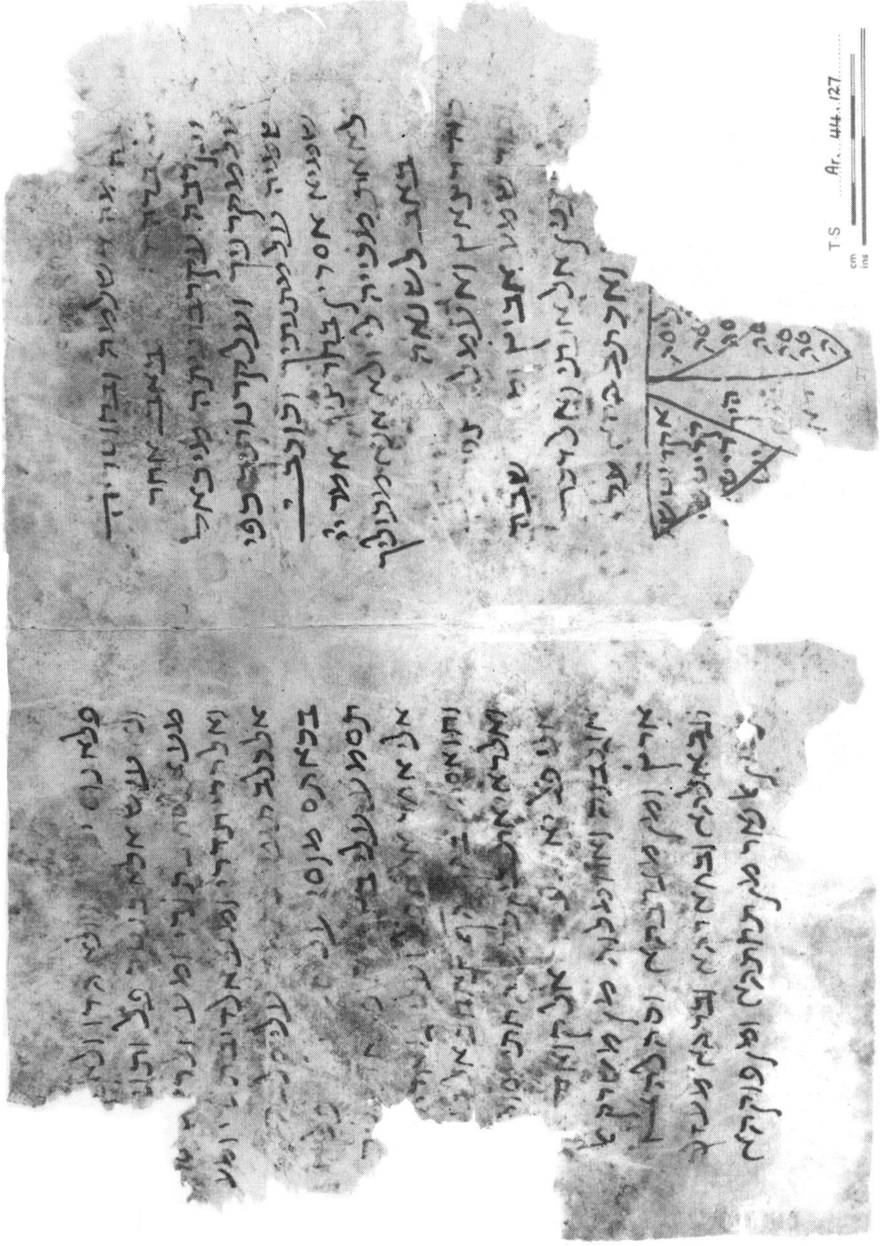

Geniza 24, pages 2 and 3

PLATE 72

Geniza 25, pages 1 and 4

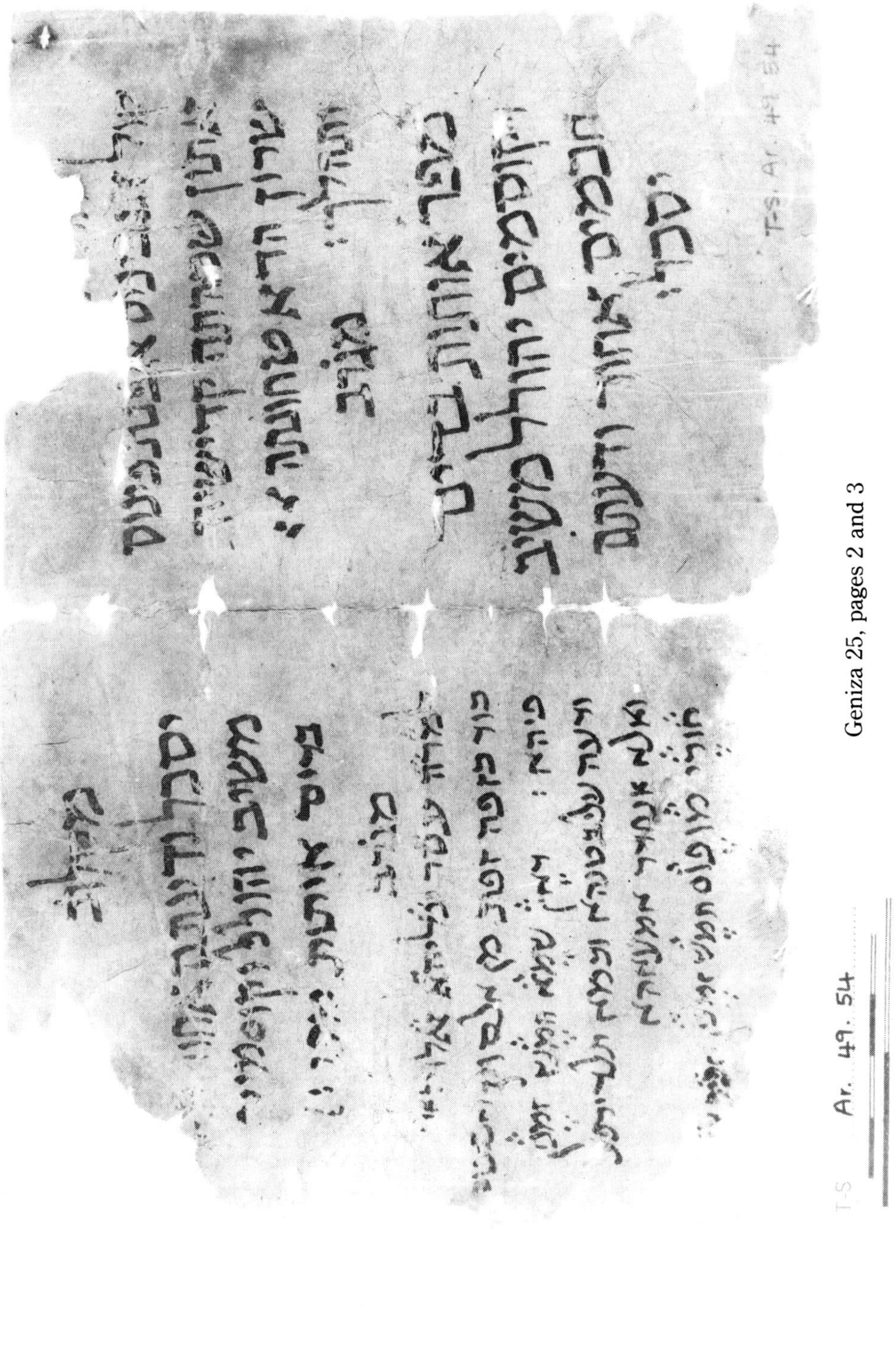

Geniza 25, pages 2 and 3

PLATE 74

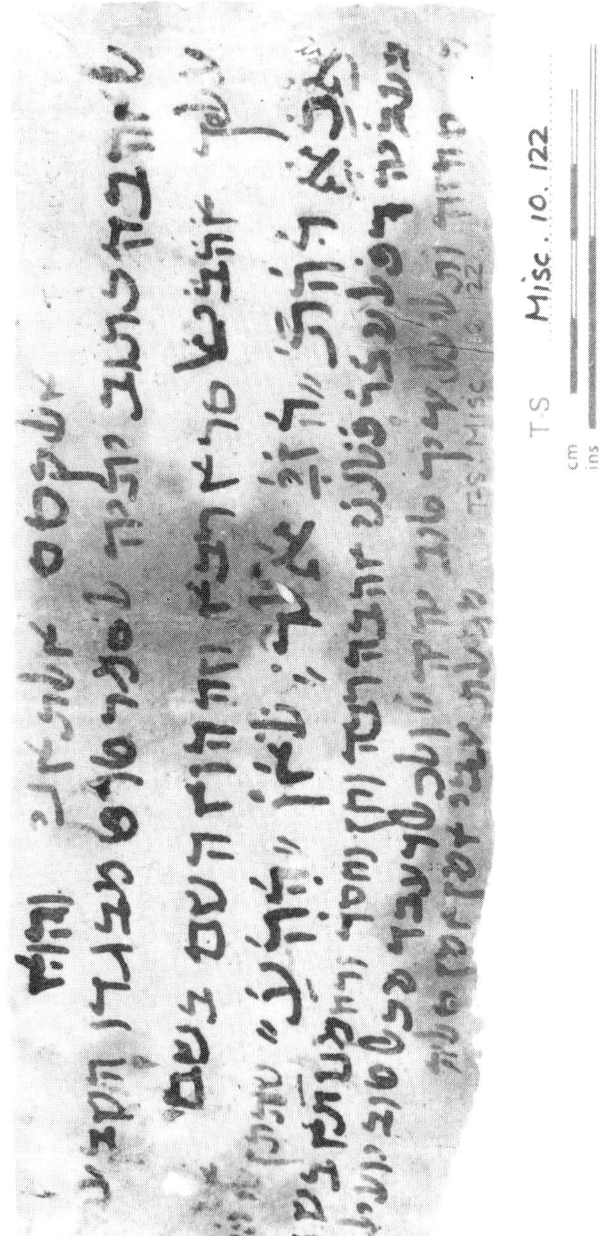

Geniza 26, page 1

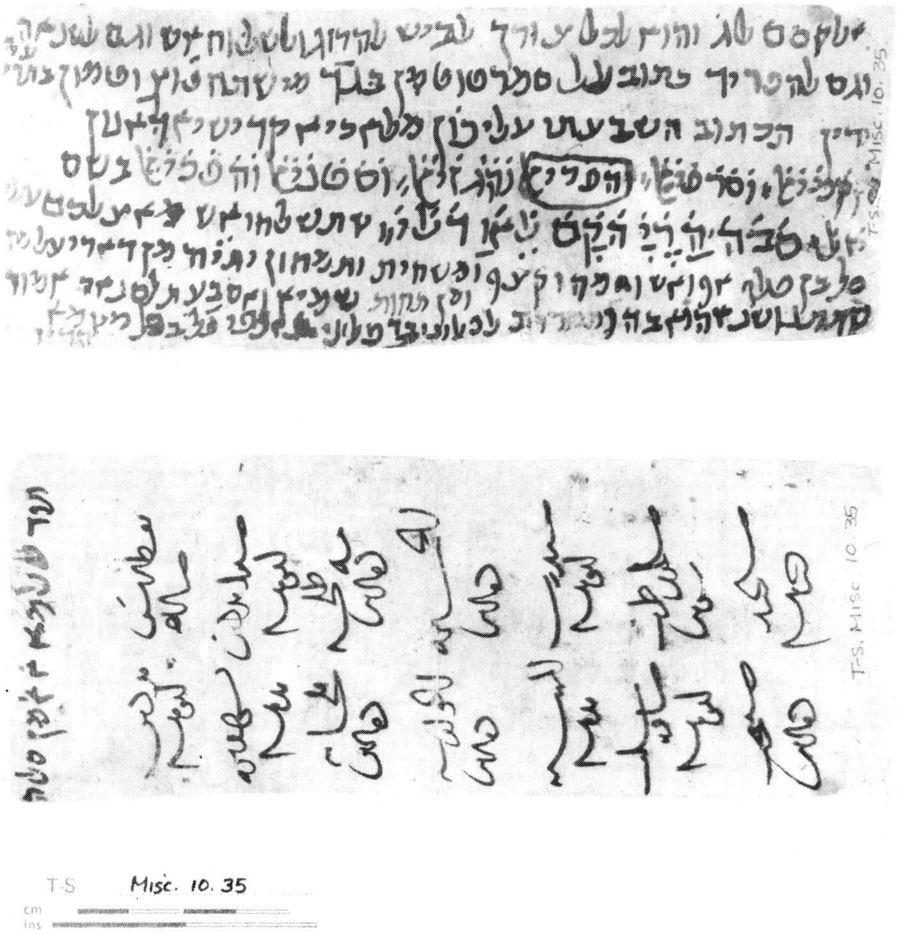

Geniza 26, page 2 (recto and verso)

PLATE 76

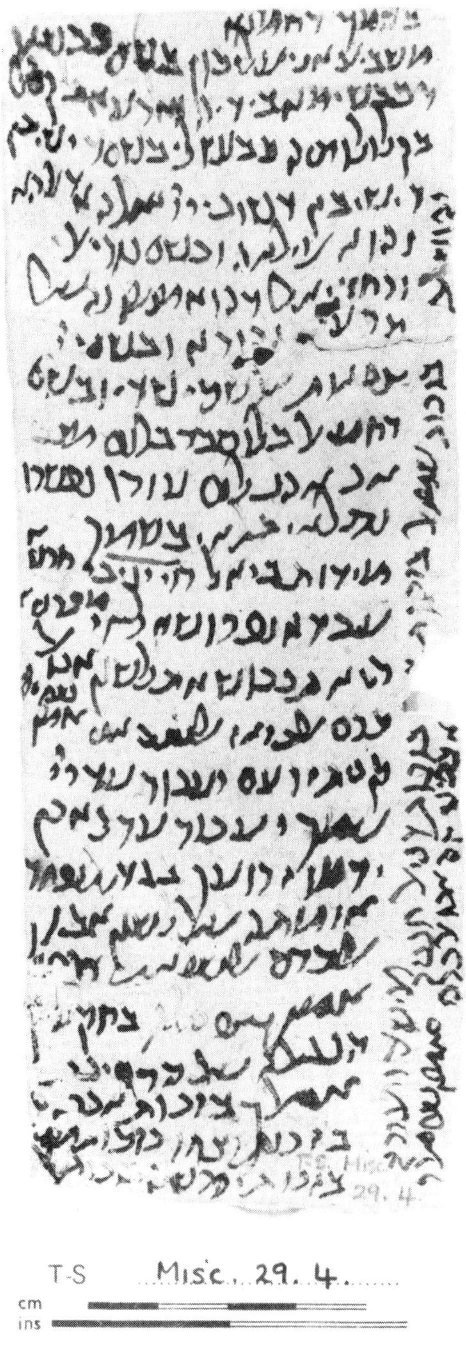

Geniza 27

Geniza 28, pages 1 and 4

PLATE 78

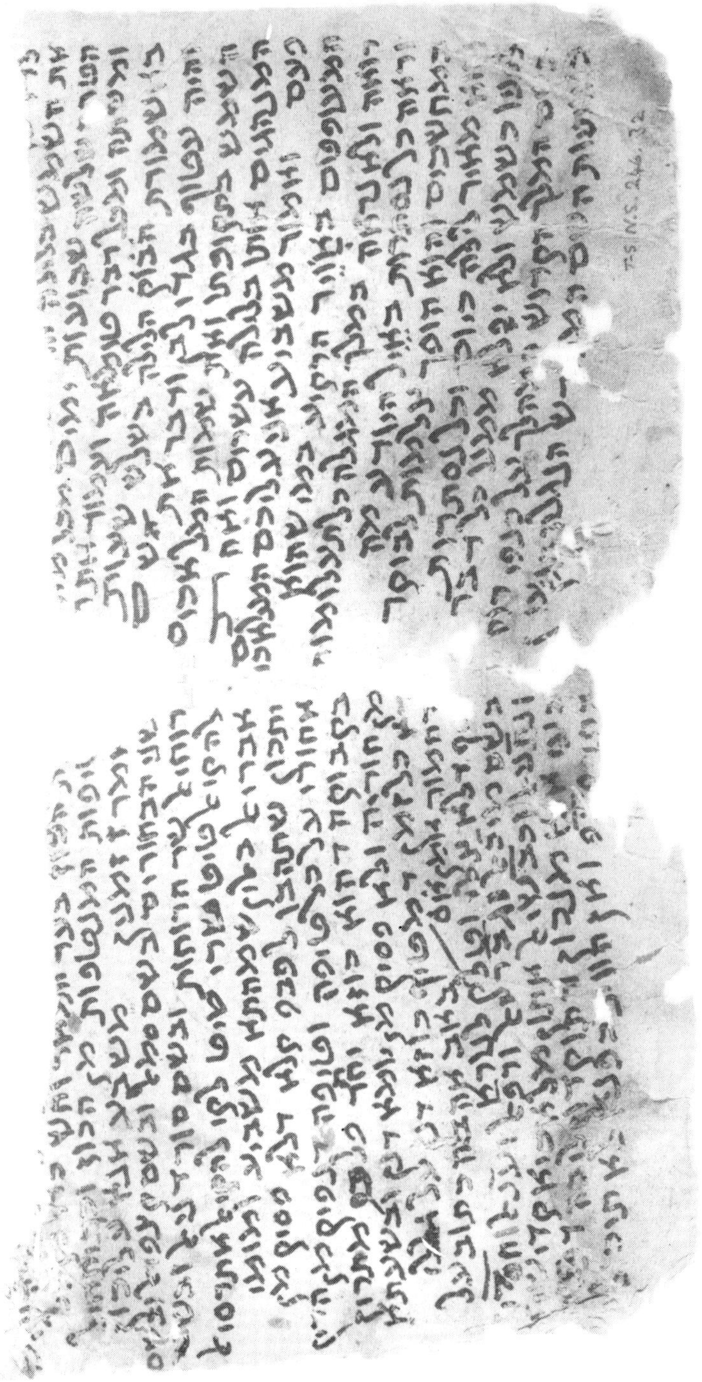

Geniza 28, pages 2 and 3

Geniza 29, page 1

PLATE 80

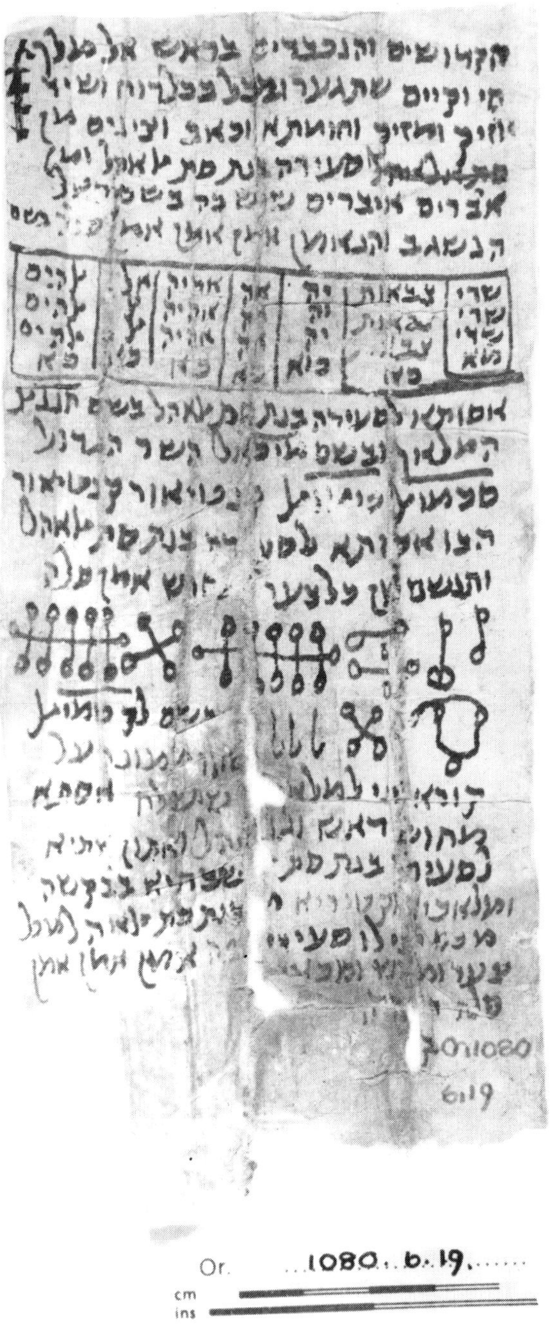

Geniza 29, page 2